# Languages for Developing
# User Interfaces

# Trademarks

# Languages for Developing User Interfaces

Edited by

**Brad A. Myers**
*School of Computer Science*
*Carnegie Mellon University*
*Pittsburgh, Pennsylvania*

with the assistance of

Mark Guzdial, *University of Michigan*
Ralph D. Hill, *Bellcore*
Bruce Horn, *Carnegie Mellon University*
Scott Hudson, *University of Arizona*
David S. Kosbie, *Carnegie Mellon University*
Gurminder Singh, *National University of Singapore*
Brad Vander Zanden, *University of Tennessee*

**CRC Press**
Taylor & Francis Group
Boca Raton  London  New York

CRC Press is an imprint of the
Taylor & Francis Group, an **informa** business

AN A K PETERS BOOK

CRC Press
Taylor & Francis Group
6000 Broken Sound Parkway NW, Suite 300
Boca Raton, FL 33487-2742

© 1992 by Taylor & Francis Group, LLC
CRC Press is an imprint of Taylor & Francis Group, an Informa business

First issued in paperback 2019

No claim to original U.S. Government works

ISBN-13: 978-0-367-45040-3 (pbk)
ISBN-13: 978-0-86720-450-6 (hbk)

Visit the Taylor & Francis Web site at
http://www.taylorandfrancis.com

and the CRC Press Web site at
http://www.crcpress.com

# Contents

**Part 2: Programming Languages for Programmers**

*General Goals*

*Models for Objects and Interaction*

*Constraints*

*Concurrency and Time*

# Preface

Computing is evolving from batch-based applications to interactive, graphical applications. However, most user interface software is still written using languages designed for writing text-based or even batch applications, such as Fortran, Pascal, C, or Ada. Researchers are investigating new approaches that may allow the next generation of computer programming languages to better support the creation of user interface software.

In addition, user interface designers are increasingly realizing that it is important to provide a high degree of end-user customization. In many cases, it would be ideal to allow end users to create their own applications. In a sense, this is what spreadsheets allow, since they can be "programmed" by their users. The success of spreadsheets shows that end users *can* learn to program, and that environments that support end-user programming can be successful.

At the SIGCHI conference in New Orleans in May, 1991, twenty leaders of the field got together in a workshop to discuss the future of languages for programming user interface software, and for end-user programming. These twenty were chosen from over 60 people who applied. The goal of the workshop was to discuss what types of computer languages would be appropriate in the future, and begin collaborations on creating these languages. This book contains the results of those discussions.

First, Chapter 1 presents an overview of the topic, and a summary of previous work. The first day of the workshop was spent with talks from the attendees. Chapters 2 through 18 contain the written papers that accompanied their talks. During the second day of the workshop, we broke into three groups to discuss various issues in depth. Chapters 19 through 21 report on the group results. Naturally, we discovered more issues than we resolved, and Chapter 22 contains a summary of the issues that were raised. We hope this will be seen as a challenge to future language designers.

In the user interface community, this book should be of interest to creators of toolkits, UIMSs and other user interface tools, as well as people creating end-user applications that want to provide end-user customization. In the programming language community, language designers would find this book useful, since future programmers will need to write modern user interfaces with their languages.

# Acknowledgements

First, we would like to thank the SIGCHI'91 conference for sponsoring this workshop, and Wayne Gray, the SIGCHI'91 Workshop Chair, for helping to organize it.

All the attendees wish to thank their organizations for supporting their attendance at the workshop.

Thanks very much to Bernita Myers and David Kosbie, who worked very hard to format this document, and convert from many different formatters into LaTeX.

# Workshop Participants

**In alphabetical order:**

Alan Borning, University of Washington
Jeffrey L. Brandenburg, Virginia Tech
James R. Cordy, Queens University at Kingston
Michael Dertouzos, Massachusetts Institute of Technology
T.C. Nicholas Graham, GMD Karlsruhe
Mark Green, University of Alberta
Mark Guzdial, University of Michigan
H. Rex Hartson, Virginia Tech
Ralph D. Hill, Bellcore
Bruce Horn, Carnegie Mellon University
Scott Hudson, Georgia Tech
Erica Liebman, Georgia Tech
Toshiyuki Masui, SHARP Corporation
Brad A. Myers, Carnegie Mellon University
John H. Reppy, Cornell University
Bob Scheifler, Massachusetts Institute of Technology
Gurminder Singh, National University of Singapore
David Canfield Smith, Apple Computer, Inc.
Randall B. Smith, Sun Microsystems Laboratories, Inc.
Brad Vander Zanden, University of Tennessee

**Organizer:**

Brad A. Myers

**Program Committee:**

Brad A. Myers
Scott Hudson
Bruce Horn

# Contributors

*Alan Borning*
(Chapter 11)
Department of Computer Science
   and Engineering, FR-35
University of Washington
Seattle, WA 98195

*Robert Boyle*
(Chapter 4)
University of Michigan
School of Education
610 E. University
Ann Arbor, MI 48109

*Jeffrey L. Brandenburg*
(Chapter 17)
Department of Computer Science
Virginia Tech
Blacksburg, VA 24061

*Bay-Wei Chang*
(Chapter 5)
Sun Microsystems Laboratories, Inc.
MS MTV29-116
2550 Garcia Avenue
Mountain View, CA 94043-1100

*James R. Cordy*
(Chapters 6, 18, 21)
Department of Computing and
   Information Science
Goodwin Hall
Queen University
Kingston, Ont. K7L 3N6 Canada

*Michael Dertouzos*
(Chapter 2)
Director, MIT Lab for
   Computer Science
545 Technology Square, Room 105
Cambridge, MA 02139

*Bjorn N. Freeman-Benson*
(Chapter 11)
University of Victoria
Department of Computer Science
Box 3055
Victoria, B.C. V8W 3P6 Canada

*Emden R. Gansner*
(Chapter 14)
AT&T Bell Laboratories
600 Mountain Ave.
Murray Hill, NJ 07974

*T.C. Nicholas Graham*
(Chapters 16, 22)
GMD
Vincenz-Priessnitz-Str. 1
D-7500 Karlsruhe 1
Germany

*Mark Guzdial*
(Chapters 4, 20)
University of Michigan
Dept. of EE and CS
1101 Beal Ave.
Ann Arbor, MI 48109

*H. Rex Hartson*
(Chapter 17)
Department of Computer Science
Virginia Tech
Blacksburg, VA 24061

*Ralph D. Hill*
(Chapters 9, 21)
Bellcore
445 South Street, Rm. 2D 295
Morristown, NJ 07962-1910

*Deborah Hix*
(Chapter 17)
Department of Computer Science
Virginia Tech
Blacksburg, VA 24061

*Bruce Horn*
(Chapters 13, 19)
School of Computer Science
Carnegie Mellon University
Pittsburgh, PA 15213-3890

*Scott Hudson*
(Chapter 7)
College of Computing
801 Atlantic Dr.
Georgia Institute of Technology
Atlanta, GA 30332-0280

*Toshiyuki Masui*
(Chapter 15)
Information System R&D Center
SHARP Corporation
2613-1 Ichinomoto-cho
Tenri, Nara 632, Japan

*Brad A. Myers*
(Chapters 1, 10, 19)
School of Computer Science
Carnegie Mellon University
Pittsburgh, PA 15213-3890

*John H. Reppy*
(Chapters 14, 20)
AT&T Bell Laboratories
600 Mountain Ave.
Murray Hill, NJ 07974

*Gurminder Singh*
(Chapters 8, 21)
Institute of Systems Science
National University of Singapore
Kent Ridge, Singapore, 0511

*David Canfield Smith*
(Chapters 3, 19)
Advanced Technology Group
Apple Computer, Inc.
20525 Mariani Ave.
Cupertino, CA 95014

*Randall B. Smith*
(Chapters 5, 20)
Sun Microsystems Laboratories, Inc.
MS MTV29-116
2550 Garcia Ave.
Mountain View, CA 94043-1100

*Elliot Soloway*
(Chapter 4)
University of Michigan
Dept. of EE and CS
1101 Beal Ave.
Ann Arbor, MI 48109

*Joshua Susser*
(Chapter 3)
Advanced Technology Group
Apple Computer, Inc.
20525 Mariani Ave.
Cupertino, CA 95014

*David Ungar*
(Chapter 5)
Sun Microsystems Laboratories, Inc.
MS MTV29-116
2550 Garcia Ave.
Mountain View, CA 94043-1100

*Brad Vander Zanden*
(Chapters 12, 21)
107 Ayres Hall
Computer Science Department
University of Tennessee
Knoxville, TN 37996-1301

*Peri Weingrad*
(Chapter 4)
University of Michigan
Dept. of EE and CS
1101 Beal Ave.
Ann Arbor, MI 48109

# Chapter 1

# Introduction

*Brad A. Myers*

In his keynote address to the SIGCHI'90 conference, Michael Dertouzos said:

> When computers first appeared, input/output commands were a minor afterthought to cohesive, often well crafted and occasionally pretentious programming languages. Today, these commands occupy over 70 percent of a programming system's instructions. Yet they, along with the user interface structures that they define, are far from cohesive, and, at least up until now, immune to standardization. We must therefore turn our thinking around and create a new breed of programming languages that are first and foremost input/output oriented and that integrate traditional processing commands into new user-oriented structures. And just as we know today that traditional commands fall into a handful of fixed categories—decision, repetition, naming, procedure definition and use—we need to search for and identify the corresponding natural classes of commands for user interfaces. [Dertouzos 90]

Researchers in the areas of user interface software have been investigating the use of special-purpose languages for programming user interfaces for many years. For example, TIGER, in 1982, was the first system that was called a "user interface management system," and it used a special

1

language called TICCL to define the user interface [Kasik 82]. Many other systems in the 1980s used BNF grammars or state transition diagrams to define the user interface (see Section 1.3). Today, researchers are concentrating on new forms of object-oriented languages and features to add to them. However, no one believes that the problem is even close to being "solved."

In addition, this research has not had much effect on the computer languages being designed by researchers who call "programming languages" their primary area of interest. I recently attended a presentation about a new programming language being designed. In the section labeled "input/output" were the conventional scanf/printf (readln/writeln in Pascal) statements. When asked if he thought these were sufficient for a modern language, the presenter replied "no," but he did not know enough about the area to do better. Some people claim that programming languages should not contain *any* I/O primitives, but rather leave it to separate packages. However, this book will show that user interface programming requires a number of important features not found in most of today's languages which cannot be relegated to external packages.

Another problem is that for applications to reach their full potential, end users will have to be able to customize and even program them themselves. Today, end-user applications are getting more and more complicated, as each release adds new features. For example, version 4.0 of the Microsoft Word text editor for the Macintosh has over 280 commands. However, users often find that what they really want is a few features from one program coupled with a few from another. If an end-user programming facility was provided that allowed the users to combine these features to create their own systems, this might solve the problem. The success of spreadsheets, which allow users to create their own programs by writing formulas and macros, shows that end users can program when given the appropriate tools, and that a product based on end-user programming can succeed.

At the SIGCHI conference in 1991 in New Orleans, a workshop was held to try to bring together user interface software specialists and programming language designers, to discuss how computer languages of the future can better support the construction of applications with modern, highly-interactive user interfaces. Twenty people met for two days to discuss this topic, and this book is a result of that discussion. The rest of the introduction motivates the problem and surveys some previous approaches.

## 1.1 Creating User Interface Software

It is well known that programming user interfaces is difficult. Studies consistently show that the user interface portion comprises about 50% of the code and development time [Myers 92b]. There are a number of reasons that software for modern user interfaces is inherently more difficult to write than other kinds of software:

**Iterative design.** Because user interfaces are difficult to *design*, the initial attempts are usually not good enough, and the interface must be re-implemented [Gould 85]. This *iterative design* requires that the user interface software be repeatedly and frequently modified. As reported by Sheil [Sheil 83], "complex interactive interfaces usually require extensive empirical testing to determine whether they are really effective and considerable redesign to make them so." The code must therefore be written so that the user interface portion can be easily changed, preferably without affecting the other parts of the software. However, most programmers find that making this separation is difficult.

**Difficult to get the screen to look attractive.** It is usually difficult to use the supplied graphics packages and libraries. As a result, achieving the desired graphical appearance can be a challenge. Techniques are required to support interactive specifications of the static and dynamic appearance and behavior of the interface.

**Asynchronous inputs.** Direct manipulation interfaces have the characteristic that the user is in control of the interface, and can perform input at almost any time. The program must therefore be able to accept input at any time. Also, the software must usually be organized with a central *event dispatcher* loop, which accepts the input events from the user, and uses the type of the event to decide which command to execute. This is quite a different software structure than for conventional programs.

**Multiple processing.** Since the program must be able to accept input events at any time, but some application procedures may take a noticeable amount of time, the software is typically organized as multiple processes, so longer actions can be executed in the background. Also, the window manager will often be in a different process than the user interface software, and may send requests to the application to redraw the windows (if they become uncovered). Dealing with multiple processes means that the programmer must deal with synchronization, race conditions, and many other problems.

**Efficiency.** All code that interfaces to the user must operate without a noticeable delay. For example, if an object is being dragged with the mouse, it should be redrawn at least 30 times a second. This means that the programmer must often deal with all the problems of real-time programming.

**Error handling.** When an error happens in a user interface, it is not acceptable for the program to "crash." An appropriate message must be shown to the user, and the system must be able to recover and continue processing. This puts tremendous emphasis on robustness in the programs.

**Aborts, Undo, and Help.** Most interfaces should allow the user to abort an operation at any time, or ask for help. This means that the software must be organized so that the appropriate information is available so the state can be restored to before the current or previous command was started, or to tell the user what is happening.

## 1.2   The Problem

This book covers two different kinds of programming: allowing end-users who do not have any formal training in programming to extensively customize their interfaces, and conventional implementation of user interfaces.

## 1.2.1 End User Programming

Users of spreadsheets and database packages write programs in the specialized languages of those systems. A large number of people have mastered the skills needed to write these programs, and it has been argued that the programmability of these tools is the primary key to their success: the user can get them to do what he or she wants. However, most other applications on computers are not programmable, and there is certainly no uniform language that can be used across different applications. Therefore, a challenge for the future is to develop a mechanism that allows end users to customize all applications.

We classify this as a style of programming because users will need program-like capabilities, such as conditionals, loops, and variables. For example, the user in a "visual shell" or desktop, like the Macintosh Finder, might want to say "delete all backup copies of files older than January 1988 if the associated original files are on the disk." This clearly requires a loop over all files, variables to hold the backup file and the associated original file, and a conditional to test the age. Since reliable natural language understanding is a long way off, we need some other way for the end user to express this request. However, there is plenty of evidence that end users find conventional programming difficult if not impossible [Shneiderman 80]. How can end users specify complex requests? We feel that programmability will be an important component of future user interfaces.

## 1.2.2 Conventional Programming Languages

We have identified two important classes of programmers who need to create user interfaces for programs: novice programmers and professional programmers. Neither has adequate tools today.

### Novice Programmers

Students who are learning to program today have used video games and computers such as the Macintosh, which have sophisticated graphics and user interfaces. When they learn to program, they expect to be able to create similar systems. However, the programming languages in use today, such as C and Pascal, have the same old I/O primitives as Fortran: read and write a string. As a result, large and complex external libraries of routines are needed to perform graphical interaction.

Current programming languages generally support simple textual input and output, and the canonical first program prints "hello world" on the screen. In most programming languages, this will be a one to three line program. For the future, however, new programmers will want to create graphical, highly-interactive programs. Therefore, our goal for a future computer language would be to make creating a blue rectangle that would follow the mouse be as easy as writing "hello world" today.

Therefore, work must be concentrated on creating the appropriate abstractions for hiding the complexities of today's window managers and graphics packages, just as languages of the present hide the complexities of how to make strings appear on the screen. What new paradigms and techniques can be used in future languages so that novice programmers can learn how to create graphical, interactive applications in the first few weeks? For example, the moving blue rectangle program should be only 5 to 10 lines.

**Programming for Professional Programmers**

A wide variety of tools have been created to help with implementing user interface software, including toolkits and User Interface Management Systems (UIMSs). Many of these have created their own new programming language. For example, the popular Xt toolkit for X, in which both Motif and Open Look are implemented, created its own object-oriented language embedded in C (see Section 1.3.2). The Garnet system defines its own embedded language using Common Lisp (Chapter 10). Current research in user interface tools focuses on object-oriented techniques, constraints, and parallelism, which should be built-in features of programming languages. Therefore, a discussion of future user interface tools must include a discussion of the design for the language the programmer will use. What are the goals, features, and characteristics for future languages for programming user interface software?

**General Problems with Programming Languages**

In summary, the problems we have identified with programming user interfaces in conventional languages include:

1. Lack of appropriate I/O mechanisms. Conventional languages still provide only limited character input and output, which supports a textual question-and-answer interaction model that is 40 years old. It is well recognized that this creates user interfaces that are modal and hard to use.

2. Lack of inexpensive multi-processing and real-time programming. Handling asynchronous input events from the user while supplying real-time feedback often requires multi-processing.

3. Ineffective object-oriented paradigms. It is the conventional wisdom that all user interface software should be programmed using object-oriented techniques. All modern user interface toolkits use this technology, but some modern languages are still not object-oriented.

4. No rapid prototyping. Many languages are designed to support the conventional software engineering model, where software is first specified, then designed, and finally implemented. However, user interface software generally requires many iterations of prototypes and re-implementation [Gould 85].

5. Inappropriate representation for programs. The textual representation of programs makes it difficult to specify graphical entities, but graphical representations to date have failed to achieve the compactness and flexibility of text.

6. Lack of various new features being investigated by user interface researchers, such as constraints, event-handlers, and incremental recomputation (these are explained in the following sections).

## 1.3   Survey

### 1.3.1   Programming Languages

Programming languages have long had embedded commands for performing input and output. However:

> Input and output are perhaps the most systematically neglected
> features of programming languages. They are usually ad hoc,
> and they are usually poorly integrated with the other facilities
> of their hosts—the languages in which they are embedded....
> The situation was bad enough before the introduction of ab-
> stract data types and interactive graphic displays, but these
> additional complications have overburdened the classical ad
> hoc input and output mechanisms beyond their design limita-
> tions. [Shaw 86]

Fortran, developed in the mid-1950s, provided sophisticated text formatting and reading facilities, so that the programmer could control the
exact format of the output and input. The roots of the model are based on
batch processing of lines of text or streams of characters. Later languages
have advanced little in this area, and still use similar mechanisms. For
example, the facilities provided by C (1972), Pascal (1975), Common Lisp
(1984), and even modern languages such as Ada (1983), Turing (1983—see
Chapter 18), and the functional language Standard ML (1985) [Milner 90],
only support text writing and reading, with varying levels of control over
the formatting. These text I/O primitives are often built-in mechanisms
because, unlike other functions in the language, they usually take a variable number of parameters. Some other modern languages, such as Mesa
[Mitchell 79], do not have *any* built-in I/O mechanisms.

The built-in primitives only support the question-and-answer style of
user interface, which is no longer very popular. The system prints a prompt
(using something like writeln or printf) and the user is supposed to type
in the answer (using readln or scanf). Notice that the program is fully in
control, and the user has no option to perform a different action, ask for
help, or revise earlier answers. To create graphical or direct manipulation
style interfaces in any of these languages, the programmer must ignore the

built-in primitives and use a separate library of routines, which is not part of the language standard.

Some argue that it is considered a good design principal to leave I/O out of the language definition and instead define it as part of the standard libraries. The lesson of PL/I shows that trying to incorporate all of the useful and reasonable semantics of I/O in a language leads to a bad design. However, as discussed above in Section 1.2.2, even without specific I/O mechanisms, there are many other features that *are* considered appropriate to be part of the design that have a significant impact on user interface software.

## 1.3.2   Languages for Programming User Interface Systems

The field of software for user interfaces has been actively researched for many years, and there are a number of good surveys (e.g., [Hartson 89b, Myers 89a, Myers 92a]) and books (e.g., [Bass 91]) about the topic. There is also an annual conference devoted to user interface software, called the ACM SIGGRAPH Symposium on User Interface Software and Technology (UIST). Since the area is so broad, this section does not try to cover all the existing systems, but rather provides an overview of the various language approaches that have been used.

From the beginning, tools for creating user interface software have used special-purpose languages. When a system includes a special language for defining the user interface, it is often called a *User Interface Management System* (UIMS). Often, the assumption is that the user interface will be programmed in this special language, but the *application* (all of the code that is not the user interface) will be programmed in a conventional language. The following sections discuss some of the forms the special languages have used.

### State Transition Diagrams

Since many parts of user interfaces involve handling a sequence of input events, it is natural to think of using a *state transition diagram* (essentially a finite state machine) to define the interface. A transition network consists of a set of states, with arcs out of each state labeled with the input tokens that will cause a transition to the state at the other end of the arc (see Figure

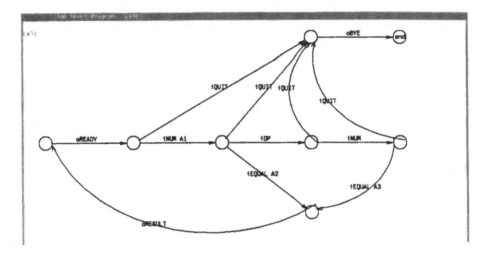

Figure 1.1:   State diagram description of a simple desk calculator [Jacob 85b].

1.1). When the user performs the action on the arc, the system goes to the next state. In order to have some action happen when the transition takes place, many systems allow the programmer to also specify on arcs or states the output that will be shown to the user, and application functions to be called.

Newman used a state transition diagram in what was apparently the first UIMS [Newman 68].   Jacob added the ability to have procedural abstraction, so that the label on an arc could actually be a call to a subdiagram [Jacob 85b]. Figure 1.1 is a view of this system.

State diagram UIMSs are most useful for creating user interfaces where a large amount of syntactic parsing is necessary or when the user interface has a large number of modes (each state is really a mode). However, most highly-interactive systems attempt to be mostly "mode-free," which means that at each point, the user has a wide variety of choices of what to do. This requires a large number of arcs out of each state, so state diagram UIMSs have not been successful for these interfaces. If the user can give parameters to a function in any order, a state transition diagram must have a different set of transitions for each order. In addition, state diagrams cannot handle interfaces where the user can operate on multiple objects at the same time

(possibly using multiple input devices concurrently). Another problem is that they tend to get very confusing for large interfaces, since they get to be a "maze of wires" and off-page (or off-screen) arcs can be hard to follow.

Recognizing these problems, but still trying to retain the perspicuity of state transition diagrams, Jacob [Jacob 86] created a new formalism, which is a combination of state diagrams with a form of event languages (see below). There can be multiple diagrams active at the same time, and flow of control transfers from one to another in a co-routine fashion. The system can create various forms of direct manipulation interfaces. However, very few state transition systems are in use today.

Because state transition diagrams are naturally graphical, most systems have allowed the user to enter them using a graphical editor. They are therefore *Visual Programming Languages* [Myers 90d]. However, some early systems required the programmer to enter the diagrams using a textual language.

### Grammars

For user interfaces that use command languages or other text-based input, it seems natural to use a context-free grammar to parse the input. Therefore, some early UIMSs allowed the programmer to define the syntax of the expected input using a BNF grammar. Tools such as YACC and LEX under Unix can then be used to generate a parser automatically. The Syngraph (SYNtax directed GRAPHics) UIMS [Olsen 83] is a system that tried to extend this idea to graphical programs, by having the syntax of the interface defined in an extended BNF. However, all of the problems mentioned above for state transition diagrams also apply to grammars. In addition, programmers usually find it very difficult to visualize the resulting sentences from a grammar. Consequently, grammars are usually only used for describing highly-constrained, textual input.

### Event Languages and Production Systems

When the user hits a keyboard key or a mouse button, window systems create an "event" structure containing various pieces of information about the input event. This structure is put in a queue, and the user interface software must take the events out of the queue and process them. Therefore, it seems natural to create a system that is organized around event handlers. Each handler is a small piece of code that is called by the system when the appropriate event occurs. Usually the event can be qualified by other conditions, for example, "left mouse button down while inside the 'Reset' button." The handler might perform some output, call an application procedure, or generate a synthetic event to cause other handlers to operate. It has been shown that event systems are more flexible than either state transition diagrams or grammars [Green 86].

The ALGAE system [Flecchia 87] uses an event language which is an extension of Pascal. The user interface is programmed as a set of small event handlers, which ALGAE compiles into conventional code. Sassafras, which implements an Event Response System (ERS) [Hill 86], uses a similar idea, but with an entirely different syntax. This system also adds local variables called "flags" to help specify the flow of control.

The HyperTalk language used to program in Apple's HyperCard is a recent example of an event language. The user writes code that is invoked when a button is hit or other event occurs. HyperTalk is further discussed in Section 1.3.3.

Event systems are much like production systems used by some AI (artificial intelligence) systems. In production systems, there are many "rules" of the form if `test` then `action`. The system repeatedly tries to find a rule whose test passes, and then executes its action. The PPS system [Olsen 90b] uses a production system approach, which is more general than an event system.

One nice thing about event languages is that they can easily handle multiple processes, which can be important in user interfaces. One of the problems with event languages is that it is often very difficult to create correct code, since the flow of control is not localized and small changes in one part can affect many different pieces of the program. It is also often difficult for the designer to understand the code once it reaches a non-trivial size. Hill [Hill 86] claims that these problems can be solved if the event language provides appropriate modularization mechanisms.

### Declarative Languages

Another approach is to try to define a language that is declarative (stating what should happen) rather than procedural (how to make it happen). Cousin [Hayes 85] and the commercial product Open Dialogue from Apollo Computer, Inc. (now part of Hewlett-Packard) both allow the designer to specify user interfaces in this manner. The user interfaces supported are basically forms, where fields can be text which is typed by the user, or options selected using menus or buttons. There are also graphic output areas that the application can use in whatever manner desired. The application program is connected to the user interface through "variables," which both can set and access.

The advantage of using declarative languages is that the user interface designer does not have to worry about the time sequence of events, and can concentrate on the information that needs to be passed back and forth. The disadvantage is that only certain types of interfaces can be provided this way, and the rest must be programmed by hand in the "graphic areas" provided to application programs. The kinds of interactions available are preprogrammed and fixed. In particular, these systems provide no support for such things as dragging graphical objects, rubber-band lines, or drawing new graphical objects.

## Constraint Languages

"Constraints" are relationships that are declared once and maintained automatically by the system. They are often considered declarative languages, since the programmer does not specify how to solve the constraints, only what the relationships should be. However, we have not included constraint languages in the previous section because they have a quite different form and use than the systems described above. Unlike Cousin and Open Dialogue, constraint languages are most often used for the *dynamic* parts of an application. For example, the programmer might declare that a line should stay attached to a box. Then, when the user moves the box, the system will automatically move the line also.

Constraint languages have been widely used to design user interfaces in research systems [Borning 86], and Chapters 11 through 13 discuss some modern constraint systems in more detail. Early constraint systems include Sketchpad [Sutherland 63a, Sutherland 63b] which pioneered the use of graphical constraints in a drawing editor in the early 1960s, and ThingLab [Borning 79, Borning 81] which used constraints for graphical simulation. More recently ThingLab has been refined to aid in the generation of user interfaces [Freeman-Benson 90c]. GROW [Barth 86] was perhaps the first user interface development system that employed constraints.

The advantage of constraint languages is that it is convenient for the programmer not to have to keep track of all the relationships and how to maintain them when changes happen. A disadvantage is that today's constraint solvers are usually inefficient in space and time. In addition, a complex network of constraints can be difficult to debug, since changing a value can have non-local effects if constraints depend on it.

### High-Level Specification Languages

Some research systems are investigating allowing the programmer to define a high-level specification of the application functionality, and automatically generating a user interface from that. For example, in IDL [Foley 88], the programmer gives the application procedures along with pre- and post-conditions for each. From these, the system can create a preliminary interactive user interface, which the programmer can then modify to be more attractive and easier to use. Mickey [Olsen 89] uses a Pascal definition of the application procedures to be called and variables to be set along with special comments, to generate a Macintosh menu and dialog-box interface.

The advantage of using high-level specification languages is that the programmer does not need to worry much about the user interface, and can concentrate on the application functionality. The disadvantages are that the systems rarely create good user interfaces, so tinkering is necessary, and the systems are limited in the forms of interfaces they can create.

### Object–Oriented Languages

Many user interface development systems are based on existing object-oriented languages. For example, InterViews [Linton 89] uses C++, and GWUIMS [Sibert 88] uses the Flavors object system in Lisp. In fact, one of the chief motivations for Smalltalk, the first successful object system, was that it would be easier to create user interface software.

In addition, special object-oriented languages have been created specifically to support user interface development. These include Object Pascal, which was created by Apple as part of the MacApp program development system [Wilson 90], and the Garnet Object System (see Chapter 10).

Also, some toolkits, such as Xt [McCormack 88] and Andrew [Palay 88], have invented their own object systems. In these two cases, the underlying language is C, and the tool developers felt that other object-oriented languages, such as C++, were inadequate, so they developed their own object-oriented systems using extensions to C.

Object-based systems typically provide the higher-level "classes" that handle the default behavior and the user interface designer provides specializations of these classes to deal with specific behavior desired in the user interface. This uses the inheritance mechanism built into object-oriented languages.

The advantages of using an object-oriented approach are well-known. The entities on the screen are naturally modeled by objects receiving messages, since they need to respond to events. In addition, the inheritance mechanism of object systems makes it easier to reuse code since standard mechanisms can be defined, and the programmer can override only those that are specific to the particular application. Virtually all modern user interface software environments are object-oriented.

### 1.3.3  Languages for End-User Programming

In the old days, computers were mostly used by programmers or scientists who knew how to program them using conventional programming languages. Today, however, the vast majority of computer users do not have any training in computer programming. However, these users find that they still need many of the capabilities that programming provides: the ability to direct the computer to perform a specific user-defined task, and to customize existing applications. Many approaches have been tried to provide this capability to users.

Clearly, the most successful end-user programming systems are spreadsheets, such as Lotus 1-2-3. Spreadsheets are enormously popular for personal-computer users, and some claim that spreadsheets are the primary reason most people buy personal computers. Spreadsheet users write programs by entering formulas into cells, and by creating macros of spreadsheet operations. Why spreadsheets have been easy to use and program has been studied by many researchers [Kay 84, Hutchins 86, Lewis 87, Nardi 90] (see also Chapter 19).

Another popular product for personal computers is database programs. These systems, such as DBASE, allow the end user to create database query programs to find information stored in the database.

The HyperCard program from Apple for the Macintosh allows end users to create applications. It is primarily good for making "forms" (called cards) containing fill-in fields and buttons. The buttons can transfer to other cards or perform other actions. If the user wants a complex action to happen, this can be programmed using the HyperTalk scripting language. However, most people who do not understand how to program have great difficulty writing HyperTalk programs.

Creating programs using graphics has long been touted as a method for making programming easy enough for end users. Many "Visual Programming Languages" [Myers 90d] have been designed to provide programming capabilities to non-programmers. For example, the LabView product for the Macintosh allows scientists to create dataflow diagrams to create a control panel for external instruments [Labview 89]. The processing of the data and control signals can be defined using icons connected by graphical wires (see Figure 1.2). Another example is Authorware, which uses a flowchart style graphical language to allow schoolteachers to design educational software [Authorware 91]. In Chapter 6, Cordy describes a new visual language, based on a functional model, rather than the imperative model used by most visual languages.

The advantages of graphical approaches are that there is usually no syntax to learn, so it is easier to create the programs, and often the two-dimensional presentation can help users understand the flow of control. In general, however, graphical programming has not been a panacea for end users. The *concepts* of programming, such as conditionals, iterations, and variables, are often hard for people to understand, and the graphical languages do not hide these. Also, graphical programs can be hard to read when they get larger than a few operations, since often the programs take up much more space than a textual program, and some forms can become a "maze of wires."

Spreadsheet systems, such as Lotus 1-2-3 and Microsoft Excel, have long allowed users to create "macros," which are a recording of a sequence of operations that can be replayed later. Research systems have investigated sophisticated macro recorders for Visual Shells [Halbert 84]. Commercial

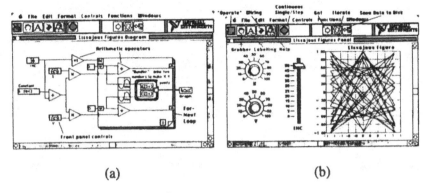

(a)                                                        (b)

Figure 1.2: A LabVIEW window (a) in which a program to generate a graph has been entered. The resulting user interface after the program has been hidden is shown in (b).

macro recorders also exist for mouse-based operating systems like the Macintosh. In many systems, the recording can be edited, and control structures such as conditionals and iterations can be added, which converts the macros into full-fledged programming systems. Sometimes the macro is recorded as a text file, and then edited directly. Other times, for example in Tempo II Plus [Tempo2 91], a series of dialog boxes is used to guide the user's editing.

The advantage of macro scripting is that the user can just operate the system normally and the commands will be remembered. The disadvantages are that this technique cannot be used to create new applications (only to more effectively give commands to existing ones), and it is difficult for users to specify control structures and variables in most macro languages.

## 1.4  Summary

In general, the existing approaches to user interface programming, either for end users or professional programmers, have proven to be quite difficult to use. Further research is clearly needed to find better paradigms and ways to present important features. The rest of this book discusses some current and future research on this problem.

# Part 1

# Programming Languages for End Users

# Chapter 2

# The User Interface is *The* Language

*Michael L. Dertouzos*

The 1970 programming manual for Dartmouth Basic describes an arsenal of some 80 instructions, 10% of which are dedicated to Input/Output (I/O). Twenty years later, the 1990 Microsoft Basic manual for the Macintosh describes some 400 instructions (including relevant toolbox calls), 70% of which deal with I/O. Figure 2.1 illustrates this difference and shows how the I/O instructions are distributed among their various categories.

Despite the obvious shift in demand, reflected by this evolutionary change, and notwithstanding current rhetoric about new software environments, little has changed in the fundamental structure of programming languages since Fortran. The step from machine language to Fortran has yet to be dwarfed by a step from Fortran to anything else! Contemporary languages still carry the same basic classes of commands for decision, repetition, binding and unbinding, arithmetic and math, procedure definition and use, as well as the separable and increasingly bulkier input output (I/O) or user interface commands. It should not be too surprising that this structural inertia is accompanied by a corresponding functional feebleness—programming productivity has barely budged beyond about 1% per year, by even the most optimistic of counts, and programming continues to be out of the reach of most people.

*Michael L. Dertouzos*

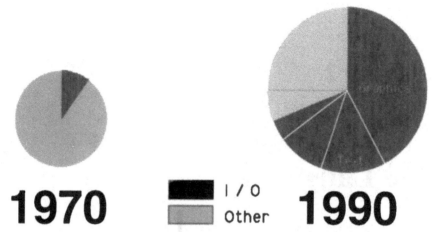

1970     ■ I / O     1990
             ▨ Other

Figure 2.1: Input/output instructions - BASIC programming language.

These observations led me, in the ACM's Conference on Human Factors in Computing Systems (SIGCHI'90) [Dertouzos 90] keynote address, to call for the creation of a new breed of programming languages that would make programming much easier, much more accessible, and much more fun than it is today, blurring the distinctions we now make between programmers and users, processors and peripherals, languages and operating systems. In my view, this can happen only if the programming language becomes **rooted in** and fully integrated with the user interface—a reversal of our traditional thinking and indeed of the title of this book which presupposes a distinction between language and user interface.

The remainder of this chapter discusses a few key characteristics that such a language should have:

## 2.1   Out–In Programming Process

An essential ingredient of this new vision is that the programming process would start with the construction of the user interface. After all, doing something purposeful by and for the user is the entire purpose of the program that is about to be born. This means that the new language should have tools that can easily create  buttons, menus, dialog boxes, windows, pictures, and sounds for input and output as well as other artifacts close to the user that are deemed natural and purposeful for the task at hand. This is clearly a creative activity with a great deal of potential and not too great a learning cost, since all the user does is select and arrange familiar gadgets like windows, buttons, and menus.

So far, I have described what in today's vernacular would be called a user interface prototyping language (e.g., *Prototyper* by Smethers Barnes for the Macintosh). Unfortunately such prototyping software stops being useful exactly at the most interesting point of the programming process: Once the interface is designed, reams of code are generated, and the user who wishes to go further must leave the familiar and personally interesting world of the interface that she has just prototyped and plunge into the antiquated, unproductive, and unbearably detailed world of conventional programming languages like Pascal, and C—a world that caters much more to what computers like rather than to what is easy and natural for people to do.

What is needed instead is the ability to proceed smoothly from proto-typing the user interface to the next natural stage—namely to what should happen when each button is activated, each menu item is selected, and each sound is made or spoken. In the language of my dreams this would be done easily by "flipping" each button that has been prototyped and specifying "behind" it what action should be taken when the button is activated by the user—akin to the spreadsheet metaphor where behind each cell may lie a formula or procedure that determines the cell's contents. This means that the programming environment of this new language **should be very rich in pre-programmed entities that can be simply selected** and that can do a lot of useful things near the I/O level of human interest. In other words, a style characterized simply by inputs, and actions caused by these inputs, which we might call **shallow programming** is good and productive and should be encouraged.

More generally, this process of **out–in** programming would continue from the user interface design to progressively deeper inner structures for more complex programs. At any time in this process, the programmer would have the ability to run the program under development with the flip of a lever, and without having to stand on his head in order to use separate build, compile, and link procedures that characterize today's development systems.

A considerably greater and more intelligent amount of compilation and run-time decision making would underlie this process, proceeding incrementally and invisibly to the user, as the program is built. This process would yield a finished prototype application, without additional fanfare, at any stage of the development process, and certainly upon its termination.

## 2.2  Total Environment Integration

Since a successful new language should survive for a long time, it should try to anticipate future developments. We are thus necessarily led to some crystal ball gazing.

Computer technology is growing in three important directions: Locally, the silicon used in computer circuits will be increasingly organized into multiprocessor architectures, roughly for the same reason that it is easier to harness many horses rather than grow one huge horse with the same total strength. Globally, these parallel computers will be increasingly interconnected to one another, forming networks at many levels of granularity, according to the aggregation of the population they serve—a single building, a building complex, or organizations spanning cities, and even continents. Finally, people will utilize tomorrow's computers only if they can easily communicate their wishes to these machines using speech, handwriting, pictures, and text and only if they can derive real benefits from such interaction.

These three observations suggest that the designers of future languages should keep in mind that the target of their endeavors is a system like that of Figure 2.2. In words: **we should strive to create programming languages and software systems that make networked multiprocessors easy to use through interaction by normal people toward the fulfillment of tangible goals.**

Accordingly, tomorrow's languages should include **integrally, rather than as afterthoughts**: (1) input/output capabilities for multiple media, (2) communication capabilities for dealing with users and servers over networks,, and (3) capabilities for controlling multiple resources. In short, future languages should include integrated access to this broader environment, for the simple reason that these capabilities will be present and should

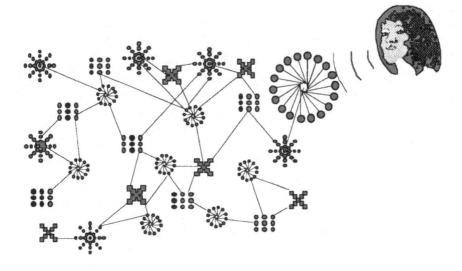

Figure 2.2: Target of new languages: networked multiprocessors that are easy to use.

be controllable by everyone. I will not discuss in this write-up the extent to which new languages should have implicit or explicit control of parallelism. The knowledge around this important issue is still accumulating. Until we know more, the new language I am after should try to achieve as much as possible implicitly, in the interest of ease of use.

## 2.3  Simplification

The combination of so many different kinds of information and information processing in new languages creates a big opportunity for designers to economize: Consider, for example, the many different commands programmers and users invoke today to name programming entities. Some of these are assignment statements within programming languages, file creation and renaming commands in operating systems, communication port naming commands, startup shell naming commands, naming of buttons, of sounds, of pictures; as well as the myriad of naming commands within some 10,000 packaged software applications. The opportunity to integrate all of these essentially identical activities under one generic naming command is suggestive of what this kind of simplification might accomplish in reducing the complexity of the immediate user environment.

A straightforward inspection of the commands found in today's languages, operating systems, communication systems, and applications reveals the following broad classes, under which commands might be combined and simplified:

**Input–output**
1. Communication with other users and programs
2. Menu selection input
3. Buttons input
4. Text input and output
5. Static picture input and output for displays, printers, and like devices
6. Window related commands
7. Sound input and output
8. Video input and output

**Internal Information - to - Internal Information**
9. Decision and control of computational flow
10. Navigation through pre-programmed entities
11. Math, functions, expressions
12. Move and Build (e.g., join, cons) commands, including procedures
13. Data and their organization (databases)
14. Error related, access control, and miscellaneous commands

There are obviously many other ways to categorize and simplify the millions of different commands in use today by applications and languages to control the computing environment. The important observation here is that under the current scheme, people have to learn new ways for expressing familiar commands for each application that they possess. Thus a central research question is "Under what categorization scheme can we make substantial gains in commonality, simplification and integration, hence in ease of learning and simplicity of use?" Good answers to this question, that minimize the number of different commands we need to remember, should act as a powerful guide in the design of new languages.

Commands are not the only targets for simplification. Common interfaces for data representation such as text, pictures, tables, graphs, charts, drawings, sounds, and video would go a long way toward simplifying the coupling of programs to one another.

With these concepts in mind, we can now see how traditional programming languages and operating systems would become blurred into a new kind of language that I call **My Virtual Computer (MVC)**, shown in Figure 2.3. The figure illustrates commands and data as standard interfaces that are accessible to users/programmers. In the figure these are drawn as **rails** to emphasize their role as solid interfaces. The rectangular solids on top of MVC represent a new class of "applications" that would plug into these rails and would run on this new platform. These applications would use the common MVC rails—command interfaces like **name** and **move** and common data interfaces like **text** and **video**. The boxes at the bottom of the figure represent the different machines, individually or in networks, on which MVC would run.

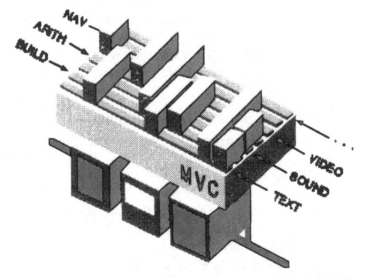

Figure 2.3: User's view of envisioned language in My Virtual Computer.

Qualitatively, the above suggestion sounds like something we already do. Quantitatively, we do it so minimally that it is essentially nonexistent: Today, each piece of application software carries along its own versions of these potentially common commands and data. I estimate that this excess baggage, whose idiosyncrasies have to be re-learned from application to application, occupies, on the average, more than 70% of each application's arsenal of command and data entities. This is a totally unacceptable learning burden, requiring people to remember the contents of 35 manuals describing essentially the same commands in slightly different ways—if they want to use fifty applications effectively!

By contrast, MVC applications would not require as much learning, since a far larger number of common commands and interfaces would be provided by the MVC rails. Users would be the real beneficiaries of this simplification, since they would be able to learn and use new application modules far more easily than is the case today.

The introduction of commands like **file, open, save, cut,** and **paste** in the Apple Macintosh is a good example of common command interfaces, as are **text** and **pict** of data interfaces. This simplification has been responsible for a good deal of the success and appeal of that machine: People appreciate knowing that there is a familiar lever in a familiar place, which when pulled does familiar things. What I am advocating here is that (1) we carry this idea far beyond the Macintosh level to **all possible common** I/O and information processing commands and (2) that we plug into these rails specialized modules that are closer to user's interests as discussed next.

## 2.4   Extensions to Specialized Concepts— Application Modules

Suppose that I ask you to

> write a small program that keeps track of my checkbook en-
> tries, including the category of expenditure of each check, so
> that the program can give me at any time a report of checks
> written and totals under each such category.

Assuming that you have understood the above request and that you are willing to comply, I have in effect programmed you to develop a desired program in less than 14 seconds. The outcome of your programming effort, using spreadsheets or, more tediously, a programming language—is likely to be acceptable to me even though I did not give you too many details.

The question of interest here is: "How is it that I can successfully program you in 14 seconds and you need 100 to 1000 times more time to program the computer?" A good part of the answer must be that you and

I share a few common concepts like *checkbook, category of expenditure, report and total,* which you understand effortlessly but must painstakingly program to a concept-free machine.

Can we evolve our programming language to get closer to this kind of easier programming? Considerably short of solving the full Artificial Intelligence problem, I believe that we can do so by letting the language grow into specialized clusters, representing various categories of specialized user interest.

Accordingly, the language I envision has natural and easy to use extensions into what today we call applications. Rather than thinking of them as applications, however, we should think of these as specialized concepts, provided by additional software modules that are fully consistent with, and plug into, the basic MVC rails. Once a set of new modules is plugged in, it will manifest itself as a new set of user interface artifacts, new commands beyond the familiar ones of the basic language/system, and other new concepts that are familiar to the specialists using that module.

Thus, if one were interested in checkbook management, one would probably get from tomorrow's application vendors a module that would handle checkbook accounting and would therefore "understand" through its built in objects **totals, checkbook, category,** and **report** as new data interfaces; and **reconcile** as a new command. Likewise, if I were interested in accounting I would get the module that knows about **journals, posting, ledgers,** and **trial balances** as its primitive entities. Whatever I plug into the MVC rails, however, I am guaranteed that it will work gracefully and seamlessly with the basic MVC language/system and whatever else I already have plugged in. Using today's vernacular, but not today's distinct application worlds which are totally oblivious to each other's existence, this means that I should be able to easily call an information service with my communications module, and just as easily transfer the historical stock quotes that I receive through this action into my spreadsheet modules for analysis and then into my charting or report modules.

The issue here is not one of mere feasibility but rather of ease and convenience, and hence of productivity gain: We are not merely asking if there exists a spreadsheet program today that happens to do all of the above actions by design (there is one). Rather, we are asking that users be able to link easily **any independently developed modules** to do what the users want to do, regardless of whether an application developer happened to think of doing the same thing. It is this property of the envisioned language to act in an integrative and cumulative way among numerous independent application modules, along with the ease with which new constructs would be developed on this base that would give the overall system its hoped for ease of use and power.

## 2.5 Conclusions

We need to get away from the current practice of simply covering up with the pretty colors of a user interface the debilitating complexity that has plagued programming since its inception. We should instead aspire to a more fundamental revolution in programming by inventing a new kind of radically different language.

Aimed at tomorrow's networked, multiprocessor architectures, such a language would integrate the entire computing environment of processor, communications, and input–output peripherals. It would simplify and incorporate as standard interfaces the commands and data representations that are common to most useful applications. It would easily extend its power via application modules to specialized domains, like accounting, design, planning, and music composition; and these extensions would be seen by users as natural additions to the standard interfaces that in many cases already represent the concepts of these higher-level activities. Finally, the modules developed for this language would be easily usable from other modules.

The programming process that would be used along with this language would be mostly in an out–in direction starting from the user interface. It would be accomplished largely through selection and easy modification of built-in or off-the-shelf objects. And it would employ substantial rapid and intelligent compilation and run-time decisions, leading to an easily tested and finished prototype at any stage of the development process.

Such a language used in such a way would blur traditional distinctions between programmers and users, among programming languages, operating systems and applications; and most important between user interface and program.

In effect the user interface would cease to exist as a separate entity and would become **the** language!

# Chapter 3

# A Component Architecture for Personal Computer Software

*David Canfield Smith*
*Joshua Susser*

## 3.1 Introduction

Today personal computer applications are written as single monolithic programs. This limits their utility to users and makes them difficult for developers to write. Personal computer software must be radically restructured. We advocate the following model. Instead of large monolithic programs, developers deliver applications as sets of independent code modules or "components." End users plug the components into a framework at run time to accomplish their tasks. The components may come from different manufacturers, be written in different programming languages, and even run on different machines on a network. The envisioned design is quite similar to that proposed in the previous chapter.

The chief benefits for users are increased tailorability and good support for multi-media documents. For developers, it eliminates the exponential growth of software complexity as they add features. Some applications are already being written this way, but the approach needs to be institutionalized. Essentially, we propose taking the concept of structured programming to a higher level: all the way up to the user.

31

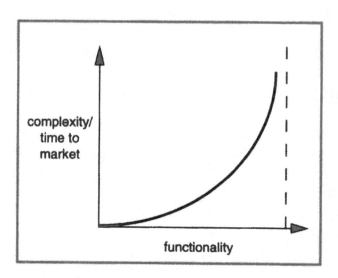

Figure 3.1: Limits on personal computer software.

## 3.2 Background: The Coming Software Crisis

The development of software for personal computers is approaching a crisis in the 1990s. The functionality of applications written for personal computers[1] is approaching the limits that current software technology can support. Applications are becoming too complex, yet developers are under continual pressure to add features in order to remain competitive. The paradox is that regardless of how many features are added, today's applications provide users with only a fraction of the help they need with their jobs.

Today applications take a long time to develop, have bugs, require lots of memory and processing power, are inflexible, don't do enough for users, do too much for users, and don't do what users want. Developers write large monolithic applications overloaded with features in primitive programming languages using primitive development tools. The more functions they add, the more complex their applications become, and the

---

[1]In fact, this is true of software for *all* computers. The Department of Defense spends $20 billion annually on ever more complex software. However, we focus on personal computer software here.

worse the ensuing problems[2] (see Figure 3.1). Fred Brooks has written an excellent analysis of software complexity:

> Software entities are more complex for their size than perhaps any other human construct because no two parts are alike... A scaling-up of a software entity is not merely a repetition of the same elements in larger sizes, it is necessarily an increase in the number of different elements. In most cases, the elements interact with each other in nonlinear fashion, and the complexity of the whole increases much more than linearly.
>
> ... Many of the classic problems of developing software products derive from this essential complexity and its nonlinear increases with size. From the complexity comes the difficulty of communication among team members, which leads to product flaws, cost overruns, schedule delays. From the complexity comes the difficulty of enumerating, much less understanding, all the possible states of the program, and from that comes the unreliability. From the complexity of function comes the difficulty of invoking function, which makes programs hard to use. From complexity of structure comes the difficulty of extending programs to new functions without creating side effects. From complexity of structure come the unvisualized states that constitute security trapdoors. [Brooks 87, p. 11]

## 3.3 Breaking the Complexity Barrier

People have worked for decades to build better programming tools: compilers, browsers, debuggers, dynamic environments, etc. These improvements are necessary but not sufficient to solve the problems with software development. What's also needed are *better ways to structure programs* so that their complexity becomes manageable. For programmers writing complex systems, it is no longer sufficient to give them just a programming language, no matter how "high-level" it is. The problem is not merely that "programming languages should also evolve in order to support the creation of modern applications," as Brad Myers states in the introduction to

---

[2]See Appendix A for an extensive discussion of the problems with current applications.

this book. The problem is to *change the nature of applications* so that they are easier to write and use.

Some people have begun to argue that there *is* in fact a silver bullet that can slay the beast of software complexity, and the bullet is pluggable components or "software ICs" as Brad Cox calls them.[3] We support this view and summarize it as follows:

> The programming problem of the 1990s will not be writing programs; it will be figuring out how to plug programs together.

Before we describe what we mean by a component architecture, we'd like to offer one additional motivation for it. Consider the following two scenarios.

### 3.3.1   A User Scenario

Most personal computer applications other than games include text editing facilities. Some are mainline text processors, such as MacWrite, Microsoft Word, and FullWrite Professional. Some rely heavily on text editing, such as MacTerminal, HyperCard, and More, although that is not their primary purpose. Some use text incidentally, such as MacDraw, MacProject, and Excel. But all differ in their details. Some allow text styles; some don't. Some have tab stops; some don't. Some are quite capable; some are quite poor. Today, if you use ten such applications, you must learn ten ways to do the very same task: edit text!

Imagine a world in which a text paragraph is a pluggable software module, usable wherever text is needed. Then you could take your favorite paragraph and plug it into each application that you use, replacing its idiosyncratic editor. You would have to learn only one text editor, and it could be the one with which you are most comfortable.

Applications built in this way would have an important characteristic: *they would simultaneously be simpler and more powerful.* They would be simpler because you would have to learn only one way to do something. They would be more powerful because you could choose a fully functional

---

[3]See for example [Zappacosta 84, Hunter 85, Goguen 86, Booch 87, Carter 87, Yudkin 88, Cox 90, Floyd 91].

module, replacing less capable ones. Techniques that claim to make programs both simpler to use and more powerful merit careful attention, if only to debunk them!

Today human factors experts have a maxim:

involve users in the design of applications.

We suggest that in the future be added:

*allow users to* **modify** *the design of applications.*

Why should users have only generic applications? Every user's job is different. Users know what they want to do; developers can only guess. It will not be sufficient in the future just to give people fixed sets of functions packaged as inflexible applications. We must provide people with *tailorable* sets of functions, which they can mix and match on a task by task basis. In fact, the term "application" probably needs to be replaced by some other term such as "task environment."

### 3.3.2 A Developer Scenario

Consider building an application that uses text incidentally, such as a spreadsheet. A user must be able to edit formulas and values, but that isn't where the value of the application lies. Spreadsheets process numbers; that's what the developer wants to concentrate his energies on, and that's where his value-added lies. Having to write a text editor is a distraction. The problem is that a text editor is a necessary part of a spreadsheet application.

Imagine a world in which developers can look in a parts catalogue for standardized pluggable components, much as do hardware engineers. Then instead of writing a text editor from scratch, the spreadsheet developer selects a standard, pre-existing text editor component. Perhaps a basic text editor component comes with the computer's system software, or maybe the developer licenses one from another vendor. At any rate, he doesn't have to write the text editor himself, so he can concentrate on the rest of the application.

Now with more time to devote to the essence of a spreadsheet, the developer may be able to implement a few extra features. He might want his spreadsheet to be able to create color graphs of results, print nice looking reports, and query databases from within formulas. Ordinarily, each of these would require a lot of work, but again components may exist that accomplish much of them already. The developer may decide not even to bundle those components with his product. Instead, he need only put in the proper hooks for interacting with them. He can rely on the user (or a system integrator) selecting components at run time. So a user who has a 5th Dimension, Triple Helix, or other kind of database component can use it from within the spreadsheet. All would have the same standard interface, so they could be used interchangeably.

Later, when the developer decides to add new features or fix bugs, he also has an easier job. He may only have to modify individual components, and that will likely be less work than changing—and *testing*—the whole application. Even for a major new release, the developer has less work to do, since he still doesn't have to modify components that are supplied by other vendors. In fact, those other components can have their own development and upgrade paths, independent of the spreadsheet itself. And when a user gets an upgrade to his text editor component, he now gets not only a better text editor, but a better spreadsheet as well.

## 3.4  A Component Architecture for Personal Computer Applications

In Apple's Advanced Technology Group, we have built a prototype of a component architecture, which we call the "Component Construction Kit (CCK)." It allows developers to build applications more simply and users to change those applications more flexibly. To test it, we've implemented over twenty components, and we've built half a dozen applications by plugging the components together in various combinations. We've implemented the prototype in the Smalltalk programming language.

### 3.4.1  Definition of a Component

A *component* is an **independent** software module having $\geq$ **0 inputs and** $\geq$ **0 outputs** which **end users** can **dynamically** connect to and disconnect from other components **at run time**. The important characteristics are

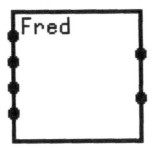

Figure 3.2: A schematic view of a component named "Fred" having 4 inputs and 2 outputs.

in boldface. Components may have any number of inputs and outputs, to give them flexibility (see Figure 3.2). *End users*, not just developers or other intermediaries, can manipulate components. Components can be dynamically connected at run time, not just at link or launch time. This is what we mean by components.

Typically, a component provides a single principal function. For example, a paragraph component provides text editing capabilities. A speadsheet cell provides arithmetic capabilities. Similarly for a video component, a graphic component, or a spelling checker. Normally components will be much smaller than today's monolithic applications, since they do not attempt to provide the hundreds of features that those applications provide.

The 20 components we've built in our prototype are all in the nature of programming tools, for examining and debugging object-oriented programming code. But they could be anything; we chose those components because they were easy to implement.

One clear lesson is that components must be written to work together. One can't just put a random collection of components together and expect something sensible to happen. We had to modify our prototype components several times in order to coordinate them. Nevertheless, it is possible to write components sufficiently generally that they can be used in a wide variety of situations.

## 3.5   The Component Construction Kit

The *Component Construction Kit* (CCK) consists of four principal elements:

- a component framework

- a component palette

- an inference engine

- a component inspector.

### 3.5.1   Framework

The *CCK framework* provides a structure within which components are connected. It provides both the system-level facilities allowing components to communicate with each other and a user-level metaphor for thinking about components.

Figure 3.3: Piece of paper with some components.

To a user, the framework is the electronic equivalent of a blank sheet of paper. When he wants to produce a document—a memo, report, drawing, spreadsheet, etc.—the user creates a piece of paper and places components on it (see Figure 3.3). He does not open several applications and cut and paste between them. He puts on the paper *all* the components he needs, and *only* those components. He may add or remove components at any time. Placing a component on a piece of paper causes it to start interacting with the other ones there without additional user work. Removing a component does not break the remaining ones; it is disconnected gracefully, and they keep working. When the user saves or mails a piece of paper, all of its components go with it. When he prints it, everything visible prints.

The framework provides a basic architecture for *all* tasks. It is a uniform way to work. Users don't deal with different applications for different tasks; they use *one* environment for all tasks.

### 3.5.2 Palette

The *CCK palette* is the source of new components. When a user needs a component for a task, he drags a copy of it from the palette and places it on a piece of paper.

Palettes make components readily available. A palette is essentially a cache of components that users have selected from the universe of possible components. There may be more than one palette, as many as users wish. A palette is just a piece of paper containing a special "palette component," but any piece of paper may be used as a source of components. However, we've created the special palette component because we've found that people like structure in palettes (Figure 3.4).

Interesting questions are: How can users discover what components exist? How can developers announce the existence of new ones? How do they get paid when people use them? Although these are still open questions, we've taken the following approach with the CCK. There is a distributed *component server* on the network. Users may open a server window and see the union of all the components available on any of the component servers. They may then drag components in which they are interested from the server window into a palette, or straight into a piece of paper. Developers announce new components by registering them in one of the component servers. A business model for components is discussed below.

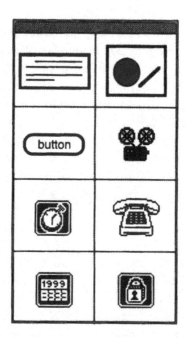

Figure 3.4: Palette of components.

### 3.5.3 Inference Engine

The *CCK inference engine* is an algorithm that automatically connects components together.

The goal is to reduce the work a user must do when he adds a component to the framework. When a user places a component on a piece of paper, the inference engine connects it to all of the relevant components that are already there (Figure 3.5). It determines what is relevant by looking at the descriptions of the inputs and outputs for the components. The descriptions contain *syntactic* and *semantic* information. The syntactic information is in the form of protocols describing the operations that can be invoked on the data passed between components. The semantic information describes the meaning of the data. Initially this just uses keywords, but someday it could be a formal specification language.

The inference engine does a pair-wise comparison of each input and output. They are said to "conform" if every operation that a component plans to do on an input is supported by the output. The output may support

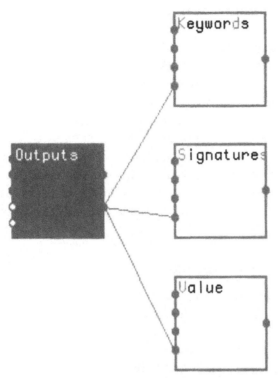

Figure 3.5: Some of the connections among components.

additional operations that the input doesn't need. The semantic information is also checked. Every semantic type (keyword) that an output produces must be accepted by an input. If an input and output conform, then they are connected.

Currently the inference engine is a simple algorithm that makes only primitive tests. However, the intention is that it is a hook into the architecture for incorporating "smart" algorithms, should they get developed, including artificial intelligence reasoning. Smarter algorithms would make appropriate connections more often, relieving users of having to correct misconnections.

Typically an output from a component will connect to inputs on multiple components. It is also legal for an output to go to two or more inputs on a single component. Similarly for inputs.

The basic communication model is multicast. When a component computes an output that it wishes to distribute, it sends it "simultaneously" to all of the inputs to which the output is connected. Since most personal computers have a single processor, the multicast is not really simultaneous but occurs in some unspecified order. Components should be written so that the order of transmission does not matter.

We have also adopted an object-oriented model for component communication. The entities that components transmit to each other are objects in an object-oriented programming language—Smalltalk in our prototype. If a component is written in a non-OOP language such as C, which is perfectly legal, the object is packed and unpacked into conventional data structures. But conceptually the medium of communication between components is objects.

### 3.5.4  Component Inspector

The *CCK component inspector* is an application designed to display and modify information about components. It has a multi-media (text and graphics) display of components, their interconnections, and their interfaces. It is useful for examining and debugging component connections.

Figure 3.6 is a screen image of the component inspector. On the left side is a schematic or "logical" view of the components on a piece of paper. Each component is represented as a box containing a name, with its inputs on the left and its outputs on the right. Connections are represented as lines between input and output dots. In the picture, the third output of the "Stack" component is connected to three other components. The "Stack" component is video reversed to show that it is selected. If the user clicks on one of the dots, the system displays its connections. If the user clicks on a component, all of the connections to all of its inputs and outputs are displayed. All connections for all components are never shown simultaneously, because the density of lines makes it look like a plate of spaghetti.

On the right side are window "panes"—subareas of the window—that display various aspects of the selected component. The first pane displays the names of the component's inputs. The second displays the names of the component's outputs; in this case the output named "context" has been selected. The third pane displays the semantic keywords, if any, assigned

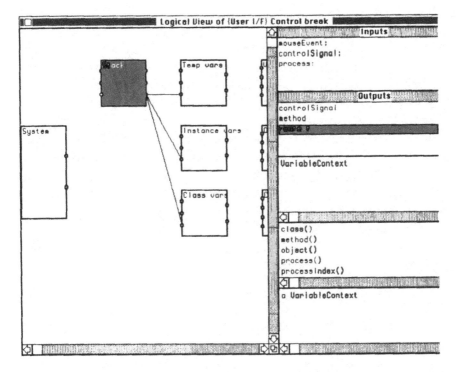

Figure 3.6: The CCK component inspector.

to the selected input or output; in this case it has the keyword "Variable-Context." The fourth pane displays the syntactic signature for the selected input or output. A signature is a list of operations that can be applied to the transmitted values; in this case stack frames are passed to components which rummage around in them and extract lists of variables using the operations class(), method(), object(), process(), etc. In an object-oriented language, these operations are messages; in a procedural language, they are functions. The final pane displays the last value communicated over this input or output. End users are not likely to understand it. We want end users to stay at the surface level. The whole point of the inference engine is to enable them to do so.

## 3.6　Component Applications

What makes a piece of paper into an "application" (if we can even use that term) is including all of the components on it necessary to accomplish some task. The applications we've built from components so far include a browser, debugger and inspector for Smalltalk code, and the component inspector. Theoretically, these tools could be used to examine C++ or other OOP code as well as Smalltalk. All are mature enough to be used for real work. We've been using them to write Smalltalk code for several months. In fact, we prefer the component tools over the ones supplied with the Smalltalk system, since they are more flexible. We routinely add and remove components "on the fly."

Throughout the project, we've been considering how to build other "applications." The classic component-based application is a multi-media document. Typical components might be:

- paragraph component (users can choose their favorite one)

- drawing editor: a coordinated set of graphical components including charts

- video component

- animation component

- sound component

- simulation component

- spreadsheet component (for arithmetic computations)

- field component (for forms and HyperCard-like uses)

- button component (for user-defined functions)

- agent components (for asynchronous user-defined agents)

- layout component (for arranging all of the above on a page)

- spelling checker (for checking the text in all of the above)

- mail component (for mailing all of the above to other people)

- interface builder (a coordinated set of components for building user interfaces).

Such components appear to fit comfortably within the CCK framework.

## 3.7 Business Model

The technical issues are irrelevant unless developers can make money selling components. But a component marketplace would be radically different from the current one. Here are a few of the outstanding questions:

- How do developers make money selling "small, bite-sized" components? They can't charge as much for a component as for a monolithic application.

- How are components marketed? Most traditional forms of advertising may be too expensive.

- How are components distributed? Packaging applications in shrink-wrapped boxes and putting them on dealers' shelves may be too expensive. Perhaps several hundred components could be bundled together on a CD-ROM, with users purchasing access keys for the components they want. Or we might take advantage of the pervasiveness of networks and bulletin boards; users could download components from bulletin boards for a fee.

A key scenario that illustrates the issues with component software is electronic mail. Suppose I create a memo containing several components, and I mail it to you electronically. What do you see when you open it? You may not own all the components that I included. An unacceptable answer is that you see a document with a bunch of holes in it. We believe that a person must at least be able to read any document created by another person, regardless of what the sender put in it.

How does this happen? Are copies of components sent with electronic mail? Developers aren't going to be happy about a lot of unauthorized copying of their code. Are components split into display and editing halves, with the display halves being freely copyable and the editing halves requiring purchase? Users are interested in hassle-free access to software. Developers are interested in getting paid for their work. These interests are not necessarily in conflict.

We would like to offer for discussion an innovative proposal from Mark Miller: charge per use software [Miller 88, Miller 91]. Like pay per view television, charge per use software charges the user a fee every time he runs a program.[4] The key features of this plan are as follows:

- All personal computer operating systems would be modified to keep track of software use.

- Centralized servers would be created to act as component registries (allowing developers to register new components and users to find out about them), distribution points (allowing users to download components to their personal computers), and billing services (allowing developers to get paid).

- One possible billing scheme (there are several) is the following. Each user purchases a credit amount from the central server. This is analogous to buying a tank of gas from a service station. Each time the user runs a component, his account is debited by a certain amount, and the developer's account credited. The key question is the size of the fee. When the account reaches zero, the user purchases a new credit amount from the server.

- During this purchase transaction, the current developers' accounts are transmitted to the server. The server is responsible for paying the developers.

- Users would no longer have to explicitly purchase software. Purchasing a component would still be an option, in which case its subsequent use would be free. But users could choose to never explicitly buy anything, except for periodic "tanks of gas," relying instead on the automatic billing facility. There would likely be a cap

---

[4]Charge per use is a concept that is independent of components; it applies to any software, including today's monolithic applications. We describe it here as it would apply to components.

on the amount users are charged for any given component, such as the list price of the component, so users would never pay more than if they bought the software outright. Various incentives could be introduced to encourage component use and experimentation, such as making the first ten minutes of the use of any component be free.

If a scheme like this were adopted, it would have a revolutionary effect on the software industry. It would radically alter the way developers build, package, market, and distribute software. But new problems require new solutions. Like any new idea, it has its strengths and weaknesses.

On the negative side:

- People don't like pay per view television, and may not like pay per use software. The key issue is the amount of money involved. If it is large, people may resist it; if it is small, people may accept it. There must be a way to cap the expense, so that users are convinced that they don't pay more than they would if they bought the software outright.

- All personal computer operating systems have to be modified.

- A server infrastructure must be set up.

- Large developers are likely to resist component software in general, since it lowers the barrier to entry which currently protects them. Small developers, however, will like it, since it allows them to enter the market. The determinant is the user; if users like component software enough to buy it, it will succeed. Developers build what sells, or they go out of business.

On the positive side:

- Charge per use is hassle-free. People are able to use any software they want. It eliminates the work of buying software.

- It solves the electronic mail problem, allowing users to view everything sent to them.

- It may actually save users money by allowing them to try out software before purchasing it. Most people have had the experience of buying a program and then finding that they don't use it, thereby wasting money.

- It may simultaneously make *more* money for developers, a seeming contradiction, by increasing sales through encouraging people to experiment with new software. The more a person uses a given program, the more likely he is to develop an attachment for it and want to own it. Currently the barrier of a large purchase price discourages such experimentation.

- It fixes the piracy problem. The Software Publishers Association estimates that the software industry loses billions of dollars each year due to the unauthorized copying of programs. The current distribution mechanism *encourages* unauthorized copying; charge per use effectively eliminates it. This is a second way in which developers may make more money. Some people go further, advocating replacing the concept of copyright with "useright." This idea is that the electronic medium invalidates the fundamental assumption of copyright law that material is difficult to copy. Copying software is no longer the issue; *using* it is the issue.

## 3.8   Open Issues

While we strongly believe that a component architecture has the potential to improve, indeed transform, the software industry, many open issues must be resolved before it becomes pervasive:

- What happens when the number of available components becomes large, in the thousands? How will users find the ones they want, or even applicable ones? This is a database problem, and we expect that its data search and retrieval techniques will be applicable. Some search criteria, however, will be unique to components. For example, users might ask to see all the components that are capable of connecting to a given component.

- How will users find out when a new component becomes available? Perhaps there could be a national directory service in which developers can register their components. Users would dial into the directory and query it. It could tell the user what's new since the last time he dialed in.

- How general can individual components be? For example, is it possible to have a general paragraph component that can be used wherever text is needed? At least part of the answer lies in standards. Without standard interfaces, developers cannot write components to be plug compatible with existing components. Many of the standards battles of the 1990s may be over component interfaces. Effective standards are a requirement for components.

- How acceptable will component architectures be to users? Are end users capable of accomplishing non-trivial tasks with components? These are complex questions involving psychological as well as computer science factors. We can imagine people saying, "It wasn't enough that I had to learn how to use applications in order to get my job done, now I have to *build* the applications too!" There are limits to how much we can ask people to do. Indeed, we expect many developers to continue to offer prepackaged sets of components, so that all users have to do is start them up. The key difference is that end users *can modify component applications if they wish to*, unlike conventional applications.

- How rich a system can one build out of components? Will the inherent complexity of software defeat the applicability of components? The only way we'll know is by building some component applications. Complexity has not been a problem in our prototype; indeed, building code navigation tools has been simpler with components than without. But we must build other types of applications before we will know the answer.

- The CCK allows components in a framework to execute on different machines in a network. How can such components be shared, so that a server need have only one copy running? How do they communicate? What is the user model?

These questions and others like them require more study. We hope that the industry will become motivated to address them.

## 3.9 Conclusions

Component architectures have the potential to make personal computer applications simultaneously simpler and more powerful. Such applications will be both easier for developers to write and easier for users to modify. The effect on the software industry could be revolutionary.

Apple's Advanced Technology Group has built a prototype component architecture and a couple of dozen test components. Writing and using components has been an enjoyable experience. We have long wanted the degree of flexibility that they give us. Writing new components has been easier than writing conventional Smalltalk code, since we can draw on the CCK framework. We can turn an existing class into a component in minutes. Adding a component to an existing application takes seconds. We prefer using our component tools to the monolithic Smalltalk tools because they are more functional and flexible. We routinely add and remove components from running applications in order to get specific information. This experience validates the expected advantages of component architectures, both from a developer's and a user's point of view.

## Appendix A - What Is Wrong with Today's Applications?

**Monolithic applications are not good for users.**

From the user's point of view, today's applications commonly suffer from a wide range of ills:

**They don't do a lot.**

Personal computers could be much more helpful to people. Today they just provide electronic analogues of traditional office functions; most of their functions could be done without a computer.

- The "big five" application areas are text, graphics, spreadsheets, databases, and communications. Relatively simple manual programs are provided in each.

- Today users must manually search unstructured text in libraries and other information sources: "tell me about..." There is little effective computer assistance.

- Today most users can't program their personal computers in any significant way. They must rely on others to write programs for them.

- Today personal computers do little to facilitate person–person communication. People find that meeting face to face is still the most successful method.

- Today personal computers are *reactive*, nothing happens until the user pokes at them. They should be *proactive*, where agents actively undertake tasks on the user's behalf.

*Today the effective utilization of the computing cycles in any personal computer over a 24-hour (or any other) period is close to zero.* Tremendous computer power is being wasted.

**They do too much.**

- Microsoft Word 4.0 contains 288 (!) named commands plus numerous unnamed ones, only a fraction of which are used by any one person.

- Ashton Tate's FullWrite Professional includes a graphics editor, in spite of the fact that there are numerous ones on the market.

**They are expensive.**

- Word 4.0 requires three 800K floppy disks. It contains a text editor, page layout editor, style sheets, front and back matter generators, table builder, spelling checker, hyphenater, dictionary, thesaurus, glossary, outliner, calculator, mail merger, menu editor, and macro maker. It costs hundreds of dollars.

- Upgrading to new releases requires lots of time and retraining on the part of the user.

- FullWrite Professional includes all of the above plus a graphics editor. The basic application alone can't fit on an 800K floppy disk without compression. It requires more than 1MB of memory to run.

**They are inflexible.**

People want help with *their specific jobs,* not with generic jobs envisioned by developers. Today users can customize applications only to the extent that developers anticipated they would want to.

- Word 4.0 is one of the best in terms of tailorability, allowing users to control the contents of menus, to assign accelerator keys to commands, and to define text styles. But it doesn't allow users to change the spelling checker it uses or even the dictionary, or the way tables are done, or to add attributes to sections, or to define tab-able fields, etc. And even the style facility, one of the industry's most flexible, doesn't allow more than one type font in a style.

- Microsoft's PowerPoint, a slide-making program, contains a graphing package to allow charts and graphs to be included in slides. But there is no way for users to add their own kinds of graphs, in spite of the fact that many users already have programs which produce graphs.

- There is no way to use (say) MacWrite's paragraph editor in Mac-Draw, or Word's hyphenater in More, etc.

**They limit the choices available.**

- The slow pace of software development reduces the number of applications that get written, resulting in fewer choices and slow software evolution.

- Large applications limit the competition. It is difficult for small developers to enter the market, since there is such a large barrier to entry.

## Monolithic applications are not good for developers.

From the developer's point of view, too, today's applications suffer from many ills:

### They are hard to write.

- Today, in order to enter a given market segment, a product must have a feature list an arm's length long. Otherwise reviewers will compare it unfavorably with existing products.

- Lots of features require lots of code, which requires large programmer teams, which introduces coordination problems.

- Today's programming tools do not work well with large programs and teams.

### They are hard to debug.

- Most monolithic applications today are 6–18 months late, largely due to the difficulty in debugging them.

- It is common for developers to issue "x.0.1" releases to fix serious bugs in the official release.

### They are risky.

Because they are hard to write and debug, they take a long time to develop. This increases the risk to developers in two ways:

- They are expensive to produce. If the product isn't a hit, the developer may lose money. The more expensive the product, the greater the risk.

- The developer can't respond to the market rapidly. The longer the time to respond, the greater the risk of lost sales.

## Some reasons for these ills.

**Monolithic structure.** The main reason is that most applications are written as single, monolithic programs. As Brooks points out, adding features to such a program causes a *nonlinear increase in complexity.* This is compounded by the following characteristic.

**Creeping featurism.** In order to compete in the market today, developers feel they must include a growing number of features in their applications. The computer press encourages this by reviewing software based on little more than checklists of features. Developers keep adding features until the schedule calls a halt or until the program can no longer be debugged.

**Bottom-up implementation.** There is no software infrastructure as there is for hardware. If you ask an electrical engineer to design a board, he will get out his catalogue and select components for it. If you ask a software engineer to design a program, he will get out his (blank) coding pad and start from scratch. (It's not quite that bad, but almost.) Programmers are forced to work from a low level of abstraction. It is analogous to hardware engineers starting with transistors.

**Primitive programming languages.** Programming of personal computers has taken a step back into the 1970s, perhaps even the 1960s, with its C and C++ languages. Even the 1960s had Algol, not to mention Lisp and Simula. The productivity gains of modern dynamic languages have yet to be widely exploited.

**Primitive programming tools.** Compounding the problem of low-level languages is their primitive development environments. It is ironic that while most personal computer applications today follow good user interface principles, the *environments* in which those applications are written do not! Adding to the problem is the complexity of the Macintosh's 1000 toolbox routines, which makes programming the Mac a challenge. The PC equivalents are, by all reports, no better.

## Appendix B - Some Existing Examples of Components

There are a number of products and projects that to some extent use software components. Here are a few of them.

- *UNIX* with its standardized file formats and integrated libraries connected via "pipes" provides perhaps the most numerous and widely-used examples of components. UNIX has stimulated the development of whole "toolboxes," since the tools are interchangeable. However, the inter-component communication is limited to text.

- Bill Budge's *Pinball Construction Set* is an excellent example of a component-based application. In fact, it's on our "10 All-Time Favorite Programs" list. Users drag pinball elements (components) such as flippers and spinners into a playing area. The elements immediately start working. Users can put as many or as few elements into a game as they wish. Everything is done by visual, direct manipulation. Everyone is able to do it.

- Deneba's *Canvas 3.0* is a true component application, albeit at a coarse-grained level. Placing a component in a certain folder causes it to be bound into the application at launch time. Deneba appears to have done a careful design of the components, so that they are reusable in other Deneba applications.

- Silicon Beach's *SuperPaint 2.0* uses components in its drawing palette. When a user places a painting tool in a certain folder before launching SuperPaint, the tool appears in the palette. Many such tools have been written, some by third parties, and some are quite imaginative.

- Macintosh's *control panel devices* (CDEVs) are components that are dynamically loaded whenever the Control Panel is displayed. Hundreds of CDEVs have been developed. All a user has to do is put them in the System Folder. Similarly the Macintosh's "inits" are components that are automatically loaded into the system "application" at boot time.

- The Macintosh *Communication Toolbox* in System 7 provides a set of components representing different communication devices and protocols. MacTerminal 3.0 uses it.

- Hewlett-Packard's *New Wave* [HP 89] includes a general component environment for writing applications for the IBM PC under MS-

DOS. It appears to be one of the best designed architectures on the market today.

- CMU's *Andrew* system incorporates the concept of pluggable components at the user level [Palay 88].

- The NeXT *Interface Builder* allows components to be connected together, which produces an Objective C interface file that is then compiled. Thus components cannot be dynamically connected and disconnected at run time. However, rumor has it that they are currently building hundreds of components.

- Apple's *Apple Events* will allow arbitrary Macintosh applications to use each other's facilities. Applications will register their nouns (data types) and verbs (commands) as Apple Events. This will provide a limited component-like interface to applications, allowing one application to access the nouns and verbs in others.

- *Fabrik* [Ludolph 88] is a component-based programming language written in Smalltalk. It was developed in Apple's Advanced Technology Group (ATG).

- Kurt Schmucker in Apple's Advanced Technology Group has built an environment in which developers can write distributed component-based applications in *MacApp*. Kurt is focusing on the problem of controlling components on multiple heterogeneous machines, including UNIX machines. The application domain is scientific visualization [Schmucker 90, Wolff 90].

- There are an increasing number of other products on the market, including Serius's *Serius Programmer*, DigiDesign's *Turbo Synth*, The Gunakara Sun System's *Prograph*, and National Instruments' *Lab View*. In addition, several companies, notably Microsoft and Claris, are developing application programming interfaces (APIs) allowing one application to talk to another. For example, *Claris CAD* can now communicate with *FileMaker*, and Aldus's *PageMaker 4.0* can use Microsoft's *Mail*.

# Chapter 4

# Design Support Environments for End Users

*Mark Guzdial*
*Peri Weingrad*
*Robert Boyle*
*Elliot Soloway*

## 4.1 Introduction

Several chapters in this book (e.g., Chapters 2 and 3) discuss the design of end user programming languages. By end users we mean people who may be experts in some domain other than software design and who want to develop software to meet their particular needs. Our focus is not so much on the programming language itself, but on the computational environment in which it is embedded. What are the features of the environment which allow end users to design interesting (and thus, complex) artifacts in a domain in which they have little expertise?

End users will be attracted to the next generation tools for two significant characteristics that we assume for these tools: rapid prototyping and concreteness. Rapid prototyping provides fast feedback on a developer's design. Though the end user will certainly make more mistakes than an expert developer, those mistakes will not be so expensive if they can be tested for, found, and corrected quickly. The direct manipulation interface of these new tools provides a concreteness that symbolic, textual programming languages lack. As programming novices who are uncomfortable and unfamiliar with the abstractions in this new domain, the concreteness of direct manipulation provides the end user with confidence that he understands what he is doing. Creating, placing, and testing computational elements such as buttons, scroll bars, and text fields assures the end user that he is creating the artifact that he desires.

The challenge for developers and researchers is how best to meet the needs of end users in these environments. End users are novices in the domain of user interfaces and programming, yet want to design and construct real artifacts as do experts in these domains. In the following section, we characterize the types of problems that novices have in software design. Beyond the relatively simple tool characteristics described above, we see the need for computer-assisted design (CAD) environments which provide support to end users, so that they can design despite the difficult problems facing novices. We refer to this new class of CAD tools as *design support environments* (DSE).

In addition, we foresee a need for these same environments to support more advanced and even expert designers. Our argument is not simply for the efficiency of one environment supporting a spectrum of user abilities. From our experience in classrooms with DSEs, we have found that the learning curve is steep. Use of the environment changes between days one and one hundred of use, and with some students, even between days one and fifty or one and ten. Therefore, support for the end user involves supporting not only the novice, but the novice developing into an expert.

Our research has focused on providing design support to a particular class of end users—secondary school students. In this paper, we describe two DSEs that we have implemented and tested in Community High School in Ann Arbor. The first is MediaText, a multi-media composition environment, which provides a non-programming example of novices working in a design environment. We then describe our experience with GPCeditor (Goal-Plan-Code Editor), a Pascal programming environment used to teach software design. [1] What we find is that there is a set of supports that must be provided to enable design by novices in a general sense.

---

[1] Community High School in Ann Arbor is led by Dean Bob Galardi. MediaText was used in physics, composition, and journalism classrooms at Community High School in

## 4.2   Characterizing End Users as Novices

We see the problem of supporting end users developing and manipulating applications in a user interface programming language as being an instance of the general problem of supporting design by novices. The particular instance of software design has been well researched, and we can identify the key novice problems in that domain.

In general, expert programmers have three types of knowledge structures that novices lack:

**Domain Knowledge:** Because of their experience, expert programmers know the components in the domain which can be used in solution of problems. They know the primitives of the domain (that is, the programming language) and the previously developed solutions which can be reused in future programs.

**Structure:** Expert programmers know how to think about their programs. They know how to identify needs, choose solutions to fulfill those needs, and synthesize these solutions into a complete program.

**Process:** Expert programmers know how to build programs. They might use top-down, bottom-up, or even opportunistic design strategies [Guindon 88], but they know how to interleave the stages of brainstorming, selecting components, synthesizing components, and debugging.

These are summarized in the first two columns of Figure 4.1. Description of novice programmers in terms of these needs follows (and is summarized in the third column of Figure 4.1).

### 4.2.1   Need Domain Knowledge

Research on novice programmers shows that one of their key difficulties is identifying components for their programs [Perkins 86]. Student Pascal programmers may realize, for example, that they need to iterate through a

---

Ann Arbor by teachers Steve Eisenberg and Tom Dodd. GPCeditor was used in a Pascal programming course taught by Bob Kinel. The classrooms at Community High used Apple Macintosh computers donated by Apple Computer.

| | Expert Programmers Have | End users Need | Expert Programmers Can Use |
|---|---|---|---|
| **Domain Knowledge** | – Languages<br>– Past programs | – Appropriate Language<br><br>√ Libraries of Reusable Components/Modules | – Powerful libraries for reuse<br><br>• Add better indices<br><br>• Add agents |
| **Structure** | – Decomposition and Synthesis skills | √ A Structure for Articulation | – Articulation of purpose for maintenance<br><br>• Identifying delocalized plans |
| **Process** | – Top-Down/ Bottom-Up/ Opportunistic | √ Provide Top-Down/ Permit Others | |

Figure 4.1: The difference between expert programmers and end users. Checkmarks indicate features addressed in this chapter.

portion of their program, but be unable to determine if they need a **repeat**, a **while**, or a **for** loop [Soloway 82]. In most cases, the student will simply use the component with which he is most familiar, likely leading the user to errors if the component is inappropriate or more difficult to use compared to others.

The DSE must provide a good index into a library of useful components. The end user uses the index to find components that might be useful in the given program, and then uses the descriptive features of the library to evaluate and choose between the possible components. Further, the library must be expandable to permit the addition of new components as the user develops them.

### 4.2.2 Need for Structure

A blank screen is a frightening thing to a novice user. An end user needs a structure in which to build a design. This structure needs to be one in which the novice can articulate the components required for the design. Education research [Brown 83, Scardamalia 89] emphasizes the importance of articulation for novices, both for understanding the current problem and for learning general strategies for dealing with similar problems. The DSE provides such a structure to encourage the user to articulate the desired design through greater levels of detail until the final design is defined in terms of primitives of the domain, in the case of user interfaces, the buttons, fields, and other items of user interfaces. The most finely detailed level of this structure are the components which, when composed, are the final design.

### 4.2.3   Need for Process

Polya [Polya 57] and others (e.g., [Spohrer 89]) have defined general models for novices of problem-solving and design that involve iteration over a number of stages. Most of these are what software engineers refer to as *top-down* design models. A typical model for software might look like this:

- Define the requirements and decompose them into subgoals,

- find the language primitives or combinations of primitives for achieving these subgoals,

- combine (compose) these components into a complete program,

- test the program,

- determine if the requirements are met.

Research has suggested that experts use a combination of methods, ranging from bottom-up (building up components in the direction of meeting subgoals, rather than defining subcomponents in terms of subgoals) to opportunistic (changing strategies depending on the currently available tools and the current most pressing problem) [Guindon 88]. End users who are experts in some domain may have a model, but generalizing and transferring design strategy knowledge from one domain to another is very difficult. The DSE needs to provide a process so that the difficulty of transferring process knowledge does not hinder the development of useful designs. The goal is to provide the user with choices within a stage, but not between what stages occur next. As will be discussed, our experience with the GPCeditor indicates that this process support must be flexible over time, so that the process support can be malleable and fade as the novice learns design skills in the new domain.

The most difficult particular process stage for both novice and expert programmers is managing interactions between components as these are integrated into the complete program [Spohrer 89]. For example, novice programmers confuse their data objects and forget the meanings they had associated with them in the various program components. The DSE supports the integration of components and the resolution of interactions between them.

## 4.3   Supporting the Novice in a Non-Programming Design Environment

Multi-media composition is similar to the process of composing text, in terms of choosing a good rhetorical structure for the purpose, developing prose, and weaving the prose into a complete composition [Hayes 86]. Multi-media composition adds the complexity of developing and weaving components of computer graphics, animations, videodisc segments, digitized sound, and other media, as well as text. *MediaText* [2] is a multi-media composition environment designed for students which has been in classes for the last year at Community High School in Ann Arbor, Michigan. It runs on Apple Macintosh and IBM PS/2 (under Windows 3.0) microcomputers.

While the students we worked with were well familiar with being consumers of multi-media from television and movies, they were novices at developing their own compositions. Thus, these students faced the same situation as do end users when they first become producers of software as well as consumers. Our experiences with MediaText, then, provide a non-programming example through which to view the general problems of supporting end users in the process of design. These problems will be revisited in the programming domain in the section on the GPCeditor. As

---

[2]MediaText was designed by Mark Guzdial and developed primarily by Jim Merz of the Highly Interactive Computing Environments (HiCE) Group at the University of Michigan, directed by Elliot Soloway. Other members of the HiCE MediaText group include Peri Weingrad, Bob Boyle, Tony Fadell, Jeff Ferguson, Sue Lott, Deborah Swanberg, Sarah Gay, and Professor Joe Krajcik of the School of Education. MediaText has been supported in part by a grant from the University of Michigan, OVPR.

summarized in Figure 4.2, the problems in supporting novices involved in multi-media composition are the same as in the software domain: Providing domain knowledge, providing a structure, and supporting a process.

| | **MediaText** | **GPCeditor** |
|---|---|---|
| **Domain Knowledge** | Domain: Multimedia (video, graphics, sound) composition<br><br>– End users are familiar with the components of the domain. | Domain: Software design in Pascal<br><br>– Explicit instruction in Pascal<br><br>– Library of Reusable Components |
| **Structure** | Simple structure of text annotation.<br><br>– No explicit articulation | A Goal-Plan Articulation Structure |
| **Process** | None<br><br>– End users are familiar with components of the domain, but not their synthesis | Support Top-Down process<br><br>– Need to support more flexibly |

Figure 4.2: Two examples of providing design support to end users.

## 4.3.1 Features and Use of the Environment

We have students explicitly designing in MediaText because construction has greater educational benefit than simply consuming presentation material. Proponents of multi-media presentation tools in education suggest that presenting information in multiple media can aid in the encoding and storing of information by providing multiple, information-rich representations that are more or less similar to the student's own representations for a concept (e.g., [Clark 85, Kozma 91]). Though we do not dispute this potential benefit, this use of multi-media tools is based on a knowledge dissemination model of education where information is "fed" to students. An emerging model of education describes the student as actively constructing her own understanding, and that this learning process is aided by having the student produce artifacts, which can be shared and critiqued by others (e.g., [Harel 90]. Constructing sharable, critiquable externalizations of their knowledge provides motivation for students. Further, construction encourages more active learning in students than the more traditional presentation-oriented, knowledge-transmission model of education.

Students use MediaText to construct their own multi-media presentations. They write their own text, select video segments, record audio clips, and compose these into the MediaText document. An important distinction between MediaText and other multi-media development systems available for this class of microcomputers is that its level of complexity is one appropriate for high school students: developing multi-media documents in MediaText is not as sophisticated as in other presentation-oriented tools (e.g., Macromind Director) and does not require the traditional programming skills necessary in more authoring-oriented tools (e.g., Apple's HyperCard). We hope that students using MediaText are gaining the advantage of exploring concepts in multiple, information-rich representations, but with the additional advantage of building these representations themselves.

### Domain Knowledge

MediaText provides no explicit support for domain knowledge. Students in Ann Arbor are relatively affluent: they are familiar with television, movies, CD players, and other forms of media. None of the media in MediaText were unfamiliar or unusual for the students at Community High School.

Support for reuse of components was through Macintosh cut, copy, and paste. An early version of MediaText provided a simple library structure with a sorted list index of named components, but students found that such a library was more of a hindrance than a help. This may have been because students in a single semester develop a small number of components, and thus don't need explicit support for reuse. Or it may be that the index needs to reflect the multi-media nature of the information. Perhaps the library would have been more useful had it provided some form of browsing, that is, providing direct experience of the media rather than simply listing the name.

### Structure

The main features of the program include a word processor that acts as the centerpiece of the document, and a *medialinks* feature that allows the user to create clickable links between the text and various media (including links to other MediaText documents as well as other applications on the computer.)

*The Word Processing Feature:* A MediaText document has two panes— a large text pane on the left and a smaller medialinks pane on the right (see Figure 4.3). The word processor built into MediaText allows for multiple styles, sizes, and fonts within the text window. The text window provides a backbone for the environment, as it can be used as the primary source of information in the document as well as providing a means of explaining how the links to other media relate to the concepts discussed in the text. The text window also provides stability to the document, whereas a document consisting purely of medialinks may seem random and unconnected to a reader unfamiliar with the content of the document. Text is thus the binding medium in MediaText. For the most part, all other media are viewed in their relation to the text. Thus, the most striking feature of a MediaText document upon first glance is that it is a traditional, comfortable application.

*The MediaLinks Feature:* Along the right edge of the MediaText document's text area is a solid bar. To the right of this bar appear icons, like those one would find on the Macintosh desktop. These are links to other media besides text.[3] This feature allows the user to illustrate her text with a variety of media types: videodiscs, computer graphics, simple (one-object) animations, sound, PICS animations, or audio compact discs.

Clicking on a link starts the associated media clip. Each link has a caption beneath it, and the icon itself informs the user what kind of media is associated with this link. For example, clicking on an icon picturing a disk starts a videodisc sequence on an attached player. These medialinks can be moved as one would a file icon on the Macintosh desktop. Once the medialink is placed, the scrollbar along the right edge of the document scrolls both the text and icons. Thus, a medialink placed to the right of a particular paragraph will remain next to that paragraph. Links can be juxtaposed with the text that describes them, but it is up to the author of the document to make any explicit connection in the text describing the relevance of the accompanying links.

---

[3]MediaText currently supports links to graphics, CD audio, videodisc players, digitized sound, simple and multi-object follow-the-path animations, and PICS animations.

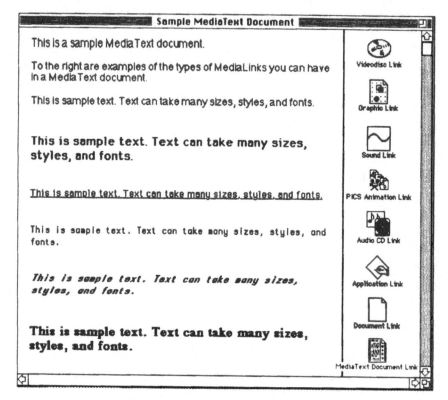

Figure 4.3: A MediaText document.

"Workshops" for the various media types are accessed through a MediaLinks menu. Each workshop allows the user to input information (as described below for each media type) including a name and description to create a "clip" which can then be stored as a medialink on the document. A medialink, once created, is completely editable—allowing the user to modify information in the clip, copy the clip to use in another document, or to delete the clip completely. Furthermore, standard workshop formats are used across media types so that users need to learn essentially one basic procedure for creating and editing clips.

The connection between non-text media and the text, or between different non-text media in MediaText is made through spatial locality. As in any text composition, two paragraphs next to one another are usually related.

A medialink is related both to the text and to the other links appearing near it. This form of relating media is comfortable, easy-to-use, and flexible, but does not explicitly articulate the purpose for the medialink and how it relates to the text and associated links.

### Process

There is no explicit support for process in MediaText. Students can explore goals, find and create media components, compose the pieces into a document, and make connections (non-articulated) between components in any order that they wish. Without support, however, we found that early student documents tended to be lacking cohesion (e.g., little connection between media and the text paragraphs adjacent), poorly structured, and without clear purpose for why one media type was selected over another. (Most student documents late in the semester tended to be improved in the integration between media elements.)

### 4.3.2   Student Outcomes

We have used MediaText in three classes at Community High School: English Composition, Journalism, and Physics. The Composition class used the multi-media capabilities of MediaText while doing the same traditional composition assignments that their classmates in other classes did. (Figure 4.4 is a sample MediaText student document from the Composition class.) The Journalism class originally planned to use MediaText as a "morgue"– a repository for all the source materials they gathered while on their "beat." But they found that the additional overhead of digitizing material and manipulating MediaText wasn't cost-effective. In the Physics class, students were asked to use MediaText to keep a multi-media chronicle of the concepts they learned in class, and they were given the option of writing a semester summary in MediaText rather than a final exam.[4]

---

[4]The final projects from the Physics class were on the whole much better documents than any of the other documents: students put more effort into organizing their work and used the media more extensively. These students were able to demonstrate that they understood the concepts they mentioned in the text by illustrating them with links to other media. Several of these students said that they didn't feel they really understood the formulas until they created animations or other clips to demonstrate the concepts at work.

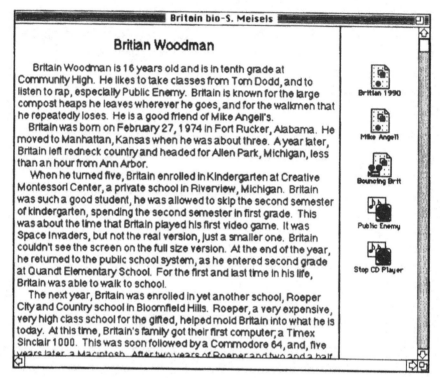

Figure 4.4: Sample student document.

The structure of MediaText led to the students' ability to immediately use it. Students had no trouble understanding the salient metaphor of use implicit in MediaText's design—that the medialinks may be considered annotations to the text. Even the students who had never used a computer before working with MediaText understood its text-centered nature and had success in producing documents by using only the word-processing features of the document.

We found that students averaged about one link per paragraph of written text, most documents only using a couple of the types of medialinks available. The Physics documents that were done in place of the final exam had closer to one link per two or three sentences. We avoided encouraging or assigning the students to use particular types of medialinks unless we had a specific suggestion as to what would work well, given what they were attempting to convey to the reader.

The most frequently used type of medialink was the Graphic/Animation link, although the Physics students frequently used videodiscs to illustrate the Physics concepts they described in their documents. Students preferred to draw their own illustrations or scan in material from magazines and books rather than using pre-created drawings ("clip art.") A number of students said they had ideas for video clips that they wanted to include in their documents, but the material was not available on videodisc.The students also noted that they would prefer to actually have all the material they linked to their documents contained "within" the document itself (as opposed to being on a videodisc or audio CD), so that there would be no difficulty for the reader to play the links. This was especially clear in the case of CD Links. Once the Sound Link feature was redone to make it possible to record directly into MediaText (this occurred about halfway through the second semester) students used digitized sound extensively in ingenious ways which tended to make their documents much more entertaining by adding subtlety to their self-expression. One student (a New Zealander) used the sound feature to let the reader know how to pronounce "Dunedin," the name of the city he was describing in a document; "It is pronounced 'due-nee-den,' not 'doon-din'," he says, scornfully.

However, students had difficulty integrating the different components. An interesting characteristic of most of the student documents is that they created the textual portion of their document so that it would stand alone, and their referrals to the medialinks were often awkward or seemed out of place in their documents—much like many students' first attempts to use quoted material in their compositions. Just as students may know that a quote is relevant to what they were writing, or as when they have been assigned to quote someone else in their work, they sometimes have difficulty working it in, not knowing how to smoothly introduce such material. Just so, many students' MediaText documents showed their seams. Generally, the links chosen were relevant to the text in terms of content: what was lacking was the ability to ease the reader's transition from the text to the media.

We were surprised at this lack of integration between the text and the medialinks in all the classes. No student made any prolonged textual discussion of a link, such as you would expect in a critical discussion of the media clip itself: the students generally used the media in an incidental fashion, many of them omitting even such helpful cues to the reader as when to click on a link, or what videodisc or external file might be required to play a link. We encouraged the students to experiment with the relationship between their text and the medialinks, even suggesting that they create documents without any writing at all. We were surprised (and disappointed) that for the most part students in this class wrote text very much as they would for any other class: writing text that would stand on its own, using standard writing devices such as paragraphs and punctuation. We think that this shows that the students were unsure (and even unaware) of how to take advantage of (and how to avoid the pitfalls of) the fact that readers of their documents interacted with the document in order to "read" it.

The model of end user programming suggested in Chapters 2 and 3 has the user combining components of various types and media into an integrated whole. Our experience with MediaText suggests that the task of integration is formidable. Providing a structure within which to think about and manipulate integration is critical for successful end user programming.

### 4.3.3   Improving the Design Environment

We feel that MediaText was successfully used by the students at Community High School. They were able to create multi-media compositions, with no previous experience in composing in such an environment. In part this was due to the familiarity the students had with the media. Students knew what graphics and video they wanted, and they created it themselves (when possible) if it wasn't available for reuse. In part, this success was due to the structure of MediaText. The MediaText document structure is comfortable, immediately accessible, and easy to understand. It's an obvious extension to the basic word-processing metaphor.

The disadvantage of this structure is that the tie between the different media types is implicit, rather than explicit. The only connection between components is due to locality, which is maintained when the document is scrolled. Articulating the connections between the components of the document might encourage more thoughtful selection of media, reflection on the relationship between the media components, and purposeful design.

We did create a version of MediaText in which the bar separating the text and the non-text media was removed. In this version, media icons could be directly inserted into the text. When students were presented with this version, less than half wanted to use the bar-less version of MediaText, and all the students felt that the default for MediaText should be the separated world. None of the students volunteered to begin using the bar-less world. When asked why they preferred the separated version, they explained that the original version of MediaText was "neat," easy to work with, and easy to understand.

We suggest that the "bar" in MediaText has important implications for end user programming. This separation eased the task of integration for student, and they felt lost without it. In a more complex world of integrating not just media components, but computational components as well, similar "bars" are needed to structure and make accessible the concept of integration in this domain.

One hypothesis for this hesitancy is the lack of process support in MediaText. MediaText provides no structure on how one develops a multi-media composition. The lack of process support is another cause for the lack of good integration between the components: without support, novices have a hard time going through the process stage of merging pieces of a design. Without a bar separating the text from the non-text medialinks, this problem is exacerbated. Placing a medialink in the bar-less world is no longer a matter of positioning a link near its corresponding text, but a matter of positioning around and within the text. The student enters the domain of page layout and desktop publishing, making the process of composition even more complex. Other multi-media composition environments [Pea 91] have noted similar problems when students work on an unstructured canvas.

In summary, the structure of MediaText permits immediate accessibility, but more articulation in the structure might provide better reflection support. Further, the addition of process support might better support the integration of media components.

## 4.4   Supporting the Novice in a Programming Design Environment

Supporting software design is an even more complex task than supporting multi-media design. We have been exploring this kind of support for over two years at Community High School with the GPCeditor.

Unlike MediaText, the *GPCeditor* (Goal-Plan-Code Editor) [5] provides tight control over the student's design process. It attempts to provide students with support for key aspects of the planning phase of software design, identifying potentially useful modules ("decomposition"), and integrating those modules into a coherent system ("composition"). Written in some 15,000 lines of LISP, it runs on an Apple Macintosh II equipped with a 19-inch or 13-inch monitor. The GPCeditor (and an associated curriculum designed expressly for the GPCeditor) has been in continuous use in an introductory programming class at Community High School since Winter semester 1988-89.

### 4.4.1  Features and Use of the Environment

The GPCeditor (seen in Figure 4.5) provides many of the features of the end user programming languages described in this book. Students using the GPCeditor do not write code. Instead, they choose program components from a library of reusable components, integrate them, and then compose the components into a completed program. Multiple representations of the developing program are provided, such as a graphical overview of the program components, textual lists, and the Pascal code itself. We can identify the kinds of supports built into the GPCeditor environment using the schema presented earlier.

### Domain Knowledge

Students using the GPCeditor are not expected to understand the domain of software development in Pascal. Component knowledge in the domain is provided through two sources.

First, the students are given explicit instruction on Pascal language constructs. A curriculum developed for the GPCeditor class is used in the high school. It emphasizes learning Pascal components while developing graphics-oriented programs (e.g., animations and Moire diagrams).

---

[5]GPCeditor was designed initially by Ken Ewing at Yale University and has been developed for the last three years by Luke Hohmann of the HiCE Group. Other HiCE GPCeditor group members include Kathy Brade, Mark Guzdial, Blake Robinson, Iris Tabak, and Professor Phyllis Blumenfeld of the School of Education. Research on the GPCeditor is supported by NSF Grant #MDR-9010362 and Apple Computer.

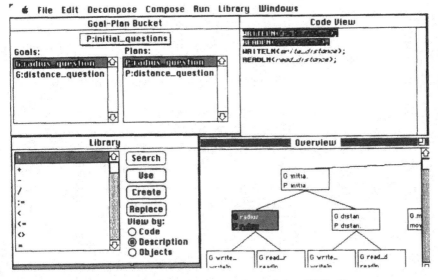

Figure 4.5: Sample screenshot of the GPCeditor.

Second, all of the standard, primitive components of Pascal are stored in the GPCeditor's plan library (lower left-hand corner of Figure 4.5). Students can browse this library to identify potential plans for achieving their program goals. As students define new plans composed of combinations of these plans, these new plans can be stored into the library for later reuse. The GPCeditor's plan library serves not only to provide the design choices for a novice user, but also provides a structure for developing the expert strategy of design component reuse.

## Structure

The GPCeditor requires students to explicitly deal with three levels of program description (Figure 4.5): *goals* (objectives that the final artifact must satisfy), *plans* (stereotypical techniques for achieving goals), and *code* (actual Pascal language constructs). A plan is made up of Pascal language statements, e.g., the GET-INPUT PLAN is made up of "writeln('please input a number'); readln(input_variable);". At the lowest level of detail, a GPCeditor *plan* is a chunk of code, where each statement in the chunk works with the other statements to achieve a particular objective (e.g., asking the user to input a value, and then accepting that value) [Rich 81, Soloway 86]. These goals and plans appear in three different representations: A linear list of goals and plans (upper left of Figure 4.5); a graphical representation of the goals and plans of the program (lower right of Figure 4.5); and the actual Pascal code corresponding to the program (upper right of Figure 4.5).

The goals and plans of a GPCeditor program define a hierarchical structure (lower right-hand corner of Figure 4.5) whose leaf nodes are the primitive components of the complete artifact. Each goal and plan in this hierarchy has a name and a description which articulates its role in the complete artifact. The goal–plan hierarchy, then, is a structure for articulation which, through stepwise refinement, results in the components of the complete artifact.

### Process

The GPCeditor was designed with a particular, top-down model of software design in mind. This model requires defining what goals the designer has for the artifact, how the designer plans to realize that artifact, and in what way these plans are composed together to synthesize the artifact. Students using the GPCeditor are held to this process through tight control realized in the menu system and representations of the environment.

In the GPCeditor design process, students must first define *goals* (what they wish to achieve) before being allowed to define matching *plans* (how they wish to achieve these goals). Before a plan can be composed into the artifact, the data objects required by the plan must be instantiated in terms of data objects used in the program. This is the process of integrating the component into the existing structure. The tools for integrating data objects with a new plan allows students to either choose to match a plan's need with an existing data object, or to define new data objects for the plan.

Students are led through this design process via tight process control realized in the menu system. The various activities of the student's design process appear as the names of the menus: First, the student *decomposes* the problem, then *composes* the solution, then finally *runs* the result. Explicitly, students are expected to define goals, and then plans for those goals, and then to compose those plans into the program. The items within the menus are enabled or disabled corresponding to the student's current design activity. For example, the menu item for creating a *New Goal* is always available in the Decompose menu, but the item for creating a *New Plan* is only enabled when a goal has been created, is selected, and has no matching plan. Variations within the process are permitted, such as creating multiple goals before creating matching plans, but the general top-down strategy is required for the student.

Based on this description, we say that the GPCeditor provides *tight* control of the various stages in the design process: one can't simply add code to the Code View, but rather the student must first identify goals, then plans, and then put the pieces together. Through this tight enforcement, students are given a process through which to work through their program.

### 4.4.2  Student Outcomes

These features of the GPCeditor provide support for end users (in our case, high school students) to design significant software artifacts. When taught using conventional techniques, students after a single semester of Pascal instruction can do little more than write syntactically correct code [Pea 86]. In the GPCeditor class, each student completes over 25 Pascal programs, ranging in size from five lines of code to over one hundred lines.

In completing these programs, students make extensive use of the support structures in the GPCeditor. They access their Pascal components (and their own, saved and then reused, plans) from the Plan Library, they articulate their designs using goals and plans, and they follow the design process embedded in the GPCeditor. In fact, the students learn these elements of Pascal, the structure, and the design process, and transfer this knowledge to similar but unsupported situations.

One indication of the student's learning of design and Pascal is that we see some generalizability to other Pascal programming environments. At the end of the semester, students in the GPCeditor class use THINK Pascal in order for us to explore the question if students can write programs without the support of the GPCeditor. If we simply count the lines of code in the final program done by the students, we see that approximately 1/3 wrote final programs at the 850 statement level, 1/3 wrote final programs at the 250 statement level, and 1/3 wrote final programs at the 150 statement level. *Thus, 2/3rds of the class were able to produce a significantly sized program without the aid of the GPCeditor.* Moreover, by and large those programs did not exhibit "spaghetti code;" rather, these programs exhibited a highly modular structure.

While students wrote code directly in THINK Pascal, students commented that they were definitely influenced by the GPCeditor experience. For example, one student noted that "I may not code in the GPC, but I think it," while another student commented that "I am seeing GPC in my mind when I write THINK."

### 4.4.3  Improving the Design Environment

The cost of the tight support in the GPCeditor is that it is not always appropriate for all students. We find that low-ability students are not yet ready to phrase their decompositions in terms of goals and plans. They require a less formal structure in which to being their problem decomposition, without creating environment objects such as goals and plans. We also find that high-ability students outgrow the support of the GPCeditor after a few months of use. They begin to take shortcuts (e.g., shorter variable names, less modularity) to reduce the development time, inflated by the additional articulation and enforced process of the GPCeditor.

We have begun to build DSE with *adaptable scaffolding* for changing the support to match the user. *Scaffolding* is a term from the Education literature that describes the support that the teacher provides to the student as he first learns a new process. The GPCeditor's supporting features are a form of scaffolding that need to adapt to the needs of a learning user. By changing the scaffolding (or allowing the users to adapt it for themselves), the DSE can support a wider range of users.

## 4.5  Summary

We have found that high school students can create quite sophisticated designs in domains unfamiliar to them, with appropriate support structures. The support structures we've described for MediaText and GPCeditor are summarized in Figure 4.2. In summary, we find that the three kinds of support most useful in supporting design by students are:

**Domain Knowledge:** In domains in which students are unfamiliar with the components, a library of reusable components is useful to provide users with a ready list of available design modules.

**Structure:** A structure in which students can articulate the purpose for the components and the connections between them is useful in helping students build complex artifacts. If an articulated structure is not provided, than a structure that builds on familiar metaphors enables the end user to function within it.

**Process:** A supported design process helps students in overcoming common novice problems, such as the inability to integrate components into a complete artifact.

We are currently exploring how these same tools can be made useful to the more expert programmer through adaptable scaffolding. Our goal is not so much to support a range of users, but to support individual users as they develop and become more skilled in these design domains. As end users design in these environments, their skills improve, and their needs change. The environment needs to change with them. Some of these changes include support for alternative process models (e.g., bottom-up and opportunistic), and computer-generated nodes in goal–plan hierarchies so as to provide the benefits of a goal–plan structure without the enforced articulation.

While not all the same tools are useful in the same ways, even expert programmers have design problems that tools such as those in the GPCeditor can help with. In particular, there is a role for component reuse libraries and structure support (summarized in the last column of Figure 4.1).

**Reuse Libraries.** Along the road from novice to expert, the end user creates a large number of programs and program components. The library in which the user stores these components for later reuse must not only permit an ever-growing repository, but must also support more powerful index structures. The problem with thousands of program plans is not just storing them, but finding them.

The successor to the GPCeditor for Pascal programming is SODA (SOftware Design lAboratory). SODA will feature much of the adaptable scaffolding mentioned earlier, but with a focus on the construction of large Pascal programs. It will provide library indices appropriate for indexing the large number of program components that experts deal with. SODA will continue to offer the flat, linear list of the GPCeditor's Plan Library, but also hierarchical and keyword indices for locating useful plans from the large repository. We are also exploring the development of agents to aid in the search for appropriate components.

**Structure for Articulation.** For experts, the structural support becomes a tool for program maintenance. As programs grow larger, maintenance on them becomes more difficult. A maintainer's task is to identify what in the program requirements correspond to what component in the program. A goal–plan hierarchy makes explicit those correspondences. In other programs we are developing, we are exploring the role goal–plan hierarchies can have in supporting program maintenance.

In conclusion, design environments for constructing user interfaces in the future must support both the first-time end user and the same user one hundred days after the first use. The first-time user has an idea of what she wants, but not how to get it. The design support environment helps by providing information on components in the domain, a structure for articulating the design, and process support including support for integrating these components. The same user one hundred days later has a better idea of what she wants, but her methods and aims have changed. She now needs support in dealing with the complexity of her new goals. The challenge to environment designers and researchers is to provide support to both kinds of users and the spectrum between within a single, adaptable environment.

# Chapter 5

# The Use–Mention Perspective on Programming for the Interface

*Randall B. Smith*
*David Ungar*
*Bay-Wei Chang*

## 5.1  Introduction

In the past decade, direct manipulation interfaces have become commonplace. It is generally recognized that these interfaces succeed because
they allow users to import intuitions from their real world experience. We
believe that there are significant advantages to taking the physical world
metaphor more seriously than does a typical direct manipulation interface.
In our work on ARK [Smith 87] and on the interface for the language Self
[Chang 90], we have concentrated on trying to portray a consistent, tangible reality: a user who subconsciously buys into this illusion does not have
to bear the cognitive load associated with the conscious awareness of the
interface. In this paper, we discuss the implications for programming that
arise from taking the physical world analogy very seriously, particularly in
regard to issues of use and mention. The task of programming is bound up
in the issue of mention vs. use. For example, when programming for the

direct manipulation context, one must have ways to mention buttons and menus without invoking (using) them. When modifying a button, one must talk *about* it, and is not then interested in operating it. Programming for direct manipulation interfaces is commonly carried out in a textual language, in which use and mention are distinct. However, a direct manipulation interface is a physical-world analog, and we argue that use and mention are not distinguished by the physical world. We argue that passing from the user interface into the textual language will always be an ungraceful act, because the two domains are fundamentally different in how they handle use and mention. We claim that forcing a distinction between use and mention into the interface has serious and evil consequences. The solution we propose is to take the real world's lack of distinction between use and mention seriously by providing programming capabilities within the direct manipulation paradigm in a way that is modeled on the physical world. What we are saying has profound consequences for the language:

(a) it must have object-oriented semantics, so that objects can directly present their own state and behavior,

(b) it must be dynamic, allowing incremental changes from the interface,

(c) it must be visual, so that all the capabilities of the language are present in the interface, and

(d) it must avoid enforcing any kind of use–mention distinction.

Features (a) and (b) are already available in a few commercial languages. We focus on the more novel claims (c) and (d), examining several ways existing visual, direct manipulation systems deal with use–mention issues. Use-mention functionality vs. use–mention distinction. We examine how use and mention functionality appear in natural language, in the physical world, and in their computational analogs: textual languages and direct manipulation. Natural language vs. the physical world. In natural language, we commonly use words and commonly mention words. For example,

```
When I said "that," I meant the red car.
```
is very distinct from
```
When I said that, I meant the red car.
```

Language is essentially symbolic or denotational: every word stands for something. Language can talk about words in the language itself: for every word W there is a quoted word Q(W) that stands for (denotes) W. It is important to note that Q(W) is distinct from W. They do not look alike, and they denote different things. Also, it is Q(W) that is used when defining W, or when modifying the meaning of W. Q(W) is our handle for "programming" in natural language. By contrast, the physical world does not of itself support a distinction between use and mention. For example, to use a knob on some device, one might grab it and twist it. To mention it (in order to change it) one might grab the knob and pull it off the device. However, the knob mentioned is the same as the knob used, so the distinction is not in the object. Is the distinction in the way I manipulate the object? Not necessarily: if I drag a paintbrush over a cloth, am I using the brush to paint the cloth, or am I mentioning the brush as I act on it to remove the excess paint? The distinction resides in the mind. This discussion is reminiscent of Heidegger's notion of "break down." By merely pointing out the existence of the paper on which this document is printed, I can cause the paper to "breakdown" from a thing used to a thing mentioned. The importance of breakdown to users of computer systems has been pointed out by Winograd and Flores [Winograd 87]. When users need to modify their natural language, they use mechanisms that force a distinction between use and mention. When users need to modify an object in the physical world, there is no special mechanism needed. Textual computer language vs. direct manipulation. In textual computer languages with enough flexibility to change the language from within itself, the use–mention distinction is also important. Perhaps the cleanest way of dealing with this is worked out in the language 3-LISP [Smith 84]. Again, it is the quoting mechanism that enables us to talk about a symbol (to mention it), and the quotes are often said to "protect it" from being used. Thus (set 'foo 3) is the way of talking about the binding of foo. The object used in "set" is not the object bound: (eq 'foo foo) is false. All of this is strongly analogous to natural language. Since LISP is a textual language, it is not surprising that its use–mention functionality mirrors that of natural language. In a similar way, we might expect use–mention functionality of direct manipulation environments to be carried over from the real world experience. However, those direct manipulation environments that can be arbitrarily changed usually are constructed by programs in some textual language. Functionality for changing the interface is available, but it is not modeled consistently within the terms of the interface. For example, the Smalltalk interface is completely changeable, but the mechanisms for doing so are at odds with the direct manipulation paradigm the interface embodies. The most direct way to change a menu in Smalltalk is to hit control-c, and dive through the resulting execution stack to find the code denoting the menu object. From there it is possible to edit lists to modify the menu, but there is no direct manipulation of the menu involved in any of this activity. The direct manipulation paradigm is abandoned, and one goes over to a linguistic domain (Smalltalk code) for programming tasks.

## 5.2   Interfaces and Language Don't Mix

What's wrong with living in a world that is partly direct manipulation, and partly textual programming? There are two serious problems that arise: the first is the automatic stifling of the everyday user's creativity and learning, and the second is the difficulty of making functionality available in the interface. Users who wish to change the functionality of their application must know essentially two systems: the set of rules and interface operations that apply to the application, and the syntax and semantics of the implementation language. This means that, for most users who only know the direct manipulation system, there is an impractically large barrier in the way of enabling them to tailor the system for their tastes and needs. It also means that the programmer–user distinction is cast into the very design of every application of the system: users have no smooth path enabling them to incrementally grow toward programming activities. The second problem with the two-system model is that functionality available in the language domain cannot be easily imported into the user domain. Once an operation is made available in the language, it must be "lifted up" into the interface explicitly. It is well-known that dealing with the interface is the bulk of the code for most systems. But might there be some way to make sliding between the text domain and the interface domain much less painful, or virtually invisible? When it comes to programming (changing, tailoring, editing) the interface, one must mention the visible interface objects, and to mention something with language, one must essentially go elsewhere, abandoning the directness of the direct manipulation paradigm. Thus there is a fundamental difference in kind which we believe will always rear its head, no matter what trickery is employed to blend a linguistic model with a direct manipulation model. So rather than try to blend the linguistic and object-centered models, we propose to give up the linguistic model completely, taking the physical world model very seriously. This opens the door to "visual programming," but we avoid the term since it implies that programming is identifiable as separate from other activities. (As we have argued above, the programming/non-programming (changing/using) distinction is not supported within the physical world, although it may be a very real and at times appropriate distinction in the mind of the user.) We have already said that most direct manipulation environments do not include much changeability within the interface paradigm. However there are a few that do, to various degrees. We survey some of the approaches that have been used in the past.

## 5.3 Examples of Use with Mention Supported by Direct Manipulation Interfaces

The few direct manipulation interfaces that provide some changeability within the interface differ in the ways they provide this functionality. We give examples of three different approaches: the modal approach, the affordance approach, and the tools approach.

### 5.3.1 The Modal Approach

In the modal approach, the interface objects can be directly manipulated in two ways: one associated with use, the other with mention. Within this paradigm, there are a variety of approaches having to do with the breadth of the mode: at one extreme we have the per-object mode, in the middle is the per-application mode, and at the end is the system-wide mode.

*The per-object mode* is exhibited by the "menu dropping" application created by the first author. In this system, any menu can be "dropped" by hitting control-m. When a menu is dropped, it essentially becomes a window, although the only cue that the menu is different is the lack of a drop-shadow (and the way it now responds to the mouse). Once dropped, a pop-up menu of operations can be invoked on the fallen menu that enables the user to add items, remove items, or otherwise edit its functionality. Of course, once this menu is dropped, the menu for editing menus becomes itself editable, and so on. The pin-down menus of the Open Look interface systems are similar, although the amount of editing they support is minimal (see Figure 5.1-a). *The application-wide mode* is exhibited by the NeXT machine's interface builder (Figure 5.1-b). A knife switch object is able to change the mode of an application from use to mention. In use mode, the mouse would slide a slider tab, in mention mode, the entire slider would get disconnected from the application and moved around by the mouse. *The system-wide mode* is exhibited by the "meta computer" Smalltalk application created by the first author. In this application, hitting control-M causes the entire computer to appear on the screen, as though one had stepped back from the display to take in the larger setting (Figure 5.1-c). Here a mouse, keyboard, and display appear. On the display are all the user's windows, though displayed slightly smaller. The user can move the virtual mouse and the cursor will track on the little display. Everything will work as before: arbitrary pieces of code can be executed in the virtual computer. The virtual computer, however, is magic: by leaving the virtual mouse aside and grabbing a window "through the glass" directly, one can manipulate display objects in a mention mode. For example, pulling the cursor arrow out through the "glass" enables the user to operate on it, editing its shape and behavior. None of these examples, (except the virtual computer) allows arbitrary changes (full programming) through the "mention" mode. But our criticism does not stop there: the modal approach, although it seems in some ways natural, is nevertheless a mode, and as such flies in the face of conventional wisdom. It is untrue to the physical world metaphor in which breakdown from use to mention occurs in the human mind, not in the world of objects. Thus what is mention and what is use is predetermined by the system, so at times repeatedly crossing the modal barrier will become tedious. The modal approach also prohibits treating different parts of an object on a different footing at the same time, i.e., using some parts while mentioning others. From that perspective, perhaps it could be said that the per-object mode sins the least.

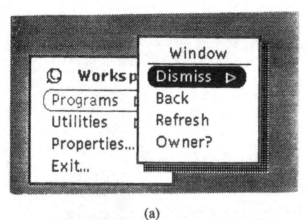

(a)

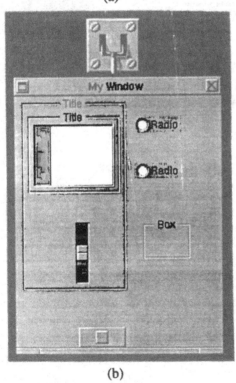

(b)

Figure 5.1: The modal approach to providing use and mention functionality enforces a use–mention distinction. (a) Pin-down menus provide a per-object mode. (b) The NeXT interface builder provides a per-application mode.

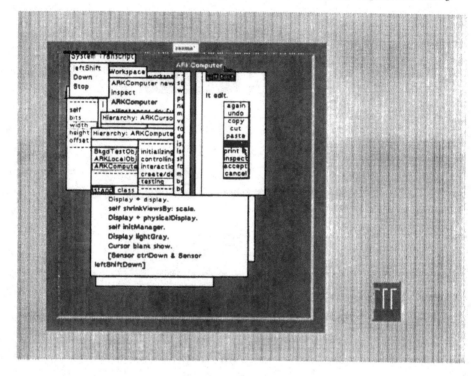

(c)

Figure 5.1 *continued*: (c) This Smalltalk "meta computer" application provides a system-wide mode.

### 5.3.2   The Affordance Approach

The term "affordance" refers to the association of a permanent knob, handle, or other object part with an appropriate function. In this scheme, each object devotes a few pixels of precious screen real estate to "mention functionality." The tear-off menus of HyperCard are an example (see Figure 5.2). Here, operations that are about the menu (moving it, closing it) are attached to regions of the "title bar" of the menu. Conventional window systems adopt this approach when they have close boxes, zoom boxes, resize corners, move regions, and pop-up menu buttons attached to the title bar or edges of the window. It is interesting to think of these systems as a

Figure 5.2: Affordances are parts of objects that providing handles for special functions. In this tear-off menu, the little title bar and close box give the user the ability to mention the menu, as opposed to use it.

historical trend. Window systems offered users increased flexibility over the older tty-style interface, because window systems enable the user to move, resize, shrink, and open the "virtual screens." These can be considered mention functions, in that they change the display objects that are tools to the user. But window systems add their own new tools: pop-up and pull-down menus. The tear-off menus begin to do for these tools what windows did for the tty-style interface. Of course we are advocating skipping to the end of this trend by making the systems arbitrarily malleable as a fundamental design principle. Again, the set of adjustments one can make to the interface through these systems is pretty impoverished. But the affordance approach would seem to have certain inherent problems: the primary drawback is the screen real estate problem: devotion of a small area (corners, edges, title bars, whatever) to programming functionality threatens to make the programming task awkward. Nevertheless, this screen real estate problem might be susceptible to conventional interface trickery: one could scroll the title bar regions, zoom in to the title bar to find it a rich landscape studded with microscopic menus, or one might pull out drawers full of buttons. A secondary concern is the scaling of this approach into arbitrary mention levels, e.g., to resize a window, I grab the corner object. How do I change the size of the corner object? Through an itsy bitsy "meta corner object" on the corner object?

### 5.3.3   The Tools Approach

In this scenario, users modify objects by applying tools directly to them. This approach is used in the Alternate Reality Kit (ARK) [Smith 87]. In ARK, users manipulate simulated physical objects, some of which are buttons. Buttons can be dropped onto an object and activated. ARK can be thought of as a kind of concrete representation of Smalltalk—any Smalltalk object can be made to appear in ARK, and any Smalltalk message can be made to appear as a button. Now because buttons are themselves just a kind of ARK object, it is possible to operate on them with other buttons (see Figure 5.3). Thus, buttons can be arbitrarily changed with other buttons. This approach is somewhat like the real world in that one often employs tools to create change. It is a less immediate effect than one can get with the affordance approach, although ARK buttons can be shrunken and left attached to an object, thereby simulating an affordance. In summary, we find several approaches for providing programming functionality within the direct manipulation paradigm. Of these, the modal approach is our least favorite as it unnaturally enforces a use–mention distinction. A final story will reinforce one of the benefits of having no use–mention distinction.

## 5.4   A Story and Conclusion

When ARK was being used to build a certain physics simulation, the first few users in a series of trials convinced the simulation's creators that their microworld would benefit by letting the users add an electric charge attribute to arbitrary objects. Adding new instance variables to objects is normally a programmer level task. The simulation designers had already started trials, so time was of the essence. But because in ARK adding instance variables is an operation that involves pressing buttons, there was essentially no work at all in adding this capability to the microworld. The users, who already understood how to manipulate and activate buttons as part of the normal interface, were given just one more button for adding an electric charge attribute. If the users had to enter a special mode to directly modify the objects, the results would have been less satisfying. If the facility was only available in the textual representation, it would have required significant work by the simulation creators to "pull up" the associated code

Figure 5.3: In ARK, buttons are the fundamental tool of the interface. Buttons can act on other buttons to modify them. Here the user has a hierarchical series of button panels that operate on the "ARKObjects" button.

into an interface function—extra work that in this case might have killed the idea for lack of time. Because there was no distinction between use and mention, the interface could be provided with arbitrary functions without requiring users to understand a whole new language, or even a new mode. We conclude by reiterating our desiderata for programming languages for the interface: object-oriented, dynamic, visual, and free of barriers between use and mention. In particular, the lack of distinction between use and mention means that designers can easily incorporate all functionality, even "programming" as part of their interfaces. It also means that users are able to smoothly grow into programmers, and are able to tailor their interfaces to their individual tastes and needs.

# Chapter 6

# Why the User Interface Is *Not* the Programming Language— and How It *Can* Be

*James R. Cordy*

## 6.1  Introduction

Portions of the user interface community suggest that if the user interface specification tools are designed perfectly, then quite naive users could specify the majority of their programs without using any programming language at all. While this is a laudable goal, and it would be a very happy world if this idea could indeed bear fruit, the fact of the matter is that specifications of even very simple user interfaces themselves, let alone more complex program semantics, will always require the full power of a programming language. This chapter demonstrates this point by setting a very simple interface problem and observing that all of the salient features of a full programming language are necessarily required in order to specify it. But all is not lost—by taking the opposite tack, and growing programming notation towards visual user interface specification rather than the other way around, we can achieve most of the advantages of the original dream. This point we demonstrate by using the visual programming language GVL [Cordy 90] to specify the example interface.

## 6.2   What Makes a Programming Language? (Semantically)

While their syntax, programming paradigm, and philosophy may vary widely, there are several features that we can say are attributes of every programming language, even if implicitly. Since all programming languages share them, we can say that these attributes form an abstraction of what a programming language is. These attributes are not accidental— rather they derive from the range of computations that we wish to be able to describe in a programming language, which, in some sense, predetermine that the attributes must be present.

The following is a proposed list of attributes of all of the things that we would call modern programming languages. The list is paradigm-independent—that is, it transcends the notions of imperative and declarative programming, and attempts to come to the essence of the semantic core of all programming languages. While there could be no complete agreement on such a list, this one is sufficiently complete and non-controversial to serve our purpose.

**Values.** The first of these, and the basis of a programming language, is the notion of a *value space*. This is simply the set of basic data objects that the language will manipulate. All programming languages have such a space. For Pascal, the value space includes integers, real numbers, Boolean values, and characters. For Turing [Holt 88a], the value space consists of integers, reals, Booleans, and text strings. For pure lisp, the value space consists of the set of all atoms. And so on.

**Structures.** The second essential attribute is the notion of em value structuring. Languages that can manipulate only atomic values are too weak to reasonably express all but the simplest of algorithms, and programming languages invariably provide some kind of structuring facility for data. In Pascal, this structuring facility includes the ability to create arrays, records, and dynamic pointer structures. In pure lisp, the structuring facility consists of the ability to build and manipulate lists.

Once a structured data space is present, the only remaining problem is the ability to express the manipulation of the data structures in such a way as to achieve a desired result.

**Decision.** The first essential requirement in expressing such manipulations is some way to make a decision. In Pascal, this is done using the **if** and **case** statements to decide what action to perform next in an algorithm. In functional languages, this is done using conditional value expressions, as in "**if** $a[i] > a[j]$ **then** $a[i]$ **else** $a[j]$". In Prolog, selection is implicit in the rule search and unification strategies of the language.

**Repetition.** Any computation that does not repeat is doomed to fixed-size data structures and to making each decision exactly once (making decisions redundant), some way of repeating or recurring is necessarily a part of all programming languages. In imperative languages such as Pascal, **while** and **for** loops serve this purpose. In functional languages, this purpose is normally served by recursion (which is argued as an essential attribute in its own right below). In logic languages like Prolog, repetition is implicit in the interpretation of each clause.

**Abstraction.** While technically a redundant feature, every programming language provides some way to name groups of decisions and repetitions. Pascal provides procedures and functions. Named functions form the very essence of functional languages, and Prolog provides abstraction through sets of rules whose heads begin with the same symbol.

**Parameterization.** Abstraction is not much use without some kind of parameterization, and every language provides some ability for parameterizing its abstractions. In Pascal there are both value and reference parameters. Functional languages have only value parameters. And in Prolog parameterization is implicit in the unification of terms with the heads of rules.

**Recursion.** Finally, the power and expressiveness of parameterized abstractions is only fully available when recursion is provided, and all modern languages provide some form of recursion. In Pascal and the other modern imperative languages both recursive functions and procedures are provided. In the functional languages, recursion is the primary method of expressing repetition. And in Prolog, recursion is implicit in the repetition strategy for rules.

## 6.3   Specifying Graphical User Interfaces— An Example

As a simple example of a user interface we might want to specify, consider an application which maintains some kind of binary tree data structure. The high-level specification of the user interface we have in mind is quite simple—the requirement is simply that the graphics screen must always show an up-to-date graphical representation of the tree in Figure 6.1. No bounds are known on the size or shape of the tree other than that it is binary.

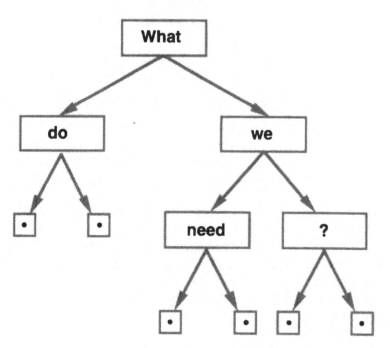

Figure 6.1: Example graphical view of a binary tree.

For the purposes of the example, we will ignore the problems of graphical layout, window and screen size and simply assume that appropriate layout, clipping and/or scrolling will be specified independently. The problem is simply to specify the graphical representation of the internal tree that we wish to see.

## 6.4 Specifying Graphical User Interfaces— What Do We need?

Given this simple example as the interface to be specified, we now ask the question, what do we really need in a facility to specify the interface? In the spirit of gradually evolving by-example style user interface tools such as HyperCard [Apple 87] to replace programming of the interface, we expect that the specification should itself be done graphically. The first step in such a specification, then, might be the drawing of the basic graphical pictures we hope to see, as shown in Figure 6.2.

Once we have these two possible pictures, we need to decide which one should be drawn depending on the particular internal binary tree at any given time. In the spirit of a by-example visual interface, we represent this decision in a graphical way, as a condition box containing each of the two alternative pictures and a condition which chooses between them (Figure 6.3). The condition box is intended to specify that if the binary tree node we are drawing is a null tree then we want to see the picture on the left, otherwise we expect to see the picture on the right.

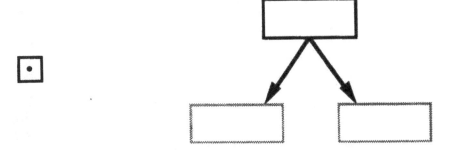

Figure 6.2: Drawings of the basic graphical pictures we hope to see.

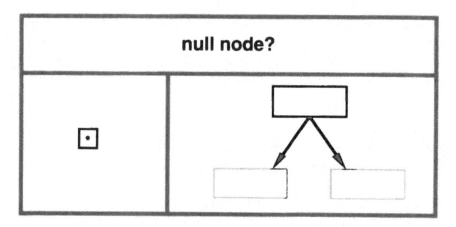

Figure 6.3: Simple by-example graphical representation of the choice between the two possible pictures of a particular tree node.

The next problem we are faced with is the question of how to specify what goes in the dotted boxes under each of the arrows in the tree picture on the right. When drawing a binary tree, each of the things hanging off a particular tree node is itself another subtree, the drawing of which can be done using the same specification. We can express this in our specification by simply giving a name to the condition box and using that name in each of the dotted boxes in the drawing of Figure 6.4.

The specification must somehow indicate that the trees that are to be drawn below are actually the right and left subtrees of the current tree node, and not simply the same node itself again. This we can specify precisely by adding names for the current node and its two children to the specification, as is shown in 6.5.

At this point we have at last a reasonably convincing specification of the drawing of the required user interface, an arbitrary binary tree. Given a root tree node, the specification fully specifies how to draw a binary tree diagram of the tree, no matter what shape or size the tree may be. Moreover, it is difficult to argue that a much simpler specification of this could be made—the whole thing consists of a box surrounding the two basic pictures and a very few labels for the parts.

We can imagine that we entered the entire specification directly on the screen using mouse and menus in a HyperCard or MacDraw-style direct

# Tree

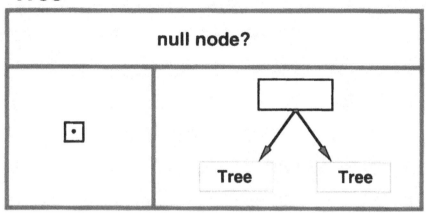

Figure 6.4: Use of a name for the specification to indicate that each subtree is to be drawn in the same way.

manipulation way, and no apparent programming has been done. The net result is a very convincing and pleasing illusion that no programming language was necessary to specify the interface.

## 6.5  Surprise!—What We Needed Was a Programming Language

Unfortunately, an illusion is all that it is. In fact, as demonstrated in Figure 6.6, the set of features we needed to do even this simple specification is in fact a complete (functional) programming language, with all of the essential attributes we listed in our original analysis of what makes one. (In fact, the notation we have used is a subset of GVL [Cordy 90], an existing visual functional language for specifying graphical output.) It has a value space consisting of the basic graphical elements such as boxes, arrows, and text labels, a structuring facility over these values consisting of the spatial relations and connections between them in a picture, a decision facility, repetition via recursion, abstraction, parameterization, and recursion itself.

The fact that the minimum we need to specify user interfaces is in fact a full programming language should really not come as a surprise. After

# Tree (this, left, right)

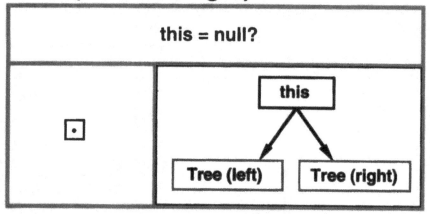

Figure 6.5: Names for the left and right subtrees of the current tree node allow some indication that it is actually these subtrees to be drawn below.

all, we know from experience that the algorithms and coding involved in the programming of a user interface is often at least as difficult as the programming of the application itself, so it should come as no surprise that the tools for specifying it must be at least as powerful.

The realization that general by-example user interface specification tools are in fact semantically programming languages also allows us to take advantage of the large store of knowledge on the design, specification, interpretation, and compilation of programming languages, the vast majority of which is independent of syntax, even multi-dimensional syntax.

Moreover, by designing future by-example user interface specification tools to be full programming languages rather than pretending that they are not and living with a limited subset of capabilities, we can be confident that **any** possible interface task can in fact be specified using the tools (though not necessarily conveniently). This fact follows from the Turing machine equivalence of such full programming languages, and is a property that many current by-example UIMS tools cannot claim without resorting to "breakout" features and hand coding.

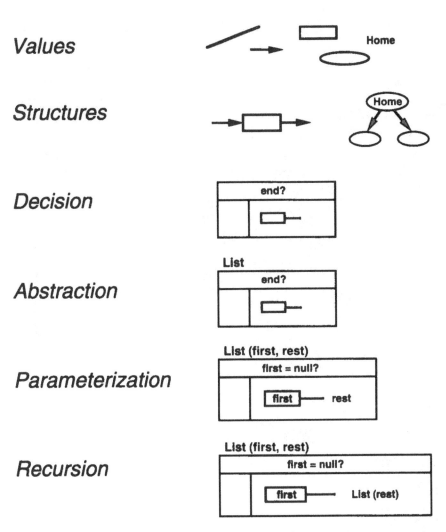

**Values**

**Structures**

**Decision**

**Abstraction**

**Parameterization**

**Recursion**

Figure 6.6: The facilities we required viewed as features of a programming language.

## 6.6    Conclusion

The possibility of evolving by-example user interface specification tools to the point of rendering programming languages unnecessary is commonly suggested these days. While this dream is an attractive and forward-looking one, it sadly ignores the fact that any such specification facility must in fact itself be a programming language to be complete, with only syntactic differences from traditional languages. By recognizing this fact in advance, and explicitly designing future by-example user interface specification tools to be full programming languages, we can both take advantage of existing linguistic techniques and tools, and ensure that the user interface specification tools we are creating will have some measure of completeness in their applicability.

# Part 2

# Programming Languages for Programmers

*General Goals*

# Chapter 7

# How Programming Languages Might Better Support User Interface Tools

*Scott Hudson*

## 7.1 Introduction

Many researchers have noted the difficulty of building user interface software. It has long been the case that the user interface portion of a typical implementation often consumes more than 50% of the total effort [Myers 92b]. In response, the last decade has seen a great deal of research in systems designed to ease this burden. User interface management systems (UIMS), interface builders, and toolkits have all emerged as viable tools to support this task. As a result, much more sophisticated interfaces can now be contemplated as a part of many applications and in fact graphical interfaces are now a requirement for many application areas. However, while the tools available for constructing user interface software have changed dramatically in the last decade, the underlying support provided by programming languages has not kept pace with these changes. In fact, many developers involved with the creation of new user interface tools have begun to feel that the languages that they are using to implement the tools do not support their tasks well and are becoming a burden. This chapter considers how this situation might be improved and how programming languages might better support the development of tools for user interface software.

I will propose an evolutionary rather than a revolutionary approach that concentrates primarily on improvements in two specific areas: object-oriented programming constructs and programming environments. Object-oriented programming has been widely recognized as an advance, but there is little agreement beyond that about which features are most important or useful. This chapter will consider this issue from the narrow perspective of tools for user interface software. I will also consider how a number of persistent problems, such as the need to deal with graphics in a graphical medium, can be best overcome. In this area, I will propose that an extensible programming environment separate from the programming language itself can best solve these problems.

In the next section, general requirements and issues will be considered. This will be followed by a section considering object-oriented constructs, then a section considering environment issues, and finally a conclusion.

## 7.2   General Requirements

Before considering specific requirements for the support of user interface tools, it is important to briefly consider how successful languages are designed. While this chapter will consider what is essentially a list of desirable features, successful language design cannot be driven simply from a list of features. Each desirable feature involves significant tradeoffs, some of which are clear from the outset, and some of which are very subtle and only become clear after experience with a language. In fact the art of language design can be seen first and foremost as the art of understanding and making the right tradeoffs.

To understand the global context in which these tradeoffs are made, it is important to review some generally desirable features for programming languages before turning to our specific requirements. Among these features are at least the following:

- Efficient runtime execution,

- Fast translation or compilation,

- Portability to, and availability on, a wide range of platforms,

- Facilities to support reuse, and

- Strong typing (and other mechanisms for early error detection and prevention).

The first two features directly illustrate the tradeoffs involved in language design—they can be, and often are, traded off directly against one another. In particular, there is often a decision to be made between compiled and interpreted languages. While an interpreted implementation traditionally has offered the fastest response to changes, I will argue for a compiled implementation for two reasons. First, with modern processors and environments (that can compile form source files stored directly in memory), compilers can now be created which provide interactive response similar to that provided by the interpreters of the past. Second, we cannot consider the user interface in isolation. Practical considerations dictate that the typical implementor will want to use one language for both the user interface and the application. Since many applications have serious runtime efficiency considerations, a compiled language is preferable and will be more widely accepted.

The third feature, while seemingly simple, is in fact one of the most constraining of the general requirements. Portability itself is not difficult to achieve. However, without actual implementations of a language on a fairly wide range of platforms there is a high risk of wasted work. Target platforms can easily become obsolete and as a result the substantial effort put into tools may have to be abandoned. While this problem may be mitigated by portable interpreters and retargetable compilers, it indicates that the language implementation task is much more difficult than might be imagined. Any suitable language will have to be implemented and maintained on a range of platforms. When combined with the need for a production quality system with tools such as visualizers, debuggers, profilers, and an interactive environment, this makes the implementation (and support) of a new language a monumental task. In fact, I argue that the task is so large that the effort is very hard to justify for a single application domain—even one as important as user interface tools. Instead, to justify the difficulty, the language must be general-purpose enough to support a range of possible applications. Again, this argues for using the same language for both interface and application and places stronger constraints on the language design.

User interfaces and tools to support them are normally large and complex pieces of software. The final two general features are characteristic of features needed to support such pieces of large software. Many of the benefits gained from object-oriented programming are derived from an increase in the facilities for reusing code. Chief among these facilities are support for strong encapsulation and mechanisms for inheritance. Encapsulation makes it possible to separate a description of *what* is to be done from the details of *how* it is to be implemented. This in turn allows implementations to be freely replaced or modified and hence increases the usefulness of inheritance. Inheritance allows implementations which perform similar operations to be reused with slight modifications to perform a new task. When new operations can be constructed as specializations of existing operations, it becomes possible to build on the work of others rather than recreating most operations from scratch.

The final feature—strong typing—is primarily a means for detecting errors earlier than would be otherwise possible. The benefits of detecting errors as early as possible should be clear. Unfortunately, most current languages have not supported strong (static) typing along with features such as late binding and multiple inheritance (which I will argue later are very important). Based on experience with new object-oriented type systems (particularly the type system of the Emerald language [Black 86, Black 87, Hutchinson 87, Black 90]), I believe that these conflicts are not intrinsic and that all these features can and should be supported together. Proving this via the design of an appropriate type system will in fact be one of the central tasks involved in any new language designed to support the features described in this chapter.

## 7.3   Object-Orientedness

Many researchers have noted the great usefulness of an object-oriented approach to user interface software. In fact, user interface software is one of the best examples of the success of this approach. I propose that at least the following object-oriented features are critical to the success of user interface systems:

- Multiple inheritance,

- Late binding or other support for substitutability,

- Static type checking,

- Separation of subtyping and inheritance, and

- Sophisticated method composition (e.g., wrappers and transparent method interposition).

Multiple inheritance greatly increases the opportunities to support reuse of code. In particular, it allows small behaviors to be created which can be used in a wider range of situations. For example, suppose a system like the Macintosh desktop interface were being created. To create file icons that can be dragged about the desktop, one might create a new "dragable_icon" object class. However, in a multiple inheritance system, it might be possible to create a class which implements dragging and another class that implements objects whose appearance is determined by an icon. A "dragable_icon" class could then be created by *mixing* the "dragable" class with the "icon" class. More importantly, a large number of other classes that provide a dragging behavior could also be implemented this way. In fact, because small individual behaviors can be implemented in separate classes, it is much easier to create a comprehensive set of behaviors for use in a toolkit.

Another important property is the support for some form of *substitutability* in the type system. This property allows objects of a given class to be transparently replaced by more specialized objects (of a subclass). This property is most often provided via the support for *late binding*. Late binding implies that the actual method (procedure) that implements the response to a message (procedure call) is not determined (bound) until runtime. This property improves the ability to support extensions of behavior. For example, in a desktop interface, a "trash can" object probably responds to a superset of the messages supported by a "folder" object. However, the implementation of the methods responding to some of these messages are probably completely different. If late binding is supported, the code which manages "folders" can be left unchanged when the system is extended to support "trash cans."

As described above, the sooner errors can be detected, the better. However, strong typing alone is not necessarily sufficient. For example, Smalltalk [Goldberg 83] is strictly speaking strongly typed (no operations are ever performed on the wrong class of data) but it performs all checking at runtime. Consequently, type errors are only caught during execution. To obtain the full benefits of strong typing, static type checking performed at translation time is required. In the object-oriented context this means that the system must be able to determine from the static program that a "method not found" error can never occur during any dynamic execution of the program. Such a guarantee is obviously very useful. The question remains as to whether static checking can be provided along with multiple inheritance and late binding. Fortunately, at least one language (Emerald [Hutchinson 87]) has provided a demonstration that this goal can in fact be accomplished.

The technical means used to implement such a type system in Emerald are too complex to describe in detail here (see [Black 86]). However, a key point that makes the solution possible is the separation of the concept of *subtyping* from that of *inheritance*. Subtyping is best defined by the property of substitutability. In terms of type correctness, an object of a given class can always be replaced by another object of a subclass. Inheritance, on the other hand, deals with a distinct concept—the reuse of code and data. Inheritance is used to specify that methods and data declarations from one class are to be used as the basis for building a new class. The "inheritance" systems found in many languages (for example, Smalltalk) combine these two distinct concepts into one language mechanism. This combination has resulted in significant confusion about these two concepts and in difficulties in deciding how inheritance should be performed. By separating these concepts, it is possible to provide a more understandable type system and to support all the features mentioned above.

The final language feature, sophisticated method composition, again provides better support for reuse. In order to make the best use of existing code, it is important to be able to have flexibility in the way a subclass method invokes its counterpart in the superclass (e.g., messages to super in Smalltalk). One example of such a flexible system is the wrapper construct found in Flavors [Moon 86]. From the user interface software point of view an even more important means of method composition is the ability to support *transparent interposition* of methods. That is the ability to intercept messages directed at an object and interpose additional behavior between the message sender and receiver. This capability is fundamentally important to user interface tools based on a data or editing model since it provides a means to transparently implement a number of forms of active data. In particular, this capability allows all manipulations of an object to be noted (via interposition) by the user interface and hence provides the opportunity to graphically depict that manipulation. Interposition can be accomplished by means of inheritance combined with mechanisms such as wrappers. However, more transparent mechanisms may also be possible.

## 7.4 Programming Environment Features

In addition to the language itself, the environment used by the programmer to interact with the language is also very important. Important features of the programming environment include at least the following:

- Support for multiple views of data and programs,

- Machine manipulatable representations of programs, and

- Dynamic compilation.

One of the most frustrating aspects of current programming languages when applied to user interface software is that entities which are intrinsically graphical or geometric in nature (for example, descriptions of dialog box layouts) must be expressed in an awkward textual form. It would be much better if the portions of code or data that dealt with geometry and graphics could be manipulated in a visual form. However, the exact nature of this visual form will vary depending on the particular entities being represented. Rather than introduce a visual component into the language itself, I propose that an environment be constructed which allows an extensible set of alternate views and editors for programs and data to be introduced. Such an environment could support a visual specification view where appropriate and a textual view elsewhere. Ideally, the various representations for a program could be interspersed as needed. In such an environment, many existing user interface tools could in fact be integrated with the rest of the language in a seamless fashion rather than being "built on top" in an awkward fashion.

Considerable attention has been given lately to tools which attempt to automatically generate user interfaces, for example from a set of application data structure definitions or application routine signatures. These systems often require that the user interface generation system be able to examine and manipulate application code. If the language or environment provides a direct machine readable representation of its programs, tools of this sort are much easier to generate. To support this, along with the multiple views described above, I propose that a language might be defined in an unconventional way. Instead of defining syntax as a part of the language, only an intermediate representation (e.g., abstract syntax trees) would be defined. All aspects of syntax would be defined by the environment. The environment, while guaranteeing to support at least one standard textual syntax, would then be free to implement as many different syntactic views of code and data as needed. As a side-effect, by defining a specific intermediate structure for programs this approach would also be providing a machine manipulatable representation of programs suitable for use by automatic generation tools.

A final environment issue involves support for rapid prototyping. User interfaces clearly need to be developed in an iterative fashion. In such a setting, it is important that the time between changing a program and being able to test the results of that change be as short as possible. The conventional approach to providing this property is to use an interpreted or mixed interpreted/compiled system. However, if we insist that the same language be acceptable for use in both the application and the interface, interpreted code may be a significant drawback. Fortunately, with modern processors, I believe that this is no longer necessary. As a general rule of thumb, response times under 1/10th of a second will normally be quite sufficient. On today's common 10 MIPS processors, this means that 1 million instructions will be available after each interaction (e.g., after each carriage return). Assuming an integrated environment that does not have to perform disk I/O, this provides sufficient time to completely compile a very substantial segment of code. When combined with the use of otherwise idle user think time, this means that in most cases full compilation can now be performed with no perceivable increase in response time over interpreted code. As a result, the benefits of interpretation and compilation can be achieved in one system without the drawbacks of either.

## 7.5   Conclusion

To summarize the main points of this chapter:

- The language used to implement user interface tools must be general-purpose so that it is reasonable to expect that the application can and will be written in the same language.

- A type system that can support strong typing, late binding, and multiple inheritance should be central to the design of any language supporting user interface software.

- Strong typing, late binding, and multiple inheritance can be handled in one type system by separating the notions of subtyping and inheritance.

- Sophisticated method composition mechanisms are useful and worthwhile.

- An environment that supports multiple views (and editors) for programs and data can resolve many of the awkward problems of dealing with graphical entities in a textual notation.

- Machine manipulatable representations of programs are needed and a language defined in a syntax independent manner can easily provide such representations.

- Dynamic compilation is now a viable alternative to interpretation.

# Chapter 8

# Requirements for User Interface Programming Languages

*Gurminder Singh*

## 8.1 Introduction

The need for a uniform user interface programming language will be well appreciated by anyone who has had to write large applications with interactive, graphical user interfaces using techniques that are currently available. Construction of such applications requires the programmer to be bi- or trilingual, requiring the knowledge of a host language, a layout language, and possibly, a dialogue language. Moreover, traffic between the host language and the user interface generally consists of sequentially controlled transfer of a large number of small pieces of information. Transfer at any higher, abstract level is generally impossible because the larger structures required in interfaces cannot directly match any structures available in the host language.

The idea of user interface programming languages is to solve these and related problems by making interface management an integral part of the programming language. This requires that the language provide control and data structure support for meeting the requirements of user interface software. In this chapter, an interface would mean a graphical interface.

Purely textual interfaces, although they are important, are not considered here.

This chapter argues for:

- an object-oriented, concurrent programming language that is suitable for developing both the user interface and the application semantics;

- a language that treats time as a first-class entity;

- a language that is interpretive and has dynamic linking capabilities.

This chapter describes problems with the existing languages followed by a discussion of characteristic features of interface software that the languages should support. Finally, recommendations are made for language facilities that can meet these requirements.

## 8.2   Problems with the State-of-the-Art

Developing an application using existing technology requires programmers to learn and program in multiple languages. The programmer has to program the  layout of the interface in a layout language (e.g., UIL [OSF 89]) or create the layout using an interactive layout program (e.g., Druid [Singh 90] ) which produces code in the layout language. The dialogue control is programmed in a dialogue language (typically, an event language) or specified using interactive tools (e.g., state transition network editors [Jacob 86], or by demonstration [Myers 90a, Singh 90]), which finally produces programs in the dialogue language. The semantics of the application are programmed in a general-purpose programming language (e.g., C or C++). Typically, the general-purpose language also acts as the host language for the layout and dialogue languages.

There are several problems with using multiple languages to build an application. The first problem is that the programmer has to be fluent with multiple languages each of which may have a different syntax, control structures, and data types. This puts a tremendous pressure on the programmer. He or she not only has to learn multiple languages, but also program in a set of languages in which the same syntactic structure may have different semantics. This makes it harder to write correct programs.

This problem is compounded by the fact that it is difficult to debug and maintain programs written in multiple languages. Typically, debugging facilities for languages depend on the features supported by the language. For programs written in multiple languages, it is almost impossible to use debuggers to help debug programs.

Another problem is that the communication of information among program components written in different languages is difficult. This is mainly because of the differences in data typing and data structuring facilities in languages. For example, a language designed for user interfaces may create a special data type for holding menu entries. When a program component written in this language needs to communicate with another language that does not understand this data type, the sender has to perform conversion to data types that the receiver can understand. Often, this is a non-trivial task. This type of conversion inhibits tight coupling among the various components of the application. For program components that need to communicate frequently, this may translate into tremendous memory and processor overhead.

Even though there are problems with using multiple languages to build applications, people still develop and use special-purpose "little languages." Little languages are programming languages or data description langauges that are specialized to a particular problem domain [Langston 90]. In the user interface software area, little languages have been developed because existing "general-purpose" languages have proven to be woefully inadequate to support user interface development. Little languages have been developed to support interface layout and dialogue control in interfaces. As discussed above, little languages, though they have advantages compared with the case where everything is developed in the host language, have their own problems. It is best to develop a truly general-purpose and complete language which provides facilities for programming not only the semantics of the application but also its user interface.

## 8.3 Characteristics of User Interface Software

Having reasoned that a complete programming language is essential, we need to identify important features of the software for which the new language will be used. For the sake of brevity in this discussion, we assume that existing "general-purpose" programming languages, such as C, PASCAL, and C++, already provide good facilities for developing the semantics of applications. So only user interface related requirements will be discussed here. This section enumerates the characteristic features of user interface software which are important for the language to support.

First, user interfaces must respond to external events (user or system generated) with guaranteed response times. Until recently, this was not seen as a serious requirement. With the advent of new interface devices, such as head-mounted displays and gesture devices, this has become one of the crucial requirements. In such devices, if the interface cannot keep up with response time requirements, the user may suffer from disorientation and display sickness. Also, to conform to some of the human factors guidelines, the user interface must respond within a specifiable delay.

Second, the user interface software must be extremely reliable. Reliability of interface software has not been emphasized in the past. This may be because until recently the interface component for critical systems (such as control of nuclear power stations, aircraft navigation, and other process control applications) has not had to deal with window systems (e.g., X [Scheifler 86] and NeWS [Gosling 89]) which are increasingly becoming big and complex. With the current generation of window systems and toolkits, reliability of interface software has become a crucial issue.

Third, user interface software is commonly large and complex. For systems with highly-interactive, graphical interfaces, the average percent of the code for applications dedicated to the user interface is reported to be about 50% [Myers 92b]. This compounds the reliability problem and means that development and maintenance costs can be very high. Despite their size, user interfaces must often achieve high computational throughput in order to meet response time constraints imposed by devices or human factors. The language therefore must be capable of efficient implementation.

Fourth, contemporary user interfaces must interface with a wide variety of I/O devices as well as applications. These devices communicate with the system in many different ways. The language should facilitate integration of new devices in the system.

Clearly, a language which can effectively support the design, development, and maintenance of such software must meet a variety of demanding requirements. The following sections discuss language features that can support these requirements. Instead of discussing general design criteria for programming languages such as readability, flexibility, simplicity, portability, and efficiency, we will focus on design requirements that emerge because of the special nature of user interface software.

## 8.4  Design Requirements for User Interface Programming Languages

### 8.4.1  Object Orientation

It is common knowledge that user interfaces are best described as a set of objects. An object-oriented organization not only helps in dealing with the size and complexity of user interface software, it also helps a great deal in implementing window systems and toolkits. An object-oriented language capable of supporting both the user interface and the application has an added advantage that it can provide standard classes of objects that can interface the user interface objects with the application objects. In most current implementations of user interfaces, this part of the interface is designed and implemented in ad hoc ways, making the maintenance of such systems difficult.

### 8.4.2  Graphical Primitives and Widgets

The language should support graphical primitives and widgets (interface objects) required for building user interfaces. Thus, programs will be developed using facilities provided by the language, independent of window systems and toolkits. Such programs can be linked to any window system and toolkit that provide "bindings" for this new language. This is probably the first step towards window system/toolkit independent interface programming. This approach is fundamentally different from toolkits such as OIT [OIT 90] and XVT [XVT 91] which create a common layer on top of several toolkits. Those "virtual toolkits" typically support the least common denominator of the lower-level toolkits.

### 8.4.3  I/O Device Programming

Another requirement is that the language should provide facilities for low-level I/O programming. In "traditional" systems, a user is invariably restricted to performing I/O operations with standard peripheral devices only (e.g., character terminals, printers, and disks). As a consequence, the designers of general-purpose languages have been able to present users with standard high-level I/O interfaces often in the form of pre-defined library procedures. A common technique is to treat all I/O as character streams which can be routed to a particular device under program control. Procedures are then provided to convert between internal data representations and external character format representations and to transfer single characters and blocks of characters to and from selected devices. Programmers thus have no opportunity to re-program I/O operations to suit their own requirements. In contrast to this picture of a traditional system, recent user interfaces present a completely different set of characteristics. The kinds of devices that a user interface uses may be many and varied (e.g., mouse, track ball, buttons, head-mounted display, data glove). In addition, the response times of the computer system to external events must be within guaranteed limits. These characteristics of user interfaces imply that a user interface language must provide facilities for programming I/O device hardware directly so that new devices can be easily accommodated and the transfer of information between the device and the application can take place at an appropriate level.

### 8.4.4  Real-Time Requirements

In certain kinds of direct manipulation and multi-media interfaces, time plays an important role. Examples include a graphical interface in which the application needs to attract the user's attention by flashing an object at a fixed frequency determined by human factors principles. This needs to be done in parallel with the user trying to accomplish another task in the same application. Implementing a simple interface like this is possible using existing programming languages, but certainly not easy. It is even harder to debug and verify such a program. Time-based feedback (e.g., updating percent-done indicator every few milliseconds) is another example which is difficult to implement.

Most programming languages provide only simple primitives for timing, such as a time-out, that do not adequately capture the complexities of time and are therefore inadequate for fully specifying and modeling timing requirements of highly interactive user interfaces [Singh 91a]. As much effort needs to be applied to appropriate timing abstractions as has been applied to objects.

To handle timing requirements of user interfaces, the programming language should treat time as a first-class entity. The term "first class entity" in this context means that time is treated at the same level as the basic data types such as integer and character. It would enable programmers to specify "real-time" requirements without having to deal with the system primitives and the system clock. The term "real-time" is used to describe any action which has to performed within a finite and specifiable delay. This would allow programmers to easily create programs that can deal with tight input-feedback loops and ensure that requirements such as flashing an object at a fixed frequency will be met by the system.

## 8.4.5 Concurrency

In view of the fact that user interfaces are naturally described as a set of concurrently executing tasks, the language should provide facilities for multi-programming. This can either be by specifying a standard interface to a multi-task operating system or by allowing multiple process systems to be expressed in the language itself. At the higher level of system design, a multi-process software organization is essential for describing user interfaces in which a number of distinct tasks can be identified. For example, a user interface may communicate with the application by messaging objects that interface UI objects with application objects. All of these objects may be executing concurrently. In order to describe such tasks in software, a notation for describing concurrent processes is required. There are several reasons why such a notation is desirable for programming user interface software.

First, concurrent programming facilities are notationally convenient and conceptually elegant for writing user interface software in which many events occur concurrently. This may happen because the user is manipulating multiple input devices as is common in virtual reality interfaces, or because the application is communicating with other applications. The second reason for a concurrent programming notation is that user interface software, which is inherently concurrent, is best expressed when the concurrency is stated explicitly; otherwise the structure of the system may be lost. Several event notations, for example the event language of the University of Alberta UIMS [Green 85] and Sassafras [Hill 86], achieve this. The third reason for concurrent programming language is that it makes it possible to efficiently utilize multi-processor architectures. It is becoming more common to use multiple processors to handle the computational needs of highly-interactive, multi-media, and virtual reality user interfaces.

### 8.4.6   Interpretive Language and Dynamic Linking

Exploratory and incremental programming are very important in interface design [Sheil 83][Singh 88]. Since there is a lack of a complete checklist of rules to design good user interfaces, much of the user interface software generally requires several iterations of prototypes and refinements to achieve user acceptability. Given the need for iteration in interface software, it would be desirable to have an interpretive language so that programs can be written and tested without experiencing compiler delays. Having an interpreter does not preclude a compiler. Once a final interface has been developed, one should be able to compile it so that programs would run faster.

Separation of the user interface from the application has been emphasized for a fairly long time [Thomas 83], [Hartson 89b]. One should be able to develop the user interface and the application semantics separately and concurrently, and load and link them dynamically to test prototypes. This can be supported by providing dynamic linking capabilities in the language.

## 8.5   Conclusions

This chapter has argued for an object-oriented, concurrent programming language which is suitable for developing both the user interface and the application. The language, in addition to providing facilities of current general purpose programming languages, should treat time as a first-class entity. This would make the programming of real-time requirements of user interfaces easy. This language should allow the low-level programming of hardware devices. This will facilitate experimentation with new devices and also provide low-level control of devices to interface programmers. The final requirement is that the language should be interpretive with dynamic linking capability. This would help with iteration in interface design.

# Chapter 9

# Languages for the Construction of Multi-User Multi-Media Synchronous (MUMMS) Applications

*Ralph D. Hill*

## 9.1 Introduction

At Bellcore we are studying the design, construction, and use of MUMMS interfaces—user interfaces that allow multiple users to simultaneously interact with a single instance of an application from multiple workstations using multiple media. Our group has focused on the problems of constructing MUMMS interfaces and has developed the RENDEZVOUS language for MUMMS interface construction. The RENDEZVOUS language is based on Common Lisp. We have extended Common Lisp with our own object system, light-weight processes, non-blocking message passing, a declarative graphics system, and a fast, multi-way constraint maintenance system. This chapter describes the design rationale behind the RENDEZVOUS language and explains how the features in this language meet the needs of programmers building MUMMS interfaces.

## 9.2  Background

Multi-User Multi-Media Synchronous (MUMMS) interfaces are user interfaces that allow multiple users working from multiple workstations to
simultaneously interact with the same instance of the same application
[Patterson 90]. This interaction may use multiple media, such as text,
graphics, audio, and video, for both input and output. We are studying the
design, implementation, and use of MUMMS applications, so that we can
provide advice on when, where, and how to use MUMMS technology. In
addition, we hope to provide both interface design guidelines and tools to
help implement the designs.

   We are focusing on MUMMS applications because, like Dertouzos in
Chapter 2, we believe that the next steps in the evolution of computer-based
tools will both help spatially separated people work and play together, and
increase the richness of input and output modalities. Traditional user
interface design and construction are tasks well-known for their difficulty.
By choosing the MUMMS focus we make our task even more difficult.

   Most of our effort to date has gone into the design and construction of
the RENDEZVOUS programming language [Hill 91]. This is a language
specifically designed for the implementation of MUMMS interfaces. Our
goal is to produce a language and supporting tools that can be used by
programmers to implement MUMMS applications of commercial size and
complexity. To date, we have built two non-trivial interfaces with REN-
DEZVOUS, and have a third under active development.

   One application that we have built with RENDEZVOUS is a multi-user
CardTable. This application allows up to four people to interact with a deck
of cards on a card table. Figure 9.1 shows Ralph's view of a two-person
blackjack game. Louis, the other player, sees a different interpretation of
the same information. In Louis's view, the card table and the cards on it
(but not the command buttons in the corners) are rotated so that Louis's
hand is at the bottom. Also, in Louis's view, the card in Louis's hand is
face up, while the card in Ralph's hand is face down.

   Users can interact with the cards via both direct manipulations that are
initiated by pointing to a card and clicking the appropriate mouse button,
and indirect manipulations that are initiated by clicking on a command
button and then pointing to the cards to act on. The supported operations

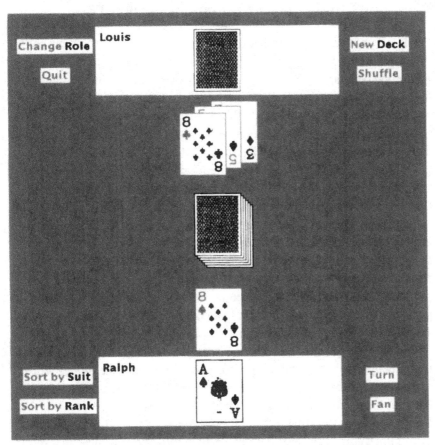

Figure 9.1: Multi-user CardTable implemented in RENDEZVOUS.

include shuffling, dealing, flipping and turning cards, gathering cards into piles, and moving cards into and out of hands. Currently the only media used in this interface are 2.5-D color graphics for output and mouse for input. The CardTable is already a compelling example of a multi-user synchronous application. We plan to add audio and video extensions that will make it a compelling multi-media example as well.

## 9.3    The Importance of Language Structures

While we believe that direct manipulation interface builders, as proposed
in Chapters 2 and 3, can and should hide much of the complexity of programming languages from interface implementors, they cannot completely
hide the programming model. Basic programming model properties, such
as whether it is object-oriented, and whether objects are processes, will
show through the direct manipulation interface builder to the person who
is trying to build an interface. These properties (and lower-level language
properties as well) will become apparent when debugging, linking in the
application, or when it is necessary to manually program interface features
that the direct manipulation interface builder does not support.

Further, we claim, and state as a goal, that there should be a range
of programming languages, from a powerful but detailed language used
by programmers to build fundamental widgets, to an easily used (but
restrictive) direct manipulation interface builder that can be used by non-
programming interface design experts. In order to facilitate migration of
personnel and experience among languages within this range, the languages
should have some commonality in their underlying model.

Because the programming model will, at some level, become apparent
to the people building and maintaining interfaces, and the model will be
shared by a number of languages, we believe it is important to begin by
designing a model that is well-adapted to the task to be performed. We
claim (without proof) that, in practice, we can derive a well adapted model
by minimizing the mental effort the interface implementors must go through
when translating from a user's view of the interface to a programmer's
view of the implementation of the interface. This measure varies with
programmers, their experience, and the task. The technique for computing
the measure will vary with the level of the language. Despite these sources
of variability, this measure is something that can be (at least informally)
measured, and should be minimized.

In order to begin designing a programming model, we must first understand the tasks involved in interface implementation. Since our interest
is in MUMMS interfaces we will concentrate on the tasks we believe are
needed to construct MUMMS interfaces.

## 9.4 MUMMS User Interface Implementation

MUMMS interface implementation is very different from many traditional programming tasks such as sorting, merging, and numerical computations. The behavior of many traditional programs can be described in terms of some number of input and output files, and the computations that must be performed on the input to get the output.

On the other hand, MUMMS interfaces are likely to be described in terms of the objects visible to the user (e.g., cards, hands, and control buttons in the CardTable), their appearances (e.g., color, size, position, and shape), and the manipulations the user is allowed to perform on them (e.g., click left mouse button to drag).

The interface implementation must display these visible objects to the users, wait for input from any of the users directed at any of the objects, and react to the input. The reaction may include updating all users' displays, and maintaining relationships among objects, such as keeping several objects attached as one of them is dragged, so that the whole group is moved. Internally, the basic actions of MUMMS interfaces are: *display* objects, *maintain* relations among objects, and *react* to user input. This is very different from the read–compute–write cycle that is common in many forms of programming.

Since user interfaces are often designed and implemented using an iterative approach, it is important that the interface implementor be able to quickly and easily change an interface implementation and see the effects of the change on the running interface. Ideally, changes that are small changes in appearance or behavior should be small changes in the implementation.

This brief discussion (and a lot of experience) leads to the list of required features presented below. Each feature is marked as being a *basic* language requirement, or supporting *display* of objects, *maintenance* of state, or *reaction* to user input.

**Object Orientation** (basic). Most user interfaces can be easily described in terms of objects (such as the cards and hands of the CardTable). Thus, we consider object orientation, with all the features described in Chapter 7, to be a requirement.

One of these features, multiple inheritance, is particularly important, but is often considered difficult to use. We have found that multiple inheritance using mix-in classes [Stefik 86] is a powerful technique for constructing graphical interactive objects. Mix-ins are a programming discipline for using multiple inheritance. When using mix-ins, there are two basic types of classes: the base classes and the mix-in classes. Instances of the base classes are complete objects in themselves. Instances of mix-ins classes would not be complete objects—the mix-ins are intended to be added to the base classes to customize or specialize them. To create specialized classes, a programmer creates a class that is a subclass of a base class and one or more mix-in classes. This new class has the properties of the base class and the mix-ins.

Using a paint store analogy, the base classes are like tinting base—it is paint and can be used as paint, but it is bland. The pigments are the mix-ins. Pigments are added to the tinting base to create the many hundreds of colors most paint stores advertise. By themselves, the pigments, like mix-in classes, have little practical use.

Multiple inheritance and mix-ins allow the construction of a basic class hierarchy of graphical classes that can then be customized by mixing in specialized behavior classes or classes that customize graphical appearance. Using this approach, it is possible to have a small and easily developed set of base classes and mix-ins that can be used to create a very large number of customized classes. Again, consider the paint store analogy. A paint store can offer hundreds of colors, in each several qualities and types (exterior vs. interior, gloss vs. matte) of paint, for a total of thousands of combinations. This is all from a small stock of tinting bases and pigments. A well designed set of base classes, mix-ins, and composition techniques can give similar flexibility to a user interface construction environment.

In addition to multiple inheritance, the object system must have features to support the description of important properties of graphical interactive objects that may not be found in other objects. For example, graphical objects are often arranged in hierarchies. The substructure of an instance of a class (its child objects) should be considered part of the class's definition, and be inherited like other class attributes (Myers also advocates this in Chapter 10). Also, there must be mechanisms for describing: their abstract relation to other objects (e.g., part-of), their appearance (and how it changes over time), and their interactive behavior. Language features that address these requirements are presented below.

**Objects as Processes** (reaction).     The objects on the display must be able to respond to a user independent of the other currently active objects and users. This requires multiple processes and some way of scheduling them so that all users are given equal access to the processor and receive rapid feedback in response to their input. Making each object a process is a conceptually simple approach that can be implemented without distorting the object-oriented programming model. This greatly simplifies the implementation of the behavior of the objects. This approach requires a very lightweight process mechanism as there may be thousands of objects.  Scheduling is also an important issue—resources must be fairly allocated, without impeding responsiveness.

**Interprocess Communication** (reaction).  Since we assume that objects are processes, inter-object communication is also interprocess communication. Thus, it is important that there be an interprocess communication mechanism that is easy to use, and, as far as possible, protects the programmer from races, dead-locks, and other concurrency problems. In particular, although user interface implementors will be writing concurrent programs, we do not want to require them to have a deep understanding of concurrency issues.

**Event-Based Input** (reaction).  The input mechanisms of traditional programming languages, such as blocking reads, are not appropriate in an environment where input may come from any of a number of users and input devices, as well as the application program, at any time. The 'select' system call in the UNIX operating system makes it possible to implement non-blocking reads from multiple sources, but it is far too inconvenient to use.  An event-driven mechanism, with a language that makes it easy to build event-handlers, would be far better (e.g., [Hill 86, Green 86]).

**Declarative Output** (display).  The programmer should never have to call a drawing primitive, such as draw-line, directly.  Instead, the

graphics system should detect changes to the descriptions of objects
(say, changes to the value of the color slot or position slot of a line, in
addition to the creation and destruction of objects), and automatically
and efficiently update the display. This automatic display update
must include redrawing any other objects that must be redrawn to
keep the display consistent. For example, when an object moves,
any objects that were obscured by the moved object at its old position
must be redrawn.

Given a declarative output system like this, the programmer only has
to describe the display that is wanted. There is no need to determine
how to draw it—that is the job of the declarative graphics system.

Declarative output should be supported for other media as well—see
Section 9.4.1 below.

**Constraint Maintenance** (maintenance). Interactive programs do not
read input and compute outputs. Most of their effort goes into
maintaining state. For example, they keep the display consistent
with underlying data and maintain relative sizes and positions in
screen layouts. Hence, user interface construction would be better
supported by programming constructs that support maintenance of
state consistency than the traditional language constructs that are
designed to support branching, looping, and data manipulation. We
believe that a constraint maintenance system should be considered
an essential element of any language for user interface construction.

Our experience suggests that the constraint system must support
(at least) these features: multi-way constraints, indirect references
(such as the pointer variables of Chapter 12), structural constraints
(or some variation thereon, see Chapter 12), and temporal constraints
[Duisberg 88]. (Chapter 11 proposes a constraint system with similar
capabilities, but employing a different model.)

The more restrictive the constraint solver, the more likely it is that
the programmers will have to be careful to avoid exceeding the limits
of the constraint solver. Our experience, and that of the developers
of DeltaBlue, suggest that a multi-way constraint maintainer can be
just as fast as a one-way constraint maintainer. Thus, a multi-way
constraint maintenance system should be supported.

Indirect references are very important when using constraints to link objects. Indirect references in constraints allow the variable that is set by the constraint, or the variables that the constraint depends on, to be determined by pointers to objects. For example, an object, **A**, may have a slot, **p**, whose value is a pointer to another object. **A** could arrange to always be the same color as the object pointed to by **p** by installing a constraint that sets the color of **A** to be the color of the object pointed to by **p**. The constraint system ensures that whenever the value of **p** changes, or the color of the object pointed to by **p** changes, the color slot of **A** is updated. This relation could also be reversed—if **A** is a color selection object, and **p** points to an object the user is picking a color for, a constraint can be installed that sets the color of the object pointed to by **p** to the color of **A**.

Along with indirect references in constraints, structural constraints are an important aid in maintaining structural consistency (e.g., keeping the user interface data structures consistent with the application data structures, see Chapter 21). The structure of the data is an aspect of state, just as the values are. Thus, just as constraints are used to maintain value consistency, constraints should be used to maintain structural consistency.

As we get more experience with animations and temporal media like sound and video, we are beginning to make use of temporal constraints. Temporal constraints are much like ordinary constraints, but they depend on the current value of real-time. In the case of animations, they can be used to establish a relationship between time and the position of an object on a display. This naturally leads to rates of motion that are unaffected by system performance. Using temporal constraints to drive animations is natural and easy.

**Real-Time Requirements** (basic, reaction). As a general user interface quality requirement, it must be possible to predict approximate response times and guarantee response within a certain time. The requirements, and the consequences of failure to meet them, are not as severe as for true real-time programming, so we hope that the elaborate techniques used in modern real-time languages are not needed. If possible, we would like to avoid adding this complexity.

Some simple real-time clock support will be needed to trigger help and advice systems. This might be needed, for example, to prompt the user with advice when he or she pauses for some minimum amount of time in the middle of an action that is normally one continuous action (see also Chapter 8).

**Libraries and Component Reuse** (basic). It must be easy to construct and use parameterized interface components. Normally, this is a consequence of using a good object-oriented language. When the language is extended with constraints and other features listed above, it is important to ensure that ease of code reuse is not sacrificed. This implies (among other things) thinking carefully about how to inherit, and override inheritance of, constraints, event-handlers, and process control mechanisms.

**Assistance Dealing with Large Numbers of Parameters** (basic). Relatively general and easily reused classes of graphical interactive objects tend to have large numbers of slots (easily 30 or more) and a similarly large number of parameters to their creation methods. The language should support some mechanism for providing default values for parameters, and making it easy to specify only some of the parameters (using the defaults for the others). Common Lisp [Steele 90] provides a mechanism for doing this in the form of keyword parameters. This mechanism allows parameters to be given as parameter-name, parameter-value pairs. Any parameter not explicitly named and given a value gets its default value. This makes simple things easy and complex things just a bit harder. For example, to create a circle of default size, color, position, etc., you need only say '(create 'Circle)'. Creating a circle of specific size and color requires a slightly more complex expression: '(create 'Circle :radius 6 :fillColor "blue")'.

**Rapid Prototyping** (basic). Since interfaces are often designed and built by iterative refinement, the programming environment must support rapid program refinement (see Chapter 7). This implies support for dynamic loading, and an interpreter or very fast compiler (see also Chapter 8). We also believe that automatic storage management (i.e., garbage collection) simplifies rapid prototyping by reducing the programmers' burden. The alternatives—forcing the programmer to manually manage storage or letting the garbage accumulate—put too much load on the programmer or the hardware.

### 9.4.1 Emerging Problem Areas

While we have been able to derive the list of requirements presented above, we know this list is not complete. We have learned that the following are problem areas to be considered, but we are not yet able to map them into a set of requirements. We expect to encounter other problem areas as time goes on.

**Synchronization of Media.** When building multi-media interfaces it is important to synchronize multiple media sources. For example, in video games, it is important to synchronize the presentation of a sound effect with its corresponding video effect. We fear it may be impossible to achieve the tight synchronization required using common workstation software such as UNIX and the X Window system [Scheifler 88]. The UNIX scheduler and the unpredictable performance of X make it hard to know when a request to draw an image on the display will be honored. Similarly, any audio server in a UNIX environment would likely have unpredictable latency. This will be a common problem for virtual reality interfaces.

**Declarative Specification of Non-Graphical or Mixed Media.** Just as it is important to have declarative specification of graphics, declarative specifications of other media, such as audio and video, should be supported. Since we do not yet have experience attempting declarative specification of temporal media, other than animation of structured graphics, we do not know what the exact implications of this will be.

## 9.5 The RENDEZVOUS Programming Model

The RENDEZVOUS programming model has been derived by iteratively refining and extending it, while actively building interfaces. We are confident that it is a solution to the problems we have encountered. This does not imply that it is a good solution to all user interface construction problems.

The model continues to evolve as we (and our clients) try to build new and different interfaces and discover new problems.

The current RENDEZVOUS programming model is based on an object system that is extended with:

- a simple 2.5-D declarative graphics system,

- a fast multi-way constraint mechanism with the additional features listed above,

- a lightweight process mechanism that allows each object to be a separate process,

- a non-blocking message passing mechanism, and

- a simple language for handling incoming events.

All these features have been smoothly integrated so, for example, constraints and event-handlers are inherited like slots and methods. As a result of this smooth integration elaborate RENDEZVOUS classes are easily parameterized and reused.

To help control the complexity of dealing with large numbers of objects, and to allow some optimizations, the RENDEZVOUS run-time architecture requires that the graphical objects in an interface be arranged (by the programmer) into an explicit tree which represents a part-of hierarchy, and implies a stacking order for overlapping objects on the display. If there really are no part-of relationships to represent, the tree can be broad and flat. But, in practice, we have found that often the graphical objects are naturally arranged into a part-of hierarchy. This hierarchy can then be used in a variety of ways, including: optimization of redrawing and picking (the part-of hierarchy is usually a graphical containment hierarchy), and run-time inheritance of graphic properties (the parts of an object often want to inherit information like color and position from their parent in the run-time hierarchy).

The graphics system builds off of the constraint system and the run-time hierarchy. RENDEZVOUS programmers never write code to update the display, they simply change the graphical parameters of objects (e.g., color, position), and edit the run-time hierarchy by adding, moving, and removing objects. The graphics system monitors changes to the objects and the hierarchy and updates the display as needed. The graphics system tries to optimize redisplay, by trying to minimize the number of objects that must be redrawn, while preserving overlapping relationships on the display. While careful hand coding can produce faster display update under some conditions, the ratio of programmer effort (zero) to performance (typically, very good) of the current automatic approach is vastly preferable to hand optimizing redisplay algorithms. (This is probably analogous to the compiled language vs. assembly language arguments of one or more decades ago. Given enough time, highly skilled programmers using low-level tools can produce more efficient code—but how often do real programmers working with real dead-lines have the time and the skill?)

The RENDEZVOUS multi-way constraint system is designed to support fast implementations and to be easy to use. The constraints are used to specify relations among slots in the objects. Constraints can be used strictly within objects, or can link values in different objects. In the latter case, the constraints are acting as a form of inter-process communication as each object is a lightweight process. To ensure correctness, this use of constraints between processes requires that any constraint propagation must happen as an indivisible operation. This is easy to implement by protecting a single constraint evaluator that is shared by all processes with a monitor or semaphore. Unfortunately, this approach may make achieving good parallelism on a multi-processor very difficult.

The constraint system includes a unique feature we find essential—the slot that a constraint updates, and the slots a constraint depends on, can both be indirectly referenced, through variables that can be set by the constraint system. For example, objects in the RENDEZVOUS run-time hierarchy have pointers to their parents. This allows the objects to inherit color information from their parent by installing a constraint that sets their color to be the color of the object pointed to by their parent field. The constraint system ensures that whenever the parent changes (possibly as a result of constraint evaluation), or the color of the parent changes, the local color slot is updated. Garnet has a similar, but slightly less general, facility; see Chapter 10. What is unique about RENDEZVOUS is this relation can be reversed—an object can set the value of the color slot of the object pointed to by its parent field. This facility could be used to have a color selector object update the color of an object it is currently attached to.

The constraint system also provides some support for structural constraints, that is, constraints that can maintain structural consistency by creating, deleting, and moving objects within a tree. While the current model needs refinement, it is being heavily used. The experience of programmers using structural constraints so far has been that they are essential for building large multi-user applications.

In the RENDEZVOUS run-time architecture, we make extensive use of indirect references to communicate between user interfaces and underlying applications. We are experimenting with the use of interprocess constraints as a declarative mechanism for assembling applications from modules. (This is related to problems identified in Chapter 3 and is discussed in more detail in Chapter 21.)

Currently, the RENDEZVOUS constraint system also has experimental support for temporal constraints, that is, constraints that relate values in objects to the value of a real-time clock. We have done preliminary testing of these constraints with some simple animations. While our model of temporal constraints needs to be refined, we are convinced that temporal constraints are a very powerful tool for constructing a wide range of animations, and must be supported.

The RENDEZVOUS model requires that every object be a (very) lightweight process. We find that this makes it much easier to control and specify the interactive behavior of objects. It would be impractical to use, say, a UNIX process for each object (since we may have thousands of objects). Instead, we partition a single UNIX process into many lightweight processes using a model derived from Sassafras [Hill 86].

Non-blocking message passing is primarily intended for communication with outside (non-RENDEZVOUS) processes, although it could be used as a general interprocess (or inter-object) communication mechanism. Input events (e.g., mouse button activity) are treated as messages that are sent to objects. Within each object, a rule-based language (derived from Sassafras) is used to define event-handlers that implement the objects' responses to the events. The responses normally do some simple computations and set local values (possibly invoking the constraint maintenance system). The responses may also include sending events to other objects. The event dispatcher is (by definition) a key component of the process scheduler. Thus, careful design can all but eliminate races and dead-locks, and allow the scheduler to minimize latency when responding to user input.

## 9.6 The RENDEZVOUS Language Implementation and Experience

The RENDEZVOUS language is built on top of Common Lisp [Steele 90]. The current version uses a simple object system that we built ourselves on top of the Common Lisp structure mechanism. We now have a fast implementation of CLOS, the Common Lisp Object System [Bobrow 88], and are building a new version of RENDEZVOUS on top of it. The new version is, as far as possible, syntactically and semantically consistent with CLOS. We have found that the CLOS Metaobject Protocol [Kiczales 91], a feature of CLOS designed to simplify extending CLOS, makes it very easy to seamlessly and portably add constraints and event-handlers to CLOS classes. Based on our experience with the two versions of REN-DEZVOUS, we believe it would be foolish for researchers, or builders of prototype language implementations, to attempt to add inheritable features like constraints and event-handlers to classes in any object system that does not support a metaobject protocol.

We use the X Window system as a device independent networked graphics system for input and output. X makes it easy to connect one UNIX process running a collection of user interfaces implemented in REN-DEZVOUS, to a number of workstations or X terminals—this is a key requirement of multi-user applications that use a centralized model like RENDEZVOUS. We are experimenting with using the audio capability of SUN SPARCstations for audio input and output.

The use of Common Lisp helps us meet our rapid prototyping require-ments. It provides dynamic loading, mixed execution of interpreted and compiled code, good debugging support, and automatic garbage collection. The keyword argument feature of Common Lisp is crucial to effective sup-port of easily overridden defaults. Common Lisp syntax supports very strict static type checking (of the level described in chapter 7), but we know of no compiler that fully implements static checking. (This may be because static checking based on full source text analysis is not part of the Lisp culture.)

Currently, there are five programmers actively using RENDEZVOUS to build user interfaces. Four of the programmers joined the team after the initial version of RENDEZVOUS was implemented. All were able to build interfaces quickly and easily. Their biggest impediments were bugs in the implementation and lack of documentation. We found only minimal difficulties with the extended object-oriented model. We hope to have fixed these problems in version 2 of the RENDEZVOUS language, in addition to adding some extensions to the existing model.

Most programmers have some initial confusion about when to use inter-object constraints, and when to send messages. We have found that the provision of a simple guideline—use events for communication with the outside world (e.g., X and the audio server), use constraints for communication within the interface—and some examples, helps resolve this confusion. This problem does leave us with some concerns though—the constraint system and message passing are two different mechanisms to communicate and synchronize among processes. Is it good to have two ways of doing the same thing? We are leaning toward yes in these cases, because one approach is event-oriented and the other has a state maintenance orientation. Each approach has its place.

Using our current (non-CLOS) system, we are pleased with the performance we are getting. Often, our bottleneck is X, not the Lisp process running RENDEZVOUS. Initial tests of our new, CLOS-based, implementation suggest that it will be at least as fast as the current version of RENDEZVOUS. CLOS probably costs us some performance, but we use better algorithms and optimization techniques we developed as we worked with the initial version of RENDEZVOUS.

Our biggest impediments to consistent real-time response are swapping and contention from other processes running on our workstations. Like X, these things are outside our control, so it is unlikely we will be able to make guarantees about responsiveness or performance. While we are still learning about responsiveness and performance issues, we believe that most currently available variations on the UNIX operating system do not provide real-time features that would allow guaranteed responsiveness, nor synchronization of media. Within the current implementation of RENDEZVOUS we partially overcome this problem by having everything run as a single UNIX process. This way, we have good control over process scheduling and synchronization for all RENDEZVOUS processes. When we have to rely on the operating system for synchronization with other processes (e.g., X server, sound server) or resource allocation (swapping), there are serious synchronization problems. We believe that, ultimately, operating systems and languages that support MUMMS interfaces will have to provide much better real-time support features, in order to ensure responsiveness and to ensure that independently generated acoustic and visual media can synchronized.

## 9.7   Future Work

The current version of RENDEZVOUS meets all of the requirements we list in Section 9.3, except it has limited support for the use of real-time to drive animations and other time-dependent interface features. We plan to add temporal constraints to help overcome this weakness.

Once we complete the second version of RENDEZVOUS, we plan to work in three directions:

- build more multi-media interfaces, to begin understanding the requirements of synchronizing media and declaratively specifying output for temporal media like audio and video,

- build higher-level tools in RENDEZVOUS, such as a multi-user, graphical debugger and a multi-user, graphical interface builder, for RENDEZVOUS, and

- informally study typical programmers building interfaces with REN-DEZVOUS, to gain insights to improve RENDEZVOUS and make it more useful to large program development organizations.

Throughout the implementation of RENDEZVOUS, we have tried to use algorithms and data structures that provide good performance. In general, we are pleased with the performance we get; however, when running the CardTable on one of our current processors, we cannot provide adequate response if four users simultaneously drag one card each. This requires one processor to track four mice and update four displays, each with four moving objects! In general, we cannot simultaneously run many high-quality graphical interfaces on a single processor. Since we expect interfaces to become more elaborate at least as fast as processors get faster we will have to find ways to distribute our multi-user interfaces across multiple processors.

## Acknowledgements

John Patterson implemented the CardTable. John Patterson and Steve Ro- hall have assisted with the design and implementation of RENDEZVOUS. They, along with Debbie Bloom and Tom Brinck, have thoroughly tested RENDEZVOUS by using it to implement a variety of interfaces.

## Appendix—Dragging Blue Rectangle

The call for participation for the workshop asked how easy it is to create a blue rectangle that follows the mouse. Here is the RENDEZVOUS code to create a window with one blue rectangle in it. When the user presses and holds the left mouse button while the mouse pointer is in the rectangle, the rectangle will follow the mouse until the button is released. This is a complete running application expressed in the current RENDEZVOUS Version 2 syntax.

```
(startAndRunView
  'BlueRectangle
  (create 'Rectangle
        :fillColor "blue"
        :addEventHandlers '(leftButtonOffsetMove)))
```

The function startAndRunView creates a window that will contain user interaction. It has two required parameters: a name for the window—in this case 'BlueRectangle, and a tree of objects—in this case, a single object. It has other optional parameters, such as the size, position, and color of the window, the workstation to display the window on, debugging and optimization parameters, and other controls. The defaults are fine for this program.

The single object in the tree of graphical objects is a rectangle. The create function creates and returns an interactive graphical object of the specified class, in this case a Rectangle. There are approximately 30 parameters for creation of a Rectangle. All are optional and have useful defaults. In this case, only two parameters are specified. The :fillColor parameter is given the value "blue." This will be translated to an appropriate color value for the display being used. The second parameter is :addEventHandlers. Its value is the list containing leftButtonOffsetMove. LeftButtonOffsetMove is a library event-handler that is used to drag objects with the left mouse button. This event-handler is added to the list of event-handlers that is already defined or inherited for rectangle.

This example illustrates the importance of optional keyword parameters in building interactive programs. The classes must have many parameters to allow customization, but each will rarely be used. Optional keyword parameters help make simple things easy and complex things possible.

Less obvious is the importance of the automatic graphics, inheritance of constraints, and the event distribution mechanism. All are used here to make a complete interactive program, but the programmer does not need to be aware of them. Also note that the running application will be a multi-process program, but again, the programmer is unaware of this and need not be worried about process and synchronization problems.

In general, with the RENDEZVOUS language and other languages with similar features (e.g., Garnet, see Chapter 10), the programmer only has to say what should happen. The language and run-time system do the rest. In this case, the code could be paraphrased as: create an interface and a window for it; call it BlueRectangle; create a rectangle, make it blue, and add the leftButtonOffsetMove behavior; make the rectangle the root of the display tree for the interface. This is very different from, and much easier than, a comparable specification in a traditional programming language where the programmer has to translate what should happen into a sequence of statements that say how and when to make it happen.

*Models for*
*Objects and Interaction*

# Chapter 10

# Ideas from Garnet for Future User Interface Programming Languages

*Brad A. Myers*

## 10.1 Introduction

The Garnet user interface development environment [Myers 90e] contains a set of tools that make it easy to design and implement highly-interactive, graphical, direct manipulation user interfaces. Garnet has a number of important features that differentiate it from other user interface tools, including an emphasis on handling the run-time *behavior* of objects (how they change when the user operates on them), and on handling *all* aspects of the user interface for programs, including the graphics displayed by the program and the contents of all application-specific windows. Garnet is implemented in Common Lisp and interfaces to the X window manager.[1] It has been in use for over two years, with at least thirty active projects using Garnet, so the ideas discussed here have been proven to be workable.[2]

Although we did not set out to create a new user interface language, we have extended Common Lisp with a special syntax for object-oriented

---

[1] In the future, we plan to interface to the Macintosh and Display Postscript.

[2] If you are interested in using Garnet, contact me at CMU, or send electronic mail to garnet@cs.cmu.edu.

programming and constraints. The input handling model of Garnet is quite different from other systems, and provides a higher level of abstraction. Furthermore, the Garnet system includes a number of interactive editors that allow a large portion of the user interface to be created by demonstration without explicitly writing code. This paper discusses these aspects of Garnet and how they might influence future computer languages and programming systems.

## 10.2   Object-Oriented Programming System

The Garnet object-oriented programming system supports a prototype-instance model for objects [Lieberman 86], rather than the conventional class-instance model used by Smalltalk, C++, CLOS, and other languages. The Garnet object system is called KR because it is implemented using an efficient Knowledge Representation system. In a prototype-instance model, there is no distinction between instances and classes; any instance can serve as a "prototype" for other instances. Other systems that have used the prototype-instance model include ThingLab [Borning 81] and Self [Chambers 89].

The advantage of the prototype-instance model is that it is much more dynamic than a class-instance model. You can create new prototypes at run-time, and easily modify the structure and values of a prototype. If there are instances of that prototype, then they are automatically changed when the original is edited. This means that the programmer can rapidly construct interfaces with simple prototypes, and dynamically modify and refine the prototypes.

All data and methods[3] are stored in "slots" (sometimes called fields or instance variables). Slots that are not overridden by a particular instance inherit their values from their prototype. This allows the methods that implement messages sent to the objects to change dynamically, which is not possible in conventional object systems like Smalltalk. In a prototype-instance system, it is only necessary to assign a new procedure to the appropriate slot of an object, and the new method will be used subsequently.

---

[3] Actually, there is no distinction between data and method slots in Garnet. Any slot can hold any type of value, and in Common Lisp, a function is just a type of value.

An instance can also add any number of new slots. Unlike conventional class-instance models, this means that the number of slots in each object is highly variable—each object can have a different number of local slots, depending on which properties it wants to inherit defaults for, and which it wants to override. In fact, the number of slots of an object can change dynamically. Slots can be explicitly removed from objects at any time. If a program sets the value of a slot that does not exist, then the slot is created automatically. The advantage of this feature is that it is easy to create slots in objects to hold local data. For example, if the color of a rectangle represents a temperature, the application can create an instance of a rectangle and then simply add a slot called temperature to it.

A disadvantage of this flexibility is that it is impossible to perform compile-time or even run-time checking of slot accessing and setting, since all slot names are legal. A common programming error in Garnet is to use the wrong slot name for accessing or setting, but this does not result in an error message, since NIL is returned or a new slot is created. Also, since slots can hold any type of value, there is little type-checking of values. In a future design, it would probably be appropriate to use a special call to create a slot, and type-check the values placed in slots.

A unique feature of the Garnet object system is the support for *structural inheritance*. Objects can be grouped into an "aggregate" object. Then, this aggregate can be used as a prototype for new objects. When an instance is made of an aggregate, Garnet automatically creates instances of all the parts, and links them together in the appropriate manner. Edits made to the prototype are automatically reflected in all instances. For example, if objects are added or removed from the prototype, the system will make the same edit to all the instances of that prototype (see Figure 10.1).

If the programmer wants new objects to be independent of the prototype (so edits to the prototype do *not* affect the instances), the built-in copy function should be used instead of the instancing function. The resulting objects look the same as instances, but there are no back pointers.

The advantages of the prototype-instance model are that it is much more dynamic and flexible than the familiar class-instance model. A high-level tool, such as Lapidary (discussed in Section 10.5), can display a prototype on the screen, and allow the user to edit it. These edits are then automatically reflected in all instances of that prototype. For

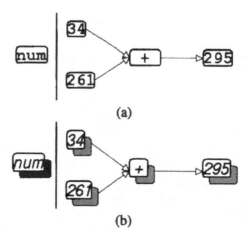

(a)

(b)

Figure 10.1: Before (a) and after (b) editing a prototype. When the prototype (shown on the left) is edited to change the font to italic and add a shadow, the modifications are immediately reflected in all of the instances (shown on the right). Note that the sizes of the boxes change in (b) because the font width is smaller.

example, the designer might be changing the standard look-and-feel of the menu prototype, and immediately all menus in the system would change accordingly. In a class-instance model, changing the class structure when there are existing instances is either very expensive or else causes the instances to be invalid.

Another advantage is the smaller number of concepts that the user must learn. The distinction between classes and instances is removed, along with the differences between class and instance variables, and "meta-messages" sent to a class instead of to instances (like "New"). Prototype-instance systems can also support either multiple or single inheritance.

A claimed disadvantage of a prototype-instance model is speed. Both Garnet and Self have demonstrated, however, that a prototype-instance system can be as fast as a class-instance system.

Since virtually all current toolkits and programming systems aimed at user interface construction are object-oriented, one would expect future languages to provide significant support for objects. Garnet shows that there are significant advantages to the prototype-instance object model, so it should be considered for future language designs.

## 10.3   Constraint System

A *constraint* is a relationship among objects that is declared once and then maintained automatically by the system when any of the objects change [Borning 86]. Constraints are a natural way to express common relationships in graphical user interfaces. For example, in an editor that supports boxes attached by arrows to each other, the user interface designer could specify a constraint that the arrows stay attached to the boxes. Then, when the boxes are moved by a program or the mouse, the system will automatically move the arrows as well. Many research user interface systems now use constraints.

Constraints in Garnet are arbitrary Common Lisp expressions, which are stored in slots of objects. When a program accesses a slot, it cannot tell whether the slot contains a simple value like a number, or a constraint that calculates the value. These formulas are "one-way" constraints, which means that if the other object changes, the object with the formula is re-evaluated, but not vice versa.

Chapters 11 through 13 of this book discuss constraints at length, so only an overview of the Garnet constraint system is presented here. Interested readers are referred to other papers [Vander Zanden 91, Myers 91c] for more details of Garnet's constraint system. The original constraint system in Garnet was called Coral [Szekely 88] but the current system is a complete redesign.

An interesting and novel feature of the constraints in Garnet is that the object referenced in the constraint can be accessed indirectly through a variable [Vander Zanden 91]. For example, a feedback object in a menu might be constrained to be the same size as whatever object it is on top of. A slot will hold the current object that the feedback should appear over. Whenever this slot is changed, Garnet will automatically reevaluate the formulas that depend on the slot, thus causing the feedback object to move.

The use of constraints in Garnet is not limited to only the position and sizes of graphical objects. Because any slot of any object can contain constraints, they are used throughout the system to control many kinds of behaviors.

The primary problems with constraints are memory usage and debugging. We find that objects often contain hundreds of constraints, most of which are needed only once when the object is first created. For example, a button might contain a constraint to keep it at a fixed offset from another button, but neither button ever moves after they first appear. Each constraint must have some memory allocated to it, however, just in case it should need to be recalculated in the future. We are now working to add a feature where the programmer could declare some properties to be constant (such as the size and position), and then Garnet will "compile-out" the constraints that only depend on constant values and thus are no longer needed.

A second problem with constraints is that when the interface does not behave in the expected manner, the debugger is rarely able to provide appropriate information for why not. Usually, the programmer knows which constraints are failing but not why they failed to compute the correct value. Therefore, more sophisticated tracing facilities would be helpful. These might show where the values used by the constraint came from. The C32 spreadsheet viewer has a rudimentary form of this [Myers 91a].

Overall, constraints have proven very powerful and successful as a low-level primitive in Garnet. We use them throughout the implementation of the system. The ability to reference objects through pointer variables has been very beneficial. Future user interface languages might incorporate constraints as a built-in primitive.

## 10.4   Input Handling

One of the most difficult tasks when creating highly-interactive user interfaces is handling the mouse, keyboard, and other input devices. Typically, window managers and user interface toolkits only provide a stream of device-dependent mouse positions and keyboard events and require that the programmers handle all interactions themselves.

Garnet provides significantly more help through the use of *Interactors*, which are encapsulations of input device behaviors.[4] The observation that makes this feasible is that there are relatively few distinct *behaviors* employed in user interfaces. For example, although the graphics can vary

---

[4]Note that this use of the term "interactor" is different from Hudson [Henry 90] and Cardelli [Cardelli 88] where the term is used for both the graphics and behavior, and is therefore a full widget or interaction technique.

significantly and the specific mouse buttons used may change, all menus operate in essentially the same manner. Another example is the way that objects move around when being dragged with the mouse. The Interactors capture these common behaviors in a central place while still being highly customizable by application programs [Myers 90c].

Although it is based on the Smalltalk Model–View–Controller idea (the Interactors correspond to the Controller), the Interactors model is quite novel, since the programmer rarely needs to write code to handle the interactive behaviors. For most kinds of interactions, it is only necessary to create an instance of an existing type of Interactor, and supply a few parameters.

We have found that it only requires about six types of Interactors to cover all the kinds of interactions used in today's graphical user interfaces:

**Choice-Interactor:** for choosing one or more from a set of items, or for a single, stand-alone button. This Interactor can be used for menus, check boxes, radio buttons, and making selection "handles" appear over objects in a graphics editor.

**Move-Grow-Interactor:** to move or change the size of an object or one of a set of objects using the mouse. This Interactor can be used for one-dimensional or two-dimensional scroll bars, horizontal and vertical gauges, and for moving or growing application objects in a graphics editor.

**New-Point-Interactor:** to enter one, two, or an arbitrary number of new points using the mouse, for example for creating new lines or rectangles in an editor.

**Angle-Interactor:** to calculate the angle that the mouse moves around some point. This can be used for circular gauges or for rotating objects.

**Trace-Interactor:** to get all of the points the mouse goes through between the start and end events, as is needed for free-hand drawing.

**Text-String-Interactor:** to input a one-line or multi-line string of text. The designer can optionally specify translations to determine the desired editing operations and the bindings to keyboard keys or buttons. This interactor supports multiple-font, WYSIWYG-style editing.

Each Interactor takes parameters so the programmer can control the mouse or keyboard events that cause it to start and stop, the optional application procedures to be called on completion, the objects that are used as the places where the Interactor should operate, and the (optional) objects that will handle feedback. For example, the programmer might create a set of text objects to be the selectable objects in a menu, and a black, XOR rectangle to be the feedback. Most of the Interactor types take the same parameters, so the programmer only needs to learn one basic mechanism. We are currently investigating how to extend the Interactors model to handle gestures and new kinds of input devices.

One quite important result of the Interactor model is that interactive, graphical programs, such as Lapidary (Section 10.5), can allow the designer to attach behaviors to objects *without programming*. The parameters to the Interactor can be specified in a dialog box or by demonstration, and then the system can create the appropriate Interactor. For example, without writing code, the designer can make objects be selectable, movable, etc., with totally arbitrary feedback objects which are drawn interactively.

The important contribution of Interactors is the discovery of the appropriate primitives and parameters so that virtually all interactive behaviors can be specified without writing code. By providing these primitives in a future user interface language, programmers could much more easily add behaviors to their interfaces. Furthermore, the Interactors model has been proven to be quite general and to scale up gracefully, so that complex behaviors can be created with it.

## 10.5 Environment

An important aspect of the Garnet system is that it is a complete environment, not just a set of language features. In the current terminology of user interface software, the features described above are part of the *Garnet Toolkit Intrinsics*. In addition, Garnet also contains two complete *widget sets*, which are collections of buttons, menus, scroll bars, etc., out of which designers can construct applications.[5] Of course, a future user interface language would have to provide access to built-in widgets, and preferably would make it easy to create new widgets.

Garnet also includes a number of interactive design tools to help create applications. These include Gilt [Myers 91b], Lapidary [Myers 89b], C32 [Myers 91a], and Jade [Vander Zanden 90]. As a result, for many parts of the application, the designer *does not need to program at all.* Instead, the desired result can be drawn or demonstrated interactively.

Gilt is a relatively straightforward "interface builder," which is a tool that allows dialog boxes and similar windows to be created interactively. A recent extension to Gilt allows the designer to demonstrate (rather than program with call-back procedures) many of the actions to be executed when a widget is operated by the end user [Myers 91b].

Lapidary [Myers 89b] is a much more sophisticated tool that allows application-specific graphical objects to be drawn and then to be given behaviors. For example, to make a boxes-and-arrows-diagram editor, Lapidary allows the designer to draw pictures of the boxes and arrows, and show how they are attached to each other. Then, Interactors can be associated with the graphics that will, for example, allow the boxes to be moved and the text labels to be edited. At all times, the designer is operating on concrete, graphical objects, which serve as examples of the types of objects that will be visible to the end user at run time. Most of the graphics and behaviors can be specified graphically without writing code. Lapidary provides iconic menus that make the most common constraints easy to specify.

The C32 tool [Myers 91a] uses a spreadsheet metaphor to help the designer create complex constraints. Menus and the mouse can be used to insert functions and references to objects into the constraints. Thus, the designer does not necessarily have to know Lisp syntax to enter constraints.

Jade is an automatic dialog box creation subsystem [Vander Zanden 90]. It is intended for when an application has lots of dialog boxes, or when dialog boxes need to generated on the fly at run time. Jade uses heuristics

---

[5]We have two sets because they have different look-and-feels. The Garnet look-and-feel is a new style, and the Motif look-and-feel looks like Motif, but was implemented entirely in Garnet.

to select widgets and lay out a dialog box given only a list of the contents and the types of the values expected.

It seems silly to require the designer to write code for things that can be better described by interactively drawing a picture. Therefore, we should expect that future user interface programming languages will include interactive tools such as those in Garnet. If the designer wants a graphical object to be part of the user interface, it should be drawn using a tool. No programming should be involved. If part of the object is parameterized and defined at run-time by the application, then the designer should be able to specify *by example* how it should look, mostly without writing code. The tools in Garnet show that this is possible.

## 10.6   Example

The call for participation for the workshop asked how easy is it to create a blue rectangle that follows the mouse. Using Lapidary, the user could create this application interactively just by drawing an example rectangle, changing the color to blue, attaching a move-grow Interactor to it using a dialog box, and then saving it all to a file. Thus, this application could be entirely created in just a few minutes *without programming at all.*

Alternatively, the designer could have ignored Lapidary and programmed this directly using the Garnet toolkit layer. If so, here is an example of the code that might have been written using the current version of the system (version 1.4). All of the properties of the objects that are not specified are inherited from the prototypes.

```
;;;       First create a window called my-window, an aggregate
;;;       called my-agg, and a rectangle called my-rect. Aggregates
;;;       are used to hold a collection of objects.
(create-instance 'my-window interactor-window
     (:aggregate (create-instance 'my-agg aggregate)))
(create-instance 'my-rect moving-rectangle
     (:filling-style blue-fill))
(add-component my-agg my-rect)  ; Add rectangle to the aggregate.
(update my-window)                      ; Display window and contents.
;;;       Create an Interactor called my-inter to move the rectangle.
(create-instance 'my-inter move-grow-interactor
                 (:window my-window)
                 (:start-where (list :in my-rect)))
    ; Start when press inside of my-rect.
```

## Acknowledgements

This research was sponsored by the Avionics Laboratory, Wright Research and Development Center, Aeronautical Systems Division (AFSC), U. S. Air Force, Wright-Patterson AFB, OH 45433-6543 under Contract F33615-90-C-1465, ARPA Order No. 7597.

The views and conclusions contained in this document are those of the author and should not be interpreted as representing the official policies, either expressed or implied, of the U.S. Government.

*Constraints*

# Chapter 11

# Constraint Imperative Programming Languages for Building Interactive Systems

*Bjorn N. Freeman-Benson*
*Alan Borning*

## 11.1 Introduction

A *constraint language* allows the programmer to specify relations that are to be maintained by the underlying system. Constraints have proven useful in building interactive user interfaces, for example, for specifying the shape and position of windows on a display, or the relation between data and displays of that data. However, other aspects of an interactive interface, for example, the sequence of actions to be taken for a given user input, are more conveniently described using an imperative programming language. We are therefore motivated to integrate constraints and imperative constructs in one language. This integration is difficult because of the fundamental differences between the two paradigms, including differences in the storage model, the computation model, the flow of control, and the data types.

In this chapter we describe these differences in more detail, and then discuss a framework, constraint imperative programming (CIP), that integrates the two paradigms. We also present a new programming language, Kaleidoscope'90, that is an instance of this framework. Kalei-

Figure 11.1: A scroll bar.

doscope'90 has been implemented, and various sample programs have been executed. Portions of this chapter are adapted from a recent conference paper [Freeman-Benson 92], which in turn is based primarily on Freeman-Benson's Ph.D. dissertation [Freeman-Benson 91]. Reference [Freeman-Benson 90a] is a preliminary conference paper on Kaleidoscope.

As a motivating example, consider the scroll bar shown in Figure 11.1. The scroll bar has "up" and "down" buttons and a "thumb." The size of the thumb is proportional to the number of lines of the document that are visible in the scrolled window. Pressing the up button scrolls the text up one line; similarly for the down button. If the mouse is clicked in the gray region above or below the thumb, the scroll bar moves by one page. Finally, the thumb can be dragged directly with the mouse to a new position.

Properties of this scroll bar that are conveniently described using constraints include:

- the position of the top of the thumb is proportional to the number of lines of the displayed document that are scrolled off the top of the window. This constraint may be coded as:

```
always: thumb.top = bar.top -
            (bar.height * (document.first_visible
                / document.total_lines));
```

- the height of the thumb itself is proportional to the percentage of the document that is visible in the window:

```
always: thumb.height = bar.height *
                  (document.visible_lines
                  / document.total_lines);
```

- the area within the thumb is colored white on the display (other constraints control the scroll bar's visibility as its window is overlapped or clipped):

```
always: thumb.interior.color = White;
```

We would like these constraints to be multidirectional and automatically maintained. For example, if the user drags the thumb of the scroll bar, the position constraint mentioned above would be used in one direction to scroll the document (thumb.top $\rightarrow$ document.first_visible), whereas if some other activity scrolls the document, the constraint would be used in the other direction to update the thumb position (thumb.top $\leftarrow$ document.first_visible). Further, the programmer should be able simply to state the third constraint, and leave it to the underlying compiler and run-time system to ensure that the graphical appearance of the thumb is maintained correctly.

Other properties of the scroll bar are more conveniently described using imperative constructs, for example, the object's behavior when the user clicks on the up button:

```
if inside(up_button, mouse.location) then
  document.first_visible :=
    document.first_visible - document.one_page;
end if;
```

Finally, some properties are most succinctly described using a combination of constraint and imperative constructs. For example, if the mouse button is pressed while the mouse is within the thumb rectangle, then as long as the button is held down, a constraint that the thumb position tracks the mouse position should be active; when the button is released this constraint becomes inactive. Naturally, during this interaction, all other constraints are maintained, in particular the display constraints that keep the screen image up-to-date. This behavior is coded as follows:

```
if ( mouse.button = down ) then
  if inside(thumb, mouse.location) then
    d := thumb.center - mouse.location;
    while ( mouse.button = down ) assert
      medium thumb.center = mouse.location + d;
    end while;
  end if;
  ...
end if;
```

## 11.2   Donor Paradigms: Imperative and Constraint

The imperative paradigm is based on the Von Neumann model of a stored program computer: an instruction processor and a data store[1] (see Figure 11.2). Each location in the value store is mapped to exactly one value. The value store can only be updated by a destructive write. Further, because each location can potentially contain a different value at any given time, we can consider the value store as a function *Time* $\times$ *Location* $\rightarrow$ *Value*. The instruction processor fetches and executes four basic kinds of instructions: *read* a value from the value store, destructively *write* a value to the value store, *compute* some function of values, and *branch* (conditionally or unconditionally) to another location in the instruction store.

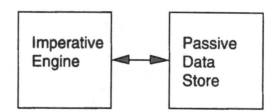

Figure 11.2: Imperative store program computer.

The constraint paradigm *per se* has no instruction processor or data store. Rather, a constraint program can be represented by a hyper-graph in which the nodes are variables and hyper-edges are constraints (see

---

[1]Without loss of generality, and to simplify the subsequent discussion, we assume that the data store is divided into an instruction store and a value store.

Figure 11.3). Each variable holds a set of values: the set of all values that are consistent with the constraint graph. However, this set is constant for a given constraint graph, i.e., the only mechanism for changing the set of values is to operate on the graph from some external driver program. The graph can thus be considered as a function *Location* → *SetOfValues* where *Location* is a variable name.

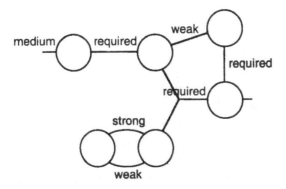

Figure 11.3: Constraint graph.

Constraint imperative programming is thus an integration of the active portions of its two donor paradigms: the imperative paradigm consists of an active instruction processor and a passive value store, whereas typical constraint systems consist of an external interface routine and an active constraint graph/value store. The CIP paradigm combines the two by replacing the imperative paradigm's passive value store with the constraint paradigm's active constraint graph, and the constraint paradigm's interface routine with the imperative paradigm's active instruction processor (see Figure 11.4).

## 11.2.1 Constraint Hierarchies

The constraint paradigm can be extended to allow both *required* and non-required, or *preferential*, constraints. The required constraints must hold for all solutions, while the preferential constraints should be satisfied if possible, but no error condition arises if they are not. A constraint hierarchy can contain an arbitrary number of levels of preference, in either a total order or a partial order, as long as the stronger constraints completely

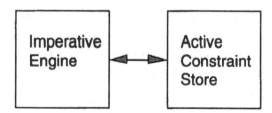

Figure 11.4: Constraint imperative programming model.

dominate the weaker ones. The solutions to a constraint hierarchy are the valuations (mappings from variables to values) that best satisfy the constraints in the hierarchy, respecting their relative strengths. An important use of constraint hierarchies in constraint imperative programming is to express weak equality constraints between successive states of a variable, so that its value doesn't change gratuitously. (This issue is discussed in more detail in the next section.) However, constraint hierarchies have many other uses as well, for example, to express default initial values, or preferences in window layout or in a scheduling application. For example, the following constraint states that the default background color of the display is gray:

```
always: weak Display.color = Gray;
```

Stronger constraints (such as the constraint on the color of the thumb in the scroll bar example) would locally override this weak constraint.

More formally, a constraint is a relation over some domain $\mathcal{D}$. The domain $\mathcal{D}$ determines the constraint predicate symbols $\Pi_\mathcal{D}$ of the language, which must include $=$. A *labelled constraint* is a constraint labelled with a strength, written $sc$, where $s$ is a strength and $c$ is a constraint. For clarity in writing labelled constraints, we give symbolic names to the different strengths of constraints. In both the theory and in our implementations of languages that include constraint hierarchies, we then map each of these names onto the integers $0 \ldots n$, where $n$ is the number of non-required levels. Strength 0 is always reserved for required constraints.

A *constraint hierarchy* is an ordered sequence of sets of labelled constraints. Given a constraint hierarchy $H$, $H_0$ denotes the required constraints in $H$, with their labels removed. In the same way, we define the sets $H_1, H_2, \ldots, H_n$ for levels $1, 2, \ldots, n$. We also define $H_k = \emptyset$ for $k > n$.

A *solution* to a constraint hierarchy $H$ will consist of a valuation for the free variables in $H$, i.e., a function that maps the free variables in $H$ to elements in the domain $\mathcal{D}$. We wish to define the set $S$ of all solutions to $H$. Clearly, each valuation in $S$ must be such that, after it is applied, all the required constraints hold. In addition, we desire each valuation in $S$ to be such that it satisfies the non-required constraints as well as possible, respecting their relative strengths. To formalize this desire, we first define the set $S_0$ of valuations such that all the $H_0$ constraints hold. Then, using $S_0$, we define the desired set $S$ by eliminating all potential valuations that are worse than some other potential valuation using the comparator *better*. (In the definition $c\theta$ denotes the result of applying the valuation $\theta$ to $c$.)

$$S_0 = \{\theta \mid \forall c \in H_0 \ c\theta \text{ holds}\}$$
$$S = \{\theta \mid \theta \in S_0 \land \forall \sigma \in S_0 \ \neg better(\sigma, \theta, H)\}$$

There are many plausible candidates for comparators. We insist that *better* be irreflexive and transitive:

$$\forall \theta \forall H \ \neg better(\theta, \theta, H)$$
$$\forall \theta \forall \sigma \forall \tau \forall H \ better(\theta, \sigma, H) \land better(\sigma, \tau, H) \rightarrow better(\theta, \tau, H)$$

However, in general, *better* will not provide a total ordering—there may exist $\theta$ and $\sigma$ such that $\theta$ is not better than $\sigma$ and $\sigma$ is not better than $\theta$. We also insist that *better* respect the hierarchy—if there is some valuation in $S_0$ that completely satisfies all the constraints through level $k$, then all valuations in $S$ must satisfy all the constraints through level $k$:

$$\text{if } \exists \theta \in S_0 \land \exists k > 0 \text{ such that}$$
$$\forall i \in 1 \ldots k \ \forall p \in H_i \ p\theta \text{ holds}$$
$$\text{then } \forall \sigma \in S \ \forall i \in 1 \ldots k \ \forall p \in H_i \ p\sigma \text{ holds}$$

We now define several different comparators. In the definitions we will need an error function $e(c\theta)$ that returns a nonnegative real number indicating how nearly constraint $c$ is satisfied for a valuation $\theta$. This function must have the property that $e(c\theta) = 0$ if and only if $c\theta$ holds. For any domain $\mathcal{D}$, we can use the trivial error function that returns 0 if the constraint is satisfied and 1 if it is not. A comparator that uses this error function is a *predicate comparator*. For a domain that is a metric space, we can use its metric in computing the error instead of the trivial error function. (For example, the error for $X = Y$ would be the distance between $X$ and $Y$.) Such a comparator is a *metric comparator*.

The first of the comparators, *locally-better*, considers each constraint in $H$ individually.

**Definition.** A valuation $\theta$ is *locally-better* than another valuation $\sigma$ if, for each of the constraints through some level $k-1$, the error after applying $\theta$ is equal to that after applying $\sigma$, and at level $k$ the error is strictly less for at least one constraint and less than or equal for all the rest.

$$locally\text{-}better\,(\theta, \sigma, H) \equiv$$
$$\exists k > 0 \text{ such that}$$
$$\forall i \in 1 \ldots k-1 \; \forall p \in H_i \;\; e(p\theta) = e(p\sigma)$$
$$\wedge \;\; \exists q \in H_k \;\; e(q\theta) < e(q\sigma)$$
$$\wedge \;\; \forall r \in H_k \;\; e(r\theta) \leq e(r\sigma)$$

Next, we define a schema *globally-better* for global comparators. The schema is parameterized by a function $g$ that combines the errors of all the constraints $H_i$ at a given level.

**Definition.** A valuation $\theta$ is *globally-better* than another valuation $\sigma$ if, for each level through some level $k-1$, the combined errors of the constraints after applying $\theta$ is equal to that after applying $\sigma$, and at level $k$ it is strictly less.

$$globally\text{-}better\,(\theta, \sigma, H, g) \equiv$$
$$\exists k > 0 \text{ such that}$$
$$\forall i \in 1 \ldots k-1 \;\; g(\theta, H_i) = g(\sigma, H_i)$$
$$\wedge \;\; g(\theta, H_k) < g(\sigma, H_k)$$

Using *globally-better*, we now define three global comparators, using different combining functions $g$. The weight for constraint $p$ is denoted by $w_p$. Each weight is a positive real number.

$$\textit{weighted-sum-better}\,(\theta,\sigma,H) \;\equiv\; \textit{globally-better}\,(\theta,\sigma,H,g)$$
$$\text{where } g(\tau,H_i) \;\equiv\; \sum_{p\in H_i} w_p e(p\tau)$$

$$\textit{worst-case-better}\,(\theta,\sigma,H) \;\equiv\; \textit{globally-better}\,(\theta,\sigma,H,g)$$
$$\text{where } g(\tau,H_i) \;\equiv\; \max\,\{w_p e(p\tau)\mid p\in H_i\}$$

$$\textit{least-squares-better}\,(\theta,\sigma,H) \;\equiv\; \textit{globally-better}\,(\theta,\sigma,H,g)$$
$$\text{where } g(\tau,H_i) \;\equiv\; \sum_{p\in H_i} w_p e(p\tau)^2$$

Finally, we define two predicate comparators as specializations of those defined above. *Locally-predicate-better* is a special case of *locally-better*, using the trivial error function that returns 0 if the constraint is satisfied and 1 if it is not. *Unsatisfied-count-better* is a special case of *weighted-sum-better*, using the trivial error function and weights of 1 on each constraint.

Reference [Freeman-Benson 91] presents an alternative formalization of constraint hierarchies. This alternative formalization uses a *filtering* model, in which successively smaller sets of valuations $S_i$ are defined, where each $S_i$ contains the valuations that best satisfy the constraints through level $H_i$.

## 11.2.2   Constraint Satisfaction Algorithms

The definition presented above is purely a specification of the set of solutions to a constraint hierarchy. To support CIP languages, as well as other constraint-based languages and applications that employ constraint hierarchies, efficient algorithms for finding these solutions are needed. In interactive applications, an incremental algorithm that modifies an existing solution to reflect a change to a hierarchy will often be a better choice than a batch algorithm that starts from scratch each time. Other axes on which constraint satisfaction algorithms can be classified include which comparator is used, and whether the algorithm produces one solution to the hierarchy or all solutions.

DeltaBlue is an incremental algorithm for producing one *locally-predicate-better* solution to a constraint hierarchy using local propagation. Since reference [Freeman-Benson 90c] is an easily-accessible description of the algorithm, we don't provide details of it here. Vander Zanden [Vander Zanden 88b] describes a related incremental algorithm for solving sets of required constraints, again using local propagation.

John Maloney's Ph.D. dissertation [Maloney 91] includes performance data for DeltaBlue on a variety of problems. One problem consists of a chain of required equality constraints linking a series of variables. There is a weak constraint at one end of the chain. Measurements were taken of the time to apply a stronger constraint to the other end (thus requiring the examination of every constraint in the chain), and then to remove this constraint. For a chain of 10,000 constraints, the time to add the constraint is 190 milliseconds; to remove the constraint, 330 milliseconds.[2] This is a worst-case situation, in which every constraint needed to be reconsidered upon a change. For more realistic cases, in which a relatively small number of constraints are affected by a change, the measured times were much smaller. A lesson of these statistics for other constraint-based languages and systems is that there is no performance reason to use one-way constraints, because multi-way constraints using local propagation is a strictly more powerful technique, and excellent incremental behavior for the constraint satisfier can be achieved.

We more recently developed another incremental algorithm, DeltaStar [Freeman-Benson 90b], that generalizes DeltaBlue. DeltaStar is actually a solver framework, parameterized by a *flat* constraint solver that provides the actual constraint solving techniques and comparison method. (By "flat solver" we mean one that handles required constraints only.) By plugging a different flat solver into DeltaStar, different hierarchical solvers can be produced quickly.

Kaleidoscope'90, a CIP language described in Section 11.4, uses the *locally-predicate-better* and *weighted-sum-better* comparators, implemented using the DeltaBlue and DeltaStar algorithms. For the underlying flat solvers of DeltaStar, Kaleidoscope'90 uses the Simplex algorithm for solving sets of linear equality and inequality constraints, and a CSP algo-

---

[2]These timings are for a C implementation of DeltaBlue running on a DECStation 5500.

rithm for constraints over finite domains [Mackworth 77] for solving the type constraints.

## 11.3 Integrating the Paradigms

### 11.3.1 Storage Model Integration

Integrating the time aspect of the imperative storage model and the constraint graph aspect of the constraint storage model results in a value store defined as a sequence of constraint graphs, one for each time interval. We can consider this store as a function *Time × Location → SetOfValues*. For notational convenience, we refer to a *Time × Location* pair as a *pellucid variable*[3] and write it as $x_t$. Thus the store maps $x_t \mapsto SetOfValues$. If all the constraints in the store have the restricted form $x_t = c$ for some constant $c$, then the store behaves like an imperative store; if time is ignored, the store behaves like a constraint graph. We have also found it useful to visualize the variables in a constraint imperative program as streams of pellucid variables, i.e., $x \mapsto \langle x_1, x_2, x_3, \ldots \rangle$. (This way of visualizing variables as holding streams of values is taken from Lucid [Wadge 85].)

In a constraint program, adding a constraint to the constraint graph asserts the constraint for the duration of the program (because there is only one such graph). However, in a CIP program, there is a separate graph for each time interval (at least conceptually). Thus, to assert a constraint for the duration of the program, the same constraint must be added to each constraint graph. This can be accomplished by keeping a table of constraint abstractions along with the time intervals during which the abstractions are to be asserted. The abstractions (called *constraint templates*) are then used to create constraints at the appropriate times. For example, at times 2 and 3 the template $\forall t, x_t + y_t = z_t$ would create $x_2 + y_2 = z_2$ and $x_3 + y_3 = z_3$. In a Kaleidoscope'90 program, the keyword always creates a permanent constraint template, the keyword once creates a constraint template that is asserted for a single time interval, and the while...assert syntax creates a constraint template that is asserted for a dynamically determined

---

[3]Pellucid: transparent, translucent. Pellucid values are useful for discussing the semantics of CIP, but cannot be directly accessed by a CIP program. Thus they are "transparent or translucent."

duration. Here are three example statements and the constraint templates that they create:

```
always: c * 1.8 = f - 32.0;
```
$$\forall t,\ c_t * 1.8 = f_t - 32.0$$
```
once: c = -40.0
```
$$t = 9,\ c_t = -40.0$$
```
while ( mouse.button = down ) assert
  c = mouse.location.x;
end assert;
```
$$t \in 9\ldots 15,\ c_t = mouse.location.x_t$$

In the imperative paradigm, the value of a variable (a location in the value store) does not change unless that variable is explicitly assigned to.[4] In the CIP paradigm this property is established by very weak "stay" constraints for each variable, i.e., $\forall x, \forall t, very\_weak\ x_t = x_{t-1}$. These stay constraints serve the role of the Frame Axioms used in AI problem solving systems. They are preferences rather than requirements—if an assignment or a stronger constraint has a different value for the variable, the stay constraint should be ignored. Without the ability to state preferential constraints, all of the constraints, including the stay constraints, would be required. This would result in all variables being write-once which, although a useful paradigm in some systems, is not the semantics that an imperative programmer expects.

Finally, to integrate destructive assignment with declarative constraints, we redefine assignment to be a *synchronic* equality constraint—a constraint between the values of variables in two different time intervals. The expression on the left side refers to the next time, and the expression on the right side refers to the current time. For example, x:=x+y becomes $x_{t+1} = x_t + y_t$. As a result, all of the computation in the data store involves constraints and no special cases are needed to accommodate assignment or other side effects. Since assignments are merely constraints, they may have complex expressions on both sides. (For example, b*c-5 := d+sin(e) becomes $b_{t+1} * c_{t+1} - 5 = d_t + sin(e_t)$.)

Because all computation in a CIP program is done with constraints, the imperative actions of *writing* to the value store and *computing* a value are

---

[4]Except in the presence of aliasing or pointers—which is why these features make it harder to describe the semantics of real imperative languages.

replaced by *adding* one or more constraints to the value store. The other operation on the value store is a *read*. In a CIP language, a read is necessary only when a value is being output to the external world or is needed to select which branch of a conditional to take. There may be many values for a variable that satisfy the constraints equally well. Since we wish to support an imperative programming style, we select one of the permissible values, rather than returning a set of all the permissible values of the variable, or backtracking through the possibilities, as in a logic program. (This choice is also more compatible with writing interactive graphical applications— a primary application area for CIP languages—as it would be difficult to display an icon on the screen at multiple locations.) The selected value is then frozen so that subsequent reads of the same pellucid variable will return the same value. (Freezing the value is equivalent to adding a required constraint that the pellucid variable be equal to a constant, i.e., $x_t = c$.)

To prevent various paradoxes in which the future modifies the past, synchronic constraints are annotated with read-only annotations so that values can flow only forward in time. (See [Borning 91] for a formal definition of read-only annotations in constraint hierarchies.) Thus x:=x+1 actually becomes $x_{t+1} = x_t? + 1$, where $x_t?$ denotes a read-only use of the pellucid variable $x_t$.

## 11.3.2 Objects

Modern programming languages support user-defined data types (often including abstract data types), and operations over those data types. Supporting user-defined data types in a general way presents a problem for constraint languages: user-defined data types do not always contain enough semantic information for the built-in constraint solvers to reason about constraints on them at their level of abstraction. Three approaches to this problem are:

1. Limit the kinds of constraints that can be applied to user-defined data types, or the power of the solver for these constraints.

2. Allow the programmer to define new solvers for user-defined data types, either within the program itself or dynamically linked to the compiled program.

3. Provide a mechanism to define constraints over user-defined data types in terms of simpler constraints, ultimately reducing them to constraints over primitive data types. This approach, which we call *splitting*, is similar to how existing imperative languages deal with user-defined data types: an imperative program ultimately defines operations over its user-defined data types in terms of operations over the primitive data types.

For example, consider a set of user-defined data types on geometric objects. We would like to define suitable constraints on these objects, e.g., point-on-line, parallel-lines, and so forth. However, a built-in constraint solver typically would not have enough information to reason about the geometric constraints at the geometric level. We could limit the kinds of user-definable constraints (e.g., to equality constraints only) or the power of the solver (e.g., to local propagation only). We could define a new solver, e.g., Kramer's solver for geometric constraint satisfaction [Kramer 91], and link it to the existing solvers in some fashion. Finally, we could define the geometric constraints in terms of primitive constraints and data types, in this case algebraically using the real numbers.

In our current design the splitting approach is used.[5] A *constraint constructor* is a procedure that defines how a particular constraint over a user-defined data type is to be split into constraints over its component parts. Those component constraints may be further split, and so on, until all the resulting constraints are over primitive types, and can be solved directly by the built-in constraint solvers.

Object-oriented languages add inheritance and dynamic binding of operation names to operations to the basic notion of abstract data types. To handle the dynamic binding of names to operations, when executed, a constraint statement in a CIP program creates a constraint template. The constraint template is bound to, and calls, one constraint constructor for each time interval. The constructor to which it is bound depends on the concrete type of the values in the pellucid variables it constrains. This dynamic binding supports object-oriented programming, and allows the

---

[5]In future CIP languages, we would retain splitting as the normal way of handling user-defined constraints. However, as Kramer's work demonstrates, solving the constraints at the appropriate level of abstraction adds considerable power; this argues for allowing special-purpose solvers to be employed as well.

concrete types of the constrained variables to change during the execution of the program. (If static binding were used, for example if the constraint template were bound to a constructor at creation time, then the concrete types of the variables would be fixed.)

| *Program* | | *Run-time* | | *Program* |
|-----------|---|-----------|---|-----------|
| statement | installs $\rightarrow$ | template | calls $\rightarrow$ | constructor |

The constraint constructor either splits the constraint into further constraint templates or, at the lowest level, generates a primitive constraint. Constraint constructors are procedures and thus may contain any legal statement or code fragment including iteration, recursion, and assignment. Each constructor executes in a nested local time scope, so that time advances affect only local variables, but not non-local ones.

In classical object-oriented languages, such as Smalltalk-80, the operation chosen for a given name is determined by the concrete type of the first argument only. (In Smalltalk-80 terminology, the method invoked by a given message is determined only by the class of the receiver.) However, this scheme is inadequate for an object-oriented CIP language, since we want to support multi-directional constraints. For example, consider a three-argument *plus* constraint p+q=r. If p were known, then the appropriate *plus* constructor could be selected based on the concrete type of p. However, if q and r were known, and p were unknown, then this would fail. Hence we use *multi-methods*, in which the operation invoked is determined by the concrete types of all of the arguments rather than just the first. (Multi-methods were first used in the CLOS extension to COMMON LISP [Bobrow 88].)

Here are two examples of constraint constructors, one that recursively defines equality for trees, and another that iteratively defines the "sum" constraint for arrays.

```
constructor =( t:Tree, v:Tree )
  always: t.value = v.value;
  always: t.left  = v.left;
  always: t.right = v.right;
end =;
constructor =( t:nil, v:nil )
end =;
```

```
constructor sum( a:Array, s:Number )
  var i, partial : Number;
  partial := 0;
  for i := a.first to a.last do
    partial := partial + a[i];
  end for;
  always: s = partial;
end sum;
```

## 11.4   A Prototype Implementation

In [Freeman-Benson 91] we describe the design and implementation of a prototype constraint imperative programming language, Kaleidoscope'90. Kaleidoscope'90 is an integration of a typed dialect of Smalltalk-80 [Johnson 86] and an enhanced version of the constraint system from ThingLab II [Maloney 89]. This initial implementation interprets the constraint imperative programming semantics directly, resulting in a robust but very slow implementation.

The interpreter is divided into three sections: a pre-compiler, an imperative engine, and a constraint-based value store. The pre-compiler converts the Kaleidoscope'90 source program into a K-code object program. There are six basic K-codes: *add* a constraint template to the active set, *remove* a constraint template from the active set, *read* a value from the value store, *call* a procedure, *branch* conditionally or unconditionally, and *advance* time. When the advance time K-code is executed (typically at the end of each source statement), each constraint template in the active set is transmitted to the constraint-based value store. Thus, a once constraint statement corresponds to a template that is added to, and then promptly removed from, the active set, whereas an always statement corresponds to a template that is added and never removed.

The constraint-based value store contains two co-mingled hypergraphs: a primitive one and a compound one. The primitive graph contains a fixed class of constraints over the primitive domains (floating point numbers and booleans). The compound graph contains a variety of hyper-edges which, together, support constraint templates over objects. As described earlier, the primitive constraints cannot be directly created by the program—instead, the program creates constraint templates which, in turn, create hyper-edges in the compound graph. These in turn are bound to the constraint constructors that create the primitive constraints. Thus, the process for determining a pellucid variable's value is first to reduce the compound graph to a primitive graph, and then to use the built-in primitive constraint solver to solve the primitive graph. The compound graph is reduced as follows:

1. Type constraints are solved to determine concrete types for the pellucid variables.

2. Constraint constructors are bound and called, based on the concrete types.

3. Constraint constructors on whole objects are executed before those on their component parts to ensure that all primitive constraints on an object are considered, including those created by constraint constructors executed on any enclosing objects.

The primitive constraint solver uses local propagation when possible. When local propagation fails, if the remaining constraints are linear equalities or inequalities over the real numbers, the solver can resort to a variant of the Simplex method adapted for constraint hierarchies.

Although the goal of this initial implementation was a proof of concept rather than an efficient implementation, we did add a few optimizations to improve its performance. One technique is to replace equality constraints by identity constraints when possible. (We can't always perform this replacement, since in an object-oriented language the programmer is allowed to redefine equality between objects.) When this substitution is used, it reduces the number of objects, pellucid variables, constraint templates, and primitive constraints that are created, and thus diminishes the overhead of reducing the compound graph and solving the primitive constraints.

Another technique we used is to combine multiple smaller constraint templates into a single larger, amalgamated template. Our motivation is that solving a large number of constraints (even simple ones) is expensive. Thus, the strict object-oriented scheme of decomposing a single constraint expression into a multitude of smaller constraint expressions, each containing a single operator, substantially increases the number of edges in the compound graph. This is obviously undesirable. Note that this amalgamation technique is similar to using a graph preprocessor to manipulate and improve the compound graph before the actual constraint solver is invoked.

These two simple techniques—replacing equality by identity, and amalgamating constraints—more than doubled the speed of our prototype implementation, and have supported our belief that better performance from our second generation implementation will be possible.

## 11.5   Related Work

We can roughly divide the related work on constraints into research on using constraints in applications, and on embedding constraints in programming languages. Applications have included interactive graphics and animation [Borning 81, Borning 86, Gosling 83, Nelson 85, Sutherland 63b], layout systems [Böhringer 90, Kamada 91, Van Wyk 82], user interface construction systems [Ege 87, Epstein 88, Maloney 91, Vander Zanden 90, Myers 88, Myers 90e, Olsen 90a, Szekely 88] (and Chapter 10), various artificial intelligence systems (see, e.g., [Mackworth 77]), and design, analysis, and simulation systems [Levitt 84, Mittal 86, Rotterdam 89, Stallman 77, Sussman 80].

In the programming language arena, one of the earliest efforts was that of Steele [Steele 80], whose dissertation describes work on a general-purpose constraint language using local propagation to find solutions. Subsequently, Leler [Leler 88] designed and implemented a constraint language based on augmented term rewriting. Lamport and Schneider [Lamport 85] propose adding constraints to an imperative language, as a uniform approach encompassing both aliasing and typing. Their primary motivation is the development of proof systems.

Recent, closely related, work is represented in this book: Horn's Siri language (Chapter 13); Hill's RENDEZVOUS language (Chapter 9); and Vander Zanden's active-value-spreadsheet (AVS) model for interactive languages (Chapter 12), which is derived from Garnet's constraint and object model (Chapter 10). All four of these models are hybrid constraint imperative systems that support automatically-maintained, multi-way constraints on objects. Kaleidoscope'90 includes constraint hierarchies, and in particular uses weak equality constraints to specify that the value of each variable should remain the same over time, in the absence of other, stronger constraints. The CIP model as we've defined it above makes fundamental use of this attribute, so that, strictly speaking, Siri, RENDEZVOUS, and the AVS model are not CIP languages; however, they are clearly close relatives. Another aspect of the CIP model is that assignment statements are constraints relating states of variables at different times. Siri takes a similar decision: event patterns define one-time assertions that may change the state of an object; in the description of an event pattern, one may reference both the current and old states of object attributes. RENDEZVOUS and AVS include both constraints and standard imperative constructs, and don't attempt to define state change in terms of constraints.

Regarding Siri and Kaleidoscope'90, some differences are as follows. First, since Siri uses only required constraints, rather than a constraint hierarchy, the user must explicitly indicate when values are to remain the same as time advances. Second, Siri uses term rewriting (as in Leler's work) as its constraint satisfaction mechanism rather than DeltaBlue and DeltaStar. Third, Siri uses a single abstraction mechanism, a *constraint pattern*, for object description, modification, and evaluation, rather than the more standard approach taken here of using separate mechanisms for these tasks. (This uniform use of patterns is analogous to their use in the Beta language [Kristensen 83].) RENDEZVOUS includes extensive support for processes and multiple users, areas that have not been dealt with in Kaleidoscope'90. The AVS model augments the basic constraint model with support for constraints on structural relationships, side effects during constraint solving (implemented using action procedures associated with active variables), and conditionally enabled constraints. These effects may also be obtained in the CIP model, but using the constraint constructor mechanism, which (at least semantically) creates a new constraint graph on each time advance. The CIP model is thus more declarative—but at a cost, the cost being either greatly reduced efficiency (if we're unlucky), or harder work for the designer of the CIP language compiler (if our current research activities are successful).

Much of the other current activity in constraint languages is based on logic programming. Jaffar and Lassez have defined a general scheme, Constraint Logic Programming (CLP), for integrating constraints with logic programming [Cohen 90, Jaffar 87]. A number of instances of this scheme have been implemented, including CLP($\mathcal{R}$) [Jaffar 90], Prolog III [Colmerauer 90], and CHIP [Dincbas 88, Van Hentenryck 89]. Two generalizations of the CLP scheme are CLP* [Hickey 89], which generalizes CLP by allowing predicates to be defined dynamically as first-class objects, and HCLP [Borning 89, Wilson 89], which generalizes CLP by including constraint hierarchies rather than just required constraints. Finally, in the cc languages [Saraswat 91, Saraswat 89] the conventional store of a Von Neumann computer is replaced by one that holds constraints. Concurrently executing agents communicate by *asking* and *telling* constraints to this store.

For a more complete discussion and a set of citations for related work, see [Freeman-Benson 91].

## 11.6   Conclusions and Future Work

We have briefly described the CIP scheme for constraint imperative programming languages, and a proof-of-concept instance of this scheme, Kaleidoscope'90. Currently, we are redesigning and simplifying the language to produce Kaleidoscope'91. In addition, we are designing a more efficient implementation, which will employ a mixed interpretation/compilation strategy. Because constraints can be added and removed dynamically in a CIP program, in general it isn't possible to remove all run-time invocations of the constraint solver, but it is frequently possible to eliminate many of them. An obvious example of this optimization is assignment to an otherwise unconstrained variable: a simple load-store instruction pair is a better choice than constructing a full compound graph, reducing it, and then solving the resulting equality constraint. Chapter 7 of [Freeman-Benson 91] discusses other compilation opportunities. Our goal is to provide an implementation of the general model (i.e., CIP) in such a way that any given program pays the cost of only the features that it uses. Once this new implementation is operational, we plan to further test the expressive power of constraint imperative programming by using it to implement selected non-trivial user interfaces.

# Acknowledgements

This work was supported in part by the University of Victoria, by National Science Foundation under Grant Nos. IRI-8803294 and IRI-9102938, by a Graduate Fellowship from the National Science Foundation for Bjorn Freeman-Benson, and by a gift from Apple Computer.

# Chapter 12

# An Active-Value–Spreadsheet Model for Interactive Languages

*Brad Vander Zanden*

## 12.1   Introduction

Conventional, batch-oriented languages lack many features that are required to support interactive computing, such as graphics, rapid prototyping, multiprocessing capabilities, and effective representations for programs, such as visual environments and object-oriented programming. However, an even more fundamental problem with conventional languages is that their foundations are typically built on imperative programming. Imperative programming forces the programmer to completely manage the flow-of-control. While this is acceptable in batch applications where the flow-of-control is centralized, fairly linear, and predictable, it is unacceptable in highly interactive applications in which the flow-of-control is distributed, highly nonlinear, and unpredictable. As the functionality of interactive applications increases, the potential combinations of operations and dialogs increases nonlinearly, inevitably overwhelming the programmer's ability to successfully manage the flow-of-control.

In many ways the distinction between batch and interactive applications is similar to the distinction between centrally planned economies and free market economies, and the lessons to be learned are similar. Batch applications are analogous to centrally planned economies whereas interactive programs are analogous to free market economies. In the batch-oriented model, the program controls the dialog—it dictates when it receives input, what type of input is acceptable, and what types of operations can be performed next. Thus the flow-of-control is centralized, predictable, and fairly linear, much as in a centrally planned economy. Imperative programming is an appropriate paradigm in this setting with its emphasis on total control.

Interactive applications overturn this model completely by placing the user in control of the human–computer dialog. Users can initiate a dialog at any time, they can maintain several different dialogs simultaneously, and they expect immediate feedback. These conditions allow dialogs to interact in many different ways, making the flow-of-control distributed, nonpredictable, and highly nonlinear, much as in free market economies. Just as central planning is inappropriate for free market economies, imperative programming is inappropriate for large interactive applications. Indeed, the difficulty software vendors are having in bringing new products to market, even with the assistance of software toolkits and software engineering tools, provides empirical evidence that imperative programming is inadequate for implementing large, complex programs.

Thus an interactive language that relies on an imperative model is doomed to failure, even if it incorporates other features designed to facilitate interactive computing. Just as successful economies have typically gravitated toward a more distributed, market-oriented model in which individuals deal directly with one another, so must models of interactive computing evolve toward more distributed control.

We believe that the spreadsheet model of computation meets these requirements. The spreadsheet model is appealing because it allows a programmer to declaratively describe relationships between a program's entities using constraints. A constraint solver automatically keeps the constraints satisfied, thus propagating changed data to the appropriate locations and handling all flow-of-control. This is a more distributed model of computation because each entity in the system is only concerned about itself and its relationships with other entities. The constraint solver acts as an automatic device that propagates this information throughout the system and keeps the system stable.

The tremendous commercial success of financial and engineering spreadsheets suggests that both programmers and nonprogrammers find spreadsheets an appealing and readily learnable model. Indeed it is now finding its way into many types of applications such as document preparation [Nelson 85, Pavlidis 85, Van Wyk 82], simulation systems [Borning 81, Barford 89], and graphical interface toolkits [Barth 86, Vander Zanden 89, Henry 88, Myers 90e, Borning 86]. Thus spreadsheets seem to present an ideal paradigm on which to base an interactive language.

However, the most commonly used spreadsheet model, in which only one-way constraints are supported, does not provide adequate support in many large applications. Indeed, as applications increasingly use one-way constraints, it is becoming clear that the ability to model multi-way and structural relationships using constraints would be quite helpful. A structural relationship expresses a relation between the structure of two or more objects. For example, it might state that a new graphical object should be created when a new node is added to a binary tree or it might state that the existence of an arrow depends on the existence of the two objects it connects.

To handle multi-way relationships, we use a multi-way constraint model that retains much of the efficiency of one-way constraint solving while providing the user with greater control over the constraint solving process. We also discuss how the active-value and spreadsheet models can be combined to provide support for constraints describing structural relationships (the active-value model is also called the *access-oriented programming* model and the *active-data* model). The active-value model allows procedures to be attached to variables that will be automatically executed when the variables change value. These procedures provide a way of implementing a structural constraint by executing the actions necessary to enforce it. For example, if the constraint controlling the existence of an object becomes false, an action procedure can be used to destroy the object. Two other paradigms for integrating multi-way and structural constraints into the spreadsheet model are presented in Chapters 11 and 13.

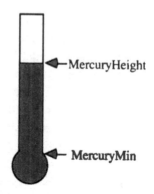

Figure 12.1: By grabbing the mercury in this thermometer and dragging it up or down, a user can change the temperature used by an application. MercuryHeight and MercuryMin are in screen coordinates. Their difference can be mapped into the actual temperature.

## 12.2   An Integrated Spreadsheet–Object Model

In this section we describe a no-frills constraint-based object system that is derived from the Garnet user interface development environment [Myers 90e]. In the next section we describe how the constraint system can be beefed up using structural and multi-way constraints.

The object model is the prototype-instance scheme described in Chapter 10. The spreadsheet model uses equations to denote relationships between two or more objects. For example, a designer might write the following equation to express the temperature as a function of the height of the mercury in Figure 12.1:

```
temperature = (MercuryHeight - MercuryMin)
```

The equations are one-way in that they compute a value and assign it to the variable on the left side of the equation. An alternative way to view these constraints is as functions that take an arbitrary number of arguments and compute a result. This result may be of any type, such as a number, a string, an object, or a list of values. The function is an arbitrary piece of code written in an appropriate language. For example, to compute the item to highlight in a property menu when an object is selected, we could write a constraint that looks at the desired property in the selected object

and returns the appropriate menu item. The following constraint computes the appropriate line-style menu item to highlight and stores it in a *selected* variable in the line-style menu:

```
line-style-menu.selected
  = case selected-obj.line-style
          dashed-line: dashed-line-menu-item
          line-1: line-1-menu-item
          line-2: line-2-menu-item
```

*selected-obj* is a pointer variable that points at the currently selected object. Pointer variables are an important enhancement that allow constraint models to achieve the equivalent of procedural abstraction in programming languages. The constraints become procedures, the pointer variables become parameters, and the constraint is invoked each time the parameters change value. In the above example, *selected-obj* is a parameter and the constraint is reevaluated whenever the user selects a new object, thus ensuring that the line-style menu always highlights the appropriate menu item.

The use of pointer variables also simplifies the integration of the spreadsheet model with the object system. First, each constraint is treated as an object, with instance variables for such things as the formula, the value returned by the formula, and pointers to the instance variable and object that the constraint is attached to. When the object system creates an instance of an object, it checks each of the object's instance variables, and if an instance variable contains a constraint, the object system makes an instance of the constraint and stores it with the appropriate instance variable in the new object. The new object can then set the appropriate pointer variables and the constraint will be customized to that object. For example, a programmer might create a prototypical arrow object that connects the centers of two boxes:

```
arrow:
    endpoint1: to-obj.center
    endpoint2: from-obj.center
    to-obj: nil
    from-obj: nil
```

When the application creates an instance of this arrow, the object system will also create instances of the constraints on `endpoint1` and `endpoint2` and store the instances of the constraints in the new arrow instance. The arrow instance will then connect any two boxes that are stored in the `to-obj` and `from-obj` pointer variables.

Pointer variables also make it easier to integrate constraints with the hierarchical object systems employed in user interface development environments such as Garnet [Myers 90e], ThingLab [Borning 81], GROW [Barth 86], and Apogee [Henry 88]. In these hierarchical systems, objects can be collected into groups called aggregates. Typically, constraints in these objects will need to reference their siblings or ancestors. For example, in the labeled box shown in Figure 12.2, the label needs to reference the rectangle in order to center itself. To facilitate these references, the object system can store pointers to the children in the aggregate and pointers to the aggregate in the children. Constraints can then navigate their way through the aggregate hierarchy by stringing together the appropriate pointer variables. For example, to center itself in the rectangle, the label could use the constraint

```
label.center = self.parent.frame.center
```

When the object system creates an instance of this labeled box, it automatically creates instances of the label and rectangle as well. The label instance will automatically reference the appropriate rectangle, since the object system will store pointers to the newly created label and rectangle in the newly created labeled box aggregate, and pointers to the labeled box instance in the label and rectangle instances.

Within this spreadsheet model, the constraint solver acts as an incremental dataflow interpreter. When a set of variables is changed, it should detect which constraints use the changed variables and reevaluate these constraints in the proper order. For example, when a new object is selected, the constraint solver must reevaluate the constraint controlling the selected item in the line-style menu. Lazy and eager algorithms for implementing the constraint solver are presented in [Vander Zanden 91].

In addition to providing an elegant framework for handling flow-of-control within interactive applications, this basic model readily supports many of the features that must be built into an interactive language:

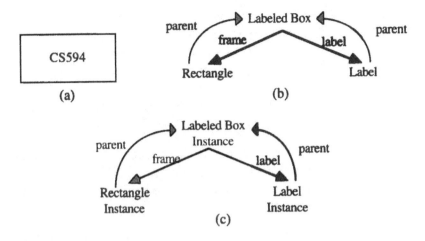

Figure 12.2: A labeled box (a), and the aggregate hierarchies for both its prototype (b) and an instance (c). The object system stores pointers to the children in `frame` and `label` and pointers to the aggregate in `parent`. The names for the child pointers are derived from the names users assign to the children.

1. Incremental Computation: Each time data changes, a constraint solver automatically identifies the affected equations, and by resolving them, automatically propagates the changed data to the appropriate places. Thus, only the affected parts of an application are recomputed, and programmers need not worry about programming the incrementality—it is done automatically by a constraint solver.

2. Parallel Computation: A constraint solver can automatically determine which constraints are independent and assign them to separate processors. Thus, programmers need not worry about parallelism.

3. Asynchronous Input Handling: Interactive applications must be able to respond to input from multiple, asynchronous devices such as mice and keyboard, and provide acceptable feedback to the user. Constraints can be used to automatically position feedback objects and propagate the side effects caused by an event to other ongoing dialogs, so they can adjust themselves appropriately.

4. Data-Driven and Declarative Format: Constraints focus on the data that is to be computed by the application and compute this data by specifying relationships between data. The constraint solver is responsible for determining the flow-of-control. Thus the programmer focuses on the high-level relationships between data and abstracts away the low-level details. This allows the programmer to more quickly develop applications, and to develop them with fewer bugs.

5. Formal Specification: Constraints allow objects and their relationships to be expressed concisely and rigorously. This formality allows the specification to serve as a design document that another human can examine and readily understand.

6. Rapid Prototyping: Since programmers need only specify the high-level relationships between objects, they can rapidly create, delete, or alter relationships, and observe their effect on the application. Thus a programmer can rapidly experiment with different designs, enhancing the probability of developing a design that potential users will find esthetically pleasing, easy to learn and use, and enhancing their productivity.

7. Amenable to Specification from Tools: A user frequently does not need to know the syntax of constraints or how to construct them since many constraints can be specified graphically using direct manipulation editors or textually via spreadsheet editors. Lapidary [Myers 89b], C32 [Myers 91a], Juno [Nelson 85], and Apogee [Hudson 90] provide several examples of such editors.

## 12.3   New Ingredients for Constraint Languages

In this section, we describe how multi-way and structural constraints can be integrated into the basic object–spreadsheet model to create what we call the active-value–spreadsheet (AVS) model.

### 12.3.1   Structural Relationships

Constraint systems currently restrict constraints to specifying the attributes or properties of data structures. However, they are not permitted to specify structural relationships that would add, delete, or modify data structures. This is due to the difficulty of developing algorithms that solve constraints which can cause side effects. Our experiences with large-scale, constraint-based applications makes it clear that structural constraints could considerably simplify the implementation of these applications. Applications and their views generally maintain separate data structures with redundant information. Although constraints can ensure that the values stored in these data structures remain consistent, they cannot ensure that the structures stay consistent. For example, if an application and a view maintain separate versions of a tree, then if the application deletes one of the nodes in its tree data structure, a constraint cannot automatically remove the corresponding node in the view's data structure. Instead, the application must either manually update the view's data structure or send the view a message telling it to update its data structure. Ideally, the two data structures would be linked via multi-way structural constraints, so if one data structure were changed, the other would be automatically changed as well. The advantages of such an approach become even more compelling when one considers that many applications have multiple views (e.g., the multi-user interfaces described in Chapter 9), and without structural constraints, maintaining the consistency of these data structures can be quite problematic.

Structural constraints can also help maintain the relationship between the objects displayed on the screen and the view data structures. Retained object models, such as that used by Garnet [Myers 90e], have a one-to-one correspondance between graphical objects on the screen and graphical objects in memory. The graphical objects in memory are typically generated from the view data structures. For example, the text items that appear in a directory browser may be generated from a list of files in the view data structures. If the list of files changes, the text items displaying these files need to change as well. A multi-way structural constraint that enforces this relationship could help simplify the implementation of the directory browser.

Active values provide one mechanism for allowing constraints to specify structural relationships by allowing side effects to occur during constraint-solving. In our scheme, any variable can have one or more action procedures associated with it that will execute when the variable's value changes. Thus, if the value of a variable is computed by a constraint, the action procedures associated with that variable will be executed whenever the constraint computes a new value. The action procedure should act as an "assistant" to the constraint solver, enforcing a constraint that the constraint solver cannot enforce by itself.

Structural constraints can be supported by allowing constraints to be placed on the structural variables of an object. Structural variables might include the object's type (e.g., rectangle, circle, aggregate), the object's components (if it is an aggregate), the object's parent (if it belongs to an aggregate), and an object's existence (perhaps indicated by a special variable). For example, an object system might store an object's type in a variable named *is-a*, an object's components in a variable named *components*, and an object's parent in a variable named *parent*. Conceivably, it could add a special variable, such as *destroy-p*, that indicates whether an object should be destroyed.

A constraint would compute the value of one of these structural variables, and an action procedure would provide the knowledge to enforce the constraint. For example, if the type of an object is changed from rectangle to circle, the action procedure can perform the bookkeeping required to make the object behave as a circle. As another example, if the *destroy-p* slot becomes true, the action procedure can destroy the object. Often these procedures will be system-supplied, in which case a programmer only has to worry about writing the constraints. The constraints will be automatically enforced by the system-supplied action procedures.

A constraint system using this style could be implemented in the following fashion. First an event will trigger an action procedure that generates a set of structural and attribute changes. Then the constraint solver gains control and starts satisfying the constraints. When a constraint causes the value of an active variable to change, the variable's associated action procedures are triggered and the constraint solver transfers control to the action procedures in an order determined by the constraint solver. The action procedures then run to completion, possibly committing side effects that invalidate constraints (for example, deleting an object that an arrow is connected to will invalidate the constraint that computes the value of the arrow's *destroy-p* variable). The constraint solver is notified of these changes, so that it may take them into account when it regains control at the completion of the action procedures. The transfer of control between the constraint solver and action procedures continues until a stable state is reached in which all appropriate constraints are satisfied and all action procedures have terminated. An interesting question is whether it is useful to allow side effects to invalidate constraints that have already been satisfied, thus forcing them to be evaluated more than once. If it is useful to allow constraints to be evaluated more than once, should there be a fixed upper bound on the number of evaluations, thus ensuring eventual termination, or should an unlimited number of evaluations be permitted, in which case the constraint solver could cycle forever?

In the model, the constraint solver is the ultimate arbiter of sequencing decisions. If an action procedure changes active variables, the procedure must return control to the constraint solver before the procedures associated with these active variables are executed. The constraint solver then decides whether to transfer control to one of these procedures, or whether to continue constraint solving. The action procedures will eventually be called. However, the constraint solver decides when they will be called. Since action procedures may access variables other than the one that triggered their execution, it is imperative that these variables be up-to-date before the action procedure is actually called.

Chapter 11 describes another way of supporting structural constraints based on constraint imperative programming. In this scheme, the application's state is conceptually recreated at each time increment, so only objects needed to satisfy the constraints are constructed at each step. For example, if an object that an arrow is connected to does not exist during a given time increment, then the arrow will not be constructed. Internally, of course, the constraint solver does not recreate the state at each step but incrementally modifies it. Thus, the programmer does not have to worry about advising the constraint solver as to how to enforce the structural constraints.

The advantage of the constraint imperative programming approach is that it is higher-level, requiring the programmer to do less work and the constraint solver correspondingly more. This reduces the time required to program the interface. The advantage of the scheme described in this chapter is that the constraint solver is told how to enforce the structural constraints, thus providing the constraint solver with greater application specific knowledge, and presumably, with greater efficiency. In addition, the system can provide default action procedures for enforcing the constraints, thus providing a higher-level interface if the programmer is not worried about efficiency.

### Examples

To illustrate the active-value–spreadsheet model, consider the following examples for a project editor that allows a user to organize a project's task:

1. Selection: When an object is selected, its properties should be highlighted in the appropriate property menus (Figure 12.3). These properties should become the current selections, so if a new object is created, it will be created with these properties.

2. Feedback: The type of selection handles that a selected object sprouts should depend on its size. Further, if the object changes size, the type of selection handles should change accordingly (Figure 12.4).

3. Deletion: If a box is deleted, all attached arrows should be automatically deleted as well.

4. Semantic Actions: The critical path should be recomputed when the task network is modified and an application function should be called once this value is computed.

We will consider first how this design can be implemented in the AVS spreadsheet model, and then compare the implementation with an implementation in a conventional spreadsheet or active-value model. The object selection design implies that a menu selection can change in one of two ways—the user directly changes it by selecting a menu item or indirectly changes it by selecting an object. An efficient way to implement this menu in the AVS model is to install a *selected* variable in the menu which contains the currently selected menu item. The menu-handler sets this variable directly when the user chooses one of the menu items. A constraint can also be attached to the *selected* variable that computes the desired menu item based on the selected object. For example:

```
selected =  case selected-obj.line-style
                dashed-line: menu-item1
                line-1: menu-item2
                line-2: menu-item3
```

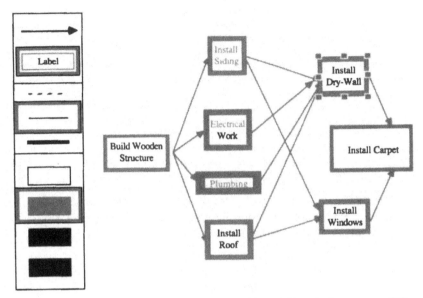

Figure 12.3: A boxes and arrows project editor. The designer can differentiate various types of tasks by using line-styles and filling-styles. For example, carpentry tasks are denoted by gray-filled boxes and interior decorating tasks are denoted by white-filled, thick-lined boxes. Although the option is not shown, the designer may attach times to the tasks indicating how long it will take to accomplish the task.

Figure 12.4: The type of selection handles should depend on the size of the object. Large objects that can comfortably accommodate selection boxes, such as the plumbing task in (a), should be ringed by eight selection boxes, while small objects that cannot accommodate such boxes, such as the iconified version of the plumbing task in (b), should be pointed at by a selection arrow.

*selected-obj* is a global pointer variable that references the selected object. When a new object is selected, the constraint will be reevaluated, potentially changing the value of *selected*. The feedback can be made to appear over the appropriate menu item by defining an *obj-over* variable in the feedback object that points to the selected menu item, and placing a constraint on *obj-over* that equates it to the value of *selected*:

```
feedback.obj-over = menu.selected
```

Constraints on the feedback's position and size would indirectly reference this selected menu item through the *obj-over* pointer variable, thus positioning the feedback object over the correct menu item.

To ensure that *selected-obj* does not point to a destroyed object, we can write an action procedure that sets *selected-obj* to nil if the object it is pointing at is destroyed:

**action-procedure**(selected-obj)
    **if** exists-p(selected-obj) == false **then** nil

The function *exists-p* returns true if *selected-obj* points to an object, and false otherwise. This constraint saves the programmer from having to remember to deselect an object in every procedure that destroys an object.[1]

The programmer can implement the feedback design by placing a constraint that controls whether the selection handles are boxes or arrows on the *is-a* variable of an object (the *is-a* variable determines the type of an object). For example:

```
feedback.is-a
    = if      selected-obj.width > threshold
         and selected-obj.height > threshold
       then selection-boxes-obj
       else selection-arrows-obj
```

Typically the object system would associate an action-procedure with the *is-a* variable that enforces the constraint, so the programmer would

---

[1]The constraint system automatically establishes a dependency from the action procedure to the selected object. When the selected object is destroyed, its "value" changes, and thus the action procedure is automatically executed.

only have to worry about writing the constraint. For example, the action-procedure might register the changed feedback object with the display manager.

The feedback must also become invisible whenever there is no selected object. A constraint on the feedback's visibility variable can enforce this rule:

```
feedback.visible = if selected-obj then true
                                    else false
```

A programmer can implement the automatic deletion of arcs when a box is deleted by attaching a constraint to each arc's existence variable that will return the value *false* when one of the boxes the arc is connected to is deleted:

```
arc.existence =     exists-p(to-obj)
                and exists-p(from-obj)
```

A system or programmer supplied action procedure can be attached to the existence variable that destroys the arc when the variable becomes false.

Finally, the computation of the critical path can be accomplished by associating a critical path variable with each task that computes the critical path to that task:

```
task.critical-path-to-me
  =   max(predecessor-tasks.critical-path-to-me)
    + task.task-length
```

The variable *predecessor-tasks* contains all tasks that must be accomplished before this task is begun and the variable *task-length* indicates the time required to complete this task. The max operator is assumed to automatically iterate through the *predecessor-tasks* list. This constraint finds the maximum critical path of the predecessor tasks and adds to it the time required to complete this task. A global critical path variable tied to all sink tasks (i.e., tasks with no outgoing arrows) can compute the final critical path:

```
critical-path
       = max(sink-tasks.critical-path-to-me)
```

This latter variable will have the appropriate application function attached as an action procedure. Such a procedure might analyze the critical path, seeking ways to reduce it. The constraints ensure that the critical path will be automatically recomputed whenever the topography of the boxes and arrows network changes or the time of a task is altered.

Note that the combination of a constraint and an action procedure can automatically keep the list of sink tasks up to date. Each task can contain a variable called *sink-task-p* that is true if and only if the task is a sink task. A constraint can compute this variable's value by querying a list of successor tasks and returning true when the list is empty:

```
task.sink-task-p
    = if task.successor-tasks == nil
      then true else false
```

An action procedure can be attached to *sink-task-p* that ensures that the task is on the sink-task list if and only if the task is a sink task:

```
action-procedure(task,sink-task-p)
    if sink-task-p
    then sink-tasks = sink-tasks U task
    else sink-tasks = sink-tasks - task
```

The create and destroy methods for an arrow will update the appropriate *predecessor-tasks* and *successor-tasks* variables. Thus the sink-task list will be automatically updated whenever the connection between tasks changes.

Finally, constraints can be used to cause the critical-path nodes to change color:

```
task.color = if critical-path-p(task)
             then black else red
```

where *critical-path-p* returns true if the task is on the critical path and false otherwise.

Compare this implementation with implementations in the conventional spreadsheet and active-value models. A spreadsheet model would require that all side effects be committed at once, and then the constraint-solver would be called to satisfy the constraints. The selection design, the visibility of the feedback, and the computation of the critical path could be handled in the same manner as the active-value–spreadsheet model handled them. However, the selection of the appropriate feedback object for selections (boxes or arrows), the deletion of arrows when nodes are deleted, and the maintenance of the sink-task list would have to be done manually by the programmer. Thus, the programmer would have to remember to check whether the same feedback object should be used when an object is resized, would have to remember to delete arrows when nodes are deleted, and would have to remember to change the sink-task list when arrows or nodes were created or deleted.

If this editor were implemented using only active values, the bookkeeping burden on the programmer would be even greater. To implement the object selection design, the programmer could associate action procedures with the *selected-obj* variable that computed the menu item that should be highlighted for each menu and store these items in the appropriate *selected* slots. The programmer would have to associate a second action procedure with each *selected* variable that moved the feedback object from the previously selected menu item to the newly selected item, and that changed the feedback's size accordingly.

To implement the feedback design, the programmer would have to associate an action procedure with the *selected-obj* variable that selected the appropriate type of feedback, and then remember to check whether the correct feedback object is being used whenever the selected object is resized.

The programmer could implement the task deletion operation by remembering to call the arrow deletion function for each of the arrows attached to the task. However, the critical path computation would be difficult to code efficiently. Ideally it should be called only once, after the task and arrows have been deleted. However, to ensure that it is called, both the task and arrow deletion procedures must call it. This is clearly inefficient since the critical path computation could be done multiple times when a task is deleted. Thus, additional code must be added to ensure that the critical path computation is only performed once.

In comparing the active-value–spreadsheet model with the conventional spreadsheet and active-value models we see that both the conventional spreadsheet and active-value models require far more bookkeeping and thus will increase software development times and decrease reliability. Additionally, slight increases in the complexity of an application can dramatically increase the software development time in either of the conventional models, but not the AVS model. For example, suppose we added the following stipulations to the project editor: multiple selections are permitted and boxes can be made to have the same sizes. This change is easily accommodated in the AVS model since constraints can automatically ensure that all constrained boxes are resized when a box is resized, and action procedures and constraints ensure that feedback objects are appropriately changed if necessary. However, the conventional active-value model requires the programmer to manually change the sizes of all the constrained boxes. And while the conventional spreadsheet model can automatically change the sizes of the boxes, it cannot change the feedback objects if some of the boxes that change size are currently selected, because constraints cannot cause side effects.

## 12.3.2   Multi-Way Constraints

The advent of large-scale, constraint-based interactive applications has made it increasingly clear that one-way constraints are incapable of supporting many behaviors required by these applications. These shortcomings have been most noticeable in applications requiring two-way flow of information between interface and application and in applications requiring various types of layout constraints. For example, one-way constraints provide poor support for multiple views of an application. A change to the application should cause all views to be updated and a change to a view should cause the application and all other views to be updated. This requires a multi-way constraint between each view and the application's data structures. One-way constraints can support the flow of information in one direction, typically from the application to the views, but this requires that the programmer attach imperative procedures to each view that updates the application when the view changes.

The commonly used practice of grouping objects into more complicated objects called "aggregates" provides a good illustration of the layout problems encountered using one-way constraints. Aggregates often compute their bounding boxes from the bounding boxes of their children and the children often compute their position from the position of the aggregate. If the aggregate is moved, its children should move as well, and if one of the children moves, the aggregate should move, as well as the remaining children. In order to accomplish this, the aggregate needs to have a constraint that computes its bounding box from its childrens' bounding boxes, and a constraint that computes the aggregate's position based on the position of all the children. Similarly, each child needs a constraint that computes its position based on the position of its aggregate. However, in a one-way constraint system, an aggregate can have only one constraint, and thus it can either compute its bounding box, or it can compute its position as a function of the position of one of its children, but that is all. Clearly, multi-way constraints are needed to support all the desired behaviors.

As another example of the utility of multi-way constraints, the designer of an aggregate object may want the formula that computes the aggregate's bounding box to be the default formula. If another positioning formula is stored in the aggregate, it will have precedence over the default formula, but if the formula is deleted, the default formula will again compute the object's position. This cannot be done in a one-way constraint system since the new positioning formula must replace the default formula. Even the solution of the application manually reasserting the default formulas when a formula is destroyed may not work because the user may not want the default formula reasserted. In a multi-way system, the user would simply destroy the default formula and this would guarantee that the formula could not be reasserted.

We have adopted a model of non-simultaneous, multi-way constraints that can be solved by graph traversal algorithms. In order to guarantee that the equations will be non-simultaneous, we stipulate that it must be possible to order the equations, such that as each equation is evaluated, it has at least one unknown variable. This requirement effectively bars simultaneous equations of the form

$$a_1 x + b_1 y = c_1$$
$$a_2 x + b_2 y = c_2$$

since there is no arrangement in which the second equation in the order would have at least one unknown. The first equation in any such order can be solved since it has two unknowns, and one of the unknowns can be forced to assume its current value. However, the second equation will then have no unknown variables and thus cannot be solved.

The motivation for the non-simultaneous restriction is that it covers most situations typically found in interactive applications and it permits the constraints to be efficiently solved using graph-traversal techniques. It is important to note that problems requiring simultaneous equations can still be expressed in our model using action procedures. For example, programmers can still enforce graphical relationships such as parallel lines or line intersection and create dynamic models of physical systems.

Even with the restriction that equations be non-simultaneous, a set of equations can have multiple solutions. A simple example is the equation `right = left + width`, which expresses a relationship between the left and right sides of a rectangle. If the right side of the rectangle is changed, the constraint solver can satisfy the constraint by changing either the left side of the rectangle or the width of the rectangle. One choice moves the rectangle, the other choice resizes it.

The problem with multiple solutions is that the constraint solver may not choose the solution the user expects. In the above example, the user might expect the rectangle to move, and the constraint solver might decide to resize it. Thus, the constraint model must give the designer some control over which solution the constraint solver chooses.

Another difficulty with multi-way constraints is that multiple constraints may be attached to a variable, only one of which should be active at any given time. For example, consider the case of the aggregate which has a formula that computes its bounding box based on the bounding boxes of its children and a formula for each child that computes the aggregate's position based on the position of the child. When a child moves, the formula associated with that child should prevail. However, when a child is added to or removed from the aggregate, the formula that computes the aggregate's bounding box should prevail. In Garnet a third case arises when the aggregate itself is moved. Garnet separates the behaviors from the graphics using an interactors model [Myers 90c]. Rather than directly changing an object's position, a move behavior sets a standard instance variable in the object that contains the computed position. The object can choose to assume this new position, assume only a portion of the position (e.g., moving only in the x or y direction), or ignore the computation by using constraints which access this instance variable. Thus, the aggregate may have a third set of formulas that compute its position based on this instance variable. If a user moves the aggregate, then this third set of formulas should prevail.

Chapter 11 discusses how constraint hierarchies can be used to provide some guidance to the constraint solver in finding the desired solution. If the constraints are given fixed priorities, one solution, such as moving a rectangle, will always be preferred over other solutions, such as resizing a rectangle. However, if in addition to priorities, we allow constraints to be enabled or disabled depending on the context, then users will gain more flexible control over the constraint solving process, and the constraint solver will be able to select different solutions based on the state of the interface.

In this expanded model, not only can designers associate a priority with a constraint, but they can also provide a condition under which the constraint is enabled. As the user manipulates an interface, these conditions will intermittently become true, thus enabling a certain set of constraints that will be passed to the constraint solver. The constraint imperative model implements this idea by using the equivalent of constraint procedures that can either build or not build a set of constraints at each step depending on the values of various parameter values.

Our approach is a bit more imperative in that the constraint is understood to always exist, but it may contain a guard that enables the constraint only if the guard's condition is true. To illustrate this idea, consider again the equation `right = left + width`. This equation has 3 solutions:

```
right = left  + width
left  = right - width
width = right - left|
```

The first two solutions cause a rectangle to move and could be associated with a "move" condition while the last solution causes a rectangle to resize itself and could be associated with a "grow" condition. Designers would indicate which condition is true when the value of `right` is changed. "Grow" mode might be activated when an end user selected a grow handle on the rectangle, and as the user dragged the right side of the rectangle, the constraint solver would solve the constraint `width = right - left`, thus causing the rectangle to resize itself. "Move" mode would be activated when the user selected a move handle, and the constraint solver would solve

the constraint `left = right - width` as the user dragged the right
side of the rectangle.

If a constraint does not have an explicit guard or priority, it will always
be active and carry a default priority. Thus, if the designer does not care
which solution the constraint solver chooses, then the user need not worry
about priorites or activation conditions. Priorities and guards must be used
only if the user wants control over the constraint solving process. One of
the advantages of using activation conditions is that the active constraints
frequently form a one-way constraint network, and thus can be solved using
efficient one-way constraint solvers. In situations where this is not the case
and a planning step is required to create a one-way constraint network,
an algorithm such as DeltaBlue [Freeman-Benson 90c] or the incremental
planning algorithm developed in [Vander Zanden 88b] can be used to order
the equations before they are solved by the constraint solver. DeltaBlue
can handle constraint hierarchies while the planner in [Vander Zanden 88b]
can solve a larger set of flat constraint networks in which all the constraints
have equal priorities. Unlike previous algorithms, these algorithms can
perform planning in real-time, even in systems involving thousands of
constraints. Thus, unless the evaluation process itself takes a long time,
there is no noticeable pause between an action instigated by the user, and
the feedback provided as a result of evaluating the constraints.

## 12.4   Comparison with Other Paradigms

### 12.4.1   Object-Oriented Programming

One might argue that the object model is sufficient to distribute the flow-of-
control in an application and, therefore, constraints are not needed. When
a change occurs to an object, it can send messages to other objects that
need to change as well. These objects can in turn send messages to the
objects they directly affect, and so on, until the system reaches a consistent
state. However, this naive method of propagating changes directly to
one's neighbors has been shown to require as much as exponential work
in the number of instance variables that must be changed. For example,
Figure 12.5-a presents an example of a list that consists of two rows of
rectangles [Henry 88]. All the rectangles should be left-aligned in their

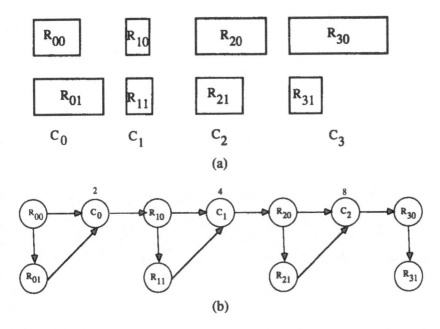

Figure 12.5: (a) A two-row list of rectangles. The rectangles in each column are left-aligned, each column has a minimum width (e.g., the minimum width for column 1 is used to compute the positions of the rectangles in column 2), and there is a fixed offset between each column. (b) The dependencies set up by these rules. For example, $R_{01}$ is left-aligned with $R_{00}$ so $R_{01}$'s left depends on $R_{00}$'s left. $C_0$'s right is the maximum of $R_{00}$'s and $R_{01}$'s right sides and the right side of the minimum column so $C_0$ depends on $R_{00}$ and $R_{01}$. The numbers above the column variables indicate the number of times they are evaluated using naive propagation.

column, each column should appear a fixed distance from the right side of the previous column, and each column must have a minimum width. Based on these requirements, the following assignments can be constructed to compute the position of each column [Henry 88]:

```
Ri0.left = Ci-1.right + col_spacing
Ri1.left = Ri0.left
Ci.right = Ri0.left +
           max(Ri0.width, Ri1.width, min_col_width)
```

In these constraints $R_{ij}$ denotes a rectangle in column $i$, row $j$, and $C_i$ denotes column $i$. Figure 12.5-b shows the dependencies set up by these assignments. If messages are implemented in a straightforward way, then when $R_{00}$ is moved, it will send messages to $R_{01}$ and $C_0$ telling them it has moved. $C_0$ will update itself and send a message to $R_{10}$ while $R_{01}$ will update itself and send a message to $C_0$. Next methods in $R_{10}$ and $C_0$ will execute. However, the method in $C_0$ is executing for the second time. If this straightforward message passing continues, $C_1$ will execute 4 times and $C_2$ will execute 8 times. In general, column $C_i$ will execute $2^{i+1}$ times. Although the message passing algorithm might be improved, it would require that the objects have more extensive knowledge of other objects' behavior, which violates the notion of data encapsulation, as well as returning to a more centralized state of control, with an attendant increase in complexity. Thus, object systems by themselves do not solve the difficult flow-of-control problem that arises in interactive applications.

The solution is to combine constraints with object systems as has been done in the active-value–spreadsheet and constraint imperative programming models, as well as in toolkits such as Garnet [Myers 90e], ThingLab [Borning 81, Borning 86], Apogee [Henry 88], and GROW [Barth 86]. The object system provides the advantages of inheritance, data encapsulation, and reusability, while the constraint system provides the advantage of automatic handling of the flow-of-control.

## 12.4.2   Constraint Imperative Programming

Many of the differences between the active-value–spreadsheet model and constraint imperative programming result from their different orientations— while both models allow programs to be more declarative than conventional imperative languages permit, the active-value–spreadsheet model is more imperative in style than the constraint imperative model. As noted in Section 12.3.1, the active-value–spreadsheet model relies on the programmer to provide action procedures to enforce structural constraints, whereas the CIP model figures out the enforcement actions itself. The CIP model uses streams to handle data, so a complete record of the program's execution is theoretically available. In contrast, the active-value–spreadsheet model uses destructive overwriting of variables so the programmer must save historically significant data. The two models also differ in their handling of time—the CIP model explicitly advances the clock when told to by the programmer, while the active-value–spreadsheet model implicitly advances the clock when the constraint solver is called. Finally, the two models treat procedures in different ways. The active-value–spreadsheet model supports traditional procedural abstraction in which constraints are procedures that consist of a set of commands parameterized by pointer variables. Constraint imperative programming supports constraint abstraction in which procedures consist of a set of parameterized constraint statements and produce as output a set of constraints instantiated with the parameters passed to the procedure.

The two models are equally expressive. By changing the variables passed to the constraint generating procedures at each clock tick, constraint imperative programming can support procedural abstraction. Similarly, a programmer can use activation conditions and action procedures in the active-value–spreadsheet model to generate sets of constraints based on the current values of variables, thus simulating constraint abstraction. The tradeoff between the two models is the usual one between abstraction and efficiency. Both models are higher-level and provide more distributed flow-of-control than conventional imperative languages. The constraint imperative model allows the programmer to abstract away implementation details, but the algorithms used to implement the constraint solver must be more general and thus the programs are likely to be less efficient and use more space. The active-value–spreadsheet model allows the constraint solver, and thus programs, to run more efficiently by providing the constraint solver with application-specific knowledge, but the programmer has to worry about implementation details. Of course, the active-value–spreadsheet model can be made more declarative by providing default implementation methods for structural constraints.

### 12.4.3   Constraint Language Programming

Several logic-oriented constraint languages have been proposed, including constraint logic programming (CLP) [Jaffar 87], HCLP [Borning 89], and the concurrent constraint family of languages [Saraswat 89]. These languages build systems of constraints by interleaving logic deductions and incremental constraint evaluation. By asserting and retracting logical statements and constraint relationships over time, these languages could conceivably be used to build interactive applications. Unlike the active-value–spreadsheet model in which constraints are manually asserted and retracted by the programmer, logic-based languages automatically assert and retract constraints via logic deductions. CLP languages offer another potentially attractive declarative paradigm, but this model is less known to most programmers than imperative programming. Also, while advances are being made in incremental backtracking, it has not been demonstrated that CLP languages can efficiently support large-scale, interactive applications.

### 12.4.4   Other Paradigms

Constraint grammars represent another variation on the spreadsheet model [Vander Zanden 89]. Programmers build successively more complicated objects from simpler ones using a part–whole hierarchy and declaratively specify relationships between the attributes of these objects using constraints. A powerful pattern-matching editing model allows the designer to manipulate these objects and modify the system of constraints. However, the constraint grammar paradigm does not support structural constraints or provide user control over the constraint solver.

A number of constraint languages aimed at non-interactive applications have been proposed and implemented, including Bertrand [Leler 88] and a language by Steele [Steele 80]. An interesting feature of Bertrand is its use of augmented term rewriting, which provides rather powerful multi-way constraint solving ability without resorting to backtracking. Chapter 13 proposes to allow this model to support interactive applications by adding memorizing techniques. Steele's language is noteworthy for its ability to produce explanations for how a constraint solution was arrived at and for providing a macro facility that allows more complicated constraints to be constructed from simpler ones, thus providing a simple form of constraint abstraction.

## 12.5   Conclusions

As interactive applications become increasingly large and sophisticated, it is becoming increasingly evident that the imperative model of computing is unlikely to provide a viable mechanism for supporting large-scale interactive computing. Thus, new paradigms of computing must be investigated. It seems that spreadsheet models provide a particularly appealing model for the implementation of interactive languages. They are easy to use and their declarative style eliminates many flow-of-control concerns, thus simplifying the development and testing of applications, and improving their robustness. Further, by adding a multi-way constraint scheme and active values, they can be made sufficiently powerful to support general-purpose programming.

# Chapter 13

# Properties of User Interface Systems and the Siri Programming Language

*Bruce Horn*

## 13.1 Introduction

The widespread use of advanced user interfaces has raised the expectations of users to new levels. Highly graphical, interactive programs with easy-to-use, intuitive interfaces, such as those available for the Apple Macintosh, have become the goal, if not the reality, in personal and workstation computing. These interfaces are usually based on three concepts: accurate and appealing visual metaphors, interaction by direct manipulation, and immediate reflection of changes in the data. Programs based on these concepts are called *reactive*, after Alan Kay's Reactive Engine [Kay 69].

One of the most important attributes of a well-designed reactive program is that the program maintains an internal model that is kept consistent with an end-user model. The end-user's model is created and modified by direct manipulation, using an input device such as a mouse to alter a visual representation. This puts the user in control, rather than the computer.

In addition, whenever possible, a reactive program should be *modeless*. Modeless interfaces allow the user to alternate between partially-completed tasks without forcing them to respond to dialogs, or to perform tedious "exit this context, enter this context" procedures to switch. Typically, modeless interfaces follow the *noun–verb* mechanism, where objects are first selected, then the operation specified. This fits in well with direct manipulation, since it avoids the specification of an agent other than the object itself (for example, the computer) that is implied in an *(agent–) verb–noun* framework; window close is preferable to (computer) close window.

A program's user interface is the bridge between the user's model and the program's model. It is simple to bridge from the program to the user: simply provide a display of the program model, using visual metaphors to build an understandable user model. Reactive programs make this bridge two-way, by allowing the program to modify its model in response to the user changing the visual representation.

Implementing reactive programs is difficult, due to the computational mechanisms that are rarely supported in existing programming languages. These mechanisms include object-orientation, multi-way constraints, multi-threading, incremental computation, meta programming, and support for real-time behavior. A new programming language is needed that addresses these requirements in a simple and uniform way.

## 13.2   Reactive Program Implementation

Reactive programming has many difficult aspects. The visual metaphors must be designed to be both aesthetically pleasing and functional; the entities in the metaphor must behave as closely to real-life objects as possible; changes in the model must be incorporated quickly, and the consequences of those changes displayed immediately; and the user must never feel that his actions have surprising and undesirable results. To achieve these high-level goals, reactive programs must address the following implementation issues:

**Use of Display and Control Objects**. In a typical reactive program, there are many basic elements of the graphical user interface that must be supplied either by the system or by the programmer: buttons, scroll bars, dialog boxes, windows, menus, rulers, palettes, and so on. The functionality of these objects may be apparently simple, but their interactions with the program are often very complicated, with many dependency chains that need to be traversed and recomputed, often explicitly. In addition, the appearance and screen layout of these elements must be carefully designed for aesthetic and practical value, and maintained under various changes such as resizing and moving.

**Modeless Interaction.** To implement a modeless interface, it is necessary to write the program so that it rarely blocks awaiting input from the user, who should be able to easily switch to another independent task. Of course, it is sometimes the case that blocking is required ("Do you really want to erase this disk?"), but generally the program should continue on, recomputing the display and internal structures that do not depend on the user's answer. Similarly, if the user performs an operation that invalidates a computation in progress, the program should restart that computation without necessarily completing it, when possible. These features can make the control flow in reactive programs quite complicated.

**Mapping User Events.** Although it is relatively easy for a program to display a model graphically, the steps required to make that graphical information reactive are substantial. Displaying a model graphically is straightforward, since it is a many-to-one function of which many valid solutions exist; a graphical display may be created in several different ways to represent the same internal state. However, an action that modifies the displayed graphics could cause many different changes in the internal model, only one of which is intended by the user. The programmer must then decide what a particular action means in a one-to-many mapping. The meaning is precisely determined by the action itself (a click, a keystroke), and the action's context (the internal program state, the current window, the selected objects, the mouse point, etc.).

**Reflection of Model and Context.** Once an action is interpreted by the program, it must reflect the consequences of that action back to the user. Updates must be continuous for objects that change over time (clocks, disk usage, network traffic, etc.). In addition, not only must the model's image be updated on the screen, but context markers that help indicate what actions are possible must be updated. These markers include the currently selected object, the currently active window, dimmed and highlighted menus, scroll bar locations, and so forth.

**Consistency Maintenance**. Because different parts of a program can be interrelated in surprisingly intricate ways to map user actions and then reflect changes in the model and context, maintaining consistency of the program model can be a challenge. There can be several hundred dependency relationships in a typical reactive program, and these generally must be specified in the program by calling update routines at appropriate points.

**Concurrency and Time**. Many interactions in programs are time-oriented: blinking a cursor twice a second; scrolling text at a comfortable reading rate; defining a double-click as two single-clicks within a quarter of a second; and animation of all kinds. Each of these tasks must execute, and be clocked, independently, with complex synchronizations between them.

Ordinary programming languages do not address all these issues well, if at all. However, it has become clear through practice that object-oriented languages come closest to providing the facilities required for the implementation of reactive interfaces, with Smalltalk being the premier example [Goldberg 83]. There are several reasons for this. First, there is a close mapping between objects on the screen and their language representations, making the creation and manipulation of display and control objects simple. Second, object-oriented programming is well suited to the *noun–verb* framework for direct manipulation. Since each object (the noun) knows itself how to perform the requested message (the verb), user actions such as clicking and dragging can be translated directly to messages sent to each object. This object-focused behavior has a consequence that the problem is discretized into objects that represent the model, and the discretization defines, and reflects, a style that is pervasive in the design of reactive programs. Finally, inheritance allows the programmer to implement objects with similar behaviors easily, while sharing common specifications. The polymorphism that results allows the end-user to treat related objects in the same way, even though their implementations may differ.

## 13.3 Toolboxes Are Not Enough

Because of the natural reluctance to design a new language solely for the implementation of user interfaces, many researchers have written interface toolboxes using existing languages. These have been successful to a certain extent, although their limitations reveal themselves quickly. Any toolbox that attempts to provide support for the consistency maintenance requirement would have to have access to the lowest levels of the program itself. Unfortunately, the boundary between the toolbox and application program isolates important information from the interface, or forces the many connections to be explicitly specified. Writing programs so closely coupled to low-level structures requires language-level support.

It will still be useful to reuse existing code written in other languages, and so there should be a facility to call out of the interface language to foreign code. However, it is essential to avoid building a large boundary between the user interface and the program that would impact the ability of the interface to manipulate the program data and reflect its state. Therefore, the language should be general-purpose enough that the call-out facility will not have to be used very often.

Most importantly, applying the standards and structures of programming language design helps to identify a fairly complete set of ideas underlying interface design, and thus a basic calculus of reactive programs. The process of designing a language for supporting user interfaces will crystallize these ideas into a disciplined, usable, and teachable form.

## 13.4 Essential Characteristics of a New Language

Any new language intended to support the implementation of reactive programs should include the following features:

**Object-Orientation.** The object-oriented framework, though incomplete, embodies many necessary features for user interface implementation. Display and control objects, in particular, are easily coded in an object-oriented style, and object-oriented implementation is well suited to the *noun–verb* interaction framework as well as the mapping of user actions through objects.

**Multi-Way Constraint Satisfaction**. There needs to be a facility for consistency maintenance. Constraints are useful for maintaining the user's view of the model and context by linking the state of the program to a screen representation and by updating dependency chains within the program itself. In addition, many aspects of user interfaces are most easily described in a declarative, constraint format, such as the spatial relationships between screen objects. Constraints, pioneered in the Sketchpad system [Sutherland 63a], have been used subsequently in many experimental systems ([Borning 79, Nelson 85, Szekely 88, Vander Zanden 88b, Myers 91c]). However, multi-way constraints, rather than a simple dependency-graph facility, are necessary for computing the forward and inverse transforms between the model and the screen representation. Although the inverse transforms could be given explicitly by the programmer in a one-way constraint language, in larger applications it quickly becomes too complex a task to determine an inverse transform without help from the system (see Chapters 11 and 12).

**Multi-Threaded**. Complicated sequencing and modeless interactions are much easier to implement if independent threads are coded separately. Tasks such as display updating and recomputation should not be blocked simply due to a dialog box's need for a user response. Asynchronous input from the user, as well as from other sources such as networks, are best handled in parallel threads, communicating higher-level information through an event queue or Linda tuple-space to the main program (see Chapters 8, 9, and 15).

**Incremental Computation**. When editing a large model in a reactive program, a user's input will often modify only a small part of the model, leaving the rest unchanged. Although the model as a whole may need to be reevaluated after a user edit, many independent subparts may be unaffected, and can be reused in the model recomputation. By caching previously-evaluated computations, and performing fast equality testing to determine when a cache entry is valid, much computation can be avoided. These and other similar techniques have been used previously in user interface constraint systems to increase performance [Vander Zanden 88b].

Many optimization techniques depend on caching information, and knowing when information needs to be recomputed, and when it does not. By providing a mechanism by which this can be determined by the system, rather than by a programmer's intimate understanding of the dependencies in the program, efficiency can be gained safely while disallowing situations that could produce inconsistent data.

Additionally, incremental computation techniques can automatically provide for simple dynamic programming, reducing the time complexity of some exponential algorithms (such as a naive recursive coding of the Fibonacci sequence).

**Meta Programming and Interpretation**. Meta programming allows the programmer to avoid reimplementing features in an application that already exist in the language. For example, dragging out a rectangle and choosing a pattern from a palette is equivalent to writing code specifying a rectangle with its size, location, and pattern. If the language that implements the drawing program can also be used to specify and interpret the screen representations of document objects and relationships as well, then much duplicated work can be avoided. Specifying objects created by the end-user directly in the programming language brings the program model closer to the user model by manipulating a program segment in exactly the same way that a user would, in an understandable form. In this way, meta programming is an extension of the object-oriented philosophy, in that it encourages a strong link between visible screen entities and actual program code.

Interpretation has the additional advantage that sophisticated end-users may be given the opportunity to program. There are many cases where the most concise and understandable way to achieve a goal is to allow the user to write small, special-purpose routines. User programmability opens up the program to applications that the original designer never imagined.

Further, meta programming and interpretation make it easier to provide tools for program development and manipulation. Being able to use reactive, direct manipulation tools for object creation and composition, such as building dialog boxes, arranging screen layout, and graphically representing control flow, can improve the utility of the system greatly (see [Myers 89b]).

**Support for Real-Time Behavior**. Threads of execution often have behavior that is time-dependent, and as such should be able to be explicitly programmed with time expressions. For example, it should be simple to write code that says that a scroll bar should scroll initially at two lines a second, accelerating at one line per second per second, and that an object moving across the screen should take two seconds to move from point X to point Y. The programming system should take care of most scheduling requirements, and should provide facilities for synchronization between threads (see Chapter 8).

## 13.5   The Siri Programming Language

These features are currently being implemented in a mixed declarative and imperative programming language called Siri. Siri (a SymbolIc Reduction Interpreter) is an object-oriented language with a simple, event-based, multi-way constraint satisfaction mechanism for consistency maintenance.

Siri provides a single abstraction for object description, modification, and evaluation called a *constraint pattern*. All kinds of objects are created and modified in the same way using constraint patterns: data objects, executable code, scroll bars, dialog boxes, graphical aggregates, and even entire documents will share the same containment structure and modification mechanisms. Therefore, the code needed to support building a dialog box will be nearly the same as is needed to support drawing figures in a document, with the only difference being the interaction code attached to the dialog objects.

Siri is a symmetric language (see [Gelernter 89]), meaning that execution occurs over the entire space of a program simultaneously, and that the same structures used for data encapsulation are also program structures. This feature allows multi-threaded execution, and provides the basis for meta programming. Because Siri is primarily declarative, multi-threading occurs automatically without having to explicitly specify independent threads.

The Siri system is a hybrid, with evaluating objects spanning a continuum from completely compiled to completely interpreted, under programmer direction. Constraint patterns can be defined, modified, and evaluated at run time by other constraint patterns for meta programming. The ability to both interpret and compile at any level of granularity allows for optimization of critical code, along with flexibility in binding times.

Concepts from many different sources form the foundation for the Siri design and implementation. The most influential include Bertrand [Leler 88], a batch constraint system that introduced augmented term rewriting; Linda [Gelernter 83], a parallel programming mechanism that demonstrated the utility of communication through tuple spaces; Beta [Kristensen 89], a programming language that consists of a single object abstraction, the pattern; and incremental computation mechanisms demonstrated by Pugh in his thesis [Pugh 88]. The idea of using continuously-changing objects in real-time interaction was inspired by Arctic [Rubine 87].

## 13.6   An Introduction to Siri

Programming in Siri consists simply of specifying objects in an object-oriented manner, with internal consistency constraints, and events by which objects may be changed. Although Siri is first a constraint system, it is not stateless as are many constraint systems; each object can have persistent information, and it can be modified by the receipt of events. Information flows in two ways: directly by sending events from object to object, and indirectly through the constraint graph. Programming in Siri is similar to programming a spreadsheet with macros: the spreadsheet provides a constraint graph, and the macros provide events which perturb the spreadsheet and cause it to be resatisfied.

Siri's syntax is based on that of Bertrand, but generalized and extended. Many of the following examples will be recognizable to anyone familiar with Bertrand.

The fundamental structure in Siri, and its only abstraction mechanism, is called a *constraint pattern*.

### 13.6.1   The Constraint Pattern

A constraint pattern consists of a label, a list of optional prefixes, the pattern body, and a list of optional type specifiers:

```
label: prefixes { body } 'types;
```

The label is a name for the object that results from the evaluation of the constraint pattern. A label may be simply a symbol, such as screenRectangle, or it may be an expression parameterized with free variables that the constraint pattern body refers to. If a label is parameterized, the object that it denotes is *underconstrained*. Its value depends on the values of the objects that are bound to the variables.

The body consists of expressions and nested constraint patterns. Expressions in Siri define relationships, or constraints between objects. Prefixes are a mechanism by which other constraint patterns may be included, much like subclassing in conventional object-oriented languages.

The expressions and enclosed constraint patterns, both defined in the body and in the prefixes, exist inside the constraint pattern, or in *pattern space*. Pattern space defines a scope within which subobjects may be directly related to each other using expressions with operators. A special operator, the semicolon, indicates that the previous expression should be asserted as a constraint on the variables in the expression. The last expression, if unasserted, is returned as the value of the constraint pattern. Expressions in pattern space are evaluated by matching with labels of patterns (whether underconstrained or nullary) and then replacing the matched subexpression with a copy of the computed object. For example,

```
myNumber: { 3 + 4 } 'number;
```

evaluates 3+4 to an object of type 'number. The expression myNumber + myNumber would evaluate to 7+7 initially by replacing the label myNumber with its computed value; the final addition returning 14 would be evaluated by a primitive operation.

If expressions in pattern space are labeled constraint patterns themselves, they may be evaluated as separate threads. Their names are visible to each other, and objects outside of the pattern space can refer to them via the enclosing pattern's label. For example, the constraint pattern

```
myThreeSums:  {
        firstSum:  { 3 + 4 };
        secondSum: { 5 + 6 };
        thirdSum:  { 10 + 2 };
        firstSum+secondSum+thirdSum
};
```

evaluates to an object whose value is 30, but which also has three sub-objects concurrently evaluated with values 7, 11, and 12. They can be referenced from outside the object by using the *dot* operator to access objects within the pattern space; myThreeSums.secondSum is the object 11. More generally, by using the dot operator, we can *enter* the object's pattern space (similar to using Pascal's with statement) and perform operations within the object's computational context. For example, the programmer can add the first two sums in myThreeSums quite simply:

```
myThreeSums.(firstSum+secondSum)
```

Labeling an existing object creates a copy of that object for local use. For example, the primitive object aNumber is defined to be a number which is not specified. Writing

```
x: aNumber;
```

simply creates an instance of a number, x, without setting x's value; further constraints will be required to determine x. We can use labeling to define the sum of three unspecified numbers by just instantiating them each as aNumber, and then specifying the sum:

```
aTriSum:  { a, b, c: aNumber; a+b+c };
```

We can then use aTriSum as an underconstrained object in another constraint pattern:

```
test: { x: aTriSum; x.(a=10; b=12; c=4); x };
```

The object test then has the value 26.

### 13.6.2    Operators

Operators are symbols or groups of symbols which define syntactic relationships between objects. The basic Siri system defines operators for arithmetic, boolean, and string operations, as well as for fundamental evaluation functions for the constraint satisfaction system.

All operators are user definable, through constraint patterns. Operators may be infix, prefix, postfix, or mixfix, allowing a wide variety of syntaxes to be created. Examples of operator definitions include

```
"_+_": anOperator commutative precedence 200;
"_!":anOperator precedence 300;
"from_to_by_": anOperator precedence 100;
```

The underbar (_) defines where operands may occur relative to the operator. While operators define the locations of their operands, they do not define what types of operands may appear in those locations, and thus all operators may be polymorphic.

Operators play an important role in labels. Although labels are often symbols (such as myName), they may also be defined by using operator expressions. For example, the expressions 3+4 and "foo"+"bar" both name the object whose label is a+b, where a and b are variables. Clearly, these two expressions need to be able to be distinguished when matching against a label with an operator expression. This is done through the type system.

### 13.6.3    Types

All objects in the system are of at least one *type*. The types define the external interface of this object which is available to users, and also specify what kinds of objects are allowed in particular contexts. Siri's type system is a predicate type system, since objects may be of many different types, depending on their interfaces. This makes the typing of objects which inherit from multiple sources quite simple: just union the types from each source. By separating the type hierarchy from the implementation hierarchy, Siri allows multiple implementations for a given type, which may be used interchangeably.

Types are used to denote what objects may match in an operator expression. This is done by tagging the variables in the label with the appropriate type. For example, integer addition may be defined by using the constraint pattern

```
a'integer+b'integer: { ... } 'integer;
```

while string concatenation is defined by

```
a'string+b'string: { ... } 'string;
```

The variables a and b are typically used in expressions in the body, thereby parameterizing the object's definition. However, the object whose label is a'integer+b'integer exists in its own right, although its value depends on what the values of a and b are. The object is under-constrained, and only produces a value when the values of a and b are provided.

Unlike most object-oriented languages, Siri may match expressions of arbitrarily mixed types. Rather than simply sending the message + to an 'integer receiver, and thus forcing the receiver to perform further discrimination on the argument to +, the entire context of the expression is examined. Multiply-polymorphic expressions are not unusual in user interface programs: situations such as adding two numbers of different kinds, or drawing a shape on a graphics device, require discrimination on the types of both arguments to determine the correct method.

Types are objects in Siri, and are defined exactly in the same way as operators. The programming environment uses types to maintain information about the kinds of interfaces which each type supports, and uses this information to help the programmer determine whether an object being used in an expression is valid or not.

### 13.6.4  Label Repetitions

As we have seen, labeling a pattern instantiates an object that is described by that pattern, and labeling an existing object makes a copy of that object. For example, by evaluating the expression x: aNumber, the object x is created. Sometimes it is useful to create a number of objects from the same pattern; an array of objects can be instantiated by using a *label repetition*.

This repetition creates a multi-part object with generated label names to reference each part of the object.

To illustrate, if we would like an array of four numbers we can write

```
myNumbers@(1 to 4): aNumber;
```

This creates an object, myNumbers, with 4 instances of aNumber as subobjects. This label repetition is equivalent to the pattern

```
myNumbers:{
        @1: aNumber; @2: aNumber;
        @3: aNumber; @4: aNumber;
};
```

Like the dot operator, the @ operator, when applied to an existing object, is a way to access the subobjects of that object. Using the @ operator, one can address the third number in the array by writing

```
myNumbers@3
```

The @ operator can be thought of as indexing into an object to return the matching subobject as the result, while the dot operator enters the pattern space of the object to evaluate an expression.

These arrays, as defined, can be used exactly as arrays are used in other computer languages. Instead of being a special structure in the language, arrays in Siri are simply objects with subobjects that are named in sequence; special syntax is provided to simplify the creation and usage of this common structure.

## 13.6.5   Constraint Satisfaction by Equation Solving

Siri's primitive constraint patterns provide basic algebra simplification and solving reductions, by rewriting complex algebraic expressions to simpler, ordered expressions. Matching on semicolons is used to determine what is being asserted, and what result is required. For example, one of Siri's primitive patterns is

```
a*x+b = 0; x: { a ~= 0; -b/a };
```

This pattern matches any assertion of the form a*x+b = 0, where the result required is x. To solve this equation we assert that a must not be equal to zero, and return -b/a as the result.

A standard example of constraint satisfaction is a temperature object, which can return its temperature in Fahrenheit or Celsius. It would typically be coded as follows:

```
aCFTemp: {
        C, F: aNumber;
        F = 9/5*C + 32;
};
```

In this pattern we have two subobjects, labeled by C and F, and a single constraint that relates them. We can use this object to compute F given C. As before, using the dot operator with parentheses to enter the object's pattern space, we can write aCFTemp. (C=100; F) to compute F given C, or aCFTemp. (F=50; C) to compute C given F. Siri uses the equation solving patterns to solve for the required object, given the other.

Siri's equation solving patterns can also solve simultaneous equations:

```
simEqn x'number y'number z'number: {
        a, b, c: aNumber;
         2*a + 4*b - 3*c = x;
         4*a - 5*b + 4*c = y;
        -4*a +   b - 8*c = z;
        a, b, c
};
```

For example, the value of simEqn 8, 2, -6 is simply the list (1.85, 1.04, -0.04).

Note that Siri's constraint system saved us a lot of work here. In a non-constraint language, we would have had to write the equivalent of

```
simEqn x'integer y'integer z'integer: {
        a: { ((9/23)*x + (29/92)*y + (1/92)*z)/2 };
        b: {   (2/23)*x - (7/46)*y -  (5/46)*z   };
        c: { -(2/23)*x - (9/92)*y - (13/92)*z   };
        a, b, c
};
```

which is much less understandable than the first representation, as well as more difficult to maintain and modify.

If Siri is unable to solve an equation, because it cannot match any reducible expressions, it is an error and is flagged by the system. This kind of error is similar to using a procedure without defining it in a conventional language. Often these kinds of errors can be resolved by adding a special constraint pattern that simplifies the expression that Siri was able to reduce to, allowing Siri to work further to solve the equation.

### 13.6.6   Prefixing Patterns

We can use aCFTemp as a prefix to another pattern, to extend its function-ality. If we want to also be able to compute temperatures in Kelvin, given we already have aCFTemp we can do the following:

```
aKCFTemp: aCFTemp {
        K: aNumber;
        C = K - 273;
};
```

This pattern is semantically equivalent to

```
aKCFTemp: {
        C, F, K: aNumber;
        F = 9/5*C + 32;
        C = K - 273;
};
```

but it is simpler, and a better factoring, to have the two patterns separate.

Multiple prefixes may be specified as well; any subpatterns of the prefixes that have the same name are assumed to be equivalent. Say two patterns, Window and GraphicsPane, each have a subpattern named boundingRect. If we prefix a new pattern, GrafWindow, with Window and GraphicsPane, Siri will assume that the two instances of boundingRect are the same, and will add the implied constraint

Window.boundingRect = GraphicsPane.boundingRect;

to GrafWindow's pattern. When Siri evaluates the pattern, this assertion will be checked; if in fact Window.boundingRect is *not* equal to GraphicsPane.boundingRect, a contradiction will occur, and Siri will flag it as an error.

### 13.6.7 References

Sometimes we would like to have a reference to an existing object, rather than a copy of the object. We can do this with the *reference* operator, ^:

```
myObjectReference: ^anObject;
```

myObjectReference can be bound to any object created from the constraint pattern anObject. By giving the name of the kind of object which will be referenced, Siri knows the types of the object for checking purposes. In addition, code may be compiled based on the object's implementation, even though some of the information is clearly unknown.

Labeling an object normally, without the reference operator, makes a copy for use within the current pattern, the client; if the definition of the object changes in any way, these changes will be propagated to all users. However, any changes that the client makes will be private to that client. In contrast, when labeling an object as a reference, any changes to the object via the reference will be visible to other clients of that object, providing an indirect communication channel between clients. References are not only for inter-object communication: if no client modifies a common object, a reference to the object can be used as a space and time optimization for those occasions that the programmer knows that a local copy is not needed or desired.

Because a reference refers to some object that may exist in the pattern space, it may be used to perform simple searches of objects within the scope. For example, if we have a database of people in a pattern D:

```
D: {
        @0: aPerson { ... };
        @1: aPerson { ... };
        ...
};
```

we can search for a particular instance of aPerson as follows:

```
Lookup: D { x: ^aPerson; x.name = "Abbey"; x };
```

By extending the pattern using D as a prefix, all of the objects in D are available in the scope of Lookup. It is as if the objects were directly defined inside of Lookup's constraint pattern, and thus visible to other constraint pattern expressions. Here, enough information is given that x is determinable, if it exists; in essence, we are constraining the reference x so that one or more of the existing objects in the scope will satisfy the constraint. Of course it is always possible to fully constrain x by asserting it to be equal to another object; in this case, no searching is necessary.

### 13.6.8   Event Patterns

Siri is an object-oriented language, and as such, objects created with constraint patterns may have state. While constraint patterns define objects and their types through expressions which are asserted to be forever true, *event patterns* define one-time assertions that may change the existing state of an object. Event patterns are specified by following the pattern label with : >, and are simply constraint patterns extended with a fixing operator, fixed, and a sequencing operator, ; >. Event patterns may only be invoked from other event patterns, in order to maintain semantic consistency.

By fixing the values of some of the objects in the constraint pattern, the programmer reduces the degrees of freedom enough that Siri can solve for the remaining values using the newly bound objects. Previous values of attributes may be obtained by using the keyword previous. The event pattern is the mechanism for a programmer to set up a context for Siri to compute new values for the unfixed and unbound objects.

Often when communicating with the outside world, particular actions must occur in sequence: a file must be opened, data written, and then the file is closed. The sequencing operator is used to force evaluation to occur in a given order. Each expression must evaluate to true, just as the semicolon assertion operator requires.

One useful event pattern is the optional pattern initially: >, which is automatically invoked by the system when an object is created. This pattern provides for initialization of state of objects without constraining their values.

In the following example, an upright rectangle is defined, with several event patterns: one to move the rectangle to a new location in a single operation, one for resizing the rectangle from its lower right corner, and one to animate the motion of the rectangle from its old location to a new one using an active value object.

The rectangle is defined by four numbers, which give the left, top, right, and bottom edges of the rectangle. Attributes such as width, height, and the center point are defined in terms of the edge coordinates.

The rectangle's location is initialized on instantiation by the event pattern initially:>, which is automatically invoked by the system. The event pattern moveTo:> simply fixes the width and height of the rectangle, and sets its center to the new center point. Siri's constraint satisfaction patterns automatically solve for the new edge coordinate values, based on the previous width and height, and the new center value. Similarly, the resizeFromCorner:> event pattern fixes the topLeft corner, and sets the bottomRight corner to the new value.

The animateTo:> event pattern takes advantage of the active object value, which is defined as a ramp that begins at zero and increases linearly to one in exactly two seconds. Because the width and height are fixed, the entire rectangle moves when the center is changed. The center attribute, being a function of the old and new center and the active object value, changes continuously over a period of two seconds, animating the object from the old to the new location. Siri's declarative graphics system takes care of screen updating, allowing the programmer to concentrate on the details of the movement.

## 13.7 Siri Design Overview

Constraint patterns play multiple roles: they define a namespace for objects to refer to each other, they are a repository for subobjects, they provide for the description of composite objects, and they are used to evaluate other constraint patterns. Labels on constraint patterns specify which subexpressions in pattern space can be matched, and they are then replaced by the object specified by the constraint pattern. Thus the evaluation of a constraint pattern occurs by repeated matching and replacement; this is accomplished through Bertrand's *augmented term rewriting* mechanism [Leler 88].

```
aRectangle: {
    -- State
    top, left, bottom, right: aNumber;

    -- Attributes
    width:  { right-left };
    height: { bottom-top };
    topLeft: {
        tl: aPoint;
        tl.x = left; tl.y = top; tl };
    bottomRight: {
        br: aPoint;
        br.x = right; br.y = bottom; br };
    center: {
        c: aPoint;
        c.x = left + width/2;
        c.y = top + height/2;
        c };

    --  Initialization
    initially:> {
        initialCenter: aPoint;
        initialCenter.(x = 200; y = 200;)
        width = 100; height = 20;
        center = initialCenter; };

    -- Event Patterns
    moveTo newCenter'point:> {
        width is fixed; height is fixed;
        center = newCenter; };
    resizeFromCorner newCorner'point:> {
        topLeft is fixed;
        bottomRight = newCorner; };
    animateTo newCenter'point:> {
        value: aRamp 0 to 1 in 2 seconds;
        oldCenter: aPoint;
        oldCenter = previous center;
        width is fixed; height is fixed;
        center = oldCenter+
            (newCenter-oldCenter)*value; }; };
```

### 13.7.1   Augmented Term Rewriting

All constraint patterns are evaluated, in no particular order, by reducing them using augmented term rewriting. Augmented term rewriting is standard term rewriting with the ability to bind values to variables within a namespace in each rule. In Siri, the role of a rule is played by a constraint pattern.

Labels and expressions are flattened into a string by traversing them in preorder, creating nodes that consist of an operator and an annotation which specifies how to find the next node in the tree. All constraint pattern labels are then compiled into tables, organized by pattern namespace contours. These tables will be used by the pattern matcher, which repeatedly matches against expressions in unreduced constraint patterns; an instantiator replaces the matched expression with the matching constraint pattern's evaluated object. A fast string matching algorithm, such as Aho–Corasick [Aho 75], is used for matching pattern labels to expressions. This algorithm allows them to be found very quickly: the time is proportional to the length of the expression being matched, and independent of the number of potential labels.

Several restrictions are made on the form of constraint labels and patterns. First, labels must obey strict left-sequentiality, in order to allow the fastest pattern matching algorithms to be used. As in standard term rewriting, constraint patterns must be restricted from introducing free variables, and their labels and bodies must satisfy similarity and non-overlapping restrictions in order to preserve confluence. These restrictions are checked by the Siri environment, when possible, and illegal structures flagged as errors when they are entered.

### 13.7.2   Linear Equation Patterns

As in Bertrand, the actual constraint satisfaction process is realized through a set of constraint patterns which transform equations into a linearized normal form using standard algebraic rules. The single assignment semantics of the augmented term rewriting system allows slightly-nonlinear, simultaneous equations to be solved, by binding an expression to a variable and replacing that variable's occurrences with its equivalent expression.

A constraint pattern may define several degrees of freedom; for each variable being solved for, all other variables are considered fixed, and a satisfaction method is executed which uses the other variables as parameters. When changing a variable, the other variables are considered free (unless specifically anchored, using the `fixed` keyword); any or all variables can be changed in order to satisfy the object's consistency requirements.

### 13.7.3    Global Consistency Maintenance

When an object is changed, due to an event changing its internal state or a modification of its defining constraint pattern, it must not only resatisfy its own internal state, but also notify dependents that it has changed. Objects resatisfy their internal state by re-reducing their pattern with the changed part of the state held constant, leaving the others variable, again unless they are specified to be fixed.

In most cases, constraint patterns which are used directly in other constraint patterns are included in-line; when this is done, the complete details of the included pattern are available for optimization and reevaluation of the composite pattern, and no communication is required. Any definitional changes cause the enclosing pattern to be reevaluated. However, when a constraint pattern is used indirectly, through a reference, only the interface is available to the client, and no optimization is possible. In this case, the constraint pattern is considered a dependent which is notified of the change of its host object, and it is requested to resatisfy itself.

### 13.7.4    Incremental Computation

The reevaluation process can be very expensive in a reactive system. Function caching and fast equality testing mechanisms are used to minimize this cost; only those subpatterns which are affected by the change need to be re-reduced. Dependents are notified by either traversing a known dependency tree (via references), or, if the structure is too large, by scanning the heap for objects which have references to the changed object. A special object format will allow the detection of object boundaries quickly while scanning the heap. This is rarely done; scanning is most often used for definitional changes.

### 13.7.5 Interpretation and Compilation

Execution occurs when a constraint pattern is reduced; the value of the constraint pattern is the object which results. Eventually, however, some low-level computation must take place. This occurs when primitive patterns, such as addition, match expressions in a constraint pattern. These patterns can be either defined as an interpreter escape (a primitive instruction), or as in-lined machine code.

As a side effect, reduction terminates in a string of primitive instructions, which are implemented by the Siri kernel, or in a string of compiled machine code instructions, either of which evaluate to the constraint pattern's value when given parameters. The original pattern is maintained in case it is redefined or needs to be re-reduced in a new context (another object, for example). Patterns can be defined for optimizing primitive or machine code sequences, by matching on instruction sequences and rewriting them to more efficient ones.

## 13.8  Related Work

Siri's implementation is based on concepts from several different systems: the most important is Bertrand [Leler 88], a batch constraint system which introduced the concept of augmented term rewriting. Bertrand is a general-purpose constraint language, and has been used for the specification of pictures, but it is not interactive, and has not been used for the implementation of user interfaces. Siri borrows much from Bertrand's augmented term rewriting and constraint satisfaction processes, which use a set of constraint patterns which transform equations into a linearized normal form using standard algebraic rules.

Siri extends Bertrand in part by supporting a fully hierarchical object organization with prefixing. This was first implemented in Beta [Kristensen 89], a language with a single object abstraction, the pattern.

Linda [Gelernter 83] demonstrated the utility of communication through tuple spaces. Siri generalizes tuple spaces to objects, allowing constraint patterns to be considered as object repositories. Object labels are used to match on objects and expressions in the shared pattern, to add, modify, or remove them.

Mechanisms for incremental computation, demonstrated in Pugh's thesis [Pugh 88], are used to reduce the cost of reevaluation of constraint patterns. Pugh considered functional programs to be the domain for his incremental computation techniques. Siri is the first system to use these techniques in a general-purpose programming language based on constraints.

ThingLab [Borning 79], a constraint-oriented, direct manipulation simulation laboratory built on top of Smalltalk, provided a language and a graphical interface for describing collections of related objects. Originally it did not directly address the user interface issue, although ThingLab has subsequently been extended for that use (see Chapter 11). ThingLab's constraints are bidirectional, but the programmer must define satisfying methods for each direction manually.

Other languages have been developed and demonstrated to be useful for simple user interface tasks. IDEAL [Van Wyk 80] used equation solving via graph reduction for the satisfaction of constraints on hierarchical objects; it was designed for layout of graphics in documents, and as such ran only in batch mode. The GROW system [Barth 86] provided constraints as an intrinsic part of an object-oriented, graphical user interface toolkit. CONSTRAINTS [Sussman 80] provided for the specification of hierarchical constraint equations for electrical circuits using local propagation. CONSTRAINT [Vander Zanden 88b] is a language with which graphical objects and subobjects may be displayed and modified, while satisfying a set of constraint equations, ordering these equations for optimal update to ensure real-time interaction. Coral [Szekely 88] is a declarative language for declaring aggregate objects and expressing unidirectional constraints between those objects. Part of the Garnet system [Myers 90e] is a unidirectional constraint language called KR [Giuse 89] built on Common Lisp.

Finally, Kaleidoscope [Freeman-Benson 90a] is the first of the constraint-imperative programming (CIP) languages, of which Siri is a member. Kaleidoscope allows the programmer to freely mix imperative statements with constraints that are to be maintained by the system. Kaleidoscope's handling of variables changing over time is more explicit than Siri's, providing a special operator to manually advance time. In Siri, time advances for the variables within an event pattern when the pattern is fully reduced.

## 13.9 Summary

The design and implementation of graphical, direct manipulation programs is a difficult process. Many different approaches have been taken to make this process simpler and more direct, from graphical toolbox routines, to application shells, to complete user interface design and implementation systems.

In the Siri system, the best ideas from the previous approaches are distilled into a simple, complete programming language, based on the event/resatisfaction model of user interface computation. Embodying the appropriate concepts into a programming language helps implementers grasp the basics of direct manipulation programming more easily, so that they may create interfaces more quickly and with fewer errors.

Several powerful language concepts have the potential of making the process of programming direct manipulation interfaces much easier. From Bertrand, augmented term rewriting and ordered linear equations provide a simple and fast mechanism for constraint satisfaction, with the potential for compilation. From Beta, the idea of an object pattern as the single abstraction mechanism makes the design of aggregate objects more consistent and general. From Linda comes the tuple-space communication method, which simplifies the communication between concurrent objects. Finally, incremental computation techniques, developed by Pugh, allow a large system to be be modified quickly, by limiting redundant computation.

These concepts are unified in a small, simple, but powerful language, Siri. The goal of this work is to show that programming in Siri can make the design and implementation of practical, advanced user interfaces faster and easier. It will be possible to create Siri programs by using direct manipulation as well: just as editing a graphics document in Adobe Illustrator creates a Postscript program that images the graphic on a printer, editing a graphic in Siri will create a Siri program that specifies the objects which, when evaluated, will display the objects in a document. This will be done by using the rewriting system to modify a document object directly, in response to editing actions by the user, while the incremental computation mechanism will be used to minimize recomputation after such edits. For specification tasks that cannot be done using the direct manipulation interface, the programmer will be able to edit the Siri program directly and see the changes on the display immediately.

It will be easy to define many threads of control which will execute simultaneously. Siri's declarative semantics will shield the programmer from the complicated flow of control that is typical of advanced user interfaces. These threads will communicate through a shared pattern which will act as a tuple-space, for objects to store and retrieve messages and other data. Again, this will be done using the rewriting system to provide a look-up mechanism in the shared pattern, and to add, change, and remove objects.

### 13.9.1   Status

The Siri system is currently being implemented in Think C for the Macintosh. An eventual goal is to rewrite all but the kernel routines directly in Siri to provide for straightforward portability between target machines.

## Acknowledgements

Thanks go to John Anderson, Randy Brost, and Blake Ward for their early comments on the Siri design. Kristen Nygaard and the Institutt for Informatikk in Oslo, Norway, provided me the opportunity to develop the ideas behind Siri in an inspiring location with interesting and friendly people. At CMU, I would like to thank Jim Morris, Jeannette Wing, and Mike Gleicher for their ongoing comments and suggestions.

This research was sponsored by the Avionics Laboratory, Wright Research and Development Center, Aeronautical Systems Division (AFSC), U.S. Air Force, Wright-Patterson AFB, Ohio 45433-6543 under contract F33615-90-C-1465, ARPA Order No. 7597.

The views and conclusions contained in this document are those of the author and should not be interpreted as representing the official policies, either expressed or implied, of the Defense Advanced Research Projects Agency or the U.S. Government.

*Concurrency and Time*

# Chapter 14

# A Foundation for User Interface Construction

*Emden R. Gansner*
*John H. Reppy*

## 14.1　Introduction

It is a cliché that the implementation of user interfaces, especially those relying on graphics, is a bane to programmers. The interface must handle a diverse set of interaction techniques involving multiple input devices and contexts, driven by the actions of notoriously asynchronous humans and usually requiring real-time feedback. In addition, the programmer must deal with how a piece of the interface works internally, how the piece connects to other parts of the interface, and how the interface connects to the actual application, all the while treading water in a vast sea of graphical details.

　　Given this situation, the thrust of interface technology has been to apply simplifying layers, in the hopes of hiding the complexity and reaching an "appropriate" level of abstraction. Figure 14.1 presents a coarse-grained taxonomy of the components that contribute to a user interface. Several layers of toolkits (e.g., **Xt** [Nye 90b], **InterViews** [Linton 89], and **NeXTstep** [NeXT 91]) are added on top of the base graphics library (e.g., **Xlib** [Nye 90a], and **DPS** [PS 90]). Special-purpose languages, constraint systems, interface generators, and interactive builders for user interfaces

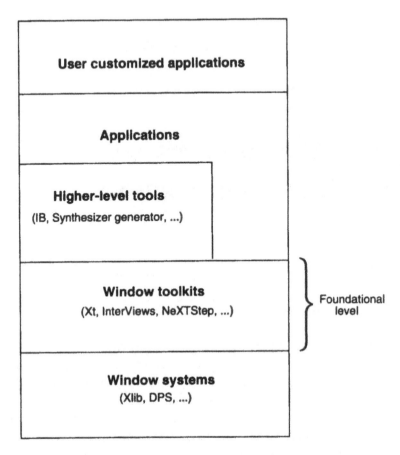

Figure 14.1: A taxonomy of user interface subsystems.

(e.g., **Interface Builder** [NeXT 91], **Synthesizer Generator** [Reps 89], and **Open Dialogue** [Schulert 88]) compose additional layers. This strategy of layering and abstraction has proven effective. In many cases, it has allowed the idealized non-programmer end user to control the graphical interface. In addition, a given layer, with the necessary functionality, aids the programmer as would the abstraction provided by any well-designed library.

By concentrating solely on layers of higher-level languages and tools and treating different foundations as largely equivalent, most current interface systems pay little attention to the need for building new low-level components and, more importantly, disregard the possible effects the foundation level may have on the entire system. Current foundations lead to an assortment of problems. For example, basic components are hard to build and complete systems are overly complex. Interactions between layers, though necessary, become difficult and poorly specified. The inherent concurrency of user interfaces is reduced to event loops and callback functions. The needs of the user interface, especially as imposed by the event loop, begin to dictate and distort the architecture of a program in a variety of ways. The design of application code ends up reflecting the user interface bias.

In the **Pegasus** system [Reppy 86], we follow a different approach, one that does not accept the present foundation models as adequate. Rather, we reconsider the base layer used for building graphical user interfaces (GUIs), and ask what the language issues for this layer are and what semantic model should this layer provide. We recognize a degree of complexity and concurrency inherent in user interfaces, and provide a foundation that allows the programmer more control over them. Specifically, we assert that a foundation for graphical user interfaces should be based on a high-level concurrent language. The language provides a unifying semantic model while mitigating against excessive layering and simplifying the interactions between layers. Processes assume their proper role as a structuring and abstraction mechanism, comparable to functions. This approach complements the subsequent addition of layers and tools for building user interfaces.

In what follows, we discuss some specific issues concerning the architecture and run-time model of a foundation for building interactive user interfaces, and what these issues imply for language design. We then describe the **Pegasus** system with its language **PML**, which instantiate these ideas for a user interface system, and provide examples of the use of the features in **Pegasus**.

## 14.2   Foundational Requirements for GUIs

When considering what language features should be provided by the foundation level, the obvious answer is that they should be a superset of the features desired in any general-purpose programming system. In particular, the language features should address the static complexity of building software and the dynamic complexity of running software. They should aid in the development of correct and understandable components; they should help the programmer reason about what the software should do. There needs to be a mechanism for structuring software into maintainable components that emphasize abstraction and promote reuse. The language should be high-level enough to relieve the programmer of handling minutiae.

The similar needs of interface and application software arise from the basic similarity of programming in these two domains. Graphical interface software is basically the same as application software, just complicated by its role of dealing with unstructured human interaction. The additional complexity does not arise so much in the graphics output, except for the wealth of details, but in program structure and control, especially as related to input handling. This similarity has frequently been ignored in developing user interface systems. Most commonly, the user interface subsumes the control flow of the program. The application-specific software must fit the mold provided by the user interface, usually that of a finite-state machine. In addition, the assumption that the two domains are intrinsically different gives rise to interface systems lacking necessary functionality. The Blit terminal [Pike 83a] provides a classic example of this situation. With the Blit, the interface portion of a program ran in its own environment, joined to the application by a serial line. The interface environment supplied a minimal process model, allowed no direct access to a file system, and, although enriched by graphics functionality, provided only a limited set of standard library functions. Because of this sparseness, writing and debugging a Blit-based program could prove an arduous chore. The clean separation of the front and back ends of a program is an admirable design goal, but it should not be arbitrarily enforced by the architecture of the user interface system.

With these general criteria in mind, we now consider the specific features we advocate.

- Concurrency is critical in allowing the programmer to cleanly structure an application and its interface to handle the asynchrony and multiple contexts of interactive use. We expand on the topic of concurrency below (see also Chapter 8).

- Strong, static typing contributes to the writing of correct and efficient programs. There is a folklore that the interactive and dynamic nature of GUIs requires weakly or dynamically typed languages. It is felt that only these models allow the flexibility needed to build libraries of interconnecting components that can be configured and used in a variety of contexts, or that can serve as the basis for WYSIWYG interface builders. Technical problems, such as providing application-specific data to be used in general-purpose callback functions, using an object-oriented programming style in a language that does not support such a style, or designing interface components that must handle arbitrary variations of data structures, seem to call for loose typing.

  We feel the benefits of strong typing are too valuable to be thrown away lightly, especially at the foundation level. In particular, the complexity of user interfaces, with the combinations of many disparate components, built at different times and at different places, begs for the ability to localize errors and prevent type mismatches that strong typing provides. The perceived rigidness of strong typing is not a significant problem if the language provides features such as polymorphism, higher-order functions, and parameterized modules. Ongoing research (e.g., [Cardelli 85b, Cardelli 89]) promises secure type systems of even greater expressiveness and flexibility.

- A side-effect-free programming style should be the norm. This is especially important in concurrent systems, where issues of interference arise. Furthermore, the use of "pure" functions and immutable data greatly increases the clarity and reliability of programs. When mutable state is required, it should be encapsulated with a well-defined and controlled interface, such as through the use of server processes.

- Higher-order functions and polymorphism are powerful tools for building abstractions and for type-safe code reuse. Using them, a programmer can express operations succinctly and in the most general form. Many parts of GUI libraries are implicitly parameterized by application-specific types and data. Lexically scoped function values supply an elegant means for handling this parameterization.

Polymorphic type systems provide the flexibility needed to strongly type generic operations, such as operations on lists.

- For programming-in-the-large, parameterized modules play a role similar to that of polymorphism in programming abstract data types, encapsulating a flexible abstraction. Modules are important for structuring large systems and controlling name spaces. In addition, many GUI libraries are not self-contained, but are a function of application-specific values and types (e.g., callback functions). Parameterized modules supports this style of library usage in a type-safe manner.

- Garbage collection frees the programmer from low-level decisions about the lifetime of objects, which results in improved programmer productivity and software reliability. Diagnosing memory management bugs, such as premature deallocation, is one of the hardest debugging tasks; garbage collection eliminates these bugs. Garbage collection also enhances software modularity, since modules do not have to keep track of references to their objects from other modules. Applicative style programming, which leads to object sharing, and higher-order functions, which require closure objects, force the use of garbage collection.

  The garbage collector should support *object finalization*, in which a value can be associated with a finalization function to be called on the value before the value's memory is freed. With this mechanism, we can extend the model of automatic storage collection to system objects such as bitmaps, fonts, etc. This is particularly important in a concurrent environment, where multiple threads may share system resources such as bitmaps and fonts.

In addition, a language must allow implementations to be efficient enough to handle the time constraints implicit in an interactive application. A user will not take kindly to a system that ignores mouse motion while it does a garbage collection or that is so slow that text windows appear to be connected by a 300 baud line.

## 14.2.1 Concurrency

The most important requirement for the foundation level of a user interface system is support for concurrency. One need only consider a sample of common interaction scenarios:

- A computationally intensive program that must periodically update its window while being able to handle external events such as window resizing.

- A program for editing and analyzing multiple views of graphs, which must allow editing on one view while applying a potentially expensive layout algorithm [Gansner 88b] to another.

- A language-based editor that uses incremental attribute evaluation to give the user immediate feedback about static semantic errors [Reps 84, Hudson 91]. Since a user's editing operation can result in an arbitrarily large number of attribute reevaluations, we must structure the evaluator so that those attributes affecting the user's view will be evaluated first and those remaining will be evaluated in the background.

These examples illustrate the principal thesis of this paper, which is that interactive programs, particularly those with GUIs, are inherently concurrent and should be written in a concurrent language (see Chapter 8 and [Cardelli 85a, Reppy 86, Gosling 89, Haahr 90]). As the above scenarios demonstrate, this concurrency is exhibited in a number of ways:

- The most common example of concurrency is in handling user interaction. This concurrency arises because users are asynchronous. Separating the application and interface into separate threads of control allows the asynchrony of users to be tamed and removes the bias towards input-driven control flow.

- In an application that provides multiple views, the different views are often independent and have their own logical flow of control.

- Window systems, such as **X**, use the concurrency provided by the operating system to allow users to interleave tasks. Interleaved computation is also useful in more tightly integrated systems, such as the graph browser mentioned above.

Sequential interactive graphics libraries, such as **Iris** [Gansner 88a] and **Xlib** [Nye 90a, Nye 90b], typically rely on event loops and callback functions to cope with the inherent concurrency of interactive applications. These control structures are essentially sequential approximations of concurrency, and can be viewed as a "poor man's" concurrency. There are problems with this approach. First, it skews the structure of the system towards the interface, since the main control loop is focused on handling user input. Second, an application may need to monitor other kinds of events, such as input on a communication port, or may want to perform some background computation. This forces the interface library to supply the hooks for all other possible events, even though they have nothing to do with the user interface. For example, the **Xt** library supplies the functions XtAppAddInput and XtAppAddWorkProc, which set procedures to be called, respectively, when input is available from a file or when the event loop would otherwise block. Of course, the programmer must insure that the procedure will return quickly to avoid delaying the handling of user input. If the programmer wants to use a procedure to do significant computation, then the procedure must handle the suspended state of computation. Another problem is the handling of composite events, such as selecting a menu item, which consists of a mouse button press, followed by mouse motion, followed by the button release. Handling composite events involves either using history-sensitive functions, or else event handlers that grab an event stream or implement some version of the main control loop. In any case, the program becomes harder to write, understand, and debug.

Another possibility is to structure the application as a collection of operating system processes and use the interprocess communication (IPC) mechanisms provided by the system. There are several problems with this approach: such processes are expensive; the cost of IPC is high; and many systems limit the number of processes per user.

We believe that the correct way to address the inherent concurrency in interactive applications is to make the concurrency explicit and provide language support for dealing with it. This approach not only addresses the concurrency in handling user interaction, but also supplies a mechanism for exploiting the concurrency inherent in the application code (e.g., multiple views, background processing, etc.).

Interactive responsiveness requires that a given task or operation cannot monopolize the processor for extended periods. Explicit coroutine switches are too low-level and cannot guarantee that a process will yield the processor. This is also a problem with relying on coroutine switches embedded in the IPC mechanisms. Compiler generated coroutine switches make it difficult to insure a fair distribution of processor time without incurring the cost of excessive numbers of switches and prevent the inclusion of "foreign" code, i.e., code processed by a compiler that does not generate the necessary coroutine switches. Based on these considerations, we believe that threads must be scheduled preemptively.

## 14.2.2   Threads Are Objects

User interface design seems to be one area where an "object-oriented" approach has a clear utility. As a result, most graphics toolkits use an object-oriented approach (e.g., **Iris** [Gansner 88a], **InterViews** [Linton 89], and **Xt** [Nye 90b]). Thus, it may seem surprising that we do not include support for object-oriented programming in this list. There are several reasons for this. The integration of object-oriented features into polymorphic type systems is still an active area of research [Cardelli 89, Mitchell 91]. A state-of-the-art module system, such as [MacQueen 84], and polymorphism provide similar interface inheritance. Most importantly, our experience, and that of others [Pike 89a, Haahr 90], suggests that concurrency and delegation provide many of the same advantages as object-oriented programming.[1] Threads provide localization of state and clean well-defined interfaces. Delegation and wrapper functions provide a way to implement inheritance. For example, the programmer could wrap a command button with a function that would override the button's geometry constraints or append to the window creation attributes used by the button. The event values provided by our particular concurrency model (Section 14.3.1) can also be composed with wrapper functions, giving another mechanism for implementating inheritance.

---

[1]This should not come as a surprise, since *delegation* was originally a concept of concurrent *actor* systems.

## 14.3   Pegasus

The language features described in the previous section have been implemented in the **Pegasus** system. This prototype system consists of a high-level, concurrent functional programming language **PML** and a rich run-time system. **PML** serves as a common base language and provides the unifying semantic model. In addition, there are various utility libraries, including a well-integrated graphics and windowing system. **Pegasus/PML** attempts to provide a high-level semantic framework for the construction of interactive software.

Not unexpectedly, the language features we are promoting for building application GUIs played a fundamental role in the development of **Pegasus**. Higher-order functions, polymorphism, and modules provided the bricks for structuring the software. Concurrency is used at all levels of the window system and libraries. We use server processes to manage resources, such as fonts, color cells, icons, etc., in order to promote sharing and automate reclamation. The garbage collector is incremental, running as a separate process. In all, the **Pegasus** system is practical in performance and functionality, while remaining modest in size and comprehensibility.

### 14.3.1   The Base Language Model

The **PML** language is a general-purpose functional language derived from Cardelli's **ML** [Cardelli 84]. It maintains **ML**'s polymorphic type system, functions as "first class" values, and expression-oriented syntax and value-oriented semantics. **PML** shares **ML**'s concrete data types, pattern matching for discrimination, and typed, value-carrying exceptions. **PML** also adopts the **SML** [Milner 90] parameterized module facilities [MacQueen 84], which provide the glue for composing software from the pieces, whether generated, hand-written or from libraries, in the **Pegasus** system.

Though close to **ML**, the sequential core of **PML** is syntactically distinct. Most of the distinctions are largely cosmetic, such as a notation for end-of-line style comments or additional syntactic sugar to delimit the ubiquitous match patterns. A more substantial modification, made in hopes of aiding the programmer, was the addition of function overloading. Ba-

sically, any time value conversion is involved,[2] there is a good argument
for overloaded functions. An an example, creating a window may involve
many parameters, many of which may be optional with implied default values. Without overloading, the programmer must provide a single function
that allows some parameters to be optional, or else provide a reasonable
subset of constructor functions, each with a distinctive name, frequently
just reflecting the subset of parameters or types involved. We felt that
such *ad hoc* solutions made a strong case for the provision of user-defined
overloading.

### Concurrency Operations

**PML** uses a fairly standard model of concurrency, derived from Cardelli's
**amber** language [Cardelli 86], with dynamic thread creation and synchronous (rendezvous) communication on typed channels. The following
code provides a simple example of the **PML** model.

```
type msg_t = oneof { msg_end | msg_val of Integer }

fun simple () = let
  channel ch of msg_t
  fun read () =
    case accept ch of
    { msg_end => ()
    | msg_val v => read ()
    }
  fun write 10 = send (msg_end, ch)
    | write  v = (send (msg_val v, ch); write (v+1))
  in
    process read ();
    process write 0
  end
```

The type declaration defines a discriminated union type, which will serve as
the type of message to be sent and received. When the function `simple` is
invoked, it creates a channel and two threads. One thread writes the values

---

[2]Constructing a value from other values, printing a value, and making a value into a
string are obvious special cases of value conversion.

0 through 9 onto the channel, using the send function, posts an end-of-communication message msg_end, and then (implicitly) exits. The other thread reads the messages from the channel, using the accept function, quitting when it sees the msg_end message and ignoring the other messages.

We believe that this model is a better fit with the value-oriented semantics of ML-style sequential languages than the shared-memory model (e.g., [Cooper 90]). In fact, the use of message passing leads to a programming style that is even more applicative than that of sequential ML programs. (See [Reppy 90, Reppy 91] for examples.) This programming style has several important benefits: by eliminating global state it improves program modularity; the applicative-style concurrent programs are easier to reason about; and the dynamic replication of services becomes trivial. The strong typing and emphasis on immutable data found in PML greatly enhances the safety of the threads.

There is a problem with the **amber** model. A programmer writing a server wants to hide the details, especially if they involve a moderately complex communication protocol. On the other hand, a client may need to synchronize on multiple servers, which typically requires breaking the communication abstraction. The solution is to extend the **amber** model in such a way that synchronous operations (e.g., receiving a message) are abstracted into first class values, called *events*.[3] The programmer creates new event values from compositions of more primitive values, and invokes a special operator for actually synchronizing on an event value. The separation of event value creation and synchronization is analogous to the separation of function definition and invocation, and provides similar expressiveness.

**Pegasus** provides the following primitive event value operations, among others.

```
delay : Time -> Event[Void]
transmit : ('a * ChannelOf['a]) -> Event[Void]
receive : ChannelOf['a] -> Event['a]
sync : Event['a] -> 'a
```

---

[3]We refer to the window system events as *input events*, to avoid confusion with these events.

The first three are used to construct event values encapsulating timeouts, writing to a channel, and reading from a channel, respectively. The sync operator is used to synchronize on an event value. The send and accept operations mentioned above are actually just shorthand for the function composition of synchronization with the corresponding event value constructor.

```
send = sync o transmit
accept = sync o receive
```

Combinators are provided for composing events in various ways. The two most important combinators are choose and handle. Selective communication is provided by the choose operator, which constructs an event value that is the non-deterministic choice of a list of events. Post-synchronization filtering is provided by the handle operator. In the simplest form, this can be used to modify the value or type of the received value. Thus,

```
handle receive ch with { 0 => false | _ => true }
```

turns an integer event value into a boolean one, mapping 0 to false and all other integer values to true. In conjunction with the choose operator, it is used to guarantee that the clauses all have consistent type and to direct control flow based on which event was satisfied.

```
channel ch_app of Integer
channel ch_user of String

choose
{ receive ch_app
| handle receive ch_user with { v => doUser v }
| handle delay t with { _ => 5 }
}
```

In the above code, synchronization on the choose event will cause the thread to wait for an integer on ch_app, a string from the user, or a timeout. In the first case, the expression evaluates to the integer. If user input is received, this is processed by the doUser function, which must return an integer value. If neither of these happens before the timeout occurs, the expression evaluates to 5.

These mechanisms allow the user to develop communication abstractions that are tailored to the application. Buffered channels, multicast channels, and RPC are some examples of user-defined communication abstractions that we have used[4].

## 14.3.2 Run-Time Support

Higher-level languages require more run-time support; in our case, there are additional constraints imposed by the desire to provide good interactive performance. As discussed above, it is necessary that the threads be scheduled preemptively. The **Pegasus** system [Reppy 86] includes a scheduler that enforces context switches at set intervals; in practice, we have found that 20 milliseconds provides a time slice that nicely balances thread responsiveness with the overhead of context switches.

We view garbage collection and object finalization as crucial features in the **Pegasus** environment. Because of the essentially real-time nature of interactive applications, garbage collection must be unobtrusive. To accomplish this, **Pegasus** provides a concurrent copying garbage collector that runs as a separate thread [North 87]. This allows memory reclamation to occur during "wasted" cycles when the user is not interacting with the system. Normally, the collector runs at a low priority. As available memory diminishes, the system increases the priority of the collector. Thanks to these techniques, the graphics system, written as user-level processes, can smoothly track the mouse while a variety of other applications are running concurrently.

## 14.3.3 Graphics System

The **Pegasus** system includes a variety of libraries of programming tools, ranging from list and string manipulation modules to hashing and tokenization modules to I/O modules to packages for pipes, multicast channels, and other concurrency abstractions. Principal among these libraries is the graphics system. This system is composed of three major subsystems. A module providing a fairly standard model of bitmap graphics serves as the foundation. This module provides for the creation of bitmaps, graphical

---

[4]For more details and examples, see [Reppy 88] and [Reppy 90].

operations on bitmaps, such as line and text drawing and bitblt, and manipulation of colormaps. This module provides a system independent base for the rest of the graphics system.

The window subsystem is built on top of the bitmap graphics module. Its role is to supply an overlapping window abstraction using virtual bitmaps (or backing store). We feel that this provides the desirable model for constructing user interfaces from collections of components. Composition and control issues in user interfaces are complex enough without the additional overhead of being able to efficiently redraw a component in response to its image being corrupted by another component. From a philosophical viewpoint, requiring widgets[5] to repair damage to its image abuses the desired independence of components and adds a gratuitous element of asynchrony. The argument against virtual bitmaps usually emphasizes memory usage. However, the window system can supply various strategies, such as "copy on write" or "parent-guided allocation," to greatly reduce memory consumption in standard usage.

We implemented virtual bitmaps in **Pegasus** using a blend of techniques described in [Myers 86] and [Pike 83b]. In any such implementation, a graphical operation performed on a window must be recursively subdivided into operations performed on a collection of on-screen and off-screen bitmaps. The bitmap operations must preserve the context of the window operation, plus adjustments for differences in coordinate systems, clipping, and special requirements of the particular operation *vis-a-vis* the attributes of the bitmap. The subdivision operation naturally fits the recursive, higher-order function style of **PML**. It is implemented as a single general-purpose function; all window operations are implemented as wrappers of the subdivision function.

Two additional features of the window system are worth mentioning. The **Pegasus** model provides a moderate collection of attributes (colors, fill style, line style, etc.) that affect the appearance of graphics operations. It is therefore convenient to encapsulate these attributes separately rather than require the programmer to supply the necessary attributes individually when invoking a graphics operation. This is a standard technique, currently most obvious in the form of graphics contexts in **X**. However, most systems

---

[5]For want of a better word, we follow the **X** usage and refer to the components as widgets.

view these encapsulations as scarce and mutable. Neither of these qualities seem compatible with the **Pegasus** model. We therefore collect the **Pegasus** drawing attributes into values called pens, which are immutable and lightweight. We also borrowed an idea from the NeWS model [Gosling 89] and provide window overlays. Using overlays, the programmer has a very clean model for handling transient output, especially when providing user input feedback.

The topmost layer of the graphics system provides the interface actually used by clients. This layer consists of a variety of servers, plus a module that provides clients with a remote-procedure call interface to the servers. How this layer looks to the application programmer is discussed more thoroughly in the next section. The principal server is the window server. In essence, the window server owns and controls the display. It is responsible for performing the calls to the underlying window system to create or destroy windows or modify the display. It is also the window server's role to provide the distribution of window system events to window clients. Abetting the window server are a mouse cursor server, which tracks mouse motion and maintains the mouse cursor glyph, a font server, to provide sharing of fonts across components, and a color server. The color server promotes sharing of colors and extends the basic color model to guarantee the existence of complementary colors in the one's-complement positions of the color map. This provides a widget with another technique for implementing feedback inexpensively.

In addition to the core graphics system, **Pegasus** also supplies the usual collection of widgets and graphical utilities for constructing user interfaces. These include text widgets, buttons, and scroll bars. There are also modules for menus, user input of rectangles and points, and affine transformations, among others.

It is worth comparing the core **Pegasus** graphics system with the interface library **Iris** [Gansner 88a]. The latter system implements comparable functionality to that provided by **Pegasus**, although it provides no support for color and a less sophisticated virtual bitmap model. It is implemented using a conventional language (C++) and a conventional design (object-oriented without concurrency). The system is three times the size of the **Pegasus** system in lines of code. We feel this reflects the additional expressiveness provided by the **PML** higher-order functions and polymorphism, the presence of garbage collection, and the use of concurrency to structure the system.

## 14.4   The Application Programmer's View

Using **Pegasus**, the programmer constructs an interface as a collection of communicating components, each involving a window and various controlling threads, and receiving input synchronously. This structure makes explicit the interactions and the underlying protocols among widgets and application code, frequently resulting in simpler and safer interactions than the single-threaded case. It avoids the input-driven bias of traditional event loops. It also allows simpler structure within each widget, as each widget can handle its input synchronously and does not have to act like a finite-state machine.

**Pegasus** further employs concurrency in dealing with the basic system events such as keystrokes, mouse motion, or resizing a window. Instead of a single stream of input events, we provide each window with three streams for mouse, keyboard, and control events. This separation reflects the natural classes of events and the way they are processed, and has been used in sequential systems (e.g., [Gansner 88a] and [Linton 89]), as well as in other concurrent systems (e.g., [Pike 89b] and [Haahr 90]). This structure avoids the need for complex stream processing routines (e.g., conditional reads and lookaheads). Typically, a widget employs a separate thread for each input stream.

Higher-order functions represent additional glue by which the programmer can structure an application or combine simpler components into complex interfaces, creating new graphical objects. For example, the interface toolkit can supply generic input event handling functions that can be specialized to a given window's requirements. Additionally, the programmer can employ wrapper functions to alter the appearance or behavior of a widget.

As an illustration of one of the advantages of the **Pegasus** approach, we focus on the mechanisms for attaching semantic actions to an interface object (e.g., attaching a text scrolling operation to a scroll bar). This is typically handled by a callback function, which is explicitly registered and unregistered by the client with the widget. From the client's standpoint, callbacks are invoked asynchronously; the client code must be able to accept the effects of a callback at any time. The callback function cannot involve time-consuming operations, lest it block the widget from handling other clients. If the programmer wishes client-specific data to be passed as an argument when the callback function is invoked, the data must also be registered with the widget, which treats the argument as an untyped pointer. Upon invocation, the callback function must convert the data back to its original type.

In **Pegasus**, a widget need only advertise an abstract event value that clients can synchronize on. There is no registration of functions or data. A client simply synchronizes on the event value. When notified of synchronization, the client has the opportunity of continuing other activities before it reaches a state at which an action associated with the synchronization is appropriate. The action executes in the context of the client's data and, thanks to the ability to spawn threads, can involve extensive computation. These semantics scale nicely to multiple clients by the interposition of a multicast channel between the widget and its clients. No change to the widget is necessary. Sometimes circumstances call for the explicit use of callback functions, but **Pegasus** allows the programmer to avoid most of the drawbacks. The programmer can use higher-order functions to package client-specific data, in a type-safe manner, in the callback's closure, and threads allow the callback function to invoke arbitrarily long computations.

### 14.4.1  Concrete Examples

To describe the usage of **Pegasus** in more concrete terms, we turn now to two applications of the system. *Bounce* is a simple program that illustrates the use of concurrency in **Pegasus**. The program has a video game-like interface. The user can use the left button to create a new head that bounces around within the window. The vector determined by the points at which the button is depressed and released is used to calculate the speed and initial direction of the head. If the user clicks the middle button on a head, the head disappears. The use of the right button produces a pop-up menu, allowing the user to delete all of the heads or exit the program. A snapshot of bounce is presented in Figure 14.2.

The implementation of bounce is fairly simple using **Pegasus**. There is a command thread for handling user input, a head server thread, and

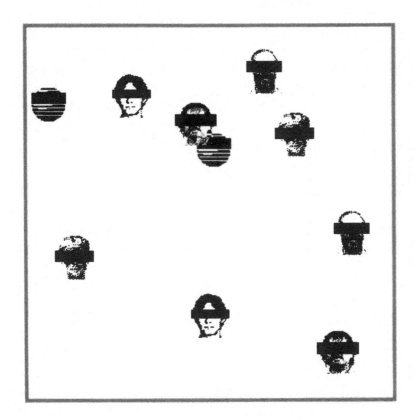

Figure 14.2: Bounce.

a display thread for maintaining the placement of the head glyphs in the window. When the user creates a new head, the command thread spawns a new head process. The new process requests a head glyph from the head server, and then just loops, calculating a new position, and telling the display thread to erase its head from its current position and draw it in a new position. When the user attempts to remove a head, the command thread broadcasts a message on a multicast channel. The message is either a conditional delete command along with a point, or an unconditional delete command. Each head process receives the message. For the former message, the process will erase its image and exit if the point is within its bounding box; for the latter message, every process will exit. We also note that, thanks to the concurrency and preemptive scheduling of **Pegasus**, when the command thread instantiates the pop-up menu, the heads continue to bounce unaffected behind it.

For a more complex and realistic example, let us look at **Graph-o-matica**, an interactive tool for analyzing and viewing directed graphs, which has been implemented on top of **Pegasus**. In the current version, **Graph-o-matica** provides the user with two kinds of windows: command windows, which provide a terminal-style, language interface to a command shell, and view windows, which provide a view on a 2D layout of a graph. There can be multiple command windows, a given abstract graph can have more than one layout, and a given layout can have more than one view. Figure 14.3 illustrates a sample session using **Graph-o-matica**. The bottom window is a command window. The two windows above provide two views of the same layout of the same underlying graph. A view allows the user to pan and zoom (using menus and the scroll bars) on the given embedding of the graph. A layout allows the user to modify the embedding, including elision of subgraphs. If a graph is edited, either using a graphical view or from a command window, this information needs to be propagated to the layouts and views of the graph. We use the multicast channel abstraction to manage the propagation of update notifications to the layouts and from the layouts to the views. This simplifies the implementation of the graph object, since it does not need to know anything about multiple layouts. The layout objects, if they decide a given change affects them, can query the graph object for more detailed information.

The command shell is a thread that communicates with a *virtual terminal* (vtty) object. The vtty object is a good example of the need for both communication abstraction and selective communication. At any time, the vtty must be able to handle both input from the user and output from its client (the command shell). The **Pegasus** window system provides an abstract interface to the input stream, but since it is event-valued, it can still be used in selective communication.

Concurrency is also used in the structuring of the application code. Layout algorithms, for example, run as separate threads, thus allowing the user to continue other activities while waiting for a new layout.

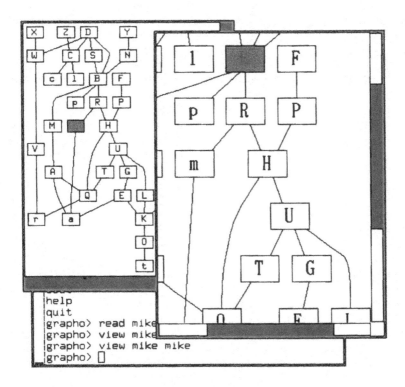

Figure 14.3: Graph-o-matica.

## 14.5 Conclusion

We have argued that a high-level concurrent language provides the desirable model for the foundation layer for structuring interactive programs. Our experiences using a higher-order concurrent language to construct interactive systems suggest this model will nicely complement work on subsequent layers and tools for interface construction (e.g., [Myers 90e] and [Cardelli 88]). We are currently involved in further developing these ideas and their ramifications [Reppy 91, Gansner 91].

## Acknowledgements

John Reppy's work was supported, in part, by the NSF and ONR under NSF grant CCR-85-14862, and by the NSF under NSF grant CCR-89-18233.

# Chapter 15

# User Interface Programming with Cooperative Processes

*Toshiyuki Masui*

## 15.1 Introduction

Many of the problems in creating user interface programs can be solved by using multiple processes communicating through a global data space. This chapter shows how current problems can be effectively solved by *Linda*[Carriero 89, Carriero 90], a parallel execution language primitive which supports the communication between processes through a common global data space called the *tuple space*. It also shows that this approach can be applied to a wide range of user interface programming without using a language specially designed for user interface specification.

Although conventional programming languages are widely used for programming user interface software, they are far from ideal for many reasons. Chapter 1 of this book discusses several high-level features lacking in conventional programming languages for writing user interface programs. There are even low-level problems in writing user interface programs. Two examples are described below.

- **Structure and Control Flow of Application and Interface Programs**

  I/O primitives provided by most conventional programming languages (e.g., Fortran, C, Pascal, Lisp, etc.) are simple and they can handle only one character stream at one time with a single de-' vice, while most of the language features are for calculation and program flow control. Simple I/O primitives work well with old terminal-based programs whose main job was calculation. Recently, however, I/O devices have become complicated and more calculations are required for better interaction. The emphasis of writing programs has moved to the interface part. Many application programs are now written with a set of interaction libraries called a *user interface toolkit*, so that the main part of the program is the interface part, and the application part should be called from the interface part.

Although the application part of the program can be programmed this way if its structure is simple, this programming style does not fit with complicated applications. For example, an expert system is a large complicated system and it has to interact with users in no predetermined order, since it decides what questions to ask at run time. It is usually very hard to use user interface toolkits for applications which need to control the I/O [Löwgren 89].

With conventional programming languages, the algorithm for the main program and the algorithm for the subroutine cannot be the same, since the former can control the main control flow but the latter can not. For this reason, an application program with terminal interface cannot usually be the same as the same application program with a graphic interface using toolkits.

Since there are a lot of programming techniques in writing programs which control the flow of computation, the control flow should not be changed merely by the requirements of user interface toolkits.

- **Single Input/Output at One Time**
  Conventional languages cannot handle multiple inputs and outputs at the same time. A program usually has to wait for a device until it is ready, and if there is a possibility of getting inputs from several devices, the program usually has to check all the devices to see if any of them have input data to be processed.

To prevent this, in current window systems, all the inputs are sent to the program as "events," which have the same structure for all the inputs. In this case, event-handling routines tend to become complicated, since all possible inputs are sent to the routine and it has to send proper information to other routines which really need the input.

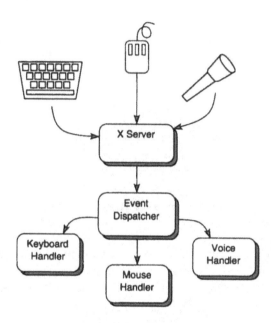

Figure 15.1: Input event handling in X window system.

The problems shown above and in Chapter 1 can be solved by using multiple processes communicating with each other through a global common space using flexible parallel execution primitives. This chapter uses the Linda[Carriero 89, Carriero 90] parallel execution primitives, and shows, with many examples, how those problems can be solved.

## 15.2 Linda Overview

We briefly introduce the features of Linda here. More detailed discussion can be found in the developers' book[Carriero 90] and article[Carriero 89].

Linda is a parallel execution specification language which uses *tuples* (sets of data) in the *tuple space* (a global space) for process communication. Linda has four language primitives and they can be used just like function calls of conventional languages. A process puts a tuple into the tuple space using the out operator. A process gets a tuple from the tuple space by issuing the in operator, where a pattern is specified in the operator, and only those tuples which match the pattern are read. The process which issued in blocks, if it cannot find any tuple which matches the pattern. Operator rd also gets a tuple from the tuple space without removing the tuple from the tuple space, while in removes it from the tuple space. Operator eval starts a new process.

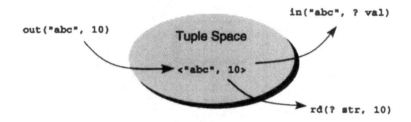

Figure 15.2: Communication through tuple space.

Processes written in different languages can communicate with each other through the tuple space, if the format of the tuples and the tuple space are the same.

Although Linda primitives are simple, they can be used as a very flexible and powerful tool for process communication and synchronization. We will show how Linda can be used for user interface programming.

## 15.3   Using Linda for User Interface Programming

### 15.3.1   Solving Control-Flow Problems

If both the application and interface parts are implemented as Linda processes, the control-flow problems shown in Section 15.1 can be solved easily. Consider the very simple database application in Figure 15.3 which returns the record of a person when his or her name and age are provided.

Here, in a C program using a simple terminal interface, the application part and the interface part are not separated at all, since interface functions (scanf(), printf()) and the application function (search()) are

```
..
printf("name? ");
scanf("%s", name);
printf("age? ");
scanf("%d", &age);
result = search(name,age);
printf("%s\n",result);
..
```

Figure 15.3: Database program in C.

intermingled. This program can easily be rewritten to the Linda program in Figure 15.4.[1]

```
                                        ...
                                        printf("name? ");
                                        scanf("%s", name);
                                        printf("age? ");
...                                     scanf("%s", &age);
in(? name, ? age);  ◄─────────         out(name, age);
res = search(name, age);  ──────►      in(? res);
out(res);                              printf("%s\n",res);
...                                     ...
```

application process                    interface process

Figure 15.4: Database program in Linda.

Here, the program at the left side corresponds to the application part and the program at the right side corresponds to the interface part. In this case, the application part and the interface part run as coroutines and both preserve their control structures. Any kind of interface process can be used with the application process as long as it puts a tuple which consists of a string and an integer into the tuple space. That is, either a simple terminal handling process or complicated text input window can be used with this small application program. In this way, using Linda, the application part

---

[1]In this chapter, Clinda (Linda implementation on C) is used for all the programming examples. The same arguments apply to all other Linda implementations using conventional programming languages.

266

---

and the interface part can be separated easily and clearly.

Here is another example of using Linda for the communication between application and interface. Figure 15.5 shows the C program that solves the famous "8-queens" problem by calling a checking function ext end(n) recursively. Every time a solution is found, it is printed at the bottom of the nested recursive call.

```
...
int queens = 8;
main(argc, argv) char **argv;
{
    int i;
    for(i=0;i<queens;i++){ col[i] = qpos[i] = 0; }
    for(i= -queens;i<queens;i++){ up[i] = down[i] = 0; }
    extend(0);
}
extend(n)
{
    int c;
    for(c=0;c<queens;c++){
        if(!col[c] && !up[n+c] && !down[n-c]){
            qpos[n] = c;
            if(n+1 >= queens)
                printqueens();
            else {
                col[c] = up[n+c] = down[n-c] = 1;
                extend(n+1);
                col[c] = up[n+c] = down[n-c] = 0;
            }
        }
    }
}
```

Figure 15.5: C program of 8-queens problem.

If you want to write a window-based program which displays a new solution on a window every time you click the mouse, and you also want to use a toolkit which calls the application part as subroutine calls, you cannot use this algorithm. You have to completely rewrite it.

On the other hand, if you want to implement this program as a Linda process with an input process which handles mouse clicks and an output process which displays the queens, you only have to modify the printqueens() line to the program below.

```
in(CLICK);
out(qpos[0],qpos[1],qpos[2],...qpos[7]);
```

Here, the input process issues out (CLICK) whenever it gets a mouse click, and the output process is always waiting for an eight-tuple by in(? p1, ? p2, ..., ? p8) to display the new positions. With this simple modification, this program can be used with any process which has the same tuple interface (see Figure 15.6).

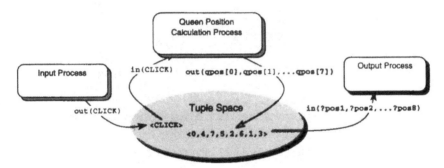

Figure 15.6: Tuple exchange in the 8-queens program.

Since Linda is simple and flexible, communication techniques other than coroutine can easily be implemented. Also, since Linda has pattern matching capabilities, more complicated communication between processes is also possible.

### 15.3.2 Parallel UI Toolkit

A parallel user interface toolkit can be constructed easily by using Linda [Masui 91]. Figure 15.7 is an example of a print format specification program which uses the toolkit.

Kanji strings can be input to the frame (text box) with a cursor. Kana–Kanji conversion can be done independently to other text boxes.[2] The "X" displayed near 手差し (manual feed) is toggled by each click in that box

---

[2]Kanji is a complex character set used for Japanese/Chinese texts, and Kana is a simple

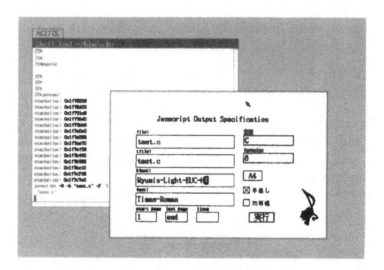

Figure 15.7: Print format specification program.

and indicates the selection of that item. Each frame corresponds to a part
of the toolkit, and a Linda process is attached to each frame.

Processes are created by eval() and then run the following loop:

```
for(;;){
    in(toolid,? eventname, ? arg);
    <actions corresponding to the tool>
}
```

In other words, each tool is always waiting for a tuple. A simple tool like a
checkbox is programmed as in Figure 15.8. After a tool object is created, a
Linda process executing an infinite loop is invoked, and other application
processes communicate with the tool through the tuple space. The value
(on or off) of the checkbox can be read by other processes via a rd()
statement like this:

```
int v;
rd(cb, ? v); // get the current value of v
```

---

character set for Japanese. As there is no straightforward way to specify a Kanji character
from an ASCII keyboard, a two-step method is usually taken. An ASCII string is converted
to a Kana string first, and the Kana string is converted to a Kanji string of the same
pronunciation.

```
for(;;){
    int value;
    in(toolid,? eventname, ? arg);
    if(eventname != MouseDown) continue;
    in(toolid, ? value)
    <toggle the value>
    out(toolid, value)
    <draw or erase the check mark>
}
```

Figure 15.8: A simple checkbox tool in Linda.

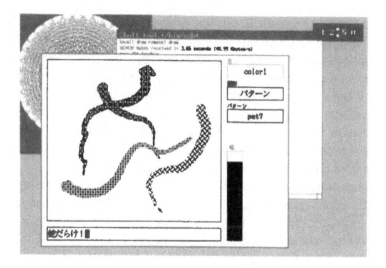

Figure 15.9: Bitmap editor.

A color bitmap editor using the toolkit is shown in Figure 15.9. The slide-bar at the right side titled 幅 (width) is a tool for specifying a value. The value can be changed not only by moving the mouse over the slide bar, but also by keyboard input. In this example, the value corresponds to the width of the line drawn by the mouse in the main drawing area. In Figure 15.9, "snakes" are drawn by drawing contiguous circles by dragging the mouse while changing the width via the keyboard. This can only be done using parallel execution of both tools[Hill 87b].

The application program (in this case, a drawing program) consists of an infinite loop waiting for a tuple for the application which indicates that a mouse button is pressed. Once the tuple is received, it checks what color is currently selected, and repeatedly reads the position information of the mouse and the size information from the slide bar through the tuple space, and draws filled circles until it receives a tuple which shows the release of the mouse button. This kind of simple control structure is possible because the application is running in parallel with other tool objects. With existing single-threaded toolkits, the drawing function called from the main loop in the toolkit library must always remember its state (e.g., idle, button-pressed, mouse-moving, etc.) and perform an appropriate action every time it is called.

Unlike existing toolkits, this toolkit does not restrict the control structure of application programs, and separation between the interface part and the application part is supported. For example, the Linda version of the 8-queens program introduced in Section 15.3.1 can run with this toolkit, while it can also run with a completely different type of interface like the terminal interface. Figure 15.10 shows the interface programs for terminal and window interface. This example clearly shows how the application part is separated from the interface part, and different interface programs can be used for the same application program.

In this way, the interface part provided by this toolkit can be separated from the application part, and the control structure of the application part is not restricted by the toolkit. These are great improvements to existing toolkits, where the application cannot be reused for other interface programs, and the structure of the application is restricted to subroutine functions.

## 15.4   Solutions to Other Problems

In the previous section, we have shown that the control-flow problem is solved, and the interface part and the application part can be separated with our approach. Although Linda is not a panacea to all existing problems in creating user interface programs, it can provide solutions to some problems.

```
<definitions>
main()
{
    <initialization for 8-queen>
    eval(extend(0)); // invoke 8-queen solver
    for(;;){
        // there's no input for this interface.
        // solutions are printed as soon as they are
        // found.
        out(CLICK);
        in(?p1,?p2,?p3,?p4,?p5,?p6,?p7,?p8);
        printf("%d %d %d %d %d %d %d %d\n",
                p1,p2,p3,p4,p5,p6,p7,p8);
    }
}
```

(a) 8-queen with terminal interface

```
<definitions>
int click();
ExecBox *e;
main()
{
    <initialization for 8-queen and toolkit>
    eval(extend(0)); // invoke 8-queen solver
    // create a execution box which invokes
    // click() every time a mouse button is
    // clicked on it. a process is created
    // automatically.
    e = new ExecBox(posx,posy,w,h,click);
    for(;;){
        in(?p1,?p2,?p3,?p4,?p5,?p6,?p7,?p8);
        <draw a chess board on the window and
         display the queens at positions
         specified by p1..8.>
    }
}
click()  // invoked by a mouse click
{
    out(CLICK);
}
```

(b) 8-queen with window interface

Figure 15.10: 8-queens program with terminal and window interface.

### 15.4.1   Supplement to Existing Languages

Chapter 1 lists a number of reasons why conventional programming languages are not appropriate for writing user interface programs and a new language is needed. Here, we list the problems again and how they can be solved by using conventional programming languages with Linda.

1. **Lack of appropriate I/O mechanisms**

   As we have shown in Section 15.1, the main reason why I/O mechanisms in conventional languages are inappropriate is they are based on a simple model of "a character stream between the program and the device." As we have shown in the previous section, this problem can be solved by using powerful parallel execution primitives. For example, `in` of Linda can be regarded as a powerful input mechanism, since it can get any structure of data from the tuple space, and also many processes can wait for many inputs at the same time.

   The CSP model of Squeak[Cardelli 85a] and the event model of Sassafras[Hill 86] can also handle multiple I/O devices at the same time, but those communication mechanisms are not as flexible as Linda. Moreover, the languages used in those systems cannot be used with conventional programming languages. As we have shown in Section 15.3, parallel execution primitives like Linda can solve the weakness of I/O mechanisms of conventional programming languages.

2. **Lack of inexpensive multiprocessing and real-time programming**

   As we have shown in the previous sections, multi-processing is a very important feature required for user interface programs. Using the rather new techniques of lightweight processes and threads, implementing inexpensive multi-processing features in conventional languages is not difficult.[3] Also, though real-time programming is not usually supported by conventional languages, research in real-time operating systems will make it easier to use those features in conventional languages.

---

[3]Clinda can be implemented in C using the MACH C-thread library.

### 3. Ineffective object-oriented paradigms

Object-oriented languages have been used more and more for many application programs. Existing applications written in C are easily modified to C++, and those written in Lisp are modified to CLOS. Using simple primitives like Linda with an object-oriented language which is most suited to the application would make the development of a large system much easier. Also, just as Reppy (Chapter 14) pointed out, parallel execution inherently supports some degree of object-orientedness. Linda well fits into the structure of conventional object-oriented programming languages.

### 4. No rapid prototyping

Rapid prototyping is most needed for the design of dialog and graphic representation. A state transition language (e.g., Flex[Masui 91]) can be used with conventional language to make dialog design easier. A graphic representation design tool like a graphic editor can be created separately from the application language. This can be considered as an environment issue, since those tools are not only useful to the design of the user interface, but also useful for any program development. Thus, they should be implemented as separate tools and they should work cooperatively with conventional programming languages.

### 5. Inappropriate representation for programs

Textual representation seems to be the most effective way to write complicated application programs, and this will also be true in the future. Although graphical representation may be nice for specifying graphic interaction, most application programs consist of pure calculations and graphical representation is not good for them at all. Since one representation technique might be suited for one part of the system and another representation technique might be suited for another part, it is better to use as many representation techniques as required and combine all of them using parallel execution and other techniques.

6. **Lack of various new features being investigated by user interface researchers, such as constraints, event-handlers, and incremental recomputation**

   Although these features are quite useful for certain systems, some applications may not require one feature at all, while they require other features. Therefore, features like these should not be implemented as standard languages features, but as separate languages or libraries. One feature may be implemented in a library. Another may be implemented as a preprocessor to a conventional language. Others may be implemented as processes running with the application. It would be better not to put all the features into one language or one system.

## 15.4.2   Using Multiple Languages

Conventional computer languages have been designed to solve a range of problems effectively. For example, C is suited for efficient calculation, Prolog is suited for reasoning, and SQL is suited for database handling. On the other hand, many features are required for user interface programs and it is very difficult to define a small set of features required for all needs. For example, a computer graphics system not only requires a good user interface, but also requires very fast processing speed. Such a system cannot use a single user interface language if it is slower than conventional languages, even though it provides a lot of useful features required for the interface part. As another example, an application which handles a database may want to use SQL in addition to the language in which the application is written. In these cases, using more than one language is preferable to using a single language for the whole system. In this way, since there is a best language or tool for each problem, *using multiple languages and tools cooperatively would be better than designing a single user interface language.*

The multi-language approach is well-known for practical applications. For example, a compiler construction tool *YACC* on UNIX accepts a BNF-like language with a notation similar to an attribute grammar, while C can also be used for usual computations. Since the BNF notation in YACC is powerful enough to write the syntax and C is a powerful general-purpose language, YACC has been widely used to build compilers. There have been many compiler construction tools which did not take this approach and tried to put all things into one tool. They did not become popular, since those tools may have been useful for creating the compilers of some classes of languages, while they were not useful at all for other classes of languages.

There are several ways to use multiple languages cooperatively. For example, one language can be implemented as a preprocessor for another. Another approach is for processes written in different languages to run in parallel communicating with parallel execution primitives. Linda is a good framework for the latter.

### 15.4.3 Plug-In UI Modules

In Chapter 2, Dertouzos introduces the idea of plug-in modules for constructing user interface software. Plug-in modules should be easily put into and removed from common "interface buses."

This is very easily implemented using Linda. The tuple space can be used as the bus, and only the structure of tuples should be defined to be used as "plugs." Any programming language can be used to implement the module, as long as it uses the same protocol.

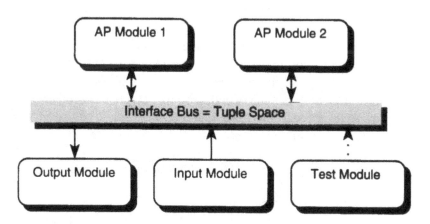

Figure 15.11: Plug-in modules and common interface bus.

Not only application modules and interface modules can be plugged into the bus, but also test modules and logging modules can be easily plugged into the common bus.

### 15.4.4   CSCW and Network User Interface

Although the tuple space looks like a shared memory, there exist many efficient implementations of Linda on distributed computers connected to a network.   On such a network, multiple users in different places can communicate with each other through the tuple space, just like using a single machine. This is a great advantage for creating software supporting CSCW. If you write user interface software which handles multiple inputs and outputs using Linda, it can be almost automatically usable as CSCW software.

## 15.5   Limitations of Linda

Linda, however, has several limitations for user interface programming. Some of them are discussed below.

- **Bandwidth of input and output**
  Input and output devices for recent advanced interfaces sometimes handle large amounts of data at a very high speed. For example, to create a virtual reality (VR), a large amount of data is sent from a data glove to the computer, and at the same time from the computer to the display. Since Linda processes can handle only one tuple at a time and a large amount of data cannot be passed efficiently between processes through the tuple space, Linda cannot be used for VR without some modification to the model. A possible solution is only using tags for the communication through the tuple space, while the actual data is passed through other communication paths.

- **Sequencing of tuples**
  The in and rd operators of Linda read any tuple in the tuple space which matches its specification. This is a nice feature in many cases, but it also causes sequencing problems. For example, in the 8-queens program shown in Section 15.3.1, if the mouse is clicked very fast

and several solutions are put into the tuple space at the same time, the output process will read one of the solutions in an undetermined order. Although in this application the order of the solutions may not be important, wrong sequencing causes problems if the order has an important meaning, like the order of input events. It is possible to preserve the order of tuples just by adding an extra "sequence number" field in the tuples, but this is an overhead compared with synchronous communication methods.

In spite of these limitations, the advantages of using Linda for user interface programming far outnumber the problems. It would also be a great research topic to extend the model of Linda so that it can be used for the wider area of user interface programming.

## 15.6  Conclusions

User interface programs can be constructed easily and efficiently by using multiple languages communicating through a global data space. Any of the conventional languages and tools can be used for this purpose by extending the languages with the Linda parallel execution primitives. This approach to creating user interface programs is applicable to a wide range of systems, from a system on a local small machine, to a large CSCW system on multiple distributed machines connected by networks.

# Chapter 16

# Constructing User Interfaces with Functions and Temporal Constraints

*T.C. Nicholas Graham*

## 16.1    Introduction

One of the chief difficulties in designing a language for the implemention of graphical user interfaces is that the requirements of such a language conflict. Among its many requirements, a language for developing user interfaces must support:

- Rapid prototyping;

- Non-determinism and concurrency; and

- Efficient implementation.

Firstly, the design of user interfaces is very dependent on user feedback: effective interface design involves testing a prototype with real users, modifying the interface based on this feedback, and testing again. Therefore, the language must support *rapid prototyping*, where interfaces can be rapidly created and modified.

Secondly, modern user interfaces must support a variety of input devices, concurrent dialogues, and even distribution over a number of machines. The language must therefore provide solid support for handling events that occur in non-deterministic order, and for *concurrency*.

Finally, an interface must be completely responsive, so that the user does not perceive delays. This implies the need for very *efficient implementation*.

Rapid prototyping often conflicts with efficient execution, since high-level prototyping languages generally contain features that are expensive to implement. Rapid prototyping with concurrent languages is also difficult, since concurrent programming is by nature complicated and error-prone, and is therefore best approached in a planned and methodical manner. It is therefore hard to achieve these three goals within a single language.

This chapter considers how techniques from declarative programming can help meet these conflicting requirements. A series of related topics are considered:

*Bridging the gap:* In Chapter 2, Dertouzos discusses the language gap between direct manipulation languages intended for users, and the programming languages intended for implementors. For programmers, there is an equivalent language gap, between the language used for rapid prototyping, and that used for production implementation. Section 16.2 considers how ideas from wide-spectrum languages can help to bridge this gap.

*Rapid Prototyping in the Large:* Rapid prototyping tools do not generally support programming in the large, that is, breaking a program into components and defining the interfaces and connections of these components. We take the same view as expressed by Dertouzos (Chapter 2) and Smith and Susser (Chapter 3) that it should be as easy as possible to connect the components. Section 16.3 discusses a simple component methodology based on concurrent objects.

*Rapid Prototyping of Concurrency:* A concurrent language must support parallel processes, communication between these processes, and synchronization of this communication. The main problems with concurrency have to do with synchronization. Section 16.4 shows how constraints in a temporal logic allow synchronization to be inferred automatically, rather than the programmer having to specify it.

A running example shows how these techniques can be applied to the implementation of a simple window manager.

## 16.2   Bridging the Gap between Prototyping and Production

Prototyping tools and languages are intended to help in the design of an application and user interface. Prototyping tools must therefore allow a programmer to rapidly create an interface, to try out the interface right away (without lengthy compilation time), and to easily modify the interface. As discussed by Hudson (Chapter 7) and Horn (Chapter 13), these requirements are very hard to meet when the resulting program needs to execute quickly, as is the case with production user interfaces.

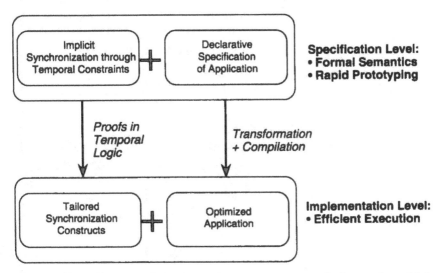

Figure 16.1: Functional programming promotes a methology where high-level constructs are used for rapid-prototyping, and are then transformed to an efficient form for production execution.

One solution to this problem is to provide one language (or system) for rapid prototyping (such as Smalltalk or Prolog), and another for production implementation (such as C++). Practical experience shows, however, that prototyping tools are most effectively used when the prototype plays some role in the final implementation: that is, when code from the prototype can be reused. One approach to this problem is to provide a language where high-level features are provided for rapid prototyping, and where *in the same language framework* low-level features are provided to achieve the required execution speed. Formal program transformation rules allow expensive high-level features to be transformed to low-level features, while guaranteeing that the semantics of the program are preserved. Such a language is called a *wide-spectrum language* [Bauer 81, Gifford 86, Jenkins 86, Odersky 90].

A wide spectrum language combines features from specification and implementation languages (Figure 16.1). We have been experimenting with *Temporal Constraint Functional Programming* [Graham 92], a language framework where the specification-level language is a functional language (called *Clock*), combined with constraints in a temporal logic to express concurrent behavior. Imperative features are introduced in a manner that preserves a local version of referential transparency [Graham 91]. Program transformation allows the programmer to prototype first using the high-level features, and then through a combination of manual and automatic transforms to create an efficient version using the low-level features. The *Clock* notation is high-level enough that it can be easily produced, modified, and understood. The compiler used for *Clock* programs [Chakravarty 91] is fast enough to be suitable for rapid prototyping purposes.

The "glue" that holds together this transformation process is a formal model for interactive programs. By giving a formal semantics to the high-level functional language, a program serves at the same time as a specification and a prototype implementation. Through the semantics, a solid foundation is given to the notion of "semantic-preserving" transformations.

Once the rapid prototyping stage is completed, the optimizing version of the compiler can be applied, where, in conjunction with automatic and manual transformations, a version suitable for production use can be obtained. We are interested in a variety of transforms—in addition to the traditional functional language transforms [Burstall 77, Thompson 89], transformations over the communication and synchronization structure of the program are conceivable. For example, in Section 16.4 we show a transformation that infers a concurrent implementation of a window manager from a sequential one.

We now give an introduction to the principles of functional programming, and an overview of how to introduce input/output and concurrency into a functional language.

## 16.2.1    Why Functional Programming?

Functional programming has a number of advantages over imperative programming, some of which are also discussed by Gansner and Reppy in Chapter 14. Modern functional languages provide a set of high-level constructs such as list data structures, higher-order functions, static polymorphic typing, pattern matching, and lazy evaluation. The defining characteristic of functional programming is that functions are a mapping from some domain of data onto some co-domain of data. Functions are *referentially transparent*, meaning that the application of some function $f$ to some argument $X$ will give the same result, no matter at what point of the program the function is applied. This referential transparency property means that functional languages have have no explicit control flow: for example, in the application:

$$f(g(X), h(Y))$$

it makes no difference in which order $g(X)$ and $h(Y)$ are evaluated (they can in fact be evaluated in parallel). Similarly, in the application

$$map(f, L)$$

the function $f$ is applied in non-deterministic order to each element of the list $L$.

Referential transparency simplifies sophisticated static analysis such as dataflow analysis, memory usage analysis, and automatic parallelization. This makes for better results and more confidence in the correctness of the results [Cousot 77, Hudak 87].

Finally, most program transformations require referential transparency. For example, to conclude that the expression

$$f(X) + f(X)$$

can be optimized to

$$f(X) * 2$$

we need to know that $f(X)$ has no side effects, and has the same value regardless of the context in which it is evaluated.

More practically, some of the more powerful features of functional programming only work in the absence of control flow [Swarup 91]. In particular, lazy evaluation is a very powerful and useful tool, but becomes incomprehensible in the presence of side effect bearing constructs that must be evaluated in a specific order. This is a key reason why we prefer not to combine functional and imperative features in the style of ML (as proposed in Chapter 14), or Lisp (Chapter 10).

For an excellent summary of modern functional progamming, we refer the reader to Hudak [Hudak 89a].

### 16.2.2   Input/Output and Concurrency in Functional Languages

We are experimenting with a functional language called *Clock*, a language based on Guarded Term ML [Lock 89], extended to provide constructs for interaction and concurrency. *Clock* is described in detail elsewhere [Graham 92], so we shall just give an overview of the features of the language here.

The philosophy behind *Clock* is that functional programming is successful for programming in the small. However, for programming in the large, one requires the ability to talk about persistent state (such as file systems), to communicate in an asynchronous manner with a variety of input and output devices, and to split the program on the basis of abstract data types, objects, or some other form of module system. This leads us to an object model, where a program is organized as a set of processes that communicate via asynchronous communication channels (or streams). Each process (or component) is a purely functional program which takes a set of streams as input, and gives a set of streams as output. The communication structure of programs is expressed via constraints in a temporal logic, called *interaction logic*. Constraints can specify how components are connected, how the communication between components is synchronized, and monitor-style sharing of global state.

In *Clock*, temporal constraints are used as a meta-programming feature, where constraints guide the evaluation of a set of pure-functional computations. Programming in the small is on the level of the process. A process is a pure functional computation, whose value always consists of a request to the I/O system, and a follow-up process to be forked once the request has been fulfilled. Temporal constraints sequence and synchronize these I/O requests and the concurrent creation and execution of processes. Thus, a functional "program" is actually a (possibly infinite) set of pure functional programs, each of which executes as a process, and the synchronization of which is guided by temporal logic constraints.

The I/O constructs in *Clock* are based on Perry's result continuations [Perry 89] and constructs for non-determinism similar to those in PFL+ [Gordon 89]. These constructs form the *machine language* level of interaction: we provide the *Clock* programmer with much higher-level abstractions based on these constructs (Section 16.3).

Non-determinism is required in a concurrent environment to reflect the many possible ways in which the I/O of two processes may be interleaved. Constraints can be written over these non-deterministically generated I/O traces, thus introducing a form of synchronization. In *Clock*, a set of predefined *component types* provides implicit temporal constraints, in the style of Burton [Burton 88]. These component types are described in Section 16.3.

The type of a *Clock* program is always *ioRequest*, a request to the I/O system paired with a process fork directive. After a process executes to termination, the resulting I/O request is served, then the new process is forked. The fork request consists of a function that is to be applied to the result of the I/O operation; such a function is usually called a *continuation function* [Hudak 88, Perry 89]. For example, a request to read a value and then perform some computation based on it looks like:

```
read (stdIn, errorC, fn X => f X)
```

Here the continuation function fn X => f X is applied to the result of the read from stream *stdIn*. (The function *errorC* is also a continuation function, to be applied in the case that the read fails.) This method introduces implicit sequentialization: here the read request must be served before any I/O activity resulting from the application of the continuation function.

As well as the usual *read* and *write* operations, there is the *any* I/O request, which takes a list of processes as parameters, and non-deterministically chooses one of them to be executed, and the *all* I/O request, which executes all of a list of processes in parallel.

The following example shows a very simple *Clock* program.

**Example 16.2.1 (Non-Deterministic Merge)** Consider we wish to construct a process whose job it is to merge two infinite streams and produce a third stream with the merged values. We do not care in which order the elements are merged, so the implementation is non-deterministic, and free to pick whatever order it chooses. We would write this as a function with type:

```
type merge :: inputStream # inputStream
                   # outputStream
             -> ioRequest.
```

That is, a process that takes two input streams and an output stream, and executes indefinitely. In fact, the program describes an infinite sequence of processes, each of which performs one step of the merge, then forks another instance of itself.

```
fun merge (In1, In2, Out) ->
    let mergeStep
        = any(copy(In1,Out,errorC, mergeStep),
              copy(In2,Out,errorC, mergeStep))
    in mergeStep.

type copy :: inputStream # outputStream
                   # failCont # successCont
             -> ioRequest.
fun copy (In, Out, ErrC, SuccC) ->
    read(In, ErrC,
             fn ValToBeCopied
                 => write(Out, ErrC, SuccC)).
```

Here, the *any* construct non-deterministically chooses between a copy of one element from the input stream *In1* onto the output stream *Out*, and a copy from *In2* onto *Out*. The recursive definition of *mergeStep* carries on this copying indefinitely. The arguments to *any* are processes, i.e., functional expressions to be evaluated.

For comparison, a general survey of proposals for I/O in functional languages can be found in [Hudak 89b].

## 16.3   Rapid Prototyping in the Large

The basic I/O primitives described in the last section are low-level and flexible. Thus, they are not appropriate for rapid prototyping, but can be more successfully used to build higher-level constructs tailored to the programmer's domain. As the basic constructs are so low-level, they also lend themselves well to the transformation methodology suggested earlier in this chapter: the general, high-level constructs available to the user can be mapped to more efficient configurations in terms of the basic constructs.

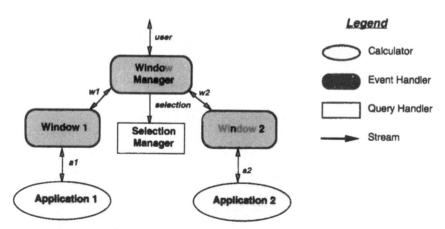

Figure 16.2: Component organization of a window manager and two applications.

As high-level constructs, we define a set of *component types*, each with a set of predefined temporal constraints. Section 16.4 shows how these constraints allow concurrent programming without the user having to explicitly program synchronization. For the time being, we shall ignore issues of concurrency, and act as if the implementation is purely sequential.

In order to introduce the component types, we walk through a simple example (adapted from [Green 86]) of the implementation of a window manager (Figure 16.2). We restrict our window manager to having two windows. Each window has an application program of some sort attached to it. The window manager maintains a concept of *focus*, where inputs are directed to whichever window has focus; the user can change focus, directing all subsequent outputs to the other window. Additionally, there exists a *select/stuff* facility between the two windows. Conceptually, a selection buffer is shared between the windows. If the user does a text selection in one window, the buffer is updated; if the user does a stuff in either window, the current buffer contents are written to that window. We can implement the selection buffer via a *selection manager*, where selection updates and requests are sent from the windows through the window manager.

This example is used in the next section to show how a set of predefined component types can be used to help a user structure programs in the large.

### 16.3.1   Informal Overview of Component Types

We shall base this simple example on four types of communication streams, and three types of components. The predefined stream types are:

*Input Stream*:  Used to carry input events to processes.

*Output Stream*:  Used to communicate outputs resulting from computation.

*Query Stream*:  Used to request some form of non-local state (e.g., requesting the current selection).

*Notification Stream*:  Used to update non-local state (e.g., announcing an update of the current selection).

For convenience, streams usually come bundled together. If a particular stream group is called $s$, we use the names $s_i$, $s_o$, $s_q$, and $s_n$ to refer to the input, output, query, and notification streams in $s$, respectively.

A set of predefined *component types* are available, where a component type is defined simply by what kind of streams it uses (Figure 16.2).

The simplest component is a *Calculator*, which is connected to an input stream and an output stream. Calculators are typically non-interactive programs, taking an input and producing an output. For example, a compiler would be a calculator that takes a source text, and produces an object text; a database program would be a calculator that takes a query, and returns a set of matching data. Because of this simple interface, calculators lend themselves well to a pure-functional implementation.

*Event Handler* components are connected to one of each of the four stream types. These are organized like traditional event handlers in the style of Green [Green 86] or Hill [Hill 86]: events are taken from the input stream, and are either passed to children (through their input streams) or processed locally. Notifications and requests may be generated as a side effect of this event handling. Event handlers may have any number of children, which may be of any component type. This means that a given event handler must be able to process or forward any requests, notifications, and outputs coming from children components. In Figure 16.2, the two windows and the window manager are implemented as event handlers.

*Query Handler* components are similar to monitors: they encapsulate data, and provide exclusive access to that data based on requests. Query handlers are connected to a notification stream (to receive notification of a state change), and a query stream (to receive requests for data). In Figure 16.2, the selection manager is implemented as a query handler.

As shown in Figure 16.2, components can be combined in a tree structure. This structure may not always be efficient, but is simple and therefore appropriate for rapid prototyping. Transformations that optimize routing and communication patterns should be used to provide a more efficient production implementation.

This briefly introduces the components. The following section indicates how these components are annotated with implicit temporal constraints to ensure that they provide the correct synchronization behavior.

## 16.4   Rapid Prototyping of Concurrency

While the sequential implementation of the window manager shown in Section 16.3 does the job, we would much prefer a concurrent implementation, so that if, for example, application 1 is a database program performing a lengthy search, the user should be able to change focus to window 2, and work there while the search is taking place. Further, we do not wish the programmer to have to specify that the implementation is concurrent: the *Clock* compiler should work out for itself that a concurrent implementation is possible.

The concurrency issues are initially quite straightforward: the window manager, the windows, and the two applications can execute as separate processes, communicating in a tree structure via streams. The window manager reads from the *user* stream, passing the commands on to the window which currently has focus; if the user changes focus, subsequent commands go to the other window. The windows each wait on their input streams, consuming input as it arrives.

Once we introduce the *select/stuff* facility, however, we run into problems of synchronization. Consider that the user does a select in window 1, then a stuff in window 2. According to our concurrent implementation, window 1 is under no obligation to process the select immediately (window 1 may be busy doing its database search, for example). Meanwhile, window 2 is under no obligation to wait for window 1 (this was the whole point of the concurrent implementation). Therefore, window 2 could potentially perform the stuff before window 1 performs the select, as a result, stuffing the old buffer contents into window 2. To solve this problem, we need some sort of synchronization to indicate that certain kinds of communication take priority over others. Our approach will be to annotate each component type with temporal constraints that specify correct behavior, and from the possible implementations to choose a concurrent one.

We first introduce the constraint logic, and then show how the component types are annotated. The treatment of interaction logic and the examples that follow are entirely informal; a more formal treatment may be found in [Graham 92].

### 16.4.1  A Stream Logic

The functional description of a concurrent program provides no restrictions on the order in which communication events take place. To express these constraints, a second level of description is used. Here, assertions are written in a temporal logic about the events that occur on the I/O streams. These streams are treated as queues: values arrive at some time, and are processed, either immediately, or at some arbitrarily later time. (For example, if the stream is being fed by a keyboard, values may be processed as soon as they are typed, or may be buffered arbitrarily until the program processes them.) Streams thus model asynchronous communication channels.

Temporal logic [Galton 87] is a modal extension of classical logic, where special temporal operators have been added. The logic presented here, *interaction logic*, is loosely based on Gabbay's USF logic [Gabbay 87].

---

*The following predicates are defined over streams. These allow constraints to be written over the state of streams in a particular time instant:*

| | |
|---|---|
| $pending(s)$ | (item available on stream $s$) |
| $enter(s, v)$ | (item enqueued on stream $s$) |
| $exit(s, v)$ | (item dequeued from stream $s$) |
| $older(s_1, s_2)$ | (first item on $s_1$ arrived later than first item on $s_2$) |

*The usual classical connectives are available:*

| | |
|---|---|
| $\neg p$ | (negation) |
| $p \wedge q$ | (conjunction) |
| $p \vee q$ | (disjunction) |
| $\forall x.p$ | (universal quantification) |
| $\exists x.p$ | (existential quantification) |

*and two temporal operators are available to express temporal relationships between events:*

| | |
|---|---|
| $\Diamond p$ | (sometime $p$) |
| $p \ll q$ | ($p$ precedes $q$) |

Figure 16.3: The primitives of stream logic.

---

Formulae in stream logic have an implicit reference to the current time. For example it is possible for the formula

$$hungry(brad)$$

to be true in the current time (Brad is hungry now), to be false in 10 minutes, and true again in an hour. This differs from classical logic, where $hungry(brad)$ is either true or false, always. We can use the whole range of standard classical operators; for example:

$$hungry(brad) \supset eats(brad, praline)$$

says that whenever Brad is hungry, he eats a praline. This is a *constraint*: as long as in *every* time instant where $hungry(brad)$ holds, $eats(brad, praline)$ also holds, then the constraint holds over all time. The logic additionally provides special temporal operators. For example,

$$\Diamond hungry(brad) \supset buy(brad, pralines)$$

states that if sometime in the future Brad is going to be hungry, then Brad buys pralines now. (The "$\Diamond$" operator is read as *sometime*.) Temporal events can also be sequenced, as in:

$$hungry(brad) \supset (eats(brad, praline) \ll \neg hungry(brad))$$

which states that if Brad is hungry, then he must eat a praline before he stops being hungry. (The "$\ll$" operator is read as *precedes*.)

We additionally provide a set of predefined predicates over streams. If at a particular time, a value is buffered on a stream $s$ waiting to be processed, we say $pending(s)$ is true at that time. If a process outputs a value to stream $s$ at a particular time, we say that at that time $out(s)$ is true. If a process inputs a value from stream $s$ at a particular time, then we say that at the time $in(s)$ is true. If the next available value on stream $s_1$ has been pending for longer than the next value on stream $s_2$, then $older(s_1, s_2)$ is true.

Figure 16.3 summarizes the operators available in stream logic. A more formal definition of the logic is available in [Graham 92].

## 16.4.2   Components and Constraints

Returning to our problem of synchronizing the window manager of Figure 16.2, we see that the challenge is to ensure that if an input to one window generates a notification or query, then that notification or query be handled by the selection manager before any notification or query resulting from a later input in the other window. To guarantee this synchronization, we associate a set of temporal constraints with every event handler component. These constraints are implicit: the *Clock* programmer need not be aware that they are there. It is up to the implementation of the *Clock* language to ensure that they are observed.

These constraints state the following two rules:

- If the event handler is going to produce a *query* as a result of the current computation, then notifications of other processes (except for children of this process) are disabled;

- If the event handler is going to produce a *notification* as a result of the current computation, then queries and notifications of other processes (except for children of this process) are disabled.

These rules are expressed as follows in the temporal logic:

**Definition 16.4.1 (Event Handler)** *A component of type Event Handler, attached to stream s, is implicitly annotated with the following temporal constraints:*

$$
\begin{aligned}
eventHandler(s) \; &\overset{\text{def}}{=} \; goingToQuery(s_q) \; \supset \; onlyChildrenMayNotify(s_n) \\
&\wedge \; goingToNotify(s_n) \; \supset \; (onlyChildrenMayQuery(s_q) \\
&\qquad\qquad\qquad\qquad\qquad \wedge \; onlyChildrenMayNotify(s_n)).
\end{aligned}
$$

*where*

$$goingToNotify(s_n) \; \overset{\text{def}}{=} \; out(s_n) \ll finishedEvent(s).$$

$$goingToQuery(s_q) \; \overset{\text{def}}{=} \; out(s_q) \ll finishedEvent(s).$$

$$finishedEvent(s) \; \overset{\text{def}}{=} \; \neg\Diamond in(s_i) \supset (\neg\Diamond out(s_o) \wedge \neg\Diamond out(s_q) \wedge \neg\Diamond out(s_n)).$$

*and*

$$onlyChildrenMayQuery(s_q) \; \overset{\text{def}}{=} \; \forall s' . ((\neg child(s', s) \wedge s_q \neq s_q') \supset \neg out(s_q')).$$

$$onlyChildrenMayNotify(s_n) \; \overset{\text{def}}{=} \; \forall s' . ((\neg child(s', s) \wedge s_n \neq s_n') \supset \neg out(s_n')).$$

□

The predicates *goingToNotify* and *goingToQuery* indicate whether this process will in the course of the current execution produce a notification/query respectively. The predicate *finishedEvent* indicates whether the process will require further input before generating output of any sort.

The constraints for calculators are comparatively simple:

**Definition 16.4.2 (Calculator)** *A component of type Calculator, attached to stream s, is implicitly annotated with the following constraint:*

$$calculator(s) \stackrel{\text{def}}{=} \neg goingToQuery(s_q) \wedge \neg goingToNotify(s_n).$$

□

This constraint simply indicates that calculators do not perform queries or notifications.

The constraints for query handlers indicate that the requests and notifications are handled in first-in, first-out order (*fifo*).

**Definition 16.4.3 (Query Handler)** *A component of type Query Handler, attached to stream s, is implicitly annotated with the following constraints:*

$$queryHandler(s) \stackrel{\text{def}}{=} fifo(s_n, s_q) \wedge fifo(s_q, s_n).$$

*where*

$$fifo(s_1, s_2) \stackrel{\text{def}}{=} older(s_1, s_2) \supset (in(s_1) \ll in(s_2)).$$

□

Using the constraint *child* to express the tree structure of our window system, we can then define the complete window system constraints as follows:

$$eventHandler(user) \wedge eventHandler(w1) \wedge eventHandler(w2).$$
$$queryHandler(selection).$$
$$calculator(a1) \wedge calculator(a2).$$

$$child(w1, user) \wedge child(selection, user) \wedge child(w2, user).$$
$$child(a1, w1).$$
$$child(a2, w2).$$

### 16.4.3 Implementing the Constraints

Now consider that we wish to implement these constraints. The predicate *finishedEvent* is straightforward to implement: we just need to know whether the process handling an event has terminated or not. The predicates *othersMayNotQuery* and *othersMayNotNotify* are also not problematic: they simply give directives to the scheduler that output requests on the given query/notification streams are to be blocked.

We have a problem, however, with the predicates *goingToNotify* and *goingToQuery*, whose values depend on the *future* action of the event handler. Knowing whether a process will some time in the future generate a notification or query is in general equivalent to the halting problem. We must therefore be satisfied with transforming the constraints into more restrictive constraints, whose behavior is, if not maximally concurrent, at least guaranteed to be correct. We shall consider two possible transformations. The first is simple and generates some concurrency, and the second is a refinement that generates far more concurrency.

### 16.4.4 Atomic Event Handler Implementation

Our problem is that we cannot implement the predicates *goingToNotify* and *goingToQuery*, since they require knowledge of the future execution of the program. To be able to implement the *eventHandler* constraint, we will replace these predicates by the conservative approximations *mightNotify* and *mightQuery*($s$) respectively. These predicates are conservative in the sense that they indicate that a notification (or query) *may* occur in the future, but not that it definitely will. Thus, we will only allow concurrent behavior when we know that no notifies/queries are going to occur. With the conservative definitions, we sometimes unnecessarily restrict concurrency, but are sure not to introduce any synchronization errors. We redefine *eventHandler* with the conservative predicates:

$$
\begin{aligned}
eventHandler'(s) \;\overset{\text{def}}{=}\;\; & mightQuery(s_q) \supset onlyChildrenMayNotify(s_n) \\
\wedge\;\; & mightNotify(s_n) \supset onlyChildrenMayQuery(s_q) \\
& \wedge\; onlyChildrenMayNotify(s_n).
\end{aligned}
$$

This version of *eventHandler* is more difficult to satisfy than the original. That is, less I/O behaviors are admitted under the new definition.

One way of being sure that a component will not generate a query or notification is knowing that the component has finished execution and is awaiting new input. This can be expressed in stream logic as:

$$mightQuery(s_q) \; \overset{\text{def}}{=} \; \neg finishedEvent(s).$$
$$mightNotify(s_n) \; \overset{\text{def}}{=} \; \neg finishedEvent(s).$$

The effect of this definition is a strict sequentialization of the program. When a component is given an input, no component other than that component and its children is permitted to perform queries or notifications until the component has executed to completion.

The set of new constraints using *eventHandler'* instead of *eventHandler*, which we will name $\mathcal{F}'$, can be proved correct by demonstrating that every I/O behavior that meets the constraints $\mathcal{F}'$ also meets the constraints $\mathcal{F}$.

### 16.4.5  Concurrent Event Handler Implementation

The solution of Section 16.4.4 is rather unsatisfactory. Imagine that the application $a_1$ from Figure 16.2 is performing a database search that will take 10 minutes to complete. Under the last definition, all inputs to window 2 are suspended until the search terminates. The database, however, does not generate any notifications or queries (by definition as a *calculator* component), and therefore need not interfere with window 2. The current definitions of *mightQuery* and *mightNotify* guarantee not to give us synchronization errors, but at the cost of too much concurrency. We would therefore like to find better definitions that give us more concurrency while continuing to provide correct synchronization.

We first define the *waitingForChildren* predicate to express that an event handler is executing, but requires inputs from its children before it can continue. This is the same as saying that if none of the component's children generates an output, then the component itself will never generate an output:

$$waitingForChildren(s) \; \overset{\text{def}}{=} \; \neg\Diamond in(s_i) \wedge \forall c . (child(c,s) \supset \neg\Diamond in(c_i))$$
$$\supset (\neg\Diamond out(s_o) \wedge \neg\Diamond out(s_q) \wedge \neg\Diamond out(s_n)).$$

We can then prove the following theorem, which states that if a component is waiting for input from its children, and its children will generate no notifications or queries, then the component itself will also generate no notifications or queries.

**Theorem 16.4.1 (Query and Notification Inheritance)** *If s is a stream, then*

$$waitingForChildren(s) \wedge \neg childGoingToQuery(s) \supset \neg goingToQuery(s)$$

*and*

$$waitingForChildren(s) \wedge \neg childGoingToNotify(s) \supset \neg goingToNotify(s)$$

*where*

$$childGoingToQuery(s) \overset{\text{def}}{=} \exists c \, . \, child(s,c) \wedge goingToQuery(c).$$
$$childGoingToNotify(s) \overset{\text{def}}{=} \exists c \, . \, child(s,c) \wedge goingToNotify(c).$$

□

From this theorem and from Definition 16.4.2, we can prove that for a stream $s$:

$$(waitingForChildren(s) \wedge \forall c \, . \, (child(c,s) \supset calculator(c)))$$
$$\supset (\neg goingToQuery(s) \wedge \neg goingToNotify(s))$$

That is, if a component has passed execution to its children, and all the children are calculators, then the component will not generate any more queries or notifications. This allows a new stronger definition of *mightQuery* and *mightNotify*:

$$mightQuery(s_q) \overset{\text{def}}{=}$$
$$\neg finishedEvent(s)$$
$$\wedge \quad \neg(waitingForChildren(s) \wedge \forall c \, . \, (child(c,s) \supset calculator(c))).$$

$$mightNotify(s_n) \overset{\text{def}}{=} mightQuery(s_q).$$

These definitions guarantee us that the selection and stuff commands will be executed in the correct order, while applications are permitted to run concurrently.

### 16.4.6   Summary

In order to lead to a result that is intuitively correct, we have kept this
example quite simple. Clearly, one does not need the entire apparatus
of the temporal logic to be able to infer the implementation of Section
16.4.5. However, it is not hard to imagine how more complex interactions
of components and more ambitious optimizations lead to implementations
too complex to understand intuitively. In these cases, the formal framework
helps the language implementor to approach the problem methodically, and
lends confidence in the correctness of the result.

## 16.5   Discussion

This chapter has explained how some aspects of declarative programming,
in particular the use of temporal constraints in conjunction with functional
programming, can be of aid in constructing user interfaces. These techniques show promise for the simultaneous support of rapid prototyping,
concurrency, and efficient execution in one language framework.

There are some interesting links to other work presented in this book.
For example, both Hill (Chapter 9) and Singh (Chapter 8) state the need for
some form of temporal constraints for real-time programming. Such real-
time constraints can be simply expressed in interaction logic by defining the
appropriate predicates. However, the difficulty is in the implementation.
Just as in Section 16.4.3 we had to satisfy ourselves with conservative
implementations of the window manager constraints, the same is bound
to be true with real-time constraints. How a general real-time constraint
language can be implemented is a matter for further research.

Another topic for further work is to see how much the use of interaction logic depends on the underlying functional language. Referential
transparency is critical to the sorts of transformations we do. The very lightweight processes supported by the functional notation are also important
for any sort of efficient implementation. These features could, however, be
provided within an appropriately restricted imperative language. It would
be interesting to examine, for example, a temporal-logic-based extension
to Constraint Imperative Programming (presented in Chapter 11).

This chapter presented a simple component system, and discussed automatic inference of communication and synchronization patterns among components. It would further be interesting to see if this approach could help in the problems of connecting end-user components of the style discussed by Smith and Susser (Chapter 3).

A great deal of further research is required in general to discover whether the declarative techniques described in this chapter are in fact practical. The current *Clock* implementation needs to be extended with a sophisticated optimizer that automatically performs the sorts of transformations that we have described. Case studies will then be required to evaluate the declarative methods.

*Representations for
User Actions*

# Chapter 17

# Different Languages for Different Development Activities: Behavioral Representation Techniques for User Interface Design

*H. Rex Hartson*
*Jeffrey L. Brandenburg*
*Deborah Hix*

Most of the chapters in this book address programming language issues for user interface construction. The target users of these languages range from novice (Chapter 4) to professional programmers (Chapter 11); the programming domains of interest range from application construction (Chapter 14) to end-user customization (Chapter 3). Throughout this broad area, though, the emphasis has been on user interface *implementation*.

Our research, and therefore our chapter, is concerned instead with languages to support user interface *design*—specifically, languages and representation techniques for capturing and communicating interface designs. We have developed the User Action Notation (UAN), a behavioral, task-oriented design language, as part of this effort [Hartson 90b]. One purpose of the UAN is to communicate user interface designs from interface *interaction* designers to interface *software* designers (a distinction which we will elaborate shortly). The UAN is also useful for documentation and analysis of interface designs, and we are investigating other areas of possible application.

## 17.1   Background

It is now well accepted that an iterative, evaluation-centered development process [Hartson 89c] involving rapid prototyping and usability engineering [Whiteside 88] is a much more effective approach to development of a *usable system* than the conventional top-down software development paradigm based on functional decomposition and linear life cycle phases. For a focus on the process-in-the-large, we find the term "design" limiting and prefer the term "development," which includes requirements analysis, task analysis, user definition, interface design, design representation, rapid prototyping, formative evaluation, design of interface software, and construction/coding/maintenance of interface software. Support for iterative refinement and prototyping of interface software is addressed in many chapters of this book. But software development is only one part of the overall development process, and other development tasks pose different requirements for support tools and languages.

Languages for representation of early activities (for example, task analysis and interface design) need to be oriented toward a view of the user's behavior. *Behavioral* design and representation involves physical and cognitive user actions and interface feedback—the behavior both of the user and of the interface as they interact with each other. Each behavioral design must be translated into a *constructional* design that is the computer system view of how the behavior is to be supported. Any description that can be thought of as "executed by the machine" is constructional. This includes control flow and/or dataflow mechanisms, state transition diagrams, event handlers, object-oriented representations, and many interface description languages.

In contrast, behavioral descriptions can be thought of as "executed by the user." Unfortunately, many existing interface representation techniques, especially those associated with User Interface Management Systems (UIMSs), are constructional and, therefore, do not adequately support a user-centered focus. *But it is in the behavioral domain that interaction designers and evaluators do their work.* Thus, there is a need for behavioral representation techniques—languages and supporting tools—to give a user-centered focus to the interface development process. Further, since these roles and activities must communicate with other roles and activities of the development process, there is a need for languages and tools to facilitate this communication.

## 17.2 Areas of System Development

Figure 17.1 provides one overview of relationships among various areas of interface development within the context of overall interactive system development. (This is not an architectural diagram of an interactive system or UIMS.) From the outside in, we have overall interactive system development, development of the part of the interactive system that is computer-based (including new interactive media and devices, such as novel display or force-feedback technologies), user interface development, user interface software development, and interaction development. Each of these domains of development involves its own lifecycle with its own set of processes. Except for projects to develop new computing systems or workstations, user interface developers usually find that choices of hardware and interaction devices are made independently.

In this chapter we are interested in the shaded areas of Figure 17.1: primarily the domain of abstract interaction development, in the context of user interface software development, and user interface development in general.

## 17.3 Processes, Boundaries, and Communication

Our view of the development of interactive systems parallels the traditional software engineering view of software development (Figure 17.2). In this traditional view, **systems analysis** generates **requirements** for **software design**—the definition of modules, data structures, dataflow, and operations. The software designer provides feedback to the systems analyst

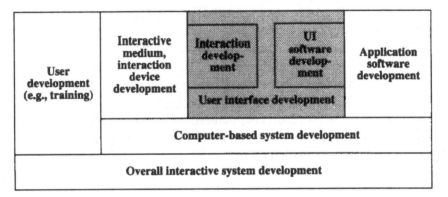

Figure 17.1: Relationships among areas of interactive system development.

by reporting any inconsistencies, omissions, or ambiguities in the requirements, and through verification that the design meets the requirements.

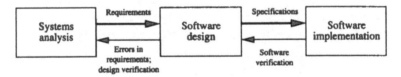

Figure 17.2: Parts of software system development.

The software design in turn provides **specifications** for **software implementation**. The software designer can receive the same sort of error feedback as described above; in addition, program verification techniques are available to confirm that the implementation meets the design specifications. Communication between these two parts of the development process has been the subject of much software engineering research, and is relatively well-understood.

The notion of separation of roles between the analyst and the software designer, and between the designer and the implementer, is very important. It is clear that the roles of analyst, designer, and implementer each require different skills and knowledge, pertaining both to the development process in general and to the specific problem domain. The division of labor and corresponding specialization of roles afforded by this kind of separation is important to support iteration within the development process. For example, if a software design is incomplete, it often seems simplest to fill in the missing details during implementation. This casts the implementer into the role of designer, however, a role for which the implementer is not necessarily qualified and does not have access to applicable design conventions, rules, and standards.

It is also fairly clear that as the size of a system under development and the number of people working on it increase, isolation between separate roles reduces side effects and unwanted dependencies. But even for small systems, and even when only one person is involved, separation among the analysis, design, and implementation roles supports a more disciplined and organized development process. Even if design and implementation are done *by the same person*, an ad hoc approach to filling in gaps can lead to inconsistencies; at the very least, it is more likely to lead to duplicated effort and problems with maintenance.

If the roles of designer and implementer are kept separate, it is easier to verify that a design is complete and correct and that the implementation satisfies that design. If the roles of analyst and designer are kept separate, it is easier to verify that the systems analysis is complete and that the requirements accurately reflect it. Applied rigorously to the entire development process, these principles of separation can lead to better designs, better code, and a better product.

Figure 17.3 expands the view of Figure 17.2 to describe the entire interactive software development process. It reflects the traditional divisions between requirements, design, and implementation, as well as the less well-defined division between interface and non-interface development.

In the **systems analysis** phase, the distinction between the user interface and the rest of the system is not necessarily as pronounced as it is during later stages of development. In an *interactive* system, the *user* is an integral part of the overall system's function, and so user activities must be considered on an equal footing with system activities. Products of the systems analysis process will include a description of functions to be performed by the system, functions the user and system together can perform, and information items the system can present to or request from the user. These will serve as requirements for non-user interface functions to be performed by the system and for design of the interactions that constitute the user interface.

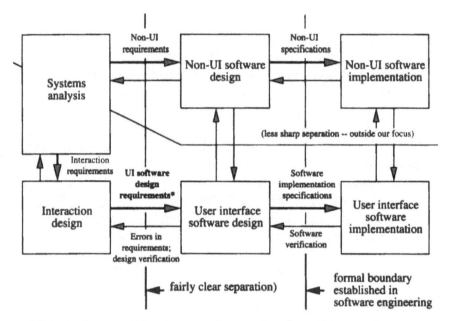

* Behavioral representations to convey these user interface software requirements to user interface software designers are the focus of our research.

Figure 17.3: Parts of interactive system development.

**Interaction design** (Figure 17.3) determines the abstract form and content of the user interface. Since interaction design focuses on how the user perceives and manipulates the system, it must rely on *behavioral representation*—a depiction of the interface in terms of user actions and observable system presentations or responses. This depiction may include tasks represented in the interface, the kinds of user actions that form the vocabulary of the interface, visual representations, interaction styles, human factors considerations, temporal aspects of tasks, and so forth. It is possible to perform some kinds of analysis on this representation, but its main purpose is to state requirements for the user interface software.

On the other hand, constructional techniques are required for **user interface software design** (Figure 17.3), which determines data structures, control paths, dataflow, and other features of the user interface software. Since this design area deals with software rather than user and system actions, the traditional tools of software engineering can be applied. Of course, there are unique language issues that do not arise in non-interactive software design; these issues, and approaches to their solution, form the main focus of this book.

The relationship between the interaction design and interface software design processes (the lower path in Figure 17.3) parallels that of the systems analysis and non-interface software design processes (the upper path in Figure 17.3). Interaction design provides **requirements** for the interface software design to fulfill (see asterisk in Figure 17.3). These requirements, since they describe the behavior of the user and the interface, must be expressed in behavioral terms. The interface software design process can provide corrective feedback to the interaction design process if it uncovers omissions, ambiguities, or inconsistencies in these requirements. Further, the interface software design can guide the construction of a prototype, which can then be evaluated for usability as part of the iterative development paradigm. While it is possible to generate a prototype from the interaction design, this will only provide a shallow facade; prototypes incorporating information from the software design process can provide a more accurate and complete representation of the final system, which can lead to more efficient and effective evaluation.

The user interface software design process produces specifications for implementation of the user interface software. The relationship between these two development arenas is precisely the same as that between conventional software design and implementation, and the same techniques can be used to communicate between them.

The boundary between interface and non-interface development (Figure 17.3) is not nearly as clear as the boundaries among analysis, interaction design, software design, and software implementation. First, systems analysis must straddle the border between the interface and non-interface parts of the system. Systems analysis, by definition, is concerned with the entire system. And since the user is an integral part of an interactive system, the systems analysis process must consider the user's actions and perceptions as well as the computer-based aspects of the system. Effectively, the systems analysis process must embrace all of Figure 17.1.

In addition, while it is generally agreed that some degree of separation between interface and non-interface *software* is desirable, it is frequently necessary that the border drawn between them is arbitrary. As the semantic processing associated with each user action or system presentation becomes more complex, it is easy for non-interface logic to creep into interface parts of a system. If we guard against this, then functionality concerned only with the interface begins to creep into the non-interface software. This problem has been considered at length elsewhere (for example, [Hartson 89a]).

During the *interaction* design process, these issues of software architecture should be of no concern to the interaction designer, because they are (or should be) invisible to the user. The interface is all that the user sees, and as long as that interface fits its design requirements, it makes no difference how the interface is implemented. The application might be written in Smalltalk to follow the Model–View–Controller paradigm, or it might be written in C with randomly sprinkled calls to X library routines, or it might be built from tiny gears and springs; in fact, all three approaches have led to successful implementations of an analog clock display.

But it certainly *is* important to provide language features, software architectures, and development techniques to help maintain a disciplined relationship between user interface software and non-interface software. The true importance of support for interface software design and implementation becomes apparent during the process of iterative refinement. If evaluation reveals that some aspect of a user interface must be changed, the usual body of software engineering experience makes it obvious that a well-structured design and implementation of the interface software will be easier to modify than a poorly-structured implementation. Further, the better the separation between interface and non-interface software, the less deeply changes to the interface design will propagate through the design of the rest of the system. And the less time and effort it takes to modify the interface implementation, the more iterations will be possible within a given time, and (ideally) the higher the quality of the final application.

## 17.4   Interaction Design as a Separate Role

Previously, we discussed the separation of roles in the development of non-user interface software (the top half of Figure 17.3). Many of the same kinds of issues arise in the development of the user interface itself (the bottom half of Figure 17.3).

The difference between the skills of an interaction designer and those of a software designer (even an interface software designer) is perhaps more pronounced than the difference between systems analysis and software design skills. Experts on interaction design and evaluation should not need to know about software design, and software experts should not need to know about interaction issues. If a suitable method of communication between the two roles is available, it becomes unnecessary for designers to have expertise in both of these two essentially unrelated fields.

Further, the visibility of the user interface leads to an additional argument for separation of development roles. As in the case of non-user interface software, both the interaction design process and the interface software design process can yield incomplete, ambiguous, or inconsistent specifications. Without a clear separation of roles, it is possible that missing parts of the design might be carried out in an arbitrary and ad hoc manner, each implementer supplying little pieces of design without a way to ensure consistency with the other pieces. The non-interactive part of the software system may be able to absorb a certain amount of this undisciplined design activity without outwardly visible negative effects on the end product, but the uniformity and internal consistency of the code may suffer, a detriment to software maintenance.

In the user interface, on the other hand, even small details can be visible to the user of the final product. When different interface software designers or implementers resolve the same interface ambiguity in different ways, the result can be an inconsistent, confusing, and unsatisfactory interface.

If the interaction design process, the interface software design process, and the interface software implementation process are kept separate, interface software implementers will not arbitrarily and inconsistently resolve incomplete interaction specifications. Instead, the interface implementer feeds back a complaint to the interface software designer; if the interface software designer determines that the fault is in the interaction specification, then the problem is returned to the interaction designer, who can resolve it correctly.

This may seem like an obvious approach, but it is not often followed. This may be true partly because a large share of highly interactive interface designs are still for relatively small systems, and there is a perception that small systems allow a less formal and less structured development process.

Many experimental languages, support environments, models, and tools are tested with these relatively small applications—paint programs, text editors, or games, mostly developed by an individual or a handful of people over a few months or years. While many interesting phenomena and useful achievements can be demonstrated in this realm, it is utterly different from the real-world realm of large-scale, multi-user, multi-function integrated software systems involving hundreds of person-years and millions of lines of code. In this arena, separation of development roles is a matter of survival; software engineering researchers have known this all along, and HCI researchers must keep it in mind.

To develop large systems, it is necessary to define and delimit the separate roles in the development process. To develop good interactive systems, it is necessary to have an iterative development methodology that allows successive improvements to the user interface. Since this means the different roles must communicate repeatedly, we need some representation technique which can communicate designs from one stage to the next. As stated previously, communication between the interface software designer and the interface software implementer is within the domain of software engineering. Communication between the interaction designer and the interface software designer (the path marked with an asterisk in Figure 17.3) must express behavioral concerns, though, and so it requires new and different techniques. It is this area of communication that is the focus of our work, and the User Action Notation is one of the techniques we have developed to facilitate it.

## 17.5   Design Representations

The difference between behavioral design representations (for interaction design) and constructional design representations (for user interface software design) can be difficult to sort out, because there are so many different kinds of representation techniques, each for a different purpose. Each type of representation uses its own perspective to describe the same thing: what is happening in the user interface. For example, suppose the user clicks the mouse button when the cursor is on an icon. This is seen from a behavioral view as a user action within a task, but in a constructional view this is an input event received by the system, and in an implementation view this can be seen as something that fulfills a condition that triggers a function within a toolkit widget. When the icon is highlighted, it is seen as perceptual feedback in the behavioral view, and as system response output in the constructional view, due to a default function or perhaps a callback in the implementation view.

A storyboard scenario is usually thought of as behavioral, because it depicts a procedure, task, or action performed by the user. On the other hand, a state transition diagram is constructional because it is based on a view of interaction that casts the system in a role of waiting in some state for an input which, when received from the user, causes a state change. In the past the most common interface representation techniques have been constructional [Green 85, Green 86, Hill 87a, Jacob 85a, Jacob 86, Olsen 83, Sibert 88, Wasserman 85, Yunten 85].

Task analysis methods are behavioral and, therefore, have the potential to be used for design representation. However, they were not originally intended for this purpose, and would require some adaptation to be suitable. For example, hierarchical task decomposition used in task analysis does not usually carry procedural or temporal information. Operation sequence diagrams represent only sample instances of interaction. Scenarios are usually employed only informally to get an early impression of look, feel, and behavior, but it is possible that they could be modified to play a more formal part in design representation [Hartson 90a]. Other behavioral representation schemes include GOMS [Card 83], Command Language Grammar [Moran 81], TAG [Green 89], the keystroke model [Card 80], action grammars [Reisner 81], and the work of Kieras and Polson [Kieras 85]. These, however, are intended more for analysis (e.g., predicting user performance of existing designs) than for capturing and communicating designs as they are developed. Nonetheless, some of these techniques have seen some use for behavioral design representation (e.g., GOMS).

## 17.6 The User Action Notation

The User Action Notation (UAN) is a behavioral, user-oriented, task-oriented notation that describes the behavior of the user and the interface during their cooperative performance of a task [Hartson 90b]. The primary abstraction of the UAN is a *user task*. A user interface is represented as a quasi-hierarchical structure of asynchronous tasks, that is, tasks with independent sequencing. User actions, corresponding interface feedback, and state information constitute the lowest level. As actions are composed into tasks at higher levels, abstraction hides these details. At all levels, user actions and tasks are composed via temporal operators which represent sequencing, interleaving, concurrency, and other allowable arrangements of user behaviors in time.

The UAN does not address all aspects of interface design. For instance, it says little about the physical appearance of interface items, and does not necessarily provide a compact representation of interface *modes* (different states of an interactive system in which the same user action has different effects). Other behavioral description techniques, particularly scenarios, storyboards, and task transition diagrams, exist to represent these aspects of the interface. These additional behavioral representation techniques can be used to complement the UAN in a complete behavioral design.

In the realm of description of user behavior, though, the UAN is a powerful tool. The UAN is more concise and precise than natural language, and users report that it is easy to learn to read and write [Hartson 90b]. Its symbols and idioms have been chosen to be mnemonic and intuitive. A simple example will illustrate the basic appearance of UAN behavioral descriptions.

The Macintosh Finder provides a direct manipulation interface to a hierarchical file system. (We choose our examples from Macintosh software because it is perhaps the best known direct manipulation interface. The UAN is by no means restricted to describing Macintosh-style interfaces.) Files are represented by icons, and can be manipulated by corresponding manipulations of the icons. For example, to delete a file, the user drags the file's icon onto another icon representing a trash can ("dragging it into the Trash"). The file's icon disappears, and (eventually, unless it is rescued) the file itself is deleted. We can describe "deleting a file" in prose as:

1. Move the cursor to the icon of the file to be deleted. Press and hold down the mouse button. The file's icon will be highlighted, indicating that the file is selected.

2. With the mouse button held down, move the cursor. An outline of the icon follows the cursor as you move it around.

3. Move the cursor over the Trash icon. The Trash icon will highlight.

4. Release the mouse button. The Trash icon will change (to a "stuffed can"), and the file icon will disappear.

The UAN description of these steps is:

1. ~[file_icon]Mv

2. ~[x,y]*

3. ~[Trash]

4. M^

In the first line, ~[file_icon]Mv indicates moving (~) the cursor into the context of the file icon ([file_icon]) and pressing the mouse button (Mv). In the second line, ~[x,y] indicates moving the cursor to some arbitrary position, and * (Kleene star indicating iterative closure) indicates that this can be repeated any number of times. In the third line, ~[Trash] indicates moving the cursor to the context of the Trash icon, and the fourth line indicates releasing the mouse button.

Of course, this describes only user actions; it provides no indication of feedback, state changes, or connections to non-interface application logic. To represent these aspects of interface behavior, we adopt a tabular representation with four columns, one for each aspect:

| Task: delete a file | | | |
|---|---|---|---|
| User Actions | Interface Feedback | Interface State | Connection to Computation |
| ~[file_icon] Mv | file_icon! | selected = file_icon | |
| ~[x,y]* | outline(file_icon) > ~ | | |
| ~[Trash] | Trash! | | |
| M^ | erase(file_icon); Trash!! | selected = Trash | mark file for deletion |

In the first line, **file_icon!** indicates that the file icon is highlighted (!), and **selected = file_icon** indicates that the interface's notion of "the currently selected object" should be updated to indicate that the file icon is now selected. In the second line, **outline(file_icon) > ~** indicates that an outline of the icon follows (>) the cursor's (~) movement. In the third line, **Trash!** indicates that the Trash icon is highlighted. In the fourth line,

**erase(file_icon)** and **selected** = **Trash** have the expected meanings, and **Trash!!** indicates an alternate highlight (!!) for the Trash icon—in this case, a "stuffed" appearance. **mark file for deletion** in the fourth column indicates an action to be performed outside the interface, and thus serves as a connection to the non-interface part of the application.

## 17.7   Details of the UAN

At the lowest level, as just shown, the UAN describes physical user actions performed with physical devices. The symbols used to represent an interface design depend on the devices the interface uses and the actions the user can perform with them. For example, a button or key can be pressed and released; each action may convey a separate signal, or a single signal may be sent either upon pressing or releasing the button. Devices in this class include mouse buttons, keys on a keyboard, triggers, and "puff and sip" tubes. The symbols v and ˆ are used as shorthand for press and release, respectively. A click, or a press immediately followed by a release, can be represented as **vˆ**, as in **Mvˆ** to indicate a mouse click.

We refer to actions at this level as *primitive user actions*. This does not imply that these actions *can*not be broken down further into subtasks. It is simply a declaration that we *do* not choose to break them down further. In a sense, they form the basic vocabulary of an interface and its UAN description.

As another example of user action with a device, contemporary direct manipulation interfaces usually include some sort of two-dimensional pointer that controls a cursor. User actions that cause *cursor movement* are described in terms of the cursor destination. For example, the user action of moving the cursor to a point (x,y) on the screen is denoted by ˜[x,y]. It does not matter what particular device or user actions are involved in this motion—whether the device used is a mouse or a touch panel, whether the user picks up the mouse during the movement or not. It is possible to break such tasks down further, and the UAN can still be used at those lower levels, but this is usually not of interest to the designer.

It is also important to note that cursor movement is assumed to be *path independent*. Only the destination of the move is important; nothing is stated about intermediate locations the cursor visits. This convention reflects the way in which pointing devices are most often used: the user's perception of the cursor and kinesthetic sense of the pointing device control a feedback loop which allows the user to sense and correct (rather than avoid) positioning errors.

The notation [X] denotes an abstract *context* of item X in the interface. This context is the "handle" by which the object may be selected or manipulated. It may be the object itself, as in the case of an icon, or it may be a grab handle attached to either end of a line segment, or it may be any other finite and recognizable region.

It might seem that since cursor movement is path independent, the common UAN idiom ˜[x,y]* ˜[Item] is redundant. Since path independence means that the cursor can follow any path to the context of Item, "move to any arbitrary position any number of times" is naturally a part of "move to the context of Item." The justification for specifying arbitrary movement before movement to a destination is revealed in the "drag to the Trash" task example above. There are *two* types of feedback for dragging the icon: the outline following the cursor wherever it goes, and the highlighting of the Trash when the cursor is over it. To specify that the outline follows the cursor even before the cursor reaches the context of the Trash, we factor out the arbitrary motion between the icon's original position and its destination, the Trash. Dragging an object is represented by X > ˜ (object X follows the cursor).

The common feedback operation of highlighting an object X is represented by X!, and dehighlighting (removing the highlighting which already exists) by X-!. The exact nature of highlighting is not specified, but is determined elsewhere. Other idioms include X!-! to indicate blinking the highlight and X!! to indicate an alternate form of highlighting.

These low-level vocabulary items can be combined to form higher-level task descriptions. Since direct manipulation interfaces can involve several concurrent or interleaved operations, the UAN provides composition operators to represent these relationships. The most basic temporal relationships, in order of decreasing temporal constraint, are sequential execution, order-independent execution, interruptible execution, interleavable execution, and concurrent execution. These relationships are characterized formally in [Hartson 92].

At every level of abstraction, it is sometimes desirable to state that a task can only be executed when a particular set of conditions is satisfied. In these cases, a *viability condition* can be specified before the first entry in the user action column. This condition consists of a boolean expression followed by a colon. The boolean expression will often refer to interface state, but may also connect to non-interface (computational) parts of the system where necessary.

Figure 17.4 [Hartson 92] summarizes the basic UAN vocabulary.

## 17.8   Example: Dialog Box

As a larger and more interesting example, consider the task of selecting a Macintosh file to be opened. A file is identified by the volume on which it resides, the directory containing it (within the volume's hierarchical file system), its name, and its type. To be able to select any file on any volume, the user must be able to select a volume, a directory on that volume, and a file within that directory. There are several approaches to this task.

In the Macintosh Finder, volumes and directories are represented by icons and windows. Each volume or directory can be **opened** by manipulation of its icon to display a window of its contents; each file or directory (**folder**) it contains is represented by an icon, and the appearance of the icon is determined by the file or directory type. In some development systems, a file can be specified by a textual pathname like those used in command-line-oriented systems. Within an application, though, files are usually selected through a **dialog box** which provides a compact way to display and negotiate volumes, paths, and file lists. It is this latter approach to file specification, specifically as followed by Microsoft Word, which we will examine in detail.

As we have said before, the UAN can be used both in design of new interfaces and in analysis of existing ones. We are not the Word designers, and the UAN was not used to support the design of Word. However, since the thrust of our current discussion involves design, we will pretend for the time being that we are recapitulating the design process followed by human interface workers at Apple and Microsoft. We have had no contact with these workers, and we apologize in advance for any misrepresentations which may ensue.

| Symbol | Meaning |
|---|---|
| ~ | move the cursor |
| [X] | the context of object X, the "handle" by which X is manipulated |
| ~[X] | move cursor into context of object X |
| ~[x,y] | move the cursor to (arbitrary) point x,y outside any object |
| ~[x,y in A] | move the cursor to (arbitrary) point within (relative to) object A |
| ~[X in Y] | move to object X within object Y (e.g., [OK_icon in dialog_box]) |
| [X]~ | move cursor out of context of object X |
| v | depress |
| ^ | release |
| Xv | depress button, key, or switch called X |
| X ^ | release button, key, or switch X |
| Xv^ | idiom for clicking button, key, or switch X |
| X"abc" | enter literal string, abc, via device X |
| X(xyz) | enter value for variable xyz via device X |
| ( ) | grouping mechanism |
| * | iterative closure, task is performed zero or more times |
| + | task is performed one or more times |
| { } | enclosed task is optional (performed zero or one time) |
| OR, I | disjunction, choice of tasks (used to show alternative ways to perform a task) |
| : | separator between condition and action or feedback |
| A B | task A and B are performed in order left to right, or top to bottom |
| A (t > n) B | task B is performed after a delay of more than n units of time following task A |
| (A I B)* | choice of A or B is performed to completion, followed by another choice of A or B, etc. |
| A & B | tasks A and B are order independent (order of performance is immaterial) |
| A → B | task A can interrupt task B |
| A ⇒ B | task A is one-way interleavable with B (A can interrupt B and execute, but not vice versa) |
| A ⇔ B | task A and task B are (mutually) interleavable |
| A ‖ B | task A and task B can be performed concurrently |

| Feedback | Meaning |
|---|---|
| ! | highlight object |
| -! | dehighlight object |
| !! | same as !, but use an alternative highlight |
| !-! | blink highlight |
| $(!-!)^n$ | blink highlight n times |
| @x,y | at point x,y |
| @X | at object X |
| @x,y in X | at point x,y in (relative to) object X |
| display(X) | display object X |
| erase(X) | erase object X |
| outline(X) | outline of object X |
| X > ~ | object X follows (is dragged by) cursor |
| X >> ~ | object X is rubber-banded as it follows cursor |

Figure 17.4: Summary of some useful UAN symbols.

Figure 17.5 shows the MS Word Open... dialog box. (We call it Open... because the menu choice which can be used to invoke it has that name.) It provides a display of the current volume, the current directory, and the contents of the current directory, as well as some other information. It serves as an *arena* in which tasks associated with selecting a file can be performed. These tasks include specifying a volume, a directory, an individual file, and the type of file access desired.

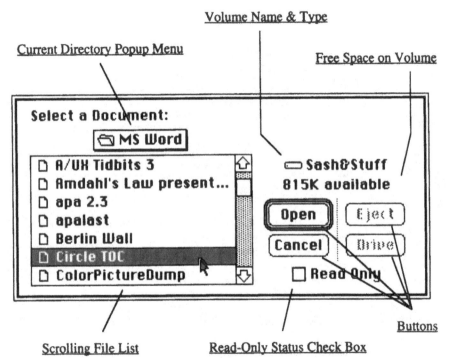

Figure 17.5: The Microsoft Word Open... dialog box.

It would be possible to prompt the user for a volume, then a directory, then a file name, but this violates several design principles. It makes the user do extra work when one or more of these values is unchanged from some default or previous value; it makes it harder to provide small, incremental, reversible steps for completing the task; and it fails to support or take advantage of the perceptual abilities of the user in conjunction with the Macintosh's display capabilities. It is possible to present information about all three values at the same time, starting with reasonable initial values, without confusion. And given this presentation, it is reasonable to allow the user to move among subtasks in whatever order is convenient. This determines the UAN representation of the highest-level task associated with the dialog box:

| Task: Use Open Dialog Box | | | |
|---|---|---|---|
| **User Actions** | **Interface Feedback** | **Interface State** | **Connection to Computation** |
| (Select Volume<br>I Select Directory<br>I Select File<br>I Specify Read-Only Status)* | | | |
| Confirm<br>I Cancel | hide dialog box | restore previous focus | pass along file name or cancellation notice |

The user can perform the volume, directory, file, and status specification tasks any number of times, in any order. Then, performing the Confirm or Cancel task terminates the Use Open Dialog Box task. Note that for the four tasks composed in the first row, the feedback, state, and computation columns are empty; feedback, state, and computational information for these tasks will be represented in their respective expansions.

This is not a complete list of tasks associated with the dialog box at the highest level. We omit some subtasks that can be associated with opening a file. For example, non-Word files ordinarily do not show up in the list of files which can be opened; there is a way to make these files appear. In our research work we have described these tasks without difficulty using the UAN, but there is not enough space here to elaborate them. For the same reason, we will fully expand only one subtask: Select Volume.

The Select Volume task should allow the user to specify different volumes—disks or other devices on which files reside. As part of this task, the user should be able to eject diskettes and insert new ones. Since there are typically only a few volumes available at one time, it is acceptable to provide an operation for stepping through them in sequence, rather than presenting them all in a list (although some users of today's hardware environments might argue this point). Composing these three tasks, which again may be performed any number of times in any order, yields:

| Task: Select Volume | | | |
|---|---|---|---|
| **User Actions** | **Interface Feedback** | **Interface State** | **Connection to Computation** |
| (Shift to Next Volume I Eject Current Volume I Insert New Volume) * | | | |

Again, feedback and other information will be provided in the expansions of these tasks.

It is necessary to provide some means to specify a shift to the next volume, ejection of the current volume, or insertion of a new volume. Since inserting a diskette is sufficient to invoke (in fact, carry out!) the insertion task, and since the other two tasks represent single events, it is reasonable to provide a button for changing volumes and a button for ejecting the current volume. It is also desirable to provide keyboard shortcuts for actions triggered by screen buttons; we will indicate these shortcuts as well in the task descriptions for Shift to Next Volume and Eject Current Volume. Most configurations of the Macintosh cannot handle diskette insertion through software, so there is no keyboard shortcut for that task.

| Task: Shift to Next Volume | | | |
|---|---|---|---|
| **User Actions** | **Interface Feedback** | **Interface State** | **Connection to Computation** |
| more_volumes_available: trigger_button(Drive button) I click_key(D) | display name, icon and free space of new volume (Figure 17.5) | current volume = next available volume | get next available volume and its info |

The viability condition on this task states that it can only take place if there is more than one volume available. If this condition is not true, the Drive button will not function, and it will be "greyed out" to provide a visual indication that it is disabled. (In fact, this is the state of the Drive button in Figure 17.5.) The logic for setting the state of this button will be specified in the Eject and Insert tasks, which are the only ones that can change the pertinent system state.

The feedback column specifies informally that the name of the new volume and an icon indicating its type should be displayed in the proper position in the dialog box. The actual layout of the information is shown in Figure 17.5; as stated here and in other chapters, a picture is sometimes much better suited than a textual language for description of this sort of layout information. (A picture is worth a thousand page layout commands.)

The screen picture complements the UAN description by portraying the appearance of interface elements; the UAN description complements the screen picture by specifying precisely what each element represents and when and how it changes.

The notion of "current volume" has meaning to the interface, and so it is updated as part of the interface state specification. It may be necessary to consult with non-interface code to obtain information about the "next volume," and that is indicated in the last column.

**Task:** Eject Current Volume

| User Actions | Interface Feedback | Interface State | Connection to Computation |
|---|---|---|---|
| current_volume_ejectable: trigger_button(Eject button) I click_key(E) | display name, icon and free space of new volume; if new volume NOT ejectable then grey out Eject button; if not more than one available volume then grey out Drive button | current volume = next available volume | eject volume; get next available volume and its info |

The Eject Current Volume task is only viable if the current volume can be ejected from its drive. If it can be, the volume is ejected, and the next available volume becomes the current volume. (We avoid for brevity the case in which there there are no available volumes—a system with no fixed drive, for example.) An appeal to non-interface facilities is necessary to perform the actual ejection. If the new current volume is not ejectable, the Eject button is greyed. Further, since the viability condition for this task would no longer be satisfied, the E-key shortcut would also be disabled. Similarly, if there remains only one available volume, the Drive button will be greyed (since toggling among one volume is dull at best).

**Task:** Insert New Volume

| User Actions | Interface Feedback | Interface State | Connection to Computation |
|---|---|---|---|
| drive_available: choose diskette and insert it into drive | display name, icon and free space of new volume; ungrey Eject button; if more than one available volume then ungrey Drive button | current volume = new volume | get info from new volume |

The Insert New Volume task requires a precondition because a diskette can only be inserted if there is an empty drive available. If there is, then inserting the diskette makes its contents available as a new volume. This volume automatically becomes the current volume, so that the user does not have to use the Shift to Next Volume task to get to a diskette's contents once it is inserted.

A designer *could* use the UAN to break down the task of "choosing a diskette" (and, for that matter, inserting the diskette into the drive). This sort of user activity is not generally considered to be within the domain of the interface; but because it is behavioral activity, it can be represented with a UAN-style table, even though it would not use any of the standard UAN notation. Further analysis of these sorts of tasks may sometimes be important; for example, a task that required the user to hold down keys on opposite ends of the keyboard while inserting a diskette would be easy to specify, but very difficult to perform.

It should be mentioned that these subtasks that make up the Select Volume task can also be used in other tasks—even some tasks the interface designer might not have considered. For example, the user might learn to use these operations as a "find a floppy with enough space" task, which would involve repetitively inserting a floppy, checking the "space available" indication, and ejecting it if it is too nearly full. Formative evaluation might recognize this task, integrate it into the task description for the interface, and perhaps provide some shortcuts to make the task easier.

The trigger_button and click_key tasks can be expressed in terms of primitive user actions:

| Task: click_key(key) | | | |
|---|---|---|---|
| User Actions | Interface Feedback | Interface State | Connection to Computation |
| key v^ | none | | |

| Task: trigger_button(button) | | | |
|---|---|---|---|
| User Actions | Interface Feedback | Interface State | Connection to Computation |
| NOT button!!: | | | |
| ~[button] | | | |
| Mv | button! | | |
| ( | | | |
| [button]~ | button-! | | |
| ~[button] | button! | | |
| )* | | | |
| M^ | button-! | | do action for (button) |

Here, **button!!** represents the greying highlight which indicates that a button is disabled. The task involves more than simply "clicking on the button" because it is possible to move the cursor outside the button while the mouse button is pressed. If the cursor is moved back into the screen button's context before the mouse button is released, the task completes; otherwise, if the mouse button is released while the cursor is outside the button's context, the task does not complete.

This is obviously far from a complete description of the dialog box. The full description—including the Select Directory task, the Select File task, and their interaction with the scrolling file list and directory popup menu—is very much larger than this. This is a simple reflection of the fact that there is really a great deal of complexity in this interaction design—a design should be as simple as possible, but no simpler. Our experience, and that of others, indicates that the UAN allows a more concise, precise, and understandable representation than natural language. And since it is behaviorally oriented, the UAN is inherently better suited for *interaction* design than are traditional *software* design languages.

## 17.9   The Need for Design

It is said that "real programmers can write Fortran in any language." Similarly, we might say that "real interface programmers can implement **vi** (or the user affront of your choice) in any software environment." It is important for us to create languages and environments that better support the design and implementation of user interfaces. But the only way to ensure that the resulting interfaces are truly usable is to place the *design* of those interfaces in the hands of *designers*—people who know about people—and provide a means of communication between these interaction designers and the software designers who actually bring the interface to life. Behavioral representation techniques in general, and the UAN in particular, are an important step toward this goal.

# Acknowledgements

The authors thank Dr. Antonio C. Siochi, the proud father of the UAN and other remarkable children. We also thank the National Science Foundation, which is funding the continuation of this research.

*Syntax*

# Chapter 18

# Hints on the Design of User Interface Language Features—Lessons from the Design of Turing

*James R. Cordy*

## 18.1   Introduction

The Turing programming language [Holt 83, Holt 88a, Holt 88b] is a general-purpose programming language designed at the University of Toronto. Designed to be a successor to Pascal, Turing resolves many of the perceived difficulties with Pascal such as the lack of string handling facilities, type-safe variant records, modularity, concurrency, and type-safe separate compilation. Turing is intended to combine the conciseness and simplicity of Basic at the lowest level with the power to implement real production software at the highest. The goal was to design a language that can serve the entire range of programming tasks, all the way from a teaching language for children to production software tasks such as compilers, operating systems, and complex user interfaces. To the extent that it has met these goals, there is much to be learned from the design of Turing about how other languages can be designed to be simple, concise, and expressive while at the same time providing great power and complexity.

## 18.2  Turing

Turing is designed to include the best features of modern systems programming languages such as Euclid [Lampson 77] in a convenient general-purpose programming language.

Turing was explicitly designed to resolve many of the perceived difficulties with Pascal. For example, Turing provides convenient string handling, it provides modules, it has type-safe variant records (called unions), dynamic parameters and arrays, concurrency, exception handlers and type-safe separate compilation. Turing has been described as simpler than BASIC at the lowest level, while at the same time more powerful than Modula for the experienced programmer.

Turing is designed to be a general-purpose language, meaning that it is potentially the language of choice for a wide class of applications. As a result, it includes general-purpose features such as convenient floating point arithmetic, powerful string manipulation, and easy to use simple and formatted stream input/output.

Turing is designed to be well suited for teaching programming. It has a no-frills syntax that is simple, concise, and readable while at the same time highly expressive. It is easy to learn, use, and teach, and is designed to be at home in the interactive environment.

The hints below describe some of the design techniques used to aid in the achievement of these seemingly conflicting goals, give concrete examples of the effect these techniques have had on the design of Turing, and make observations about how these techniques can be applied in the design of language features appropriate for aiding in the construction of complex graphical user interfaces.

## 18.3  Achieving Conciseness

One of the areas in which the goal of ease of learning most affected the language is in the area of syntax. Turing is designed to have a concise, "streamlined" syntax which avoids wordiness. As observed by [Weinberg 71], the compactness of the notation used to express a program can have a great effect on its perceived complexity, even if the algorithm expressed is inherently very simple. It is surprising that, in this age when the importance of a really well engineered user interface is so universally acknowledged, language designers continue to ignore the importance of good syntax, often brushing it off as "just syntactic sugar."

The design of Turing achieves a tight conciseness through the use of several techniques. The first, perhaps most obvious (hence most often overlooked) of these is the simple *avoidance of syntactically redundant symbols* whenever possible.

For example, the use of program headers such as the "program" in Pascal has been avoided. A simple program to output the word "hi" is written in Turing as:

```
put "hi"
```

Contrast this with Pascal, in which the same program is written as :

```
program   P (output);
begin
     writeln ('hi')
end.
```

Another example is the lack of semicolons or other punctuation between statements in Turing. While this may seem a trivial point, one of the acknowledged problems with Pascal is the difficulty in remembering the rules for the placement of semicolons. For example, although statements in Pascal are generally followed by a semicolon the final end is required to be followed by a period instead. Turing avoids this kind of problem by not requiring semicolons or other punctuation following statements at all. Unlike BASIC, Turing does not require physical line boundaries between statements either, and thus retains the free-format properties of Pascal as well.

This avoidance of redundancy can be extended to the semantic domain as well. For example, a variable declaration which has an initial value has no need for a type specification because the type must obviously be the type of the value. This leads to a much more concise, readable form of declaration which has the additional advantage that it encourages initialization as well. For example:

```
var i := 1
var s := "hi there"
```

In each case the type of the declared variable is inherited from its initial value. In the realm of user interface specification, we can imagine using a syntax in which the attributes of a complex interactive graphical object, such as a window and all its associated handling methods, could be cloned in a similarly straightforward way:

```
var  redRectangle  := blueRectangle
redRectangle.color (red)
var  editWindow2 := editWindow1
```

In the first example, *i* is of course of type **int** and *s* is of type **string**. Of course, an explicit type specification could have been given in either case, for example, to restrict *i* to an integer subrange:

```
var  i : 0 .. 10 := 1
```

Which leads us to the second major way of achieving conciseness, *avoiding detail through the use of optional information and defaults.* This goal is much more difficult than it sounds and involves considerable use of user feedback and statistical analysis to get it right (and if you get it wrong it can be disastrous!)

In Turing, the statistically most common case is typically the default, with options ordered by decreasing frequency of use. For example, the "put" statement of Turing was designed to capture all of the power of PL/I formatted output while retaining the simplicity and elegance of BASIC's free-format output. The following four put statements output the value of the real variable *r* with increasing constraints on the output format:

```
put r          % outputs value in simplest form, no
               % blanks, e.g., 42
put r:10       % outputs value right justified in a
               % field of width 10, e.g., bbbbbbbb42
put r:10:2     % outputs value right justified in a
               % field of width 10 with 2 digits to
               % the right of the decimal point
               % e.g., bbbbb42.00
put r:10:2:2   % outputs value right justified in a
               % field of width 10 with 2 digits to
               % the right of the decimal point
               % and a 2 digit exponent
               % e.g., bb42.00e00
```

This example also points out the use of *extensional syntax* (i.e., consistently using the : as a marker for further detail) rather than traditional bracketed syntax. This again helps achieve a conciseness and enhances the perceived simplicity of the notation.

Moreover, extensional syntax plays an important part in the effective use of options because it allows the casual user to be blissfully unaware of the detailed options which are not of interest at his or her user level. This will be even more important when referring to user interface concepts, where, for example, the user who simply wants to create a simple blue rectangle moving across the screen will not want to be bothered with the many other detailed attributes that a rectangle (or indeed a region, window, or display) might have.

## 18.4 Consistency

It has been said that "consistency is the mark of a small mind," but lack of consistency is also a major indicator of psychological complexity. Psychologists tell us that the perceived complexity of a system is inversely proportional to the number of exceptions to the rules of the system. In language design, this means that "rules" of the language, whether syntactic or semantic, should be as consistent as possible. This observation leads to several design rules that help achieve a consistent design.

*Syntactic consistency* is perhaps the simplest of these to achieve. Simply put, it means that, as much as possible, similar concepts should use similar notation in a similar way. An example in Turing is the consistent use of the phrase "end X" to close each construct "X," which applies consistently throughout the language, as in **if..end if, case..end case, loop..end loop, for..end for, record..end record, union..end union,** and so on. (Note that these consistent structuring brackets also serve to reduce syntax by making **begin .. end** blocks almost entirely redundant in Turing.) The only exceptions to the rule are **begin..end, procedure** P **.. end** P, and **module** M **.. end** M, which differ for traditional reasons too strong to ignore.

*Orthogonality* is another way of achieving consistency of design. Simply put, orthogonality insists that different features should as much as possible be independent of each other. In the Turing design, syntactic orthogonality is readily evident in the different levels of abstraction, statements, procedures, and modules. The construction rule for the next level of abstraction is always the same: simply enclose the existing source text in the brackets for the next level, for example any sequence of declarations and statements in a procedure, and any sequence of declarations, statements, and procedures in a module.

A more striking example of the use of orthogonality to achieve consistency is the *position independence* of sequences of declarations and statements in Turing, which gives a very simple code construction rule. For example, the sequence of declarations and statements:

```
var fahrenheit :    real
get fahrenheit
const celcius : =  (fahrenheit - 32)  *  5/9
put celcius
```

can be made conditional by simply embedding it directly in an if:

if *temperatureCalculationDesired* then

```
var fahrenheit :    real
get fahrenheit
const celcius : =  (fahrenheit - 32)  *  5/9
put celcius
```

end if

repeated by embedding it verbatim in a loop:

loop
    exit when *eof*

```
var fahrenheit :    real
get fahrenheit
const celcius : =  (fahrenheit - 32)  *  5/9
put celcius
```

end loop

or abstracted by simply embedding it in a procedure:

**procedure** *convert*

```
var fahrenheit :    real
get fahrenheit
const celcius  : =  (fahrenheit - 32) * 5/9
put celcius
```

**end** *convert*

Other examples of consistency in the Turing design include the legality of all types in all contexts, for example, as array elements, parameters to procedures and result values of functions, the use of the identical keywords **get, put, read, write,** and **seek** to describe file opening modes in **open** statement as are used in the input/output statements of those modes themselves, and consistent use of parentheses as mapping brackets in function calls, array subscripts, and collection pointer dereferences.

In the context of user interface features, the need for consistency and orthogonality is even greater since the number of distinct concepts is so inherently large. The careful splitting and layering of user interface handling features into orthogonal subsets will be a difficult but very important design task.

## 18.5 Locality

Psychology also tells us that perceived complexity can be reduced by grouping related things physically close to one another, and avoiding remote references whenever possible. This is the *principle of locality*, and is reflected in the design of Turing by the removal of the distinction between statements and declarations, and the introduction of run-time values for constants.

Even though Turing retains the traditional declaration-before-use, static strong typing and nested block scoping rules of Pascal, and the change is a purely syntactic one, declarations in Turing conceptually act like executable statements that dynamically introduce a new symbol until the end of the scope. This is the model in the mind of the Turing programmer, and removes the distinction between declarations and statements, thus reducing the total number of concepts in the language and yielding a greater perceived simplicity.

Declarations as statements increases locality of Turing programs by allowing sequences of statements to locally capture whole semantic concepts, rendering them portable (as we saw in the position independence example) and easy to remember. For example, the sequence of statements:

**const** *temp* := *x*
*x* := *y*
*y* := *temp*

is legal at any point in a Turing program, is independent of context, and completely captures the concept of a swap of two variable values, no matter what their type or internal structure. The **const** statement declares a new constant with the type and value of the variable x. In Pascal, this kind of local conceptual chunking is simply impossible because of the necessity of remotely declaring "temp" as an artificially global variable and explicitly typing it.

Declarations as statements also encourages naming of anonymous but meaningful intermediate expressions. For example, the Pascal statement:

*writeln ( round ( fahrenheit*-32) *5/9) ) ;

can be written in Turing as:

**const** *celcius* := *round ( fahrenheit*-32) *5/9)
**put** *celcius*

Other examples of locality in the Turing design include the fact that every language construct, including loops, the **then** and **else** clauses of **if** statements, and each alternative of a **case** statement automatically introduces a new scope. This keeps the scope of declaration of local variables and constants very small and local and avoids the distracting wordiness of **begin** ... **end** statements.

One of the failures of existing general-purpose user interface toolsets such as X and its windowing packages is the inability to do this sort of local abstraction, even when the language supports it. In these packages it is often necessary to refer to remote and even hidden library symbols frequently even in simple drawing applications. The user interfaces themselves, on the other hand, normally are structured such that operations happen very locally, for example to one particular window or object, and such objects each have their own local environment on the screen. A good design for user interface language features would reflect these natural locality properties of the objects themselves in the source code that manages them.

## 18.6   Define-by-Example

Another way of achieving a good measure of "naturalness" in a language design is by liberal use of the *define-by-example style*. We have already seen in the syntax of Turing variable and constant declarations an example of this style in the Turing design, in which the type of a variable or constant is inferred from an example of the kind of value that the variable is to hold, as in:

**var**  $x := 1$

Another example is the consistency of the syntax of formal parameter declarations in Turing, which is identical to the syntax of the corresponding variable and function declarations. For example, a procedure that takes a variable and a function as parameters might be declared as:

**procedure** P ( **var** x : **int, function** f (x : **real**) : **real**)

where the syntax of the formal parameters "**var** x : int" and "**function** f (x : **real**) : **real**" are identically syntactic examples of the declarations of arguments that can be passed to the procedure. In addition, the choice of commas rather than the semicolons of Pascal in the formal parameter list is another example of the define-by-example guideline, since all calls to the procedure will also use commas to separate arguments.

Define-by-example is also the flavor of the simple but powerful stream output statement of Turing, the **put** statement. Like all features of Turing, the **put** statement is designed such that the most common cases have the simplest and most concise syntax. This implies, for example, that the default is for the put statement to output an entire line rather than just part of one. In Pascal and PL/I, the default is to output only parts of lines. If the user wishes to output an end-of-line as well, he must explicitly say so in addition to giving the values to be output. (In Pascal, he must use

*writeln* instead of *write*, in **PL/I**, **put skip** instead of simply **put**.) If the
Turing programmer wishes to continue output on the same line (a much
less common case), then he says so explicitly using the continuation marker
".." at the end of the put statement. For example:

```
put "The value of x is : ", x
```

will output a complete line, whereas:

```
put "The value of x is : " ..
```

says that the program will output more on this same output line.

Unlike BASIC and Pascal, Turing default output does not put any
spaces around output items unless they are explicitly specified. Thus
Turing has the property that output statements form an example "template"
for the output line they create. So, for example, the statement:

```
put "The value of x is ", x,
        " and the value of y is ", y
```

simply and completely defines every character to appear on the output line.
There is no question in the programmer's mind about spacing or formatting
since it is explicitly given.

In the context of language features for user interfaces, the most important opportunity for define-by-example is the definition of graphical objects
in the language. It is clear that directly drawing an example of the object
that you would like to see on the screen is simpler and more intuitive than
trying to define it indirectly through its mathematical attributes or generating functions. As evidenced by the many mixed mode tools such as
MacWrite, Framemaker, and Interleaf on the market that allow graphical
objects directly in the text, there is no reason that our language features
should not include the direct insertion of graphical objects into the program
itself, and I would encourage the use of this technique to impart a natural
show-by-example flavor to the user interface features of the language.

## 18.7   Basic Types

One of the most powerful ways of providing clarity and brevity in a language is by the *appropriate choice of basic built-in abstractions* such as

types. In the case of Turing, the most striking example of this is the inclusion of the varying length **string** data type and its operations as primitives of the language. As for most general-purpose languages, it was expected that upwards of 80% of the programs written in Turing would be primarily text-handling rather than number-handling applications. Pascal and its successors, with the exception of Modula-3, fail miserably in this regard, forcing users to deal with shovelling characters about to achieve even the simplest concatenation or substring operation on text. In Turing, the basic string operations are built in, and text-handling algorithms are clearer, shorter, and much less bug prone as a result. For example:

```
const sentence := ''Algorithms are much less bug
                   prone as a result.''
const muchpos := index (sentence, "much")
put sentence (1 .. muchpos - 1)
            + sentence (muchpos + length ("much")
            + 1 .. *)
```

outputs the sentence with the overused word "much" removed from it.

In the context of features for user interface programming, it is clear that at least some basic types for graphical objects should be built in to the language, and much thought should be given to the set of the most common operations on such objects in the hope of notationally building these operations into the language.

## 18.8 Conclusion

We have outlined only a few of the basic design principles that were used to achieve a measure of conciseness, expressiveness, and readability in the design of the Turing language while retaining great power in the notation. Other principles used included *layering*, which refers to designing features in such a way that more complex, structured features for programming-in-the-large build upon the previous simpler features in layers of expected expertise such that the user of the language at any one level need not be aware of the higher levels at all, and perhaps the most important design tool of all, *user feedback*, which tells us that we should not arbitrarily freeze a language design before we have extensive experience with its use in practice and have redesigned in response. In the case of Turing, the design was tuned by user feedback for more than three years before finalizing it.

We have tried to demonstrate some of the design principles that have been successful in rationalizing the relatively successful design of Turing. In retrospect, the design criteria and their effect on the design may make the process seem easy and obvious. Nothing could be further from the truth. The design of a new programming language, and even more so new language features, is a difficult and time consuming task for which there are no right answers. The design criteria often conflict and the choice of the right compromises is anything but straightforward. In the end, like the design of good user interfaces, it requires a rare combination of psychology, linguistics, mathematics, intuition, artistry, and experience that only the user community can really teach us about.

# Part 3
# Workshop Reports

# Chapter 19

# Report of the "End-User Programming" Working Group

*Brad A. Myers*
*David Canfield Smith*
*Bruce Horn*

The "End-User Programming" Working Group consisted of:

Alan Borning (University of Washington)
Jeffrey L. Brandenburg (Virginia Tech)
Michael Dertouzos (Massachusetts Institute of Technology)
Bruce Horn (Carnegie Mellon University)
Scott Hudson (University of Arizona)
Brad A. Myers (Carnegie Mellon University)
David Canfield Smith (Apple Computer, Inc.)
Randall Smith (Sun Microsystems Laboratories, Inc.)

## 19.1  Introduction

As the number of computer users in the world continues to grow—
approaching 100 million—the task of providing software for them grows

343

too. It is reminiscent of the problem facing the phone companies in the 1930s. They projected that at the current rates of growth, by the end of the century the switchboards would be miles long and they would have to employ every female in the country to work them. The solution was to make telephone users become their own operators, leading to the development of dial phones and telephone directories. It worked; the number of switchboard operators per capita has been drastically reduced.

Today we have a few thousand software developers trying to supply software for millions of computer users. It's not working. The generic software that results delivers to users only a fraction of the potential utility and power of personal computers. The solution is to make computer users become their own programmers. *There is no other way for users to exploit the full potential of personal computers.*

Obviously there are gigantic hurdles to making this happen, much larger than those faced by the phone companies. But back in the days of punched cards and JCL, there were equally big hurdles in *ever* getting a large number of people to be able to use computers. The solution to that problem was to improve the human–computer interface. This has worked so well that it's hard to imagine millions of people using computers without today's graphical user interfaces. In fact, it has spawned an entire branch of computer science. Similarly, we need to improve the user interface to programming if we hope to make it pervasive.

It's ironic that today the applications that personal computer developers write mostly follow good user interface principles, principles that have been tested and refined during the past decade. But the *process* of programming those applications does not follow those principles; the process has changed little since the 1960s. We suggest that what is needed now is for programmers to apply good user interface principles to the programming process. Only in that way will programming become accessible to a large number of people.

## 19.2   Two Kinds of End-User Programming

We discuss two signficantly different kinds of end-user programming. One, as promoted in Chapters 2 and 3, involves connecting pre-defined modules together. The other kind is embodied in HyperCard and spreadsheets

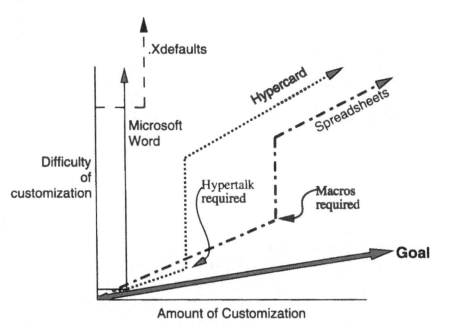

Figure 19.1: How hard is it to achieve various levels of customization in different systems?

which allow the end user to construct programs from low-level primitives. Ideally, you would like to combine both approaches, so that the end user could attach modules together, but if the modules did not perform the desired functions, then they could be "opened up" and programmed at a more detailed level.

One way to look at end-user programming is as a way to allow the users to *significantly customize* the system. For example, spreadsheets allow the user to create their own financial applications that handle the specific problem the user has in mind. Figure 19.1 attempts to give a feeling for how hard it is to customize some of today's systems.

What the figure is trying to get across is that different systems provide various levels of customization or programmability, but at some point, the user finds no further customizations are possible, or that significant new techniques are required. In Microsoft Word for the Macintosh, the user can fairly easily change the menus and keyboard accelerators for commands, but no other changes are possible. The .Xdefaults mechanism is much harder to use and is also quite limited. It allows menus, colors, and sizes to be set for various X/11 applications. In HyperCard, many things are easy to do by direct manipulation, but to do more, the user must learn the HyperTalk programming language. Similarly, with spreadsheets, at some point the user must learn the macro language. The particular scale on the diagram is clearly open to debate, but the general goal of decreasing the amount of effort required, without having the "wall" where there is a sharp bend upwards in the graph, should be clear.

## 19.3   A Few Good Interfaces

A good methodology for improving the programming interface or any interface is to look at some successful examples, distill the essence of their success, and try to apply it to the new domain. Some very powerful systems are widely used because of their excellent human interfaces. Six of our favorites are Lego blocks, spreadsheet programs, the Star/Macintosh interface, MacPaint, HyperCard, and video games.

### 19.3.1   Legos

We'll start with a product that doesn't even involve computers: Lego bricks, those tiny plastic blocks that snap together. Why is it that millions of children (and many adults) all over the world love Legos? There are important reasons that can serve as lessons to a variety of product developers:

small learning cost – One can start using Legos immediately. Legos do not require training or reading manuals.

small number of fixed interfaces – Almost everything plugs into everything else.

versatile – One can build millions of interesting things from a small number of block types.

instant gratification – People get immediate results when they snap bricks together. As soon as they connect two bricks, they have built something.

incremental planning – Little planning is needed with Legos. Designs *evolve*. This further reduces the start-up cost of building things.

kinesthetic experience – Jerome Bruner has identified three mentalities involved in thinking and learning: "enactive" (kinesthetic experience), "iconic" (visual experience), and "symbolic" (textual experience) [Bruner 66]. Legos allow users to involve their enactive (bodies) and iconic (3D objects) mentalities in construction, thereby using more of their minds.

transparent – Lego constructions are like glass boxes; all the inner workings, gears, etc. are visible to users. By contrast, computers today are pretty much "black boxes" whose workings are opaque to users.

examples supplied – Both on the cover and in enclosed instructions, every Lego set shows examples of what can be built with the pieces in the set. Note that these are not the same as typical training materials, which are generic; Lego instructions are for concrete, specific toys.

ease and speed of assembly – In the 1950s, many children used Erector Sets consisting of steel beams and nuts and bolts. Today Legos have essentially wiped out Erector Sets because it is so much quicker to build things with Legos. With Erector Sets, each joint required a nut and bolt, a time consuming screw-in-the-bolt process, and a high degree of frustration as one inevitably dropped the nut into an unreachable place. With Legos, it takes less than a second to snap two blocks together, and there are no nuts and bolts to drop.

no serious errors – Everything that is built with Legos is "correct" in the sense that it is a functioning construction whose pieces all fit together. It may not be what the user intended, but at least it does not "crash" or "trap to the debugger." The mistakes that people make are easy to undo and change.

safe – Since one can't make serious errors, Legos provide a safe environment for exploration.

fun – Building things out of Legos is fun, for all of the reasons listed
above. People spend more time on tasks they enjoy than on tasks
they don't.

### 19.3.2   Spreadsheets

Spreadsheets exhibit many of the characteristics listed above for Legos,
as indeed do all of these examples. However rather than repeat the same
characteristics for each example, we'll concentrate on new ones that were
not previously listed. It's an interesting exercise for the reader to consider
which of the characteristics listed here apply to the different examples and,
when they don't, why not. Perhaps stronger products would result if they
adhered to more of these characteristics.

visibility – The entire state of the computation is visible and available for
manipulation. There is no hidden state.

interactive – Spreadsheets are continuously evaluated, so that the computation is always up-to-date. This makes it easy to spot mistakes.

locality – The user's focus is normally on a small region: a cell. At any
one moment, the user's task is just to get a single cell correct. This
is a simpler task than dealing with a program as a whole.

modeless – There are few persistent modes that change the behavior of
the system.

no side effects – A cell cannot affect the value of any other cell directly; it
can only change its own value. Thus spreadsheet cells may be said to
"pull" the values of other cells into their computations; by contrast,
objects in an object-oriented programming language "push" values
at other objects via messages. This is a fundamental difference.

no explicit control structures – There are no conditionals or user-defined
subroutines. Functions may be invoked, but only predefined ones.
Iteration is done interactively, via successive updates. Studies show
that people have trouble with control structures [Shneiderman 80].

no explicit sequencing – Each spreadsheet cell is a separate computation independent (from the writer's point of view) of the order in which other cells are evaluated. The system is responsible for figuring out the optimal order of computation. Other studies have shown that some people even have trouble with sequences of steps.

levels of complexity – Using cell formulas is easy, but they are somewhat limited in their capabilities. Spreadsheet macros are considerably richer but also more difficult to use. This combination is an effective realization of Alan Kay's maxim: "simple things should be simple; complex things should be possible" [Kay 84].

few data types, cells are untyped – Spreadsheets use only a small number of data types: numbers, text, dates, booleans, sometimes a couple of others. Cells may hold any data type. An enormous range of computations may be produced from this small set of primitive types; in this respect spreadsheets are analogous to Legos.

user's conceptual model – The visual representation of a spreadsheet matches the user's natural model in many domains. Spreadsheets existed on paper long before they were implemented on computers.

"smart" assistance – Copying rows and columns automatically adjusts the formulas in the copied cells appropriately. This almost always gives users what they want.

multiple views – Cells may be viewed as values, as formulas, or as graphs. Different views are appropriate for different tasks. This gives spreadsheets great representational power.

### 19.3.3    Xerox Star / Apple Macintosh User Interface

The Xerox Star introduced and the Apple Macintosh popularized the concept of a graphical user interface in which computer resources are represented as small pictures or "icons." The images used are those of objects commonly found in an office: documents, folders, file cabinets, mailboxes, printers, calendars, etc. This interface has been adopted by all major personal computer and workstation manufacturers. Here are a few of the reasons for its success:

desktop metaphor – By representing computer resources as familiar office objects, the manipulation of the resources is taken out of the domain of the computer professional and put into the world of the office worker/home owner. This drastically reduces the unfamiliarity of the computer environment.

generic commands – A few commands are utilized by all application programs on the computers. In Star, the commands were Move, Copy, Delete, Show Properties, Copy Properties, Undo, Again, Help; in the Macintosh, the commands are Cut, Copy, Paste, Undo. These commands are not only implemented in all applications but apply to most objects in each application as well. This uniformity simplifies the system without reducing its power, and it reduces the learning burden on users working with multiple applications.

noun–verb interaction – Both computers adopted a style of command execution in which the operand of the command is specified first and then the command is invoked. This reduces the modalness of verb-first command systems, allows multiple operands to be specified, and makes it easy to apply generic commands.

few commands, many objects – Noun–verb interaction together with generic commands encourages the formation of systems having many objects on which to operate (the "nouns") and relatively few actions (the "verbs"). This mirrors natural languages, in which the great majority of words are always nouns. Nouns are the data; verbs are the data transformations, and therefore verbs represent much of the complexity of systems.

data interchange – The Macintosh introduced both the concept of the "clipboard" and the notion of clipboard-standard data types. This pioneered a new level of interoperability among personal computer applications.

direct manipulation – In a graphical user interface, most (ideally all) elements controllable by users are visible on a display screen. When objects are visible, they can be manipulated directly by concrete pointing actions, rather than indirectly by symbolic designation. People find direct actions to be easier.

### 19.3.4  MacPaint

what you see is what you get – The great appeal of MacPaint is its simple directness. There is only one data structure: bits on the screen. The user's sole goal is to turn bits on and off to produce the desired image. All tools have this as their function. And the entire state of the image is always visible on the screen; there is literally nothing to remember.

concrete tools – All tools in MacPaint either look like the physical objects that they emulate—e.g., pencil, paint brush, eraser—or the objects that they produce—e.g., line, rectangle, oval. This concreteness reduces the learning and remembering burdens on the user.

### 19.3.5  HyperCard

directness – One of the reasons for HyperCard's remarkable success is the directness with which users can obtain the desired appearance for their cards and stacks. Painting tools can be used directly on cards, since cards are canvases. Buttons and fields can be put on cards right among the graphics. The result is an innovative blend of visual and computational semantics.

powerful idea – HyperCard gets tremendous power from a single simple idea: a button can be linked to a card. Whole applications have been written using this as the central mechanism, for example the commercial game "The Manhole." There is even a method for defining the target card by demonstration, so that users do not have to see the script at all. This is a good example of what Seymour Papert calls "powerful idea" [Papert 80].

reduced nesting in HyperTalk – An innovation in the HyperTalk scripting language is the use of the variable "it." All functions set "it" implicitly. Subsequent statements can test the value of "it," instead of having to nest the function calls. For example, instead of

```
if foo(bar(x)) is empty then
```

one can write

```
get bar(x)
get foo(it)
if it is empty then ...
```

This reduces the complexity of individual statements. Many beginning students in computer science courses have trouble with the notion of nesting, so eliminating it is helpful.

### 19.3.6   Video Games

Tom Malone has written an excellent analysis of the appeal of video games [Malone 81]. He identifies three characteristics of successful computer games: challenge, fantasy, and curiosity. Challenge: a game must have a clear goal, and the attainment of the goal, or at least the degree of success (e.g., score), must be uncertain. Fantasy: a game must provide an emotionally appealing fantasy; it must address the emotional needs of the player. Curiosity: a game must stimulate and satisfy the player's curiosity. "Environments can evoke a learner's curiosity by providing an optimal level of informational complexity.... In other words, the environments should be neither too complicated nor too simple with respect to the learner's existing knowledge." [Malone 81, p. 272]

There are a few other aspects of games that appealed to the workshop participants:

reward – Players are rewarded for doing well. This reward is often remarkably motivating; children (and adults) have been observed playing video games well into the night.

performance metric – Typically there is a clear measure of how well the player is doing: score, level attained, number of obstacles remaining, etc.

mystery and thrill of discovery – This is what Malone means by "curiosity." Typically a player is not led by the hand through each step of a game. He or she must discover characteristics of the game and then master those characteristics.

physical action – We have already mentioned Bruner's "enactive" mentality above in discussing Legos, but we mention it again here because it is such a big element in the appeal of video games. Players take considerable pride in the development of the speed of their reflexes.

use of appropriate devices – Typically, video games use input devices which best match the action that the user is to perform: a steering wheel when the game is driving, a gun when the game is shooting, a joystick to control movement direction, etc.

## 19.4 Ideal Properties of the Language to Be Designed

By studying the successful systems described above, we have identified some features that we feel should be present in future languages for end users. Naturally, any single language is unlikely to have all of these features, but they seem like appropriate goals to strive for.

Our group's overall vision was to have:

*Multiple levels of user control that progressively provide more flexibility that empowers the end user to customize the application and its user interface to his or her particular requirements and taste.*

### 19.4.1 General Properties

#### Single Programming Language

Currently, each programmable application, such as a direct manipulation macro system, spreadsheet, or database, has its own separate programming language that the user must learn (and some, such as spreadsheets, even have more than one). Naturally, it would be better if a single programming language could be provided by the operating system, so that all applications could use the same one. Then, when the user wanted to create macros or programs for the visual shell, spreadsheets, databases, or drawing programs, the same techniques would apply (but see Section 19.4.3). Similarly, if the user is going to connect together modules (as discussed in Chapters 2 and 3), but the user wants some conditionality (e.g., use module *A* for simple letters, but use module *B* for longer documents with bibliographic references), then the same programming techniques should be available.

### Direct Manipulation

Another set of global goals relate to what is often called "direct manipulation" [Shneiderman 83]. The resulting system should allow the user to operate *directly* on viewable objects, rather than abstractly on symbols. Entities that are being referenced in programs should have a visible appearance so they can be visualized and pointed at. Even abstractions should attempt to present some kind of example, so the interface can be demonstrational [Myers 90b]. When the user operates on an object, the results should be immediately shown, so the system is interactive and incremental. Errors should be prevented whenever possible, and when made should provide useful feedback. Finally, the system should have good aesthetics and kinesthetics, so users find it pleasing to look at and operate.

### Ease of Use

Naturally, we would like the programming language to be easy to use. Based on the ideas from spreadsheets, we view the most important properties of this as being:

Low learning costs: It must be very easy for users to get started doing simple things, and doing more difficult things should only require a small investment in learning.

Fast assembly: It should not take much time to create useful programs.

Instant gratification: Users should see results immediately. Even with small efforts, useful and interesting programs should be created.

Some techniques that we identified that can be useful for helping to make a language easy to use include:

- Allowing the user to perform actions by direct manipulation. If the operation is an abstraction, then possibly allowing the user to operate on an example which represents the abstraction may work.

- Providing appropriate notations. One reason spreadsheets are easy to use is that they allow the user to type mathematical expressions to represent arithmetic. For other domains, it will be necessary to use notations that are similarly familiar to users.

- Using user's knowledge. A related point is that the language should take advantage of the knowledge that users have from the domains. For example, most users will know arithmetic and its symbology (as in spreadsheets), and there is much domain-specific knowledge that can be used for specialized applications.

- Using graphical, as opposed to textual, representations. In general, people find graphical notations easier to understand, and this can alleviate the syntax errors that are frequent problems with textual notations (but so can a syntax-directed editor). Section 1.3.3 of the introduction discussed visual languages in depth.

- Integrating programming with the user interface. In many programming-by-example and macro systems, to create a program, the user can execute the commands of system in the normal way. A new environment does not have to be learned to enter and execute programs.

### 19.4.2   Properties Relevant to the Module Architecture

Chapters 2 and 3 presented an architecture that allows pre-programmed modules to be connected together by the user. The following goals are relevant to this architecture.

**Full Coverage**

In the system of Chapter 3, the modules themselves must be programmed by professional programmers. However, it would be desirable if the end user could also create new modules and modify the existing modules. Therefore, we would like the architecture to allow users to "open up" the modules, and modify the internals also, which would probably be composed of more primitive modules. At each level, the user would probably need to learn more about programming and the workings of the module, but we hope there will not be a "wall" that prevents most users from making further progress.

It is possible that different programming languages would be needed at the different levels. The top level might simply be a direct manipulation way to put modules together. At the lowest level, some sort of general programming language might be needed. In between, the languages used should be accessible to the end users, so they can go down as far as possible. Ideally, there will be a smooth transition from one language to another, so only a small fraction of the users are lost. If at any point, a large fraction of the users are unable to master the new language, then this is a "wall," which is undesirable.

Of course, this capability would have to be balanced against a commercial vendor's desire to keep the internal implementation of the module a secret, and the difficulty of presenting internal implementation in an understandable form. However, just allowing one level of customization (attaching modules together) seems unnecessarily restrictive, and designers should strive for more!

### Ease of Searching

As noted in Chapter 3, an environment that contains many modules and primitives that can be put together will make it difficult for the user to find the appropriate pieces. Sophisticated, possibly intelligent, searching mechanisms will be needed to help users identify appropriate modules for their current tasks and goals. We can envision a networked database that contains descriptions of all commercial and "freeware" modules. When the user enters a description of the task or goal in some easy-to-use language (maybe even a natural language like English), the database would return a list of the relevant packages, along with prices and other information. If a package was needed that the user did not already have, it could be retrieved off the network, and the user's account would be charged appropriately.

### Communication

We feel that it will be essential that modules be able to work concurrently. However, the current mechanisms available to programmers to synchronize and control multiple processes are much too difficult for end users. Therefore, the modules should not require the end user to deal with synchronization issues.

### 19.4.3 Properties for the Language

A language to be used by end users should probably have significant differences from a language designed for professional programmers. However, some of the important characteristics of "professional" languages should be retained. Based primarily on our judgement of the important features of spreadsheets, we have identified the following important properties that a programming language for end users should have. These are, of course, in addition to the general goals discussed above in Section 19.4.1.

#### Few Side Effects

One important feature of spreadsheet formulas is that there are no side effects; the formula simply returns a value that goes into the cell. This makes it much easier to know the effect of a change to a formula. However, it is not possible to have a system which is totally side effect free, especially since saving information in a database or showing information on the screen is a side effect.

Therefore, the goal is to *minimize* the use of side effects, and to make it easy to *trace* and *debug* the effects of any action. There should be clear cause-and-effect relationships that can be viewed by the user.

#### Smooth Transition between Languages

It would be desirable if the user only had to learn one language which would work for all applications, but special-purpose languages, such as the formula language in spreadsheets, are often easy to learn because they rely on domain-specific notations and knowledge. There is clearly a tradeoff here. One clear goal, however, is when there *are* multiple languages, there should be a smooth transition from one to another. Ideally, the overall structure of the languages should be similar, and learning one language should provide significant help for users when learning the next language. In addition, it should be possible to call procedures in one language from another (the database language might want to access values in a spreadsheet, for example).

## Abstraction Mechanisms

One important lesson from conventional languages is the need for procedural abstraction. It must be possible for users to identify a part of a program, hide its implementation, and declare its parameters. For example, in a graphical program, the user might select some set of the program statements, declare them to be a procedure, and then draw a new icon to represent them.

## Unobtrusive Typing

There was some disagreement at the workshop about whether static typing is a good thing or not. Spreadsheet cells can hold any type of value, and conversions are performed automatically. The object system described in Chapter 10 is also untyped. However, some authors (Chapters 7 and 14) call for static type checking.

An advantage of static type declarations is that it makes it easier for the system to handle connections and conversions. If it knows that one module produces a string, and another accepts an integer, it can provide an error if the user tries to connect them. Also, declaring the types can be a form of documentation. On the other hand, most people feel that it is annoying and time-consuming to declare the types. One compromise is to infer the types, rather than requiring them to be specified. The Turing language infers the types from constant values (Chapter 18), and Peridot [Myers 88] infers types from example values.

## Simple Control Structures

Research has shown that non-programmers have trouble with the *concept* of control structures [Soloway 82], so considerable effort must be directed at presenting them in a way that users can understand. In spreadsheet formulas, the system automatically determines the flow of control from the formulas. In macro languages, the sequencing of operations is simply the order in which they were demonstrated. Some systems, such as Peridot, try to infer when iterations and conditionals are needed, and others provide simple dialog boxes or commands to add these to sequential programs.

Ideally, control structures would be entirely hidden from users. When this is not possible or desirable, then they should be presented in a way that the users will understand.

# 19.5 Open Issues in Programming Languages for User Interfaces

Although many of the structures and features of programming systems for user interfaces are agreed upon, there are still a number of open issues that require further study. Some of these issues are strictly language-level, while others address requirements of the surrounding implementation environment. The following sections summarize some of these issues.

## 19.5.1 Applications vs. Components

One ongoing debate concerns whether a particular set of functions should be considered an application or a set of communicating components. Most systems currently are built up of a single program which calls library routines to perform specific tasks; this program is difficult to modify, even by programmers, and the approach leads to monolithic applications that re-implement features that exist in a variety of other programs. The other approach is to use small components that are connected together by the user. Each component would provide a small piece of functionality, say, text editing or the maintenance of a scrolling list, and the components would share data with each other and perform their own operations on the data. However, no one has ever produced a system this way, so it is not clear how to make one.

## 19.5.2 Intelligence

What kinds of intelligent assistance would be useful in user interfaces, both at the user and the programmer level? Simple macro facilities are available for such systems as the Macintosh and Hewlett-Packard's New Wave system, but they are quite low-level, and do not generally have the ability to interpret the graphical displays and make decisions based on the current context. Typically, they record and play back user events, automating only those tasks that consist of a well-defined set of actions. In contrast, some macro systems, such as Tempo II for the Macintosh, can retrieve and act on certain kinds of information in the environment, such as the contents of the clipboard. However, most of the state of the system is invisible to the executing macro, which must execute blindly, performing the same actions regardless of the state of the environment. An additional limitation is that macros are controlled directly by the user, who activates them specifically to perform a given task.

The logical next step would be to evolve macros into intelligent *agents*, which can be activated by specific changes in the environment, such as the appearance of electronic mail that matches a certain specification. Agents may also be helpful as entities in the programming environment; for example, update agents may be defined to handle window redrawing when a window is exposed, and various kinds of recomputation agents may be activated on demand. In order to be able to implement such agents, systems must become much more open, with a consistent mechanism for naming and accessing states of all kinds. It is also not clear how to provide the intelligence to the user.

Other issues related to intelligence are intelligent help. For example, the system might supply automatic guidance about how to perform the programming if the user gets stuck.

### 19.5.3   Transitioning Levels

Another open issue concerns the transition from the pure user level, which is typically a non-programming task, to some sort of programming. Situations where this would be desirable include automation of a repetitive task; extension of the current application to perform a function not anticipated by the original program designer; or simply to customize the application and its user interface to different requirements or personal taste. This topic is extensively discussed throughout this book.

As in Chapter 2, one would like to be able to directly manipulate the user interface to gain access to the functionality behind each screen item. To do this, one must be able to somehow shift from "use" to "mention" (Chapter 5) in order to change the intent of the manipulation of the object. In

HyperCard, there is a global switch on a menu item which tells the system that it is now operating under "mention" mode, in order to manipulate buttons, fields, and backgrounds, and to access scripts written in HyperTalk. In this case, the use–mention mode is explicit, and for each screen entity there is a piece of code that is run when the object is activated.

In more advanced user interfaces, however, there is not a one-to-one correspondence between a screen entity and a piece of code to be run. Instead, the entire context must be taken into account when deciding what function is going to occur. For example, in the Macintosh Finder, double-clicking on a screen object can mean many things: a disk or folder opens, showing its contents; an application runs; and a document loads its application, and then itself. This polymorphism is convenient and useful for the user, but makes the situation more complicated for someone who is interested in modifying the functionality of the system.

Aside from the issue of use vs. mention, or even pinpointing the functionality that is to be changed or extended, it is still a very steep drop from the direct manipulation world of HyperCard to the complex scripting language of HyperTalk. As soon as the user steps into the world of HyperTalk, standard computer science concepts such as sequencing, iteration, variables, scoping, and side effects must be grasped in order to create even simple programs. One would rather have several levels which are progressively more detailed and powerful (and possibly complicated) than a swift descent into a morass of low-level commands and textual programming language concepts. In addition, it would be helpful to maintain the style of programming and interaction introduced in the base application as long as possible. Again, programming-by-example systems show that there is potential to allow a class of programming tasks to be handled without having to describe low-level details in a separate "programming" mode.

### 19.5.4 Component Interconnection

There are many different ways in which components could be connected and composed. However, this brings up the difficulty of communication between the components, and in particular, the specific protocols which would be used for each composition. For example, components within components would be useful for hiding implementation and packaging functionality; how should the outer component share information with the inner components? In well-designed interfaces it should be easy to embed more complicated objects inside linear textual structures, such as pictures, mathematical equations, animations, sounds, and so on; what protocols are necessary for communication of placement and sizing information? The Andrew system [Palay 88] has addressed some of these problems, but the architecture is not fully component-based.

### 19.5.5   The Connection Model

An issue related to component interconnection is the connection model. In the Component Construction Kit (Chapter 3), components are connected together via wires which allow objects to be transmitted from component to component. These wires are automatically connected by the system. This approach has several advantages: the communication paths are visually described; no naming of components need occur; and the paths are inherently two-way. However, a disadvantage is that it is more difficult to connect, and understand the communications between, spatially-distant objects.

  To solve this problem, a message-passing mechanism might be useful. In this case, objects are named, and their communications described via a recipient and a message. A disadvantage of this method is that messages are typically one-way channels; a two-way channel must be set up using two one-way messages.

### 19.5.6   Data Formats

As more and more distinct kinds of media are used in presenting information, there will be a demand for more data formats for describing that information. The Macintosh provides objects called *resources* which are typed data; initially, less than two dozen different resource types were described, and only two were expected to be handled in communication between applications: "TEXT" (a text string) and "PICT" (picture). Now there are over a hundred different resource types used in the Macintosh system, with thirty or more different types in a single application. However, only a very small number are common to all applications and used for communication purposes (i.e., Dertouzos' "rails"—Chapter 2).

The issue is to determine what kinds of data formats should be available in a user-interface programming environment, how new formats can be added to the system, and how existing formats can be used by applications. In particular, should subtyping be allowed? If so, how can subtyping be accomplished so that languages of all kinds can interpret the information provided by both the main type and its subtypes?

### 19.5.7   Data Formats for Rails

Given the large number of different data formats that can be used by particular applications, what formats are most useful for communication between applications? Although all data formats should be able to be communicated, a subset of all types could be chosen as a common standard to minimize the difficulty of program implementation. It is clear that unformatted text and pictures are far too limiting, and that a more comprehensive set of basic types needs to be supported by all cooperating programs.

### 19.5.8   Typing

An issue completely separate from the issues of data formats and rails is the issue of typing within a programming language. Languages such as HyperTalk are typeless. In the case of HyperTalk, all data are stored as strings, and interpreted as necessary in the particular context (such as arithmetic, string concatenation, and so on).

In Smalltalk, each object is an instance of a particular class; the class is used as a context to determine the meaning of a message. For example, the draw message can be sent to a circle or a rectangle, and the appropriate graphic will be created. Although objects are typed by their class, it is not necessary to declare variables as holding only objects of a given class. This provides flexibility in allowing a single variable to hold many different kinds of objects, but can make it difficult to compile programs efficiently. In contrast, systems such as Trellis-Owl require all variables to be declared to be a particular type.

For many inexperienced programmers, being able to use variables without declaring their types is easier and more convenient initially, while the program is just starting to be written. Later in the programming process, the added rigor of typing is useful for finding some kinds of errors in the program logic. A type system for a user language should be optional, allowing both modes of programming when each is appropriate.

### 19.5.9 Data Interchange vs. Intelligent Objects

Another unresolved issue has to do with whether objects simply consist of data which is passed around, whether they include code to interpret that data, or at an even higher level, whether they provide functions for display and editing when appropriate. The Macintosh chose the first mechanism; objects ("resources") are passed around between programs, and it is up to each individual program to interpret the data as it sees fit. One advantage of this approach is that a particular piece of data is not restricted to a predetermined set of interpretations or views: any application can interpret the data in a new way. A disadvantage of the approach is that an object can be sent to a recipient who has no idea how to interpret it or even display it.

The Andrew system [Palay 88] chose the opposite mechanism: bringing the program with the data. In this case, the data always knows how to display itself (and possibly edit itself) within an Andrew document. The advantage here is that if you receive an object in a document, you are guaranteed to be able to view and edit it. Because of this, applications need not interpret objects that are more complicated than, say, plain text, since the programs for displaying those objects are always available. Although this approach does not, *a priori*, prohibit an application from reinterpreting the object and displaying it in a new way, the additional effort required can discourage programmers from providing new functionality.

### 19.5.10 Which Programming Paradigm?

Most graphical user interfaces are built using object-oriented techniques, if not object-oriented languages. Is there a benefit to using the newer language paradigms for user interface programming? Languages such as CML (Chapter 14), Kaleidoscope (Chapter 11), Siri (Chapter 13), and Prolog may prove to be excellent foundations for the creation of user interfaces.

### 19.5.11 Detailed Design

The final issues have to do with how the actual detailed design of a program is accomplished by a non-professional programmer. There are many challenges to making detailed programming achievable to users:

- Some application semantics are inherently non-visual. Having to do mathematics, for example, may be a barrier to some users.

- Programming concepts such as side effects, abstraction, flow of control, and so on may be difficult to understand initially.

- Users may not even understand the basic mathematics necessary for even simple user interface tasks.

- Many more objects are visible to a programmer than are visible to a user. The details of how objects work and interconnect can be daunting.

- Having to deal with debugging may be difficult, since debugging a program often requires the exposure of the interpretation mechanism to the user.

- Some apparently small changes can require diving to great depths in the system, and therefore intimate understanding of the internal works.

- Dealing with real-time issues, such as display updating and direct manipulation interaction, can also be difficult, as it brings in yet another dimension of programming that must be understood at a sophisticated level.

These problems are basic to the programming task, and no simple answers are apparent.

## 19.6 Conclusions

While there are clearly a large number of problems and research issues, we believe that end-user programming is highly desirable and possible. An important caution, however, is that end users want to get tasks done; their job isn't to program. Therefore, programming must be a way for users to perform their tasks more effectively, and not create complexity and a host of new problems for them. If this is achieved and an appropriate paradigm is found, the success of spreadsheets shows that end-user programming can revolutionalize the way that computers are used.

# Chapter 20

# Report of the "User / Programmer Distinction" Working Group

*Mark Guzdial*
*John Reppy*
*Randall Smith*

The "User/Programmer Distinction" Working Group consisted of:

T.C. Nicholas Graham (GMD Karlsruhe)
Mark Guzdial (University of Michigan)
Toshiyuki Masui (Carnegie Mellon University)
John Reppy (Cornell University)
Bob Scheifler (Massachusetts Institute of Technology)
Randall Smith (Sun Microsystems Laboratories, Inc.)

## 20.1 Introduction

Software rarely satisfies all of the needs of its users. For this reason, many software packages provide mechanisms for user customization (such as specifying colors) and extensions (such as providing a mechanism to bind

367

a special function key to a series of commands). The final extrapolation of this customizability is for users to actually *program* their applications, to add extensions or even to create new applications. This can be an intellectually challenging task. One proposed technique, promoted in Chapters 2 and 3 of this book, is to build applications from independent components, that can be individually purchased and combined by users. Our working group was charged with the task of examining the barriers (social, psychological, and technical) that hinder users from programming their applications. In particular, we discussed the component approach and dealt with factors that might enhance or impede its success.

In this report, we first examine the barriers to user programming. The software component strategy is one approach to overcoming these barriers (discussed in detail elsewhere in this volume). We discuss two others: *embedded languages* and *demonstrational programming*. The software component approach requires end users to assemble their applications in such a way that their needs are met, while the other two approaches are designed to give the user the option of modifying existing applications.

## 20.2   Challenges to Blurring the User/Programmer Distinction

There are two classes of barriers to user customization of software applications: technical problems in the design and implementation of customization mechanisms, and social and psychological problems in the use and marketing of user programmable applications. Although there was some discussion of the technical barriers, our group primarily focused on the social and psychological problems, which can be further refined into three general categories:

*Task differences:* Differences in the kinds of problems being solved.

*Domain differences:* Differences in skills, training, and knowledge.

*Market challenges:* The conflict between preserving proprietary technical information and exposing the internals of applications.

We now discuss these various barriers in more detail.

## 20.2.1   Technical Problems

For software components, the key technical difficulty is providing a mechanism for facilitating the correct connection of components. This is essentially a problem in type checking. While modern languages, such as Modula-3 [Nelson 91] and SML [Milner 90], provide sophisticated module systems, it is likely that a much more powerful typing mechanism is required. In particular, the operational behavior of components should be specified as part of their interface. Type systems with this power are an active area of research (e.g., [Cardelli 89]). Another problem is reliability; a reusable component must be robust enough to work in situations unenvisioned by their authors. This will require advances in programming practice and a shift to higher-level implementation languages.

As noted above, the other style of supporting customization is to provide a mechanism for end users to "program" their existing applications. Essentially this means that some portion of the application must be implemented as an interpreter.[1] The amount of the system that is interpreted dictates how much can be customized.

## 20.2.2   Task Differences

End users and application programmers have different objectives when they use a computer. For the end user, the focus is on solving a specific problem that she is interested in, computing a budget using a spreadsheet, for example. The application programmer has a much wider audience, namely the end users of her application. This means that the application programmer is searching for general solutions. Furthermore, programmers must keep future evolution of their application in mind. We discuss these differences in more detail below.

### Specific vs. Flexible

The programmer's environment is necessarily more complex than the end user's since it cannot assume task domain restrictions. The solution of particular problems permits a specific, domain-centered approach. The

---

[1]For applications embedded in an "open" system, such as Smalltalk and Lisp, incremental compilation is available.

end user's environment can be tailored to ease interactions by taking advantage of restrictions within the task domain. Programmers, however, require flexibility since they deal with the common substrate upon which these domain-specific interfaces are built. Therefore, the path from the user's level to the programmer's level necessarily leads toward increasing flexibility and complexity.

### Direct vs. Symbolic

End-user applications that feature direct manipulation interfaces provide access to objects in the application through direct pointing. Each object in the domain is instantiated, with a manipulatable, on-screen representation. The programmer's domain is more abstract. For example, programmers deal with abstract menus that can contain any number of items and generic applications for which error handlers must be built. The programmer's domain requires symbolic reference, as opposed to end user's direct pointing.

### Mapping Non-Visual Semantics

A user-interface programmer is concerned with constructing the mapping between the application domain and the underlying computer primitives. In many cases, the mapping is not complex: there is a one-to-one mapping between computational objects and graphical representations, which the end user directly manipulates as domain-specific objects. But other domains do not have such clean one-to-one mappings, perhaps because there may be too many objects to construct one-to-one mappings or because the domain-specific objects have no obvious graphical representation (for example, as in higher-dimension mathematics). In these domains, the task of the programmer is to construct mappings that will be understandable and useful to the end user, while the end user's focus is on use of the mapping, not its design.

### 20.2.3  Domain Differences

Programmers and end users have different skills, training and knowledge; i.e., their domains of expertise are different. Moving from one domain to the other requires learning new skills. The complexity of having programmers shift application domains is a common software engineering problem, and the shift from end user to programmer requires a similar shift. It may be possible to build the knowledge into the development environment, or to layer the programmer levels such that the knowledge needed for changing the environment at each level might only be a small increment from the level before. Each of the differences identified below, while occasionally subtle, is a subset of programming knowledge that end users typically do not possess.

### Mathematics

Programming is an inherently mathematical activity. It involves intellectual techniques, such as abstraction, specification, recursion, and logic, that are typically learned as part of a mathematical education. Furthermore, many implementation techniques and algorithms rely on mathematical models. In graphics programming, for example, matrix algebra plays a dominant role. Even if we remove the obvious, surface level mathematics, we are left with a substrate of programming that is steeped in mathematics. For example, conditionals are phrased in terms of Boolean ANDs and ORs, data is typed by integer or real or array, and functions are defined iteratively or recursively. Many end-user domains do not require this level of math understanding, and practitioners in those domains will have a larger knowledge gap in tackling programming tasks. Mathematics is so pervasive in computer science that inventing an environment that does not require math expertise by programmers may require creating new metaphors for computation.

### More Objects

Programmers looking at a user interface see more objects than do end users, because a single interface for an end user is made up of many interacting components for a programmer. For example, where an end user sees a window, a programmer sees a graphic port, scroll bars, a close box, and window operations such as opening, redrawing, and closing. The shift from end user to programmer necessitates a shift in awareness of the interface which raises the number of components in that interface. The knowledge difference is not only in identification, use, and manipulation of these additional components, but also in the abstraction mechanisms for dealing with the complexity of greater numbers of interacting components.

## Complexity of Modifying Code

Modifying software is difficult because of interactions. A seemingly simple change to a low-level component that is used frequently throughout the environment can cause a ripple effect resulting in radically different system behavior. Many domains suffer from these sorts of interaction problems (e.g., the interactions of drugs in medicine), and the solution is often for greater training and more system-wide understanding on the part of the practitioner. However, end users who are only interested in making their specific changes to the environment will probably not have nor want a system-wide understanding. Thus, end-user programming is made even more complex than programming is for programmers, since end users are inexperienced and without tools for working with interacting code elements.

## 20.2.4   Market Challenges

The problem for constructing a market of computational components is in allowing users to manipulate those components. When users can manipulate components, component suppliers must provide more than just the components. Suppliers must consider what goes into the development of that component, and how that development process can be made available to the end user.

### Development Information Is Baggage

Delivering executable binaries is not an option in a world in which end users expect to be able to manipulate components at a subcomponent level. While the development tools themselves (e.g., editors, browsers, and debuggers) might be built into the environment, the component manufacturer must include information on the modularization of the component, the meaning of these modules, and the source code (or its equivalent). This raises the size and cost of these modules.

## Warranty Invalidation

What is the component manufacturer responsible for if the end user can manipulate the components? One simple response, used by computer equipment manufacturers, is that any modification of the component invalidates the warranty. But since these components are software, there is potential for a user to copy a subcomponent and use it elsewhere. Does the manufacturer's warranty on a component extend to subcomponents as well? The cost to users both for such extended warranties and for the technical support required to support users through such manipulations of components might be tremendous. Further, identifying problems that are the manufacturer's responsibility becomes even more complex when these problems are interacting with user changes. How does a manufacturer's technical support group determine with whom the responsibility lies for a problem?

## Protection of Investment

A key question when considering a computational component market is what is being sold and how the manufacturer's investment is protected. If the manufacturer is selling a piece of code, it may be within the user's rights to copy the code and reuse it in as many applications as the user wishes. If the manufacturer is licensing the use of a piece of code, the license will need to be defined recursively to cover the subcomponents as well. The task of reverse engineering and constructing a clone product is facilitated when the subcomponents are available for study. The legal problems of look-and-feel copyrights and patents become more complicated if the "look" is computational functionality and the "feel" is how the component is invoked.

## Dependence on Shared Components

A component market requires these components to assume certain extant, shared facilities in the environment. But if the environment itself is constructed of malleable components, then it may be that these shared facilities have been changed in ways that make the use of new components impossible. This is already a common problem in environments such as

Smalltalk or Lisp Machines where low-level features can be manipulated. A component market can only exist if the individual potential buyer might be able to use the component regardless of other components or low-level component changes.

## 20.3   Embedded Languages

Providing user programmability of applications requires providing a programming notation to the user. One common and successful way to do this is to use an *embedded language* in the application [Ousterhout 90, Beckman 91]. The basic scheme is to embed an interpreter for a simple, usually untyped, programming language in the application. The use of an interpreted untyped language makes such features as dynamic loading, dynamic binding, and programs as data fairly easy to implement. The embedded language provides a layer between the user's command language and the application's internal operations. Two binding mechanisms are required: one to provide a binding between user actions, such as keystrokes and mouse clicks, and programs; and one to provide hooks so that programs can manipulate the application's state and visual representations. (These roughly correspond to the controller component and model and view components, respectively, in a Smalltalk user interface [Goldberg 83].) The binding at the application/language level is fixed by the application designer; the binding between user actions and programs is customizable. By off-line editing of start-up scripts, and possibly by interactive programming, users can customize their applications in sophisticated ways. But the lack of typing and abstraction mechanisms means that these languages do not scale well to large programming tasks; thus it is doubtful that embedded languages, as they exist now, can provide the basis for complete user programmability.

### 20.3.1   Some Examples

In this section we examine several examples of the use of embedded languages in interactive applications.

## Elisp

The most successful example of an embedded language is Elisp [GNU 90], which is embedded in the GNU Emacs editor [Stallman 86]. The great popularity of GNU Emacs is owed, in large part, to its user programmability. Emacs consists of a core, written in C, which provides a bytecode interpreter Elisp, which is a dialect of Lisp. In addition to standard Lisp features, Elisp provides mechanisms for handling text and edit buffers. One might even view emacs as being implemented in Elisp, and view the core as the Elisp run-time system (although it is clearly specialized towards text processing).

The user programmability of emacs has been exploited to build a huge range of interactive interfaces to common user tasks. Examples include language specific editing modes, file system browsers, debugger interfaces, and appointment calendars.

Despite the great power of Elisp, there are still places where the mechanism falls short of providing total user programmability. For example, if a user wants to add pulldown menus to emacs, she must modify the core implementation, which is written in C, and recompile the whole system. Furthermore, the system is limited to textual interfaces; there is no support for graphical objects.

## WOOL

The Generic Window Manager (GWM) also uses a Lisp dialect for providing user programmability [Nahaboo 89]. Using *Window Object Oriented Lisp* (WOOL), users can customize GWM to give the look-and-feel of any of the other standard window managers (e.g., twm or motif). In addition, WOOL can be used to add menus to existing applications.

## Tcl

One of the dangers of embedded languages is the proliferation of different language designs. If each application has its own language, then the user will have to master a new syntax, semantics and programming style for each application she wants to customize. Even though these languages might be simple, this is still an excessive burden. It also seems unnecessary, since these languages all have the same basic mechanisms at their core: conditionals, procedures, variables, etc. They only need differ at the application interface. Ousterhout has developed an application independent language for embedding in tools, called *Tool command language* (Tcl) [Ousterhout 90]. The Tcl implementation consists of an application independent C library, which provides the Tcl parser and interpreter, and an application specific part, which consists of a set of application specific commands and a mechanism for dispatching Tcl programs to the interpreter.

Tcl has been used to implement a toolkit for X11, called Tk, which is similar in function to Xt [Ousterhout 91]. Applications built on top of Tk can provide users with both static and dynamic access to all aspects of the user interface.

## 20.3.2   Addressing the Challenges

This section discusses how the embedded languages approach might be used to address the social and psychological challenges described in the first section.

### Task Differences

Embedded languages allow end users to program specific solutions to their problems. The effort of programming, however, makes it worthwhile to find general solutions that can be reused in a number of cases. Thus, the end user who does significant programming must develop an application programmer-like focus.

### Domain Differences

Embedded languages do not really address the complexity of programming. For simple, application specific tasks, the existence of the right hooks may make the application program easy to write. For example, writing an Elisp script to perform a global editing operation is made much easier by the existence of regular expression matching. The simple design and small set of constructs make embedded languages easier to learn than most general-purpose languages, but it is this simplicity that makes these languages unsuitable for more complex programming tasks.

One might imagine a more powerful embedded language that might include previously missing mechanisms (such as typing and abstraction). Such a language would provide the power that current embedded languages lack, but would pose an even more formidable learning task for the end user. Current embedded languages (as discussed below) are tightly coupled to the applications in which they are embedded, thus providing a conceptual *domain bridge* for users moving from simply using an application to customizing it. But the addition of complex mechanisms means that users making such a shift must incur the domain differences discussed earlier.

Thus, while embedded languages offer a proven solution to the problem of blurring the user/programmer distinction, there are clear limitations to this approach. As users become more ambitious in their efforts to customize their applications, they will eventually hit the limitations of their language and programming skills.

### Market Challenges

Embedded languages seem to offer a reasonable solution with respect to the market challenges discussed in Section 20.2.4.

**Development baggage**   Embedded languages carry with them the problem of providing development support and debugging. If user programming is kept off-line, then other tools, such as text editors, will provide the development environment. Because these languages are untyped and interpreted, the size of a simple debugging tool ought to be fairly small. If a common embedded language is used for multiple applications (à la Tcl), then the cost of the development and debugging support can be amortized over multiple applications.

**Warranty invalidation**   The more power and flexibility provided by the embedded language, the more rope users have to hang themselves with. The vendor is presumably responsible for the correct behavior of the application core and for the behavior of vendor supplied embedded programs, but not for any user-written programs or user modifications to vendor programs. Vendors might choose to provide hot-line support for user efforts to customize their application.

**Protection of investment**   By providing a pre-compiled form of embedded programs, vendors can protect their proprietary software, while still allowing the user to replace a vendor component with a user version. Vendors may choose to release source for some components as a way of providing users with modifiable templates.

### 20.3.3   Summary

While embedded languages allow users tremendous power in customizing their application, users are still limited by the hooks provided by the underlying application and by their ability to shift domains. Furthermore, programming in an embedded language may be easier for simple tasks, but for more complex features, it is fraught with the same complexities that the application programmer must face.

## 20.4   A Programming by Demonstration Scheme

We offer here a "paper design" of a system that addresses a number of the challenges listed in the first section. We assume in this example an underlying language and environment like those of modern Lisps or like Smalltalk, in which the user is able to modify all parts of the environment, including any application, the window system itself, or even low-level file system code. Although users have all the basic tools necessary to directly inspect and incrementally modify almost anything in these environments, this is not enough to soften the path from user to programmer: the syntax and semantics of the implementation language are in the way. All the user knows is use of the application: how to operate menus, press buttons, and the like.

One approach discussed by the working group is to explore the expressive power of interfaces for describing computation, that is, to provide a *programming by demonstration* scheme. Such a system avoids the psychological complexity of requiring the user to learn a new set of concepts, since, presumably, the user must have a model in which pressing a button somehow invokes a procedure on the object under the button. In a programming by demonstration scheme, we can present that procedure to the user, not as a chunk of text, but as a movie: a demonstration of the cursor pointing and clicking away on various objects. Similarly, the user might define a new procedure by recording a movie of actions that the system might encode as a procedure.

We can use a typical scenario for describing such a system. Imagine a user sitting at his computer with mouse in hand, windows on screen, while manipulating icons, activating buttons and menus, and selecting text. However, he discovers a need for an "undo" item on his edit menu. To implement the new feature, our user holds down the *meta* key on his keyboard, and selects "cut" from the edit menu. Immediately, a window pops up with some code in it, the code for the "cut" procedure. A second window appears with computational objects associated with this code (e.g., representations of data objects, as in *Pygmalion* [Smith 75]) with a computational mouse pointer.

The user needn't read the code *per se*. Instead, he chooses to have it "demonstrated." The system plays back the actions associated with each statement in the code using its own mouse pointer and objects on the screen. Variables and data structures referred to by the code are represented by icons in a window alongside the code. As the routine is played out, the mouse glides from one icon to the next, itself activating buttons or invoking menus to call further procedures.

As the system's demonstration continues, the user can see the corresponding statement in the source code get highlighted. Thus the source code text is present alongside the demonstration. Unlike other demonstration-based systems [Myers 90b], we imagine that this system can also demonstrate code execution. This provides a *demonstrational debugger*, which the end user can use to step through the code. At any moment in the demonstration process, our user can stop, reverse the playback, or interrupt to create his own source code. The user creates new statements in a way that feels similar to conventional macro recording facilities.

There are two differences we note between macros and programs in the Lisp and Smalltalk systems we are taking as our assumed underlying environment: programs support arbitrary variables, while macros do not; and programs are compiled, while macros are expanded. We list the second one only to dismiss it immediately. Languages with incremental compilation are now commonplace, and there are existing demonstration style interfaces that generate compiled code. It is rather the variable issue that troubles demonstration style programming. How does the system know that a user's reference to a menu might stand for this specific menu, as opposed to an arbitrary screen object? How does the system generalize from the specific?

Much interesting work has been done on the problem of generalizing in demonstration style programming. A standard approach is to give the system a kind of domain knowledge that enables it to infer meanings: the system generalizes to variables automatically. However, in this scenario, let us presume that our user can somehow mark objects that are variables. The code generator will notice the user's gesture to a marked object, and generate code referring to the variable, as opposed to a constant.

The automatic generation of textual code for the user to see is an important feature of this system. The user can modify code by directly manipulating the screen objects, or by editing the text itself. Because he can see the text associated with his actions, he can gracefully make the transition from the demonstrational into the textual writing of code. Eventually, we imagine our user would be able to take apart an application by direct manipulation until the underlying source code is exposed, then edit the text directly. Thus, the user will have bridged the domain gap and become a conventional style programmer.

### 20.4.1   Addressing the Challenges

Given this scenario, now let us look at each item on the list of barriers to blurring the user/programmer boundary, to see exactly what has been addressed and what has been left wanting.

**Task Differences**

**Specific vs. flexible**   If the programmer's task is to create a text editor with his programming tools, the end user's task is to create a document with the text editor. The two tasks are different in an important way: the programmer works with much more abstract stuff in the computer. This system offers some help by always representing the objects of the program as visible entities on the screen. Even abstractions appear concrete. For example, an icon stamped with a 3 can represent a variable if so marked in this system: the corresponding textual representation might be "x." Thus the abstract notion of "number" is being represented by what has been called an "exemplar." The advantage is that the exemplar exhibits the behavior of the object to appear when the code is run. The benefits of exemplars are similar to those of the use of prototypes instead of classes in object-oriented systems.

**Direct vs. symbolic**    By having both the textual (symbolic) and graphical (direct) representations of objects, the transition between the two is made easier. Thus our user may spend some time in the direct manipulation mode with his system, and change to the textual as needed. The transition still exists, but the mechanisms of the system make the mapping explicit.

**Mapping non-visual semantics**    How should one represent abstract procedures and objects on the screen? This is partly addressed by our demonstrational system, because any display object can be inspected as text: the two representations allow the revelation of the mapping from text to object. Although the problem of how to naturally represent an "append-only read–write stream" is not solved, it is not necessary to work with the visual representation if the textual seems more appropriate.

**Domain Differences**

**Mathematics**    It is necessary to understand math in order to program, and this system does nothing directly to install this knowledge in the mind of the user. It may at best facilitate his acquisition of this knowledge. (For example, our user can see a demonstration that "cubed" means a number times itself times itself.)

**More objects**    Visual programming is plagued by what has been called "the spaghetti ball problem." A procedure that, represented textually, fills a page of text may involve a screen full of icons, typically with lines running between them. However, the visual component of the demonstration system will be better off than typical visual programming languages: each expression is executed in turn, and there is no need to keep the visual representations of earlier and later expressions on the screen. So instead of representing an entire procedure, our system must represent only one expression at any given moment. This does not mean however, that the user's "more objects" problem is completely solved: he may have to understand and deal with more object once he is "under the hood" than he did while he was "driving."

**Complexity of modifying code**    Although our system may facilitate the user's understanding of a particular chunk of code, it does not give him any leverage on appreciating the wide ranging effects of a change. This design also leaves open the question of how complex relationships are browsed, i.e., what in the system invokes this procedure, and when?

### Market Challenges

None of the market problems are addressed by the demonstration system. However, if end users who might use such a system are sufficiently enamored of their life as user programmers, they may refuse to buy anything but decomposable software. Thus, software vendors would have no choice but to respond to the desires of the marketplace, even though the thought may make them uncomfortable.

### Summary

The programming by demonstration system succeeds in some areas, but seems to contribute little in others. Most notably, the domain differences category (and arguably, the market challenges category) seem to be tough nuts to crack in general. An unsurprising conclusion can be drawn from this discussion: programming involves a special kind of skill, and there is little the computer can do in the way of representation to get that knowledge across. The computer can, at best, facilitate the uphill struggle along the path from user to programmer. It remains to be seen how gentle that slope can be made.

## 20.5   Conclusion

There is always going to be a tradeoff between choice and complexity. Programming will never be an easy task; providing the user with more options means that she must make more decisions. It may be possible to provide a very high level mechanism, such as components, for users to assemble custom applications, but mixing and matching the components will still be a complex task. Furthermore, for such an approach to be robust requires advances in type systems and programming practices.

In this chapter, we have reviewed some of the barriers which prevent end users from becoming programmers. In our discussion of the component-based, embedded languages, and programming by demonstration approaches, we have noted no one single approach which addresses all the barriers. The component-based approach deals best with the task boundary by eliminating it entirely: what the end user does is what the programmer does. None of the approaches completely deals with the domain boundaries that lie between end users and programmers, though both the embedded languages and demonstration approaches provide some aid. Only the embedded languages approach resolves the marketing challenges raised.

One hope for addressing the task and domain challenges may be look-and-feel standards, which limit the design space and thus reduce the number of choices. Of course, this, in effect, limits customizability. In the final analysis, it may be that the best one can hope for is shifting the user/programmer distinction to allow for more user flexibility.

# Chapter 21

# Report of the "Linguistic Support" Working Group

*James R. Cordy*
*Ralph D. Hill*
*Gurminder Singh*
*Brad Vander Zanden*

The "Linguistic Support" Working Group consisted of:

Jeffrey L. Brandenburg (Virginia Tech)
James R. Cordy (Queens University at Kingston)
Mark Green (University of Alberta)
H. Rex Hartson (Virginia Tech)
Ralph D. Hill (Bellcore)
Gurminder Singh (National University of Singapore)
Brad Vander Zanden (University of Tennessee)

## 21.1   Introduction

The Linguistic Support group chose as its goal a modest, immediately-achievable design for integrated linguistic support to aid professional applications programmers in 1) specifying and implementing user interfaces to their programs; and 2) specifying the connections between the user interfaces and the underlying application programs. Despite a wide range of different backgrounds and experiences in the group, a surprising level of agreement was reached. We observed that a model based on separating the application semantics from the user interface, and then providing explicit mechanisms for connecting the separated components, adequately described a large proportion of interface techniques and tools used by members of the group.

The notions of separation and dialog independence have been around for a long time [Thomas 83]. For much of this time, researchers and practitioners have been struggling to simultaneously achieve the advantages of separation or dialog independence, and provide the necessary connections between the components. In our discussions we found that most of the members of our group experienced some level of success in achieving both goals. Success was usually achieved by using advanced programming techniques or linguistic models to declaratively (as opposed to procedurally) specify connections between the user interface and the application.

We assume an underlying run-time architecture with explicit separation of user interfaces from applications. We propose the use of declarative linguistic structures to specify the connections between these components. Based on the experience of members of the group in using techniques like those we propose, we believe that our proposal provides good support for the construction of WIMP (Windows, Icons, Menus, and Pointing) interfaces. We include in this belief, interfaces with extensive direct manipulation interaction with the application or application information. The applicability of our proposal to non-WIMP interfaces is less certain. Only a small number of our group members have experience building non-WIMP interfaces, making it difficult to comment from a broad experience base. However, those group members that have experience building non-WIMP interfaces use techniques like those we propose.

The underlying principles of our proposal can be implemented in a variety of ways, and allow a wide range of user interface specification techniques. The full range of techniques, from specification via programming to constructing graphical specifications via direct manipulation, have been demonstrated. We believe that the language features our proposal requires are immediately implementable using existing language and interface tool technology.

## 21.2 Goal of the Group

The group's goal has two major motivations:

- dissatisfaction with the lack of even the most rudimentary user interface support in existing application programming languages, and

- given independent development of applications and user interfaces (possibly with different languages and tools), the lack of a consistent semantic model relating the user interface to the application.

Since there is not even basic language support for performing the tasks that are of most interest to us, we feel it is best to choose a very conservative goal. A conservative goal increases the likelihood that our proposals will influence new language designs. Given the current situation, we feel that immediate progress is more important than establishing a long-term research direction.

Our broad goal is to suggest linguistic features that allow the specification of graphical user interfaces within the programming language framework, and which address the two problems identified as motivations. In so doing, we hope to develop a consistent semantic model which simultaneously integrates existing user interface specification technology and is familiar to, and usable by, application language programmers.

Our discussions emphasized mechanisms for connecting the user interface to the application. Other important issues, such as event handling and display management, were not discussed. While a consensus may be achievable on event-handling models and display management techniques, time constraints and our desire for modest goals combined to prevent thorough discussion of these topics.

## 21.3 Scope

In keeping with our modest goals, and desire for immediate practical results, we adopted a narrow focus. Currently, we are interested in providing linguistic support embedded in programming languages used by professional programmers to build WIMP style interfaces. As far as possible, we wish to base our work on known practical methods, emphasizing the

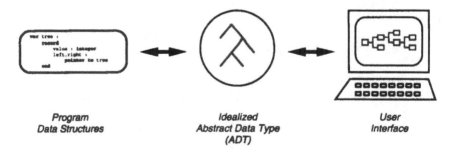

|  Program       |        Idealized        |    User    |
| Data Structures |   Abstract Data Type   | Interface  |
|                 |         (ADT)          |            |

Figure 21.1: The Descartes model.

research progress and results of the last five or so years of work in UIMS and related tools.

In the long run, it will be necessary to address non-WIMP interfaces, and non-programming interface developers. In keeping with our goal of being practical, however, we leave these issues to future workshops.

## 21.4   Architecture

It has long been recommended that the implementation of user interfaces be separated from the implementation of the underlying applications. There are good software engineering and user interface design reasons for this separation. Recommendations from this separation have come from researchers in both of these areas, e.g., [Shaw 83, Thomas 83, Hartson 89b].

Many years ago, the Descartes project [Shaw 83] suggested a total separation of user interface specification from the application program with ideally passive, automatic links between the two. The links would be based on an ideal abstraction of the data space (in the form of an abstract data type or ADT) that may or may not be physically represented (Figure 21.1).

The Descartes design was driven by three principles concerning relations between the underlying application and the display. The first principle states that there should be a strong linkage between the display and the client program. At all times, the display should reflect the current state of the displayed variables. The second principle has to do with the decoupling of the application from the interface. It suggests that the I/O interface be separable from the client program so that it is straightforward to replace one display with another display or with a different kind of interface. The third Descartes principle deals with the separation of policy from instance. This principle means that stylistic policy should be separable from the layout decisions for any particular interface. Descartes implements these principles based on the model shown in Figure 21.1.

A similar structure to Descartes', using an explicit representation of the application data, was proposed by [Dance 87], in an effort to overcome the limitations of strict separation when trying to provide rapid feedback that incorporates information from the application.

While neither the Descartes nor the Dance model have found widespread success, more recent systems with similar ideas, such as Weasel/GVL [Graham 89], UofA* [Singh 91b], RENDEZVOUS [Hill 92], and CON-STRAINT [Vander Zanden 88a], have shown that this basic architecture, especially when using declaratively specified links, may now be practical.

Even stronger, we believe that separation and the use of passive links is necessary for other reasons. The number of languages available for application implementation is growing. Given the continuing growth in the number of application areas and corresponding programming notations, this is not likely to stop. This means it is unreasonable to expect that every application will be coded in a new language simply because the language contains good user interface features. Therefore the features we design should be as orthogonal as possible to the rest of the application language, so that they can easily be attached to any language.

## 21.4.1 Paradigm

Our paradigm to maintain orthogonality between user interface features and the application programming language is to treat the ADT model as the interface between the application and the user interface. The critical issue is the connection between the ADT model and the application program, and the connection between the ADT model and the user interface. The Weasel/GVL "conceptual view" model suggests that a declarative specification of these transitions has several advantages. The most important advantages of a declarative specification are ease of programming and reusability of the user interface and application components that results from the sparability of the declarative connections from the components.

In the case of Weasel/GVL, this declarative specification takes the form of a visual pure functional program (see Section 21.5.4). In UofA* [Singh 91b], a specification of the application semantics is used to generate these connections (see Section 21.5.2). In the case of Sassafras [Hill 86], this specification uses a declarative rule-based system (see Section 21.5.1). In user interface systems that support constraints, this connection can be achieved with a set of declarative constraints, e.g., [Myers 90e, Hill 92, Vander Zanden 89] (see Section 21.5.3).

### Application ⟷ ADT

The critical issue in the transition between the application and the ADT is synchronization. The problem is knowing when it is necessary and/or legal to update in each direction. In the case of output, the question is when to sample the state of the program to update the state of the ADT. For input, the question is reversed.

It has been demonstrated that, using declarative specifications, each of these transitions can be achieved automatically without any explicit synchronization being introduced into the application [Cordy 90, Singh 91b, Hill 92, Vander Zanden 88b]. For the application programmer, this has the advantage that his/her application need not be disturbed by the presence of, or a change in, the user interface.

For this reason, we suggest that linguistic constructs that support a purely applicative specification with automatic, implicit synchronization should be used in the construction of WIMP interfaces. In the long-term, we recognize that explicit synchronization will be necessary to provide a full range of user interface capabilities, and a synchronization controller like that used in Sassafras may be necessary. How to handle such explicit synchronization features in a way that is not obtrusive for the application programmer remains a research topic. In the case of virtual-reality interfaces, synchronization problems are exaggerated by the need for hard real-time support to keep the displays synchronized with user input.

### ADT ⟷ User Interface

In the second transition, between the ADT and the user interface, the critical issue is the specification of the graphical presentations of the information in the ADT, and the mapping from user gestures and commands to updates of the ADT. Both tasks can be viewed as pure functional tasks: a functional mapping from a sequence of ADT states to a sequence of user interface states, and a functional mapping of user interface states into a sequence of ADT states. This suggests that some form of pure function mapping is appropriate. (This is not the same as saying a functional programming language is required. For example, most constraint systems can be used to implement the functional mappings.)

For the applications programmer, it seems probable that the best way to specify the graphical properties of the interface is to use a graphical, by-example, construction tool, such as Peridot [Myers 90a], Lapidary [Myers 91c], or Druid [Singh 90]. On the other hand, some aspects of the interface itself, notably complex types of behavior, may be better handled by a textual specification of the constraints to be met.

We suggest that, for the short term, the language features for specifying user interfaces be designed as a mixed visual/textual language. The graphical objects would be drawn by example, and the constraints and relations among them added by textual programming. In the long-term, it is not clear whether a text or graphical specification will be the best and most general strategy. In particular we do not know the best way to specify the objects in non-WIMP interfaces. For example, for objects that will appear in a virtual reality, it may be easier to use mathematical specifications than to draw them (in a by-example system) in enough detail to look real from all angles at all viewing distances. Research to explore drawing and demonstration approaches to virtual object specification is just beginning [Singh 92].

Even having decided upon a declarative, mixed text/visual specification, there is still a wide range of possibilities for the declarative linguistic paradigm to use. Various systems have demonstrated the viability of each of functional [Graham 89], rule-based [Hill 86], constraint-based [Vander Zanden 89, Hill 92], and equational systems for this purpose.

## 21.4.2  Specifying Feedback

A weakness in the separation-based paradigm we have chosen is the difficulty in specifying and modeling good semantic feedback without disturbing the application. This is a long-standing problem that has been addressed, with limited success, before (e.g., [Dance 87]). We have explicitly avoided this issue for the moment since we know of no convincing general solution that could both be immediately adopted to practice and provide the features we have envisaged above.

For the short term, we suggest that the specification of interactive feedback could use a model like that of Garnet's interactors [Myers 90c], which package the short-circuit input feedback into the input primitives of the user interface specification language. This ensures rapid low-level feedback, and provides conveniently packaged low-level interaction. It leaves untouched the ongoing research topic of providing rapid semantic feedback.

While we do not have suggestions for linguistic paradigms that we know will simplify the problem of providing semantic feedback, we believe that our proposal is no worse than any other in this respect. Further, some current research suggests that linguistic structures similar to those we propose may lead to some improvements in this area.

## 21.5   Example Systems

Brief descriptions of some prototype user interface construction tools and languages that inspired, or conform to, our proposal follow.

### 21.5.1   RENDEZVOUS

The RENDEZVOUS [Patterson 90, Hill 91] language and architecture have been designed for the construction of multi-user synchronous interfaces. These are interfaces where several users simultaneously interact with a common set of data. In terms of our proposed architecture, there is one set of "program data structures" (the application program) that is shared among several users who interact with it simultaneously. The RENDEZVOUS architecture is an extension of our proposal in that there is one ADT per user (or, more correctly, one ADT per view, since one user can have multiple views onto one application).

The RENDEZVOUS language is object-oriented Lisp that has been extended with concurrency features, constraints, and a declarative graphics system. The constraint system is linked with the process scheduler, so that constraints can be used for interprocess communication.

In RENDEZVOUS, a *view* must be a collection of RENDEZVOUS objects. These objects are typically graphical and interactive (i.e., they have an associated display appearance and behavior). There is (at least) one view per user. The view presents a graphical representation of the application data to the user, and permits the user to interact with the data. Each view is a lightweight process.

The *application* is another lightweight process. The views are linked to the application with constraints. If the application is written in REN-DEZVOUS, the application can be totally unaware of the views and the constraints that connect the application to the views.

In RENDEZVOUS, constraints fill the role of the ADT. The constraints carry information between the views (the user interfaces) and the application, and transform the data representations as necessary. In order to perform the transformations, the constraints must have a model of the data that is being transformed. This model, which is implicit in the code but explicit in the design, is the ADT.

The RENDEZVOUS architecture is strongly consistent with our proposal. It has a strict separation with an implicit ADT. There are declarative connections between the components with implicit synchronization, and the application code does not have to be changed to add a new or different interface. There is also support for rapid low-level feedback within the objects in the views. Support for semantic feedback is an important research issue for RENDEZVOUS—if one user changes the state of the application, the other users' interfaces should be updated immediately.

The RENDEZVOUS architecture is inconsistent with our proposal in several ways. It does not currently support graphical specification of interfaces. More importantly, RENDEZVOUS is currently very tightly tied to its Lisp base. It is not easy to use RENDEZVOUS from programs written in other languages. This has been done, but it may require modifying the existing application to communicate with RENDEZVOUS.

The RENDEZVOUS language and architecture have been in use for approximately two years and two large applications have been completed. At the present, there are eight users. None has had difficulty with the fundamental architecture—separation with declarative, passive links and automatic synchronization. This leads us to believe that these aspects of our proposed architecture should not be difficult for application programmers to grasp and use.

## 21.5.2   UofA*

The UofA* UIMS [Singh 91b] works with a high-level, declarative description of the semantic commands supported by the application. A semantic command description includes command name and all the arguments required for executing the command. Based on this description, UofA* automatically produces a design specification of the user interface and implements it. The user interface thus generated can be refined using interactive graphical facilities provided by the UIMS to improve the interaction with the user.

The UofA* UIMS is aimed only at graphical user interfaces. Within this domain, it only supports interfaces that access the commands that manipulate the application data. It does not account for the design of the presentation, or direct manipulation, of application data. This part of the interface must be designed by the interface designer and hand-coded, or generated by another system. Even within graphical interfaces, it cannot produce all kinds of interfaces. Examples of interfaces built using UofA* include a distributed network editor, a paint program, and a fish animation system.

The UofA* generated user interfaces communicate with the applications by sending and receiving tokens. A token has a token id and a token value. The user interface sends tokens to the application to control command execution. When the application wants to present information to the user or when it wants to affect other changes in the interface (e.g., change the maximum value of a slider, disable menu items), it sends output tokens to the user interface. The presentation component of the user interface interprets the output tokens and converts token values into graphics that is presented to the user. The run-time system of the UIMS manages the token queues and coordinates the flow of tokens between the user interface and the application. In addition, the run-time system maintains a global set of values that are used by the dialogue control component and are sent to the application when a command is ready for execution.

The UofA* approach to interface generation and management is based on a high-level semantic definition. In UofA*, the communication between the interface and the application is specified in terms of the information that the application needs to obtain from the user. The interface definition does not specify the I/O events necessary to achieve this exchange of information. In the UofA* UIMS, more work is shifted from the application to the UIMS, which is responsible for gathering low-level device inputs, converting them into tokens for the application, and displaying the application data. As a result the application does not need to deal with low-level device input/output primitives. This provides for a better framework for integrating applications.

In UofA*, there is a weak coupling between the interface and the application. That is, the interface, after it has collected all the information required to execute a command, communicates with the application. This makes it difficult to provide rapid, semantic feedback.

The UofA* approach to communication between the interface and the application is similar to the model discussed in Section 21.4—the UIMS maintains a set of global state variables that are shared between the interface and the application. These variables are a physical manifestation of the ADT. As a result of this architecture, significant parts of the presentation and dialog control components can be changed without affecting the application and vice versa.

In UofA* the links that communicate between the user interface and application are automatically derived from the application's semantic definition which forms the main input for the UIMS. Even though the links are procedurally implemented (with token passing) the user interface implementor's and application programmer's views are of a declarative system.

UofA*, in its current form, implements a fairly loose coupling between the user interface and the application. It could easily be modified to provide a tighter coupling allowing rapid semantic feedback. This can be achieved by providing a Druid-like [Singh 90] run-time structure which is capable of communicating more frequently and smaller grains of information.

### 21.5.3 Constraint Grammars

Constraint grammars are an extension to attribute grammars that support the specification of user interfaces [Vander Zanden 88a, Vander Zanden 88b]. The extensions support directed graphs rather than trees, multi-way rather than one-way constraints, and the manipulation of the directed graphs using a powerful transformation editing model based on pattern recognition. Constraint grammars are conducive for specifying applications whose data structures can be naturally represented as directed graphs. This covers a fairly large range of applications since directed graphs naturally model lists, sets, trees, and of course, directed graphs.

Systems based on constraint grammars use the productions (from the grammar portion of the constraint grammars) to generate the application and interface data structures, the constraints to compute semantic and display information, and the transformations to alter the data structures. From both the interface designer's and application programmer's viewpoint, the data structures are encapsulated in a package, the transformations are a set of messages or procedures that manipulate these data structures, and the attributes are the exported portion of the data structures. Multi-way constraints provide the glue that ties these attributes to the application and interface. The constraints compute the attributes' value based on the information contained in the application's and interface's data structures. They also convey the information contained in these attributes to the application and interface.

Thus the constraint grammar model successfully separates the application from its interface by encapsulating the data structures which are common to the application and user interface in a single package and allowing them to communicate with the data structures via constraints and operate on the data structures via transformations.

The constraint grammar model adheres to the basic form of our proposed architecture in that there is an ADT that encapsulates the data structures common to both the application and user interface. The transformation model provides the connections from the application and interface to the ADT, and constraints provide the connections from the ADT to the application and interface.

However, the current incarnation of constraint grammars does not precisely conform with our proposed architecture since the application and interface do not maintain separate data structures but rather share the data structures in the ADT. This setup has both advantages and disadvantages. Three advantages are the saving of space due to only one set of data structures, lack of consistency problems that arise when duplicate data structures are maintained, and the removal of the synchronization problem of when to update the duplicate data structures. Several disadvantages are the problem of providing semantic feedback without irrevocably altering the application's current state, some complexity in providing multiple views since separate data structures might support different views more easily, some added complexity in the application because customized data structures might be able to support it more easily, and the necessity of rewriting existing applications in order to add an interface to them.

The reason for the common data structure requirement is that the constraint links from the ADT to the interface and application cannot induce side effects, they can only convey information. One solution to this problem is to allow the transformation model to work on the application and interface data structures as well as the ADT. Thus the user could provide transformations for modifying the ADT, and two other sets of transformations for modifying the application's and interface's data structures based on changes to the ADT. A more attractive solution is to extend the constraint model so that it can specify structural relationships as well as data relationships. In this case, the constraints would automatically change the application's and interface's data structures in response to structural changes to the ADT's data structures. This extension to the constraint grammar model would bring it into conformance with our proposed architecture. In addition, it would eliminate problems associated with not being able to customize data structures without introducing synchronization or consistency concerns (synchronization would occur when the constraint solver is invoked and the constraint solver would automatically keep all data structures consistent). It would significantly reduce the amount of code that must be rewritten in the application, especially if the constraints used the same syntax as the language the application is implemented in. The issue of providing semantic feedback would not go away but additional research could probably make it disappear as well.

Constraint grammars have been successfully implemented in CONSTRAINT, a system that automatically generates a direct manipulation interface for an application from its constraint grammar specification [Vander Zanden 88b]. A handful of programmers have used it to generate a number of graphical applications that demonstrate the ability of constraint grammars to specify simulation systems, program visualization systems, visual programming environments, and the semantic and display characteristics of input devices. The programs for these interfaces typically required several hundred lines of code and typically were completed with a few hours of effort. We found that debugging time was frequently quite short since the programs are at the specification level, with the CONSTRAINT system transforming them into operating graphical interfaces. Thus debugging was limited to errors in the overall design rather than implementation errors. In general the programmers expressed happiness with the constraint grammar model and found it relatively easy to learn and use.

### 21.5.4   GVL

GVL (Graphical View Language) [Graham 89, Cordy 90] is a graphical, functional language used to specify output. GVL is used to specify conceptual views of output, which map the data state of an application program to a display view.   Such conceptual views may be debugging views of internal data structures, simple algorithm animations, or production output such as dynamic visual editor screens and diagrammatic representation of computation results. The conceptual view model is based on separating a program's output from the program itself. The program consists of a set of modules, encoded in the language of choice of the application programmer (e.g., C, Turing, Ada, etc.).   The program contains no output statements, only data structures and algorithms to manipulate the data structures.

A separate output specification maps the contents of a program data structure to a display view. As the data structure is modified, the display view is automatically updated. Conceptual views can be thought of as a data probe, the software equivalent of a logic probe. Each probe continuously senses the data state of the program and maps it to a display view. The display view is an abstraction of the data structure, and serves the functions of the ADT. It represents some facet of the data structure that is of interest to the programmer. The name conceptual view comes from this idea of abstraction. A data structure can be mapped to multiple different output views. For example, the data structure implemented in a stack module may be mapped using both a specification which maps to an array diagram with a cursor, and simultaneously by another specification that shows the same data structure as a stack.

As the data structure is modified throughout the execution of the program, the display is implicitly updated.  These updates are based on the invariant assertion of the module being displayed: when the invariant is false (i.e., an update is taking place), it is illegal to update the display. When the invariant is true, the module's data structure is guaranteed to be in a consistent state, and the display can be updated. Therefore, it is sufficient to update the display every time the module's invariant changes from false to true, which corresponds to the module being exited.

Conceptual view specifications are expressed in two parts. First a specification written in GVL expresses how the current state of the data structure is to be mapped to a set of display primitives such as boxes, lines and text. The mapping specification does not necessarily constrain the location or sizes of these primitives. Then a set of built-in layout rules are applied to this form to determine the actual display. Layout rules determine any unconstrained sizes and positions, and resolve how to fit large displays when the physical display device is too small.

The GVL language itself is a visual language based on pure functional language principles. There are a number of basic graphical primitives such as lines, arrows, text, and so on, and various attributes that can be applied to them, as well as higher-level linguistic constructs. In general, the basic primitives represent themselves, and must appear exactly as they are drawn in the GVL function.

GVL uses the concept of a coordinate space in a way analogous to the concept of scope in traditional programming languages. A coordinate space is simply an area of display space. A display whose position is unconstrained is restricted to being displayed within the coordinate space in which it is specified. Three language constructs introduce a new coordinate space: function definitions, boxes, and the cond (short for condition) function. (Note that since boxes can be nested, so can coordinate spaces.)

Weasel [Graham 88] is a prototype environment using GVL with the Turing programming language [Holt 88a]. Weasel/GVL has been very successful in specifying output and debugging views for a large number of applications, including interactive board games, simple visual text editors, data structure debuggers, and concurrent system animators as well as various kinds of simple static graphical output such as bar charts. Work is presently under way to extend the GVL conceptual view model to include input views specified and synchronized in a way analogous to output conceptual views.

### 21.5.5  Linda

The tuples in the tuple space of Linda, as discussed in Chapter 15, can be physical representations of the ADT. Thus, Linda can be the basis of a system with architectural properties that are similar to our proposal.

## 21.6  Summary

We believe that a practical linguistically-based user interface specification package, that can be used by professional application programmers, is achievable without further research. This package would be based on existing technology, perhaps derived from the example systems of the previous section, and could be semantically integrated with several existing programming languages. The technology base would include: an architecture that separates interactive software into application and user interface components, passive, declarative techniques (e.g., constraints or functional programming) to link the components, and a mix of graphic and textual user interface specification techniques. While the system we envisage would be best suited to WIMP interfaces of a modest kind, we believe this represents the vast majority of current application program interfaces. This wide applicability implies the potential for significant impact. Thus, it would represent a tangible contribution of the user interface community to the production of software, by helping to close the gap between the strong ability of programming languages to structure and manipulate data, and their lack of ability to express interaction of those structures with the outside world.

# Chapter 22

# Future Research Issues in Languages for Developing User Interfaces

*T.C. Nicholas Graham*

## 22.1   Introduction

While the workshop certainly did not solve all outstanding linguistic issues in user interface construction, a surprising consensus was reached as to what the problems are that need to be solved. Solutions to many aspects of these problems were proposed in the technical papers presented in Chapters 2 through 21. This chapter summarizes the issues the workshop participants found to be important, and relates them to the arguments provided in the technical papers. It is hoped that this collection will be of use to other researchers in user interface construction, and will form a stimulus for further research.

The chapter is divided into the following four (somewhat overlapping) categories of issues:

- General Language Issues: What are general features and approaches required in languages for the construction of user interfaces?

- End-User Programming: How do we support the customization and programming of user interfaces by the non-programmer?

- Non-WIMP Interfaces: How do we support interfaces involving such features as concurrent dialogues, three-dimensional output, non-standard input devices, and animation under real-time control?

- Programming in the Large: How should interactive programs be organized, and what are the software engineering concerns particular to the programming of interactive systems?

## 22.2   General Language Issues

Before creating a new language, there are a number of basic philosophical questions that have to be considered. Some authors in the book propose mixed-language systems, while others argue that one language alone suffices. There are arguments in favour of extending existing languages rather than inventing a new one. It is open what sort of environment should be provided: where the boundary (if any) should lie between language and environment, and what kind of language processing technology should be used.

There exist more pervasive language questions, such as to how much can be done declaratively, what kind of typing should be provided, how constraints can be integrated into a language, and the role of object-orientation in constructing user interfaces.

### 22.2.1   A New Language, an Extended Language, or a Toolkit?

Before considering what features are useful in a language for user interface construction, a language designer must consider the issue of whether to build from an existing language, to design a completely new language, or to attempt a language-independent toolkit approach. Each of these approaches has advantages, indicating a need for further research to better understand this issue.

Designing a new language provides the opportunity to build everything correctly from scratch. When grafting new ideas (such as constraints or object-orientation) onto an existing language, one has to support the new ways of thinking within the old framework. It may be that supporting the mindset of the old language restricts the new concepts so severely as to make them unattractive.

Alternatively, creating a new language is expensive and time-consuming. Unfamiliarity and poor implementations may severely inhibit the acceptance of the language.

Another approach is the use of toolkits, which can be fairly language independent. Horn (Chapter 13) argues that toolkits are insufficient—the main problem in creating interfaces is not the graphics, but in maintaining consistency of the data state in the presence of multiple input channels and multiple threads of control. Toolboxes, since they are not integrated into the programming language, cannot supply any aid for consistency maintenance. Masui (Chapter 15) indicates that toolkits can be acceptable when integrated correctly—such as using the Linda model.

## 22.2.2  Should We Have Multiple Languages or a Single Language?

It is still unclear whether user interfaces should be constructed in the same language as application programs, or whether multiple languages should be used. The main advantage of the multi-language approach is that different languages can be specialized to perform different tasks: computation may be best done in a traditional imperative language, while dialogue specification may be more appropriately expressed in some other language. Multiple languages can be combined in interesting ways: one language may be, for example, a meta-language, influencing the way in which the first language operates. Examples of such approaches in this book are the GVL model where output specifications operate over data structures in the application programming language (Chapter 6), interpreting user commands as meta-programs (Chapter 13), and the use of temporal constraints to influence the execution of functional programs (Chapter 16). Other authors (Chapters 12,9) argue the utility of separate, declarative specifications for output. Multiple languages can also be combined into one framework through a unified communication model, such as Linda (Chapter 15).

The main disadvantages of multiple language systems are that the user must learn several different notations, and that it is hard to debug and maintain multiple languages. Further research is required to see if these problems with the multiple language approach can be overcome.

### 22.2.3   How Should the Environment Look?

As well as the language itself, there are many questions as to what kind of programming environment should be provided to support the language. A programming environment must support a series of somewhat conflicting features. User interfaces are created through successive refinements. There must be a tight edit/execution cycle so that minor changes in an interface can be tested immediately. Execution must also be very efficient, due to the real-time constraints of user interfaces. The book discusses several directions for the general view of an environment, leaving a broad scope for future experimentation.

Hill (Chapter 9) stresses the need for dynamic loading and automatic garbage collection. Horn (Chapter 13) suggests the novel approach of using an interpreter, and implementing user actions as meta-programs that generate program code.

Another solution is to have two implementations, an interpreter for rapid-prototyping, and a compiler for efficient execution—here there is the problem of making two implementations of the same language exactly the same. Even with languages that have a formal semantics, this is very hard to achieve; problem areas are typically treatment of erroneous programs, meta-programming, and interfaces to external software. Additionally, modern compilers execute so quickly that interpreters in the traditional style are becoming ever less interesting.

Hartson *et al.* (Chapter 17) point out the importance of integrating better support for behavioral notations in the programming environment. Tools could be provided to support graphical syntax for these notations; the transition from behavioral to programming notations could be eased by environmental support.

### 22.2.4   How Should Constraints Be Integrated?

Several chapters of the book suggest that constraints be included in a language for user interfaces. Virtually every proposal is different, indicating the need for intensive research to determine the appropriate role for constraints.

The proposals differ on three axes: should constraints be:

- One-way or Two-way?

- Integrated or Meta?

- Classical or Temporal?

Two-way constraints present a relation among a collection of objects: if the state of any one object changes, the state of the others is automatically changed such that the constraint continues to be satisfied. One-way constraints are directional: a constraint is attached to a particular object. When the state of other objects is updated, the object with the constraint may be modified to satisfy the constraint, but not vice versa.

The issue of whether one-way or two-way constraints are better appears to be tied to the issue of whether constraints are integrated into the language or considered to be a meta-construct. In the approaches discussed by Hill, Myers, and Vander Zanden (Chapters 9, 10, 12), constraints are *integrated* right into the language: they act over the data structures of the program and are activated as a course of execution. In this sense, a constraint is operating as a command within the programming language, and actively changes the values of objects. This leads to the problem that two-way constraints may in effect introduce unexpected side effects. A data object may be referenced and indirectly modified by constraints at arbitrary locations in the program code. Integrated, two-way constraints therefore violate the locality principle of good programming language design (Chapter 18), leading these authors to adopt one-way constraints.

Another approach is to have constraints operate at a meta-level, restricting the freedom of non-deterministic programs. For example, in Freeman-Benson and Borning's approach, variables actually represent a stream of values; constraints always affect the value of the next element in a particular stream, a value that has not yet been determined (Chapter 11). In my own approach, constraints operate over the non-deterministic I/O behavior of processes, restricting possible inputs and outputs (Chapter 16). In all these approaches, therefore, constraints reduce non-determinism, rather than effecting change. When constraints are a meta-construct, one-way constraints are uninteresting: since the constraints have no side effects, there can be no danger of introducing unwanted side effects.

Constraints may be based on *classical* logic, allowing the expression of spatial relationships between objects that hold at any time in the program execution. *Temporal* constraints are based on some form of temporal logic, where temporal relations between objects can be expressed as well as spatial ones. This allows the sequencing of events, and the specification of real-time behavior. The main disadvantage of temporal constraints is that they are hard to implement—an area undergoing considerable research. There is also very little experience with users programming in a temporal constraint language. Chapters 16 and 9 discuss the addition of temporal constraints to influence real-time behavior.

### 22.2.5  How Much Static Typing?

One of the traditional tradeoffs in systems intended for rapid-prototyping is the issue of whether to include static typing or not. Static typing provides early error detection, improves execution efficiency, and aids the readability of code (Chapters 7, 14). Untyped or dynamically typed languages have the advantage of being flexible, and not hindering the programmer with (intentionally) redundant detail (Chapter 10). Untyped languages are generally appropriate for rapid prototyping, whereas static typing is generally considered to be indispensible for programming production systems. User interface languages typically need to span the gap between rapid prototyping and production implementation, leading to an unresolved question of how much typing to include.

### 22.2.6  Is There a Role for Functional (Declarative) Programming in HCI?

There is currently a great deal of interest in using declarative languages in the construction of user interfaces. In this area, future work is required to determine whether declarative languages are expressive enough to program user interfaces conveniently, whether declarative languages can be implemented efficiently enough to meet the demanding requirements of graphical user interfaces, and whether declarative languages are easy enough to use to gain acceptance in the general programming community.

Declarative languages are defined as having no notion of control: they specify the *result* of a computation without giving an algorithm to achieve it. Declarative specifications can be functional, or relational (usually expressed in some logic). Declarative languages allow programming at a very high-level, and support program transformation methodologies that allow high-level, inefficient programs to be transformed into efficient ones. This allows programmers to prototype quickly, and then to achieve efficiency through transformation rather than reimplementation. The strong mathematical basis of declarative languages affords a much greater degree of security than traditional languages.

Direct manipulation of time is, however, problematic within a declarative framework such as constraints or functional programming. Declarative specifications are by definition free of control flow or temporal aspects: they are simply a specification of the desired results. Thus, for example, a constraint might specify that two objects are to be a certain distance apart from one another, but would not specify how much time is permitted to the satisfaction of that constraint following a change in one or other of the constraint's parameters. Worse, declarative specifications are so high-level that a programmer cannot typically estimate how long execution will take. Hill (Chapter 9) discusses the need for temporal constraints to fill this need. I describe (in Chapter 16) the use of constraints in a temporal logic to guide the execution of functional programs; it is open as to whether one could practically extend this notation to describing real-time constraints.

Another possible approach (Chapters 12, 9, 6) is the use of declarative notations within more traditional languages to implement the output component of a user interface.

### 22.2.7 Is Object-Orientation Useful for User Interfaces?

Many of the papers in the book deal with issues of object-oriented programming. Although Gansner and Reppy (Chapter 14) argue that object-oriented programming is too much of a research topic to warrant inclusion in current languages, it is almost uniformly accepted by the authors that object-oriented techniques are indispensible to user interface programming.

One of the general goals in constructing software is to map the behavioral domain as naturally as possible to the constructional domain (Section 22.5.1). This is exactly the software process supported by object-oriented analysis and design, where an analysis phase first identifies the "natural" objects in terms of the user's domain, then allows construction of the software in terms of these objects, and in terms of the terminology of the user.

Object-oriented *programming* is however only the last stage of object-oriented analysis and design. At the programming level, object-oriented languages provide good support for code reuse (through inheritance and dynamic binding), and for incremental software development. There is as yet, however, no experience with the long-term maintenance of object-oriented programs.

It is still open how object-orientation should be supported in a programming language for user interfaces, particularly to best support the need for rapid development times required for user interfaces, and the wish to be able to experiment with different designs.

One of the primary means of abstraction in object-oriented programming is the concept of class, which allows an object *type* to be defined. Classes can then be instantiated into objects. Chapter 10 discusses the issue of how in rapid prototyping, it is more natural to work with concrete objects, and then later abstract the objects to a class. The prototype-instance model of objects provides automatic abstraction of instances to classes, so that any object can be used as if it were a class. The problem with this approach is that since there is no explicit class declaration, there is less typing information available to an implementation, leading to greater difficulty in detecting and locating programming errors. It is a research issue as to how to best reconcile this desire for flexibility with the desire for robust software.

A further issue is how to separate the concept of subtype from that of inheritance (Chapter 7). Traditionally, the notion of subtype is bound to that of inheritance. This sometimes leads to unnatural object hierarchies, where inheritance cannot be used as much as one would like, since it would lead objects not to be assignable as desired.

## 22.3   End-User Programming

A major theme in the workshop was how to make the programming or customization of user interfaces more accessible to the end user. In the context of end users, even the traditional term *programming* is inappropriate—it is unreasonable to expect the user to deal with any sort of programming language. There is much discussion in the book of how tasks that have been traditionally in the realm of programming can be presented in a non-programming framework. Tools exist, such as interface builders and HyperCard, that are more appropriate to non-programmers. These tools are typically limited in what they can do, such that after some point an escape mechanism must be used to a more traditional programming language.

One should not fail to note that ultimately, we are all end users. Even programmers use computers as tools, and also wish to create simple interfaces and customize applications with a minimum of fuss.

### 22.3.1 Making Abstractions Understandable to End Users?

The fundamental concept behind programming is that of abstraction: variables are an abstraction for data; procedures denote some general process over unspecified data. Ideally, end users should be working in a concrete world, directly manipulating user interface components instead of abstractions of user interfaces. This is a hard problem, since the system must in some way deduce the general case from the concrete examples that the end user has specified. How to achieve this goal is still a very open research issue, although the book provides some ideas.

Smith, Ungar, and Chang (Chapter 5) coin the distinction between *use* and *mention*, where *using* an object involves manipulating it directly, or demonstrating its behavior by example, whereas *mentioning* an object—naming it and referring to it by name—is in effect programming with it. The authors argue that for a user, this distinction should not exist, and offer a series of possibilities for avoiding it. Cordy (Chapter 6), however, demonstrates that the full power of programming must be available to the user interface creator, including selection and repetition. If *use* is the only paradigm available, then the system must infer general rules from examples, leading to problems when more than one generalization is possible.

Guzdial and Soloway (Chapter 4) offer a wealth of practical advice on creating environments for non-programmers. They particularly emphasize the need for concreteness and a very controlled design cycle for the beginner. A process called *scaffolding* can be used to remove constraints, and allow the expert user more freedom. The authors argue that with today's systems, naive users seldom become experts, but that through carefully designed scaffolding, users would be more inclined to make the effort to learn more about a system.

### 22.3.2    Are Component-Based Applications Suitable for the End User?

Two chapters are devoted to the concept of allowing end users to create and customize applications from a predefined set of components (Chapters 2, 3). The idea behind this approach is that application specific modules can be bound together to create new applications. The components themselves would probably have to be actually programmed, but by having a library with sufficient existing components, all performing fairly small tasks, an end user could create sophisticated software by combining components.

While issues to do with component-based programming are discussed in Section 22.5.4, some open questions are specific to end-user programming. It is important that users be able to collect and connect components in a completely transparent way. The component approach requires some sophistication on the part of a user to be able to collect and assemble the right components to perform some task. It is also not clear whether users would see a benefit to being able to customize their own applications, or whether they prefer to have a turn-key application which will operate as soon as it is loaded from a disk.

## 22.4    Non-Wimp Interfaces

WIMP interfaces are defined as those based on Windows, Icons, Menus, and Pointing. Much of the effort in tools for user interface construction has been directed to supporting this style of interface. However, there has been comparatively little investigation as to how to extend tool and language support to concurrent and distributed dialogues, multi-dimensional output devices, real-time constraints, three-dimensional graphics, multi-media interfaces involving video and sound, and non-standard input devices such as data gloves.

A great deal of the work in non-WIMP interfaces reported in the book deals with problems of distribution, concurrency, and real-time. Concurrency is required for interfaces with concurrent dialogues, or that are distributed over a number of workstations; real-time support is required for interfaces with temporal requirements.

## 22.4.1 What Kind of Concurrency Do We Need?

In general, concurrency is required in user interfaces to handle multiple input devices, and multiple threads of control in programs. More recently, work has taken place in distributed user interfaces, where different users on different (perhaps significantly separated) machines cooperate to perform some task (Chapter 9), and in virtual reality, where computation is so intensive that it is distributed over several specialized processors.

Traditional support for concurrency in user interfaces has been based on event handlers, where each thread of control must be able to handle events from any source. There exist many languages that allow programming of concurrency, by providing constructs to support the explicit creation of processes, and communication and synchronization between processes. Most of these languages were designed to build operating systems, a quite different task from the construction of user interfaces.

Several chapters in the book look at the issues of concurrency in user interfaces, and what special characteristics a user interface language should have to support concurrent programming. The basic issue is how best to trade off high-level programming versus efficiency and flexibility.

The most commonly used approach is that of windowing systems, which typically provide some limited support for concurrent dialogues through event handlers, and access to explicit processes provided by the operating system (see Chapter 14). This level of support is too low-level for convenient programming of concurrent or distributed user interfaces, leading to the conjecture that true concurrency primitives should be built into a language. Additionally, processes must be lighter weight than those provided by the operating system, meaning that they should be provided by the language.

Masui (Chapter 15) recommends the use of a general model for communication and synchronization, where distribution is transparent, and where multiple languages can be supported within the general model.

We thus see that there is general agreement that some sort of general support for concurrency is required, but it is an open issue requiring further research to determine what form this support should take.

### 22.4.2   Can We Support Concurrency Transparently?

Given the need for some form of concurrency in user interfaces, can support
for concurrency be given in such a way that the user not be aware of it explicitly? A number of chapters in the book propose that through declarative
descriptions, a concurrent implementation can be derived without the user
explicitly programming the concurrency. The main problem in systems
with multiple sources of input is not handling the inputs themselves, but in
maintaining a consistent state in the presence of multiple threads of control
(Chapters 13, 9). Thus many aspects of concurrency could be handled by
constraints that specify what is the notion of a consistent state. Thus, as
inputs occur, they are handled by some traditional method such as event-
handlers or interactors, while consistency between concurrent threads is
maintained through constraints.

   An alternative declarative approach is suggested in Chapter 16, where
synchronization of processes is achieved by placing constraints on the I/O
behavior of the processes, restricting non-determinism.

   Hill argues, however, that practical experience shows that both constraints and more traditional message passing primitives are required. He
argues that while state-maintainence is naturally expressed in terms of
constraints, event-handling is more naturally expressed in terms of explicit
communication (Chapter 9).

   More experience with constraints will be required to determine how
practical it is to use constraints for implicit communication and synchronization.

### 22.4.3   Supporting Time and Temporal Aspects?

All user-interfaces have some real-time component—be it constraining
the system to respond to the user within some prescribed time, or detecting whether two mouse clicks were close enough together to constitute
a double-click action, or as complex as deadline-scheduling of processes
over a network. Much work is required to determine how to give flexible
and expressive support for real time in a language, while maintaining the
ease of programming required for prototyping user interfaces.

   Various chapters give requirements for a notation for the manipulation
of time. The "real time" must be available system-wide, to allow direct

calculation of how long a particular activity has been under way. Estimates must be available of how long a particular piece of code will require to execute, to support scheduling. Some ability to preempt processes must be available, as well as an ability to dynamically inform processes that they must provide a result immediately (e.g., through degrading the quality of the result). Singh (Chapter 8) goes further, to recommend that time be treated as a first-class object, supporting some form of temporal constraints without direct reference to the system clock. Such constraints could perhaps be expressed in a temporal logic (Chapter 16).

It would appear likely that the support required for user-interface programming is simpler than general real-time programming. How such restrictions can be reflected in support for real-time in user interfaces is a matter for further research.

## 22.5  Issues of Programming in the Large

Much of the earlier research in language support for user interface construction dealt with issues in programming in the small. Research concentrated on such issues as designing toolkits and window systems, generating widgets by demonstration, and dialogue specification. With some very notable exceptions, less work has been done on the general organization of large programs with complex user interfaces. Issues of programming in the large include problems of how to make user interfaces reliable, how to support reuse of existing user interface software, how to specify the behavior of user interfaces, how to connect user interfaces to applications, and how to organize component-based architectures.

### 22.5.1  Translating from Behavioral to Constructional Domains?

A traditional issue in software engineering is how to describe *what* a program is to do, rather than *how* it is to do it, and how to bridge the gap between such a specificational notation and a programming notation. In user interface construction, a similar approach has been developed, where the *behavioral* domain is that of the user, based on the vocabulary of the application, and the *constructional* domain is that of the programmer, based on the vocabulary of implementation tools and techniques. These behavioral specifications have yet to achieve any realistic acceptance, leading to the issue of how best to specify the *behavior* of a program separately from its implementation, and how to translate in some methodical fashion from this behavioral specification to an implementation.

Hartson *et al.* offer one approach to specifying behavior (Chapter 17). Specifications in this language describe possible user actions, and the effects these actions will create.

### 22.5.2   How Do We Make User Interfaces Reliable?

Programs with sophisticated user interfaces are typically complex and therefore difficult to code correctly. Therefore, special care must be taken to make such programs reliable. Traditional methods such as formal specifications or program synthesis are difficult to apply to user interface construction, because of the need to support rapid prototyping and rapid modification. Little concrete work has been done in this area; however, some possible approaches were suggested in the book.

Some advantage may be gained by using high-level declarative languages, where there is less chance of making errors (Chapters 9, 14, 16). Programming by demonstration also holds some promise, since there is no programming involved at all. Demonstrational approaches have their own difficulties, in that they always involve some component of inference, which is not guaranteed to do what the programmer intended.

### 22.5.3   Connecting Application Code to Interface Code?

Many proposals over the years have dealt with how to generate or infer interface code from a high-level description. There is still much work to be done on how to attach this user interface code to an application program. This issue raises the main question of how interactive programs should be structured from an architectural point of view: where is the dividing line between user interface and application, how should the two communicate, and how should the two be synchronized?

One point of view strongly represented at the workshop is that there should be no application program at all—that everything should be done in the user interface (Chapters 2, 3, 5). This approach clearly has the advantage of avoiding the connection problem altogether. As discussed in Section 22.3, recent work aims at extending the programming functionality available in the user interface; how far this approach can extend is a matter for further research.

The questions of communication and synchronization between user interface and application also have no easy answer, and would appear to depend on the nature of the application. The application and the user interface must typically share some information, involving some kind of communication protocol between them. Communication should be easy to specify, but also must be efficient. Synchronization of the user interface and the application is a problem: typical organization of interactive programs allows a mixed-control model, where sometimes the application is dominant, and sometimes the user interface. It must somehow be possible to specify when each is permitted to be dominant, and when communication between the two is allowed. Ideally, this should be allowed in a high-level manner, not through explicit programming.

A number of directions are proposed within the book as possible approaches to solving these problems. Horn and Vander Zanden (Chapters 13, 12) recommend that constraints be used to connect applications and user interfaces. Vander Zanden's constraints are actually expressed as sets of functions, from the user interface to the program and back again, and are therefore similar to the functional views discussed by Cordy (Chapter 6). Hill argues alternatively for similar declarative output specifications, but prefers the flexibility of event-based input (Chapter 9).

Even more high-level is the approach of interactors in the style of Garnet (Chapter 10). Myers raises the question of whether the Garnet interactors are sufficient, and if not what would need to be added. The tradeoff between these approaches is that of simplicity versus flexibility. Interactors are much easier than event handling, but cannot be used to solve every problem; constraints are clearly high-level, but more practical experience is needed to evaluate whether the constraint approach is sufficiently flexible and efficient.

### 22.5.4   How Do We Solve the Practical Problems
###          with Components?

Several chapters (2, 3, 9) discussed the idea of a software architecture
based on components drawn from a library and connected in some implicit
way. This approach allows applications to be unbundled, and provides the
user the opportunity to customize and extend applications. There are many
exciting prospects for further research.

Many technical obstacles exist. Primarily, how does one connect components? If the user is to be doing the connection, an implicit method is
clearly preferable, where the user simply selects which components he/she
would like to have, and the system joins them together (Chapter 3). It
would appear impossible, however, for such a system to work in general,
requiring further investigation as to how the connection can be achieved in
as transparent a manner as possible.

Further problems are of a more organizational nature. To work, components must be easily available, inexpensive, and easy to combine. It
is critical that interfaces be standardized between components, so that
components from different vendors can be combined in a straightforward
manner. Issues of copyright and distribution of components will have to
be addressed. If components are available over a network, some method
must be invented to easily arrange for payment.

### 22.5.5   How Do We Support Reuse?

Programming user interfaces offers a wide spectrum of reuse of code—
perhaps far more than traditional programming domains. Parts of user
interfaces operate similarly between programs, and between different functions within one program. It not only saves programming time but also aids
in guaranteeing consistency of the user interface if the same code can be
reused in such situations. While many of the problems in reuse are general
problems currently being researched in the software engineering community, some approaches are particular to languages for user interfaces.

With the component approach (Section 22.5.4), thousands of components can be available, which alone or in combination may perform some
required task. Here, the basic building blocks of reuse are provided, but
the problem is how to find which blocks can be used. Some interface is

needed to a library of components so that appropriate components can be found.

Another level of reuse can be gained through a functional approach (Chapters 16, 6), where the semantics of a piece of code is defined only by its functional interface, rather than being bound in intricate ways to shared data structures or other environmental characteristics. When combined with polymorphism, functions lend themselves to reuse. With this approach, the programmer must inevitably face the difficult task of anticipating how code may be reused in the future. The problem of finding appropriate functions in a library is also present.

## 22.6   Conclusions

High-quality user interfaces have ceased to be an exotic curiosity found only in research labs or extravagantly priced products. As more and more people have begun to use computers, the marketplace has begun to expect that programs be flexible, easy to learn, and easy to use. In the '90s, the software crisis is being extended to a new frontier: how to cheaply and rapidly produce high-quality graphical user interfaces.

The current tool and language support for developing user interfaces is usable only by expert programmers. Such programmers are rare, and their time is expensive. Worse, experts at *programming* user interfaces are not necessarily experts at *designing* user interfaces. It is therefore necessary to simplify the process of constructing user interfaces, and to make the tools more accessible to the designers, and even the users, of the interface. Tools must better support rapid development and modification of user interfaces, so that the interface can be repeatedly tested and improved.

Meanwhile, end users are performing more and more programming-like tasks. Users wish to be able to customize interfaces, to extend them with new commands, and to combine different programs into one environment. More aspects of the construction of user interfaces must therefore be removed altogether from the domain of programming, and turned into simple, direct manipulation activities that can be performed by the end user.

The authors of this book have attempted to show what the current issues are in languages for developing user interfaces, and have offered an overview of the current research in the field. The individual chapters show sometimes a close consensus, sometimes significantly differing ideas as to where work should go. Summaries of these positions were given in a set of three group reports. Finally, this chapter has attempted to collect a list of the outstanding issues in designing languages for user interfaces, indicating where work remains to be done.

It is hoped that the work presented in this book will be of help to other practitioners and researchers, and will be a step forward in our goal of making it easier and cheaper to create effective user interfaces.

# Bibliography

[Aho 75]  A. Aho and M. Corasick.  Efficient String Matching:  An Aid to Bibliographic Search. *Communications of the ACM*, 18(6):333–343, June 1975.

[Apple 87]  Apple Computer, Inc. *HyperCard User's Guide*, 1987.

[Authorware 91]  Authorware Inc., 1991. 8400 Normandale Lake Blvd., Suite 430, Minneapolis MN 55437, (612) 921-8555.

[Barford 89]  Lee A. Barford and Brad T. Vander Zanden. Attribute Grammars in Constraint-Based Graphics Systems. *Software—Practice and Experience*, 19(4):309–328, 1989.

[Barth 86]  Paul Barth.  An Object-Oriented Approach to Graphical Interfaces. *ACM Transactions on Graphics*, 5(2):142–172, April 1986.

[Bass 91]  Len Bass and Joelle Coutaz. *Developing Software for the User Interface*. Addison-Wesley, Reading, MA, 1991.

[Bauer 81]  F.L. Bauer, M. Broy, W. Dosch, R. Gnatz, B. Krieg Brückner, A. Laut, M. Luckmann, T. Matzner, B. Möller, H. Partsch, P. Pepper, K. Samelson, R. Steinbrüggen, M. Wirsing, and H. Wössner. Programming in a Wide-Spectrum Language: A Collection of Examples. *Science of Computer Programming*, 1(1):73–114, 1981.

[Beckman 91]  Brian Beckman.  A Scheme for Little Languages in Interactive Graphics. *Software—Practice and Experience*, 21(2):187–207, February 1991.

[Black 86]  Andrew Black, Norman Hutchinson, Eric Jul, and Henry Levy. Object Structure in the Emerald System. In *Proceedings of the ACM*

*Conference on Object-Oriented Programming Systems, Languages, and Applications*, pages 78–86, November 1986.

[Black 87] Andrew Black, Norman Hutchinson, Eric Jul, Henry Levy, and Larry Carter. Distribution and Abstract Types in Emerald. *IEEE Transactions on Software Engineering*, 13(1), January 1987.

[Black 90] Andrew Black and Norman Hutchinson. Typechecking Polymorphism in Emerald. Technical Report 90-34, University of Arizona, Department of Computer Science, December 1990.

[Bobrow 88] Daniel G. Bobrow, Linda G. DeMichiel, Richard P. Gabriel, Sonya E. Keene, Gregor Kiczales, and David A. Moon. Common Lisp Object System Specification. X3J13 Document 88-002R, June 1988.

[Böhringer 90] Karl-Friedrich Böhringer. Using Constraints to Achieve Stability in Automatic Graph Layout Algorithms. In *CHI'90 Conference Proceedings*, pages 43–52, Seattle, April 1990. ACM SIGCHI.

[Booch 87] G. Booch. Reusable Software Components. *Defense Electronics*, 19(5):53–60, May 1987.

[Borning 79] Alan Borning. ThingLab—A Constraint-Oriented Simulation Laboratory. Technical Report SSL-79-3, Xerox Palo Alto Research Center, July 1979.

[Borning 81] Alan Borning. The Programming Language Aspects of ThingLab; a Constraint-Oriented Simulation Laboratory. *ACM Transactions on Programming Languages and Systems*, 3(4):353–387, October 1981.

[Borning 86] Alan Borning and Robert Duisberg. Constraint-Based Tools for Building User Interfaces. *ACM Transactions on Graphics*, 5(4):345–374, October 1986.

[Borning 89] A. Borning, M. Maher, A. Martindale, and M. Wilson. Constraint Hierarchies and Logic Programming. In *Proceedings of the 6th International Logic Programming Conference*, pages 149–164, Lisbon, Portugal, June 1989.

[Borning 91] Alan Borning, Molly Wilson, and Bjorn Freeman-Benson. Read-Only Annotations in Constraint Hierarchies. Technical Report 91-07-04, Department of Computer Science and Engineering, University of Washington, July 1991.

[Brooks 87] Frederick P. Brooks. No Silver Bullet, Essence and Accidents of Software Engineering. *IEEE Computer*, 20(4):10–19, April 1987.

[Brown 83] A.L. Brown, J.D. Bransford, R.A. Ferrara, and J.C. Campione. Learning, Remembering, and Understanding. In W. Kessen, editor, *Handbook of Child Psychology: Cognitive Development*, pages 77–166. Wiley, New York, 1983.

[Bruner 66] Jerome S. Bruner. *Toward a Theory of Instruction*. Harvard University Press, Cambridge, MA, 1966.

[Burstall 77] R.M. Burstall and J. Darlington. A Transformation System for Developing Recursive Programs. *Journal of the Association of Computing Machinery*, 24(1):44–67, January 1977.

[Burton 88] F. Warren Burton. Non-Determinism with Referential Transparency in Functional Programming Languages. *The Computer Journal*, 31(3):243–247, 1988.

[Card 80] S.K. Card and T.P. Moran. The Keystroke-Level Model for User Performance Time with Interactive Systems. *Communications of the ACM*, 23(7):396–410, July 1980.

[Card 83] Stuart K. Card, Thomas P. Moran, and Allan Newell. *The Psychology of Human–Computer Interaction*. Lawrence Erlbaum Associates, Hillsdale, NJ, 1983.

[Cardelli 84] Luca Cardelli. Compiling a Functional Language. In *Conference Record of the 1984 ACM Conference on Lisp and Functional Programming*, pages 208–217, August 1984.

[Cardelli 85a] Luca Cardelli and Rob Pike. Squeak: A Language for Communicating with Mice. In *Computer Graphics*, volume 19, number 3, pages 199–204, San Francisco, July 1985. Proceedings SIGGRAPH'85.

[Cardelli 85b] Luca Cardelli and P. Wegner. On Understanding Types, Data Abstraction and Polymorphism. *ACM Computing Surveys*, 17(4):471–522, December 1985.

[Cardelli 86] Luca Cardelli. Amber. In *Combinators and Functional Programming Languages*, volume 272 of *Lecture Notes in Computer Science*, pages 21–47. Springer-Verlag, July 1986.

[Cardelli 88] Luca Cardelli. Building User Interfaces by Direct Manipulation. In *ACM SIGGRAPH Symposium on User Interface Software and Technology*, pages 152–166, Banff, Alberta, Canada, October 1988. Proceedings UIST'88.

[Cardelli 89] Luca Cardelli. Typeful Programming. Technical Report 45, DEC Systems Research Center, May 1989.

[Carriero 89] Nicholas Carriero and David Gelernter. How to Write Parallel Programs: A Guide to the Perplexed. *ACM Computing Surveys*, 21(3):323–357, September 1989.

[Carriero 90] Nicholas Carriero and David Gelernter. *How To Write Parallel Programs*. MIT Press, Cambridge, MA, 1990.

[Carter 87] James A. Carter and James B. Tubman. Integrated Software: Past, Present, and Future. *Future Computing Systems*, 2(2):151–181, 1987.

[Chakravarty 91] Manuel M.T. Chakravarty and Hendrik C.R. Lock. The Implementation of Lazy Narrowing. In *Proceedings of PLILP, Programming Language Implementation and Logic Programming*. Springer-Verlag, LNCS 528, 1991.

[Chambers 89] Craig Chambers, David Ungar, and Elgin Lee. An Efficient Implementation of SELF, a Dynamically-Typed Object-Oriented Language Based on Prototypes. *SIGPLAN Notices*, 24(10):49–70, October 1989. ACM Conference on Object-Oriented Programming; Systems Languages and Applications; OOPSLA'89.

[Chang 90] B. Chang and D. Ungar. Experiencing Self Objects, an Object-Based Artificial Reality. In Urs Hozel, editor, *The Self Papers*. Center for Integrated Systems, Stanford University, 1990.

[Clark 85] R.E. Clark and G. Salomon. Media In Teaching. In M.C. Wittrock, editor, *Handbook of Research on Teaching*, pages 464–478. Macmillan, New York, 1985.

[Cohen 90] Jacques Cohen. Constraint Logic Programming Languages. *Communications of the ACM*, pages 52–68, July 1990.

[Colmerauer 90] Alain Colmerauer. An Introduction to Prolog III. *Communications of the ACM*, pages 69–90, July 1990.

[Cooper 90] E.C. Cooper and J. G. Morrisett. Adding Threads to Standard ML. Technical Report CMU-CS-90-186, School of Computer Science, Carnegie Mellon University, December 1990.

[Cordy 90] J.R. Cordy and T.C.N. Graham. GVL: A Graphical, Functional Language for the Specification of Output in Programming Languages. In *Proc. IEEE 1990 International Conference on Computer Languages*, pages 11–22, March 1990.

[Cousot 77] P. Cousot and R. Cousot. Abstract Interpretation: A Unified Lattice Model for Static Analysis of Programs by Construction of Approximation of Fixpoints. In *ACM Principles of Programming Languages*, pages 238–252, 1977.

[Cox 90] Brad J. Cox. There is a Silver Bullet: a Software Industrial Revolution Based on Reusable and Interchangeable Parts Will Alter the Software Universe. *Byte*, 15(10):209–215, October 1990.

[Dance 87] J.R. Dance, T.E. Granor, R.D. Hill, S.E. Hudson, J. Meads, B.A. Myers, and A. Schulert. The Run-Time Structure of UIMS-Supported Applications. *Computer Graphics*, 21(2):97–101, 1987.

[Dertouzos 90] Michael L. Dertouzos. Redefining Tomorrow's User Interface. In *Human Factors in Computing Systems*, page 1, Seattle, April 1990. Proceedings SIGCHI'90.

[Dincbas 88] M. Dincbas, P. Van Hentenryck, H. Simonis, A. Aggoun, T. Graf, and F. Bertheir. The Constraint Logic Programming Language CHIP. In *Proceedings Fifth Generation Computer Systems-88*, 1988.

[Duisberg 88] R.A. Duisberg. Animation Using Temporal Constraints: An Overview of the Animus System. *Human–Computer Interaction*, 3(3):275–307, 1987–1988.

[Ege 87] Raimund K. Ege. *Automatic Generation of Interactive Displays Using Constraints*. PhD thesis, Department of Computer Science and Engineering, Oregon Graduate Center, August 1987.

[Epstein 88] Danny Epstein and Wilf LaLonde. A Smalltalk Window System Based on Constraints. In *Proceedings of the 1988 ACM Conference on Object-Oriented Programming Systems, Languages and Applications*, pages 83–94, San Diego, September 1988. ACM.

[Flecchia 87] Mark A. Flecchia and R. Daniel Bergeron. Specifying Complex Dialogs in ALGAE. In *Human Factors in Computing Systems*, pages 229–234, Toronto, Ont., Canada, April 1987. CHI+GI'87.

[Floyd 91] Michael Floyd. The Evolution of Component-Based Programming. *Dr. Dobbs Journal*, 16(1):96–98, January 1991.

[Foley 88] James D. Foley, Christina Gibbs, Won Chul Kim, and Srdjan Kovacevic. A Knowledge-Based User Interface Management System. In *Human Factors in Computing Systems*, pages 67–72, Washington, D.C., May 1988. Proceedings SIGCHI'88.

[Freeman-Benson 90a] B. Freeman-Benson. Kaleidoscope: Mixing Objects, Constraints, and Imperative Programming. *SIGPLAN Notices*, 25(10):77–88, October 1990. ACM Conference on Object-Oriented Programming; Systems Languages and Applications; OOPSLA'90.

[Freeman-Benson 90b] Bjorn Freeman-Benson and Molly Wilson. DeltaStar, How I Wonder What You Are: A General Algorithm for Incremental Satisfaction of Constraint Hierarchies. Technical Report 90-05-02, Department of Computer Science and Engineering, University of Washington, May 1990.

[Freeman-Benson 90c] Bjorn N. Freeman-Benson, John Maloney, and Alan Borning. An Incremental Constraint Solver. *Communications of the ACM*, 33(1):54–63, January 1990.

[Freeman-Benson 91] Bjorn N. Freeman-Benson. *Constraint Imperative Programming*. PhD thesis, University of Washington, Department of Computer Science and Engineering, July 1991. Published as Computer Science Department Technical Report 91-07-02.

[Freeman-Benson 92] Bjorn Freeman-Benson and Alan Borning. The Design and Implementation of Kaleidoscope'90, A Constraint Imperative Programming Language. In *Proceedings of the IEEE Computer Society International Conference on Computer Languages*, April 1992.

[Gabbay 87] Dov Gabbay. The Declarative Past and Imperative Future. In *Temporal Logic in Specification*, volume LNCS 398, pages 409–448. Springer-Verlag, 1987.

[Galton 87] Anthony Galton, editor. *Temporal Logic and Their Applications*. Academic Press, 1987.

[Gansner 88a] E. R. Gansner. Iris: A Class-Based Window Library. In *USENIX C++ Conference*, pages 283–292, October 1988.

[Gansner 88b] E.R. Gansner, S.C. North, and K.P. Vo. DAG—A Program that Draws Directed Graphs. *Software—Practice and Experience*, 18(11):1047–1062, November 1988.

[Gansner 91] Emden R. Gansner and John H. Reppy. eXene. In *Third International Workshop on Standard ML*, Carnegie Mellon University, September 1991.

[Gelernter 83] D. Gelernter. Generative Communication in Linda. Technical Report TR-294, Yale University, May 1983.

[Gelernter 89] D. Gelernter and S. Jagannathan. A Symmetric Language. Technical Report YALEU/DCS/RR-568, Yale University, May 1989.

[Gifford 86] David K. Gifford and John M. Lucassen. Integrating Functional and Imperative Programming. In *Proceedings of the 1986 SIGPLAN Conference on Design and Implementation of Programming Languages*, pages 28–38, 1986.

[Giuse 89] Dario Giuse. KR: Constraint-Based Knowledge Representation. Technical Report CMU-CS-89-142, School of Computer Science, Carnegie Mellon University, April 1989.

[GNU 90] Free Software Foundation Inc. *GNU Emacs Lisp Reference Manual*, 1990.

[Goguen 86] Joseph A. Goguen. Reusing and Interconnecting Software Components. *IEEE Computer*, 19(2):16–28, February 1986.

[Goldberg 83] Adele Goldberg and Dave Robson. *Smalltalk-80: The Language and Its Implementation*. Addison-Wesley, Reading, MA, 1983.

[Gordon 89] Andrew Gordon. PFL+: A Kernel Scheme for Functional I/O. Technical report, University of Cambridge Computer Laboratory, March 1989.

[Gosling 83] James A. Gosling. *Algebraic Constraints*. PhD thesis, School of Computer Science, Carnegie Mellon University, May 1983. Published as CMU Computer Science Department tech report CMU-CS-83-132.

[Gosling 89] James Gosling, David S.H. Rosenthal, and Michelle J. Arden. *The NeWS book: An Introduction to the Network/Extensible Window System*. Springer-Verlag, New York, November 1989.

[Gould 85] J.D. Gould and C.H. Lewis. Designing for Usability—Key Principles and What Designers Think. *Communications of the ACM*, 28(3):300–311, March 1985.

[Graham 88] T.C. Nicholas Graham. Conceptual Views of Data Structures as a Programming Aid. Technical Report 88-225, Department of Computing and Information Science, Queen University at Kingston, 1988.

[Graham 89] T.C. Nicholas Graham and James R. Cordy. Conceptual Views of Data Structures as a Model of Output in Programming Languages. In *Proceedings HICSS-22, Hawaii International Conference on Systems Sciences*, pages 1064–1074, 1989.

[Graham 91] T.C. Nicholas Graham and Gerd Kock. Domesticating Imperative Constructs for a Functional World. In *Proceedings of PLILP, Programming Language Implementation and Logic Programming*. Springer-Verlag, LNCS 528, 1991.

[Graham 92] T.C. Nicholas Graham. Temporal Constraint Functional Programming: a Declarative Framework for Interaction and Concurrency. In John Darlington and Roland Dietrich, editors, *Declarative Programming*. Springer-Verlag Worshops in Computer Science, March 1992.

[Green 85] Mark Green. The University of Alberta User Interface Management System. In *Computer Graphics*, volume 19, number 3, pages 205–213, San Francisco, July 1985. Proceedings SIGGRAPH'85.

[Green 86] Mark Green. A Survey of Three Dialog Models. *ACM Transactions on Graphics*, 5(3):244–275, July 1986.

[Green 89] Thomas R.G. Green. Task Action Grammar. In *British Computer Society HCI Specialists Group Day Meeting on Task Analysis*, London, 1989.

[Guindon 88] R. Guindon and B. Curtis. Control of Cognitive Processes during Software Design: What Tools Are Needed? In *Human Factors in Computing Systems*, pages 263–268, Washington, D.C., May 1988. Proceedings SIGCHI'88.

[Haahr 90] D. Haahr. Montage: Breaking Windows into Small Pieces. In *USENIX Summer Conference*, pages 289–297, June 1990.

[Halbert 84] Daniel C. Halbert. *Programming by Example*. PhD thesis, Computer Science Division, Dept. of EE&CS, University of California, Berkeley, CA, 1984. Also: Xerox Office Systems Division, Systems Development Department, TR OSD-T8402, December 1984.

[Harel 90] I. Harel and S. Papert. Software Design as a Learning Environment. *Interactive Learning Environments*, 1(1):1–32, January 1990.

[Hartson 89a] H. Rex Hartson. User Interface Management Control and Communication. *IEEE Software*, 6(1):62–70, January 1989.

[Hartson 89b]  H. Rex Hartson and Deborah Hix. Human–Computer Interface Development: Concepts and Systems for Its Management. *Computing Surveys*, 21(1):5–92, March 1989.

[Hartson 89c]  H. Rex Hartson and Deborah Hix.  Toward Empirically Derived Methodologies and Tools for Human–Computer Interface Development. *International Journal of Man–Machine Studies*, 31(4):477–494, October 1989.

[Hartson 90a]  H. Rex Hartson, Deborah Hix, and Thomas M. Kraly. Developing Human–Computer Interface Models and Representation Techniques. *Software—Practice and Experience*, 20(5):425–457, May 1990.

[Hartson 90b]  H. Rex Hartson, Antonio C. Siochi, and Deborah Hix. The UAN: A User-Oriented Representation for Direct Manipulation Interface Designs. *ACM Transactions on Information Systems*, 8(3):181–203, July 1990.

[Hartson 92]  H. Rex Hartson and P. Gray. Temporal Aspects of Tasks in the User Action Notation. In *Human Computer Interaction*, volume 7, number 1, 1992.

[Hayes 85]  Philip J. Hayes, Pedro A. Szekely, and Richard A. Lerner. Design Alternatives for User Interface Management Systems Based on Experience with COUSIN. In *Human Factors in Computing Systems*, pages 169–175, San Francisco, April 1985. Proceedings SIGCHI'85.

[Hayes 86]  J.R. Hayes and L.S. Flower. Writing Research and the Writer. *American Psychologist*, 41(10):1106–1113, October 1986.

[Henry 88]  Tyson R. Henry and Scott E. Hudson.  Using Active Data in a UIMS. In *Proceedings of the ACM SIGGRAPH Symposium on User Interface Software*, pages 167–178, Banff, Alberta, Canada, October 1988.

[Henry 90]  Tyson R. Henry, Scott E. Hudson, and Gary L. Newell. Integrating Gesture and Snapping into a User Interface Toolkit. In *ACM SIGGRAPH Symposium on User Interface Software and Technology*, pages 112–121, Snowbird, UT, October 1990. Proceedings UIST'90.

[Hickey 89] Timothy J. Hickey. CLP* and Constraint Abstraction. In *Proceedings of the Sixteenth Annual Principles of Programming Languages Symposium*, pages 125–133, Austin, TX, January 1989. ACM.

[Hill 86] Ralph D. Hill. Supporting Concurrency, Communication and Synchronization in Human–Computer Interaction—The Sassafras UIMS. *ACM Transactions on Graphics*, 5(3):179–210, July 1986.

[Hill 87a] Ralph Hill. Event-Response Systems—A Technique for Specifying Multi-Threaded Dialogues. In *Human Factors in Computing Systems*, pages 241–248, Toronto, Ont., Canada, April 1987. CHI+GI'87.

[Hill 87b] Ralph D. Hill. Some Important Features and Issues in User Interface Management Systems. *Computer Graphics*, 21(2):116–120, April 1987.

[Hill 91] R.D. Hill. A 2-D Graphics System for Multi-User Interactive Graphics Based on Objects and Constraints. In E. Blake and P. Wisskirchen, editors, *Advances in Object Oriented Graphics 1*, pages 67–91. Springer-Verlag, Berlin, 1991.

[Hill 92] Ralph D. Hill. The Abstraction–Link–View Paradigm: Using Constraints to Connect User Interfaces to Applications. In *Human Factors in Computing Systems*, page (in press), Monterrey, CA, May 1992. Proceedings SIGCHI'92.

[Holt 83] R.C. Holt and J.R. Cordy. The Turing Language Report. Technical Report CSRI-153, Computer Systems Research Institute, University of Toronto, December 1983.

[Holt 88a] R.C. Holt and J.R. Cordy. The Turing Programming Language. *Communications of the ACM*, 31(12):1410–1423, December 1988.

[Holt 88b] R.C. Holt, P. Matthews, J.A. Rosselet, and J.R. Cordy. *The Turing Programming Language: Design and Definition*. Prentice-Hall, Englewood Cliffs, NJ, 1988.

[HP 89] Hewlett-Packard. Special Issue about New Wave. *Hewlett-Packard Journal*, 40(4), August 1989.

[Hudak 87]  Paul Hudak. A Semantic Model of Reference Counting and its Abstraction. In Samson Abramsky and Chris Hankin, editors, *Abstract Interpretation of Declarative Languages*, pages 45–62. Ellis Horwood, Chichester, 1987.

[Hudak 88]  Paul Hudak, Philip Wadler, Arvind, Brian Boutel, Jon Fairburn, Joe Fasel, John Hughes, Thomas Johnsson, Dick Kieburtz, Simon Peyton Jones, Rishiyur Nikhil, Mike Reeve, David Wise, and Jonathon Young. Report on the Functional Programming Language Haskell. Technical report, Yale University, December 1988.

[Hudak 89a]  Paul Hudak. Conception, Evolution and Application of Functional Programming Languages. *ACM Computing Surveys*, 21(3):359–411, September 1989.

[Hudak 89b]  Paul Hudak and Raman S. Sundaresh. On the Expressiveness of Purely Functional I/O Systems. Technical Report YALEU/DCS/RR-665, Yale University, March 1989.

[Hudson 90]  Scott E. Hudson and Shamim P. Mohamed. Interactive Specification of Flexible User Interface Displays. *ACM Transactions on Information Systems*, 8(3):269–288, July 1990.

[Hudson 91]  Scott E. Hudson. Incremental Attribute Evaluation: a Flexible Algorithm for Lazy Update. *ACM Transactions on Programming Languages and Systems*, 13(3):315–341, July 1991.

[Hunter 85]  Colin Hunter. Software Components Stem Growing Costs. *Electronic Product Design*, 6(3):49–51, March 1985.

[Hutchins 86]  Edwin L. Hutchins, James D. Hollan, and Donald A. Norman. Direct Manipulation Interfaces. In Donald A. Norman and Stephen W. Draper, editors, *User Centered System Design*, pages 87–124. Lawrence Erlbaum Associates, Hillsdale, NJ, 1986.

[Hutchinson 87]  Norman Hutchinson, Rajendra Raj, Andrew Black, Henry Levy, and Eric Jul. The Emerald Programming Language Report. Technical Report 87-29, University of Arizona, Department of Computer Science, October 1987.

[Jacob 85a] R.J.K. Jacob. An Executable Specification Technique for Describing Human–Computer Interaction. In H. R. Hartson, editor, *Advances in Human–Computer Interaction*, pages 211–242. Ablex, Norwood, NJ, 1985.

[Jacob 85b] Robert J.K. Jacob. A State Transition Diagram Language for Visual Programming. *IEEE Computer*, 18(8):51–59, August 1985.

[Jacob 86] Robert J.K. Jacob. A Specification Language for Direct Manipulation Interfaces. *ACM Transactions on Graphics*, 5(4):283–317, October 1986.

[Jaffar 87] J. Jaffar and J. Lassez. Constraint Logic Programming. In *Proceedings of the Principles of Programming Languages Conference*, pages 111–119, Munich, Germany, January 1987. ACM.

[Jaffar 90] Joxan Jaffar, Spiro Michaylov, Peter Stuckey, and Roland Yap. The CLP($\mathcal{R}$) Language and System. Technical Report CMU-CS-90-181, School of Computer Science, Carnegie Mellon University, October 1990.

[Jenkins 86] Michael A. Jenkins, Janice I. Glasgow, and Carl McCrosky. Programming Styles in Nial. *IEEE Software*, January 1986.

[Johnson 86] Ralph E. Johnson. Type-Checking Smalltalk. In *Proceedings of the 1986 ACM Conference on Object-Oriented Programming Systems, Languages and Applications*, pages 315–321, Portland, OR, November 1986. ACM.

[Kamada 91] Tomihisa Kamada and Satoru Kawai. A General Framework for Visualizing Abstract Objects and Relations. *ACM Transactions on Graphics*, 10(1):1–39, January 1991.

[Kasik 82] David J. Kasik. A User Interface Management System. In *Computer Graphics*, pages 99–106, Boston, July 1982. Proceedings SIGGRAPH'82.

[Kay 69] A.C. Kay. *The Reactive Engine*. PhD thesis, University of Utah, Computer Science Department, September 1969.

[Kay 84] Alan Kay. Computer Software. *Scientific American*, 251(3):53–59, 1984.

[Kiczales 91] G. Kiczales, J. Des Rivieres, and D.G. Bobrow. *The Art of the Metaobject Protocol*. MIT Press, Cambridge, MA, 1991.

[Kieras 85] D. Kieras and P. G. Polson. An Approach to the Formal Analysis of User Complexity. *International Journal of Man–Machine Studies*, 22(4):365–394, April 1985.

[Kozma 91] R.B. Kozma. Learning with Media. *Review of Educational Research*, 61(2):179–211, February 1991.

[Kramer 91] Glenn Kramer, Jahir Pabon, Walid Keirouz, and Robert Young. Geometric Constraint Satisfaction Problems. In *Working Notes of the AAAI Spring Symposium on Constraint-Based Reasoning*, pages 242–251, Stanford, March 1991.

[Kristensen 83] Bent Bruun Kristensen, Ole Lehrmann Madsen, Birger Moller-Pederson, and Kirsten Nygaard. Abstraction Mechanisms in the BETA Programming Language. In *Proceedings of the Tenth Annual Principles of Programming Languages Symposium*, Austin, TX, January 1983. ACM.

[Kristensen 89] B.B. Kristensen, O.L. Madsen, B. Moller-Pedersen, and K. Nygaard. Object-Oriented Programming in the Beta Programming Language. Technical report, Norwegian Computing Center, Oslo, and Computer Science Department, Aarhus University, Aarhus, Denmark, 1989.

[Labview 89] National Instruments. LabVIEW. 12109 Technology Blvd. Austin, TX, 78727, 1989.

[Lamport 85] Leslie Lamport and Fred B. Schneider. Constraints: A Uniform Approach to Aliasing and Typing. In *Proceedings of the Twelfth Annual Principles of Programming Languages Symposium*, pages 205–216, New Orleans, January 1985. ACM.

[Lampson 77] B.W. Lampson, J.J. Horning, R.L. London, J.G. Mitchell, and G.L. Popek. Report on the Programming Language Euclid. *SIGPLAN Notices*, 12(2):1–79, February 1977.

[Langston 90] Peter S. Langston. Little languages for music. *Computing Systems*, 3(2):193, Spring 1990.

[Leler 88] W. Leler. *Constraint Programming Languages: Their Specification and Generation*. Addison-Wesley, New York, 1988.

[Levitt 84] David Levitt. Machine Tongues X: Constraint Languages. *Computer Music Journal*, 8(1):9–21, Spring 1984.

[Lewis 87] Clayton Lewis and Gary Olson. Can Principles of Cognition Lower the Barriers to Programming? In *Empirical Studies of Programmers: Second Workshop*, Norwood, NJ, 1987. Ablex.

[Lieberman 86] Henry Lieberman. Using Prototypical Objects to Implement Shared Behavior in Object Oriented Systems. *SIGPLAN Notices*, 21(11):214–223, November 1986. ACM Conference on Object-Oriented Programming; Systems Languages and Applications; OOPSLA'86.

[Linton 89] Mark A. Linton, John M. Vlissides, and Paul R. Calder. Composing User Interfaces with InterViews. *IEEE Computer*, 22(2):8–22, February 1989.

[Lock 89] Hendrik C.R. Lock. An Amalgamation of Functional and Logic Programming Languages. Technical Report 408, GMD, September 1989.

[Löwgren 89] Jonas Löwgren. An Architecture for Expert Systems User Interface Design and Management. In *Proceedings of the ACM SIGGRAPH Symposium on User Interface Software and Technology*, pages 43–52, November 1989.

[Ludolph 88] Frank Ludolph, Yu-Ying Chow, Dan Ingalls, Scott Wallace, and Ken Doyle. The Fabrik Programming Environment. In *1988 IEEE Workshop on Visual Languages*, pages 222–230, Pittsburgh, October 1988. IEEE Computer Society.

[Mackworth 77] Alan K. Mackworth. Consistency in Networks of Relations. *Artificial Intelligence*, 8(1):99–118, 1977.

[MacQueen 84] D.B. MacQueen. Modules for Standard ML. In *Conference Record of the 1984 ACM Conference on Lisp and Functional Programming*, pages 198–207, July 1984.

[Malone 81] Thomas W. Malone. What Makes Computer Games Fun? *Byte*, 6(12):258–277, December 1981.

[Maloney 89] John Maloney, Alan Borning, and Bjorn Freeman-Benson. Constraint Technology for User-Interface Construction in ThingLab II. In *Proceedings of the 1989 ACM Conference on Object-Oriented Programming Systems, Languages and Applications*, New Orleans, October 1989. ACM.

[Maloney 91] John Maloney. *Using Constraints for User Interface Construction*. PhD thesis, Department of Computer Science and Engineering, University of Washington, August 1991.

[Masui 91] Toshiyuki Masui. User Interface Specifacation Based On Parallel And Sequential Execution Specification. In *USENIX'91 Conference Proceedings*, pages 117–125. USENIX, January 1991.

[McCormack 88] Joel McCormack and Paul Asente. An Overview of the X Toolkit. In *ACM SIGGRAPH Symposium on User Interface Software and Technology*, pages 46–55, Banff, Alberta, Canada, October 1988. Proceedings UIST'88.

[Miller 88] Mark S. Miller and K.E. Drexler. Markets and Computation: Agoric Open Systems. In B.A. Huberman, editor, *The Ecology of Computation*, pages 133–176. Elsevier Science Publishers B.V., North-Holland, Amsterdam, 1988.

[Miller 91] Mark S. Miller. Charge per Use Software. unpublished paper. Xerox PARC, 1991.

[Milner 90] Robin Milner, Mads Tofte, and Robert Harper. *The Definition of Standard ML*. MIT Press, Cambridge, MA, 1990.

[Mitchell 79] James G. Mitchell, William Maybury, and Richard Sweet. Mesa Language Manual. Technical Report CSL-79-3, Xerox Palo Alto Research Center, April 1979.

[Mitchell 91] J. Mitchell, S. Meldal, and N. Madhav. An Extension of Standard ML Modules with Subtyping and Inheritance. In *Conference Record of the 18th Annual ACM Symposium on Principles of Programming Languages*, pages 270–278, January 1991.

[Mittal 86] Sanjay Mittal, Clive L. Dym, and Mahesh Morjaria. PRIDE: An Expert System for the Design of Paper Handling Systems. *Computer*, pages 102–114, July 1986.

[Moon 86] David A. Moon. Object-Oriented Programming with Flavors. In *Proceedings of the ACM Conference on Object-Oriented Programming Systems, Languages, and Applications*, pages 1–8, November 1986.

[Moran 81] T.P. Moran. The Command Language Grammar: A Representation for the User Interface of Interactive Computer Systems. *International Journal of Man–Machine Studies*, 15(1):3–51, July 1981.

[Myers 86] Brad A. Myers. A Complete and Efficient Implementation of Covered Windows. *IEEE Computer*, 19(9):57–67, September 1986.

[Myers 88] Brad A. Myers. *Creating User Interfaces by Demonstration*. Academic Press, Boston, 1988.

[Myers 89a] Brad A. Myers. User Interface Tools: Introduction and Survey. *IEEE Software*, 6(1):15–23, January 1989.

[Myers 89b] Brad A. Myers, Brad Vander Zanden, and Roger B. Dannenberg. Creating Graphical Interactive Application Objects by Demonstration. In *ACM SIGGRAPH Symposium on User Interface Software and Technology*, pages 95–104, Williamsburg, VA, November 1989. Proceedings UIST'89.

[Myers 90a] Brad A. Myers. Creating User Interfaces Using Programming-by-Example, Visual Programming, and Constraints. *ACM Transactions on Programming Languages and Systems*, 12(2):143–177, April 1990.

[Myers 90b] Brad A. Myers. Demonstrational Interfaces: A Step Beyond Direct Manipulation. Technical Report CMU-CS-90-162, School of Computer Science, Carnegie Mellon University, August 1990.

[Myers 90c] Brad A. Myers. A New Model for Handling Input. *ACM Transactions on Information Systems*, 8(3):289–320, July 1990.

[Myers 90d] Brad A. Myers. Taxonomies of Visual Programming and Program Visualization. *Journal of Visual Languages and Computing*, 1(1):97–123, March 1990.

[Myers 90e] Brad A. Myers, Dario A. Giuse, Roger B. Dannenberg, Brad Vander Zanden, David S. Kosbie, Edward Pervin, Andrew Mickish, and Philippe Marchal. Garnet: Comprehensive Support for Graphical, Highly-Interactive User Interfaces. *IEEE Computer*, 23(11):71–85, November 1990.

[Myers 91a] Brad A. Myers. Graphical Techniques in a Spreadsheet for Specifying User Interfaces. In *Human Factors in Computing Systems*, pages 243–249, New Orleans, April 1991. Proceedings SIGCHI'91.

[Myers 91b] Brad A. Myers. Separating Application Code from Toolkits: Eliminating the Spaghetti of Call-Backs. In *ACM SIGGRAPH Symposium on User Interface Software and Technology*, pages 211–220, Hilton Head, SC, November 1991. Proceedings UIST'91.

[Myers 91c] Brad A. Myers, Dario Giuse, Roger B. Dannenberg, Brad Vander Zanden, David Kosbie, Philippe Marchal, Ed Pervin, Andrew Mickish, and John A. Kolojejchick. The Garnet Toolkit Reference Manuals: Support for Highly-Interactive, Graphical User Interfaces in Lisp. Technical Report CMU-CS-90-117-R, School of Computer Science, Carnegie Mellon University, June 1991.

[Myers 92a] Brad A. Myers. State of the Art in User Interface Software Tools. In H. Rex Hartson and Deborah Hix, editors, *Advances in Human–Computer Interaction*, volume 4, page (in press). Ablex, 1992.

[Myers 92b] Brad A. Myers and Mary Beth Rosson. Survey on User Interface Programming. In *Human Factors in Computing Systems*, page (in press), Monterrey, CA, May 1992. Proceedings SIGCHI'92.

[Nahaboo 89] Colas Nahaboo. *The X11 Generic Window Manager*. Groupe Bull, 1989.

[Nardi 90] Bonnie A. Nardi and James R. Miller. The Spreadsheet Interface: A Basis for End User Programming. In *Human–Computer Interaction*, pages 977–983. Proceedings INTERACT'90, Elsevier Science Publishers B.V. (North-Holland), 1990.

[Nelson 85] Greg Nelson. Juno, a Constraint-Based Graphics System. In *Computer Graphics*, volume 19, number 3, pages 235–243, San Francisco, July 1985. Proceedings SIGGRAPH'85.

[Nelson 91] Greg Nelson, editor. *Systems Programming with Modula-3*. Prentice-Hall, Englewood Cliffs, NJ, 1991.

[Newman 68] William M. Newman. A System for Interactive Graphical Programming. In *AFIPS Spring Joint Computer Conference*, volume 28, pages 47–54, 1968.

[NeXT 91] NeXT Inc. *NeXTstep Reference*. Addison-Wesley, 1991.

[North 87] S.C. North and J. H. Reppy. Concurrent garbage collection on stock hardware. In *Functional Programming Languages and Computer Architecture*, volume 274 of *Lecture Notes in Computer Science*, pages 113–133. Springer-Verlag, September 1987.

[Nye 90a] A. Nye. *Xlib Programming Manual*, volume 1. O'Reilly & Associates, Inc., 1990.

[Nye 90b] A. Nye and T. O'Reilly. *X Toolkit Intrinsics Programming Manual*, volume 2. O'Reilly & Associates, Inc., 1990.

[Odersky 90] Martin Odersky. How to Make Destructive Updates Less Destructive. In *ACM Principles of Programming Languages*, 1990.

[OIT 90] Open Interface Toolbox, 1990.

[Olsen 83] Dan R. Olsen Jr. and Elizabeth P. Dempsey. Syngraph: A Graphical User Interface Generator. In *Computer Graphics*, volume 17, number 3, pages 43–50, Detroit, July 1983. Proceedings SIGGRAPH'83.

[Olsen 89] Dan R. Olsen Jr. A Programming Language Basis for User Interface Management. In *Human Factors in Computing Systems*, pages 171–176, Austin, TX, April 1989. Proceedings SIGCHI'89.

[Olsen 90a] Dan R. Olsen Jr. Creating Interactive Techniques by Symbolically Solving Geometric Constraints. In *Proceedings of the ACM SIGGRAPH Symposium on User Interface Software and Technology*, pages 102–107, Snowbird, UT, October 1990. ACM SIGGRAPH and SIGCHI.

[Olsen 90b] Dan R. Olsen Jr. Propositional Production Systems for Dialog Description. In *Human Factors in Computing Systems*, pages 57–63, Seattle, April 1990. Proceedings SIGCHI'90.

[OSF 89] *UIL—Programmer's Manual*. Boston, 1989.

[Ousterhout 90] J.K. Ousterhout. Tcl: An Embeddable Command Language. In *Proceedings of the Winter 1990 USENIX Conference*, pages 133–146, January 1990.

[Ousterhout 91] J.K. Ousterhout. An X11 Toolkit Based on the Tcl Language. In *Proceedings of the Winter 1991 USENIX Conference*, pages 105–115, January 1991.

[Palay 88] Andrew J. Palay *et al*. The Andrew Toolkit—An Overview. In *Proceedings Winter Usenix Technical Conference*, pages 9–21, Dallas, February 1988.

[Papert 80] Seymour Papert. *Mindstorms: Children, Computers, and Powerful Ideas*. Basic Books, New York, 1980.

[Patterson 90] J.F. Patterson, R.D. Hill, S.L. Rohall, and W.S. Meeks. Rendezvous: An Architecture for Synchronous Multi-User Applications. In *Proceedings CSCW'90*, pages 317–328, Los Angeles, October 1990.

[Pavlidis 85] Theo Pavlidis and Christopher J. Van Wyk. An Automatic Beautifier for Drawings and Illustrations. In *Computer Graphics*, volume 19, number 3, pages 225–234, San Francisco, July 1985. Proceedings SIGGRAPH'85.

[Pea 86] R.D. Pea and D.M. Kurland. On the Cognitive Effects of Learning Computer Programming. In R.D. Pea and K. Sheingold, editors, *Mirrors of Minds*, pages 147–177. Ablex, Norwood, NJ, 1986.

[Pea 91] R.D. Pea. Learning through Multimedia. *IEEE Computer Graphics and Applications*, 11(4):58–66, July 1991.

[Perkins 86] D.N. Perkins, F. Martin, and M. Farady. Loci of Difficulty in Learning to Program. Technical report, Educational Technology Center, Harvard University, Cambridge, MA, May 1986.

[Perry 89] Nigel Perry. I/O and Inter-Language Calling for Functional Languages. In *Proceedings of the Ninth International Conference of the Chilean Computer Science Society and Fifteenth Latin American Conference on Informatics*, July 1989.

[Pike 83a] Rob Pike. The Blit: A Multiplexed Graphics Terminal. *AT&T Bell Laboratories Technical Journal*, 63(8):1607–1631, 1983.

[Pike 83b] Rob Pike. Graphics in Overlapping Bitmap Layers. *ACM Transactions on Graphics*, 2(2):135–160, 1983.

[Pike 89a] Rob Pike. A Concurrent Window System. *Computing Systems*, 2(2):133–153, 1989.

[Pike 89b] Rob Pike. Newsqueak: A Language For Communicating with Mice. Technical Report 143, AT&T Bell Laboratories, April 1989.

[Polya 57] G. Polya. *How to Solve It*. Princeton University Press, Princeton, NJ, 1957.

[PS 90] Adobe Systems Inc. *The PostScript Language Reference Manual*. Addison-Wesley, 2nd edition, 1990.

[Pugh 88] W. Pugh. *Incremental Computation and the Incremental Evaluation of Function Programs*. PhD thesis, Computer Science Department, Cornell University, August 1988.

[Reisner 81] Phyllis Reisner. Formal Grammar and Human Factors Design of an Interactive Graphics System. *IEEE Transactions on Software Engineering*, SE-7(2):229–240, March 1981.

[Reppy 86] John H. Reppy and E. R. Gansner. A Foundation for Programming Environments. In *Proceedings of the ACM SIGSOFT/SIGPLAN Software Engineering Symposium on Practical Software Development Environments*, pages 218–227, December 1986.

[Reppy 88] John H. Reppy. Synchronous operations as first-class values. In *Proceedings of the SIGPLAN'88 Conference on Programming Language Design and Implementation*, pages 250–259, June 1988.

[Reppy 90] John H. Reppy. *Concurrent Programming with Events—The Concurrent ML Manual*. Computer Science Department, Cornell University, Ithaca, NY 14853, November 1990.

[Reppy 91] John H. Reppy. CML: A Higher-Order Concurrent Language. In *Proceedings of the SIGPLAN'91 Conference on Programming Language Design and Implementation*, pages 293–305, June 1991.

[Reps 84] T.W. Reps. *Generating Language-Based Environments*. MIT Press, Cambridge, MA, 1984.

[Reps 89] T.W. Reps and T. Teitelbaum. *The Synthesizer Generator: a System for Constructing Language-Based Editors*. Springer-Verlag, New York, 1989.

[Rich 81] C. Rich. Inspection Methods in Programming. Technical Report AI-TR-604, MIT AI Lab, Cambridge, MA, November 1981.

[Rotterdam 89] Ernst Rotterdam. Physiological Modeling and Simulation with Constraints. Technical Report R89001, Medical Information Science, Department of Anesthesiology, Oostersingel 59, 9713 E2 Groningen, June 1989.

[Rubine 87] D. Rubine and R. Dannenberg. Arctic Programmer's Manual and Tutorial. Technical Report CMU-CS-87-110, School of Computer Science, Carnegie Mellon University, Pittsburgh, June 1987.

[Saraswat 89] V. A. Saraswat. *Concurrent Constraint Programming Languages*. PhD thesis, School of Computer Science, Carnegie Mellon University, Pittsburgh, 1989.

[Saraswat 91] Vijay A. Saraswat, Martin Rinard, and Prakash Panangaden. Semantic Foundations of Concurrent Constraint Programming. In *Proceedings of the 18th Annual Principles of Programming Languages Symposium*. ACM, 1991.

[Scardamalia 89] M. Scardamalia, C. Bereiter, R. McLean, J. Swallow, and E. Woodruff. Computer-Supported Intentional Learning Environments. *Journal of Educational Computing Research*, 5(1):51–68, January 1989.

[Scheifler 86] Robert W. Schiefler and Jim Gettys. The X Window System. *ACM Transactions on Graphics*, 5(2):79–106, April 1986.

[Scheifler 88] R.W. Scheifler, J. Gettys, and R. Newman. *X Window System*. Digital Press, 1988.

[Schmucker 90] Kurt Schmucker. The Future of Scientific Computing on the Mac. *Computers and Physics*, 4(4):359–360, July–August 1990.

[Schulert 88] A. Schulert and K. Erf. Open Dialogue: using an extensible retained object workspace to support a UIMS. In *USENIX C++ Conference*, pages 53–64, October 1988.

[Shaw 83] M. Shaw, E. Borison, M. Horowitz, T. Lane, D. Nichols, and R. Pausch. Descartes: A Programming-Languages Approach to Interactive Display Interfaces. In *Symposium on Programming Language Issues in Software Systems*, pages 100–111, San Francisco, June 1983. Proceedings SIGPLAN'83.

[Shaw 86] Mary Shaw. An Input–Output Model for Interactive Systems. In *Human Factors in Computing Systems*, pages 261–273, Boston, April 1986. Proceedings SIGCHI'86.

[Sheil 83] Beau Sheil. Power Tools for Programmers. *Datamation*, 29(2):131–144, February 1983.

[Shneiderman 80] Ben Shneiderman. *Software Psychology: Human Factors in Computer and Information Systems*. Winthrop Publishers, Cambridge, MA, 1980.

[Shneiderman 83] Ben Shneiderman. Direct Manipulation: A Step Beyond Programming Languages. *IEEE Computer*, 16(8):57–69, August 1983.

[Sibert 88] John L. Sibert, William D. Hurley, and Teresa W. Bleser. Design and Implementation of an Object-Oriented User Interface Management System. In H. R. Hartson, editor, *Advances in Human–Computer Interaction*, pages 175–213. Ablex, Norwood, NJ, 1988.

[Singh 88] Gurminder Singh and Mark Green. Designing the Interface Designer's Interface. In *ACM SIGGRAPH Symposium on User Interface Software*, pages 109–116, New York, October 1988. ACM.

[Singh 90] Gurminder Singh, Chun-Hong Kok, and Teng-Ye Ngan. Druid: A System for Demonstrational Rapid User Interface Development. In *ACM SIGGRAPH Symposium on User Interface Software and Technology*, pages 167–177, Snowbird, UT, October 1990.

[Singh 91a] Gurminder Singh. UIMS Support for Multimedia User Interfaces. In John Waterworth, editor, *Multimedia: Technology and Applications*, pages 170–198. Ellis Horwood, Chichester, England, 1991.

[Singh 91b] Gurminder Singh and Mark Green. Automating the Lexical and Syntactic Design of Graphical User Interfaces: The UofA* UIMS. *ACM Transactions on Graphics*, 10(3):213–254, July 1991.

[Singh 92] Gurminder Singh and Mark H. Chignell. Components of the Visual Computer: A Review of Relevant Technologies. *The Visual Computer*, page (in press), 1992.

[Smith 75] D.C. Smith. *Pygmalion*. Birkhauser, Boston, 1975.

[Smith 84] B.C. Smith. Reflection and Semantics in LISP. In *Principles of Programming Languages Conference*, pages 23–25, Salt Lake City, UT, 1984. ACM.

[Smith 87] R.B. Smith. Experiences with the Alternate Reality Kit: an Example of the Tension Between Literalism and Magic. In *Human Factors in Computing Systems*, pages 61–67, Toronto, Ont., Canada, April 1987. CHI+GI'87.

[Soloway 82] E. Soloway, K. Ehrlich, J. Bonar, and J. Greenspan. What Do Novices Know about Programming? In A. Badre and B. Schneiderman, editors, *Directions in Human–Computer Interaction*, pages 27–54. Ablex, Norwood, NJ, 1982.

[Soloway 86] E. Soloway. Learning to Program = Learning to Construct Mechanisms and Explanations. *Communications of the ACM*, 29(9):850–858, September 1986.

[Spohrer 89] J.C. Spohrer. *MARCEL: A Generate-Test-and-Debug (GTD) Impasse/Repair Model of Student Programmers*. PhD thesis, Yale University, March 1989.

[Stallman 77] Richard M. Stallman and Gerald J. Sussman. Forward Reasoning and Dependency-Directed Backtracking in a System for Computer-Aided Circuit Analysis. *Artificial Intelligence*, 9:135–196, 1977.

[Stallman 86] Richard Stallman. *GNU Emacs Manual*. Free Software Foundation Inc., 5th edition, 1986.

[Steele 80] Guy L. Steele Jr. *The Definition and Implementation of a Computer Programming Language Based on Constraints*. PhD thesis, MIT, Computer Science Department, Cambridge, MA, 1980.

[Steele 90] Guy L. Steele Jr., editor. *Common Lisp: The Language, 2Ed*. Digital Press, 1990.

[Stefik 86] M. Stefik and D. Bobrow. Object-Oriented Programming: Themes and Variations. *The AI Magazine*, 6(4):40–62, Winter 1986.

[Sussman 80] Gerald J. Sussman and Guy L. Steele Jr. CONSTRAINTS–A Language for Expressing Almost-Hierarchical Descriptions. *Artificial Intelligence*, 14(1):1–39, August 1980.

[Sutherland 63a] Ivan Sutherland. *Sketchpad: A Man–Machine Graphical Communication System*. PhD thesis, MIT, Computer Science Department, January 1963. Reissued May 19, 1965.

[Sutherland 63b]  Ivan E. Sutherland. SketchPad: A Man–Machine Graphical Communication System. In *AFIPS Spring Joint Computer Conference*, volume 23, pages 329–346, 1963.

[Swarup 91]  Vipin Swarup, Uday S. Reddy, and Evan Ireland. Assignments for Applicative Languages. In *Functional Programming Languages and Computer Architectures*, 1991.

[Szekely 88]  Pedro A. Szekely and Brad A. Myers. A User Interface Toolkit Based on Graphical Objects and Constraints. *SIGPLAN Notices*, 23(11):36–45, November 1988. ACM Conference on Object-Oriented Programming; Systems Languages and Applications; OOPSLA'88.

[Tempo2 91]  Affinity Microsystems Ltd. Tempo 2 Plus. 1050 Walnut Street, Suite 425, Boulder, CO 80302. (303) 442-4840, 1991.

[Thomas 83]  J.J. Thomas and G. Hamlin. Graphical Input Interactive Technique Workshop Summary. *Computer Graphics*, 17(1):5–30, 1983.

[Thompson 89]  Simon Thompson. Functional Programming: Executable Specifications and Program Transformation. *Fifth International Workshop on Software Specification and Design*, pages 287–290, May 1989.

[Van Hentenryck 89]  Pascal Van Hentenryck. *Constraint Satisfaction in Logic Programming*. MIT Press, Cambridge, MA, 1989.

[Van Wyk 80]  C. Van Wyk. *A Language for Typesetting Graphics*. PhD thesis, Stanford University, Computer Science Department, Stanford, CA, June 1980.

[Van Wyk 82]  Christopher J. Van Wyk. A High-Level Language for Specifying Pictures. *ACM Transactions on Graphics*, 1(2):163–182, April 1982.

[Vander Zanden 88a]  Brad T. Vander Zanden. Constraint Grammars in User Interface Management Systems. In *Proceedings Graphics Interface*, pages 176–184, Edmonton, Canada, June 1988. GI'88.

[Vander Zanden 88b]  Brad T. Vander Zanden. *Incremental Constraint Satisfaction and Its Application to Graphical Interfaces*. PhD thesis, Computer Science Department, Cornell University, Ithaca, NY, 1988.

[Vander Zanden 89] Brad T. Vander Zanden. Constraint Grammars—A New Model for Specifying Graphical Applications. In *Human Factors in Computing Systems*, pages 325–330, Austin, TX, April 1989. Proceedings SIGCHI'89.

[Vander Zanden 90] Brad Vander Zanden and Brad A. Myers. Automatic, Look-and-Feel Independent Dialog Creation for Graphical User Interfaces. In *Human Factors in Computing Systems*, pages 27–34, Seattle, April 1990. Proceedings SIGCHI'90.

[Vander Zanden 91] Brad Vander Zanden, Brad A. Myers, Dario Giuse, and Pedro Szekely. The Importance of Pointer Variables in Constraint Models. In *ACM SIGGRAPH Symposium on User Interface Software and Technology*, pages 155–164, Hilton Head, SC, November 1991. Proceedings UIST'91.

[Wadge 85] William W. Wadge and Edward A. Ashcroft. *Lucid, the Dataflow Programming Language*. Academic Press, London, 1985.

[Wasserman 85] A. I. Wasserman and D. T. Shewmake. The Role of Prototypes in the User Software Engineering Methodology. In H.R. Hartson, editor, *Advances in Human–Computer Interaction*, pages 191–210. Ablex, Norwood, NJ, 1985.

[Weinberg 71] G.M. Weinberg. *The Psychology of Computer Programming*. Van Nostrand Reinhold, New York, 1971.

[Whiteside 88] John Whiteside, John Bennett, and Karen Holtzblatt. Usability Engineering: Our Experience and Evolution. In M. Helander, editor, *Handbook of Human–Computer Interaction*, pages 791–817. Elsevier North-Holland, Amsterdam, 1988.

[Wilson 89] Molly Wilson and Alan Borning. Extending Hierarchical Constraint Logic Programming: Nonmonotonicity and Inter-Hierarchy Comparison. In *Proceedings of the North American Conference on Logic Programming*, Cleveland, October 1989.

[Wilson 90] David Wilson. *Programming with MacApp*. Addison-Wesley, Reading, MA, 1990.

[Winograd 87] T. Winograd and C. F. Flores. *Understanding Computers and Cognition: a New Foundation for Design*. Ablex, Norwood, NJ, 1987.

[Wolff 90] Robert Wolff. The Macintosh Scientific Computing Environment. *Computers and Physics*, 4(4):348–358, July–August 1990.

[XVT 91] XVT Software Inc. Extensible virtual toolkit (XVT). Box 18750 Boulder, CO 80308, (303) 443-4223, 1991.

[Yudkin 88] Howard L. Yudkin. Emerging Trends Present Opportunities, Challenges for Standards Development. *IEEE Computer*, 21(8):67–69, August 1988.

[Yunten 85] T. Yunten and H. R. Hartson. A SUPERvisory Methodology And Notation (SUPERMAN) for Human–Computer System Development. In H. R. Hartson, editor, *Advances in Human–Computer Interaction*, pages 243–281. Ablex, Norwood, NJ, 1985.

[Zappacosta 84] Pierluigi Zappacosta. Module-Based Software Integration: The Next Software Revolution. In *Wescon U84 Conference Proceedings*, pages 12/1/1–3, Los Angeles, October 1984. Electronic Conventions.

# Index

—— **Jones and Bartlett Books in Computer Science and Related Areas** ——

Barnsley, M., *The Fractal Transform*
ISBN 0-86720-218-1

Bernstein, A.J., and Lewis, P.M., *Concurrency in Programming and Database Systems*
ISBN 0-86720-205-X

Birmingham, W.P., Gupta, A.P., and Siewiorek, D.P., *Automating the Design of Computer Systems: The MICON Project*
ISBN 0-86720-241-6

Chandy, K.M., and Taylor, S., *An Introduction to Parallel Programming*
ISBN 0-86720-208-4

Epstein, D.B.A., *et al.*, *Word Processing in Groups*
ISBN 0-86720-241-6

Flynn, A., and Jones, J., *Mobile Robots: Inspiration to Implementation*
ISBN 0-86720-223-8

Geometry Center, University of Minnesota, *Not Knot* (VHS video)
ISBN 0-86720-240-8

Healey, G., *et al.* (eds.), *Physics-Based Vision: Principles and Practice, Color*
ISBN 0- 86720-295-5

Iterated Systems, Inc., *Floppy Book: A P.OEM PC Book*
ISBN 0-86720-222-X

Iterated Systems, Inc., *SNAPSHOTS: True-Color Photo Images Using the Fractal Formatter*
ISBN 0-86720-299-8

Lee, E. S., *Algorithms and Data Structures in Computer Engineering*
ISBN 0-86720-219-X

Myers, B.A. (ed.), *Languages for Developing User Interfaces*
ISBN 0-86720-450-8

Parke, F.I., and Waters, K., *Computer Facial Animation*
ISBN 0-86720-243-2

Ruskai, M.B., *et al.*, *Wavelets and Their Applications*
ISBN 0-86720-225-4

Whitman, S., *Multiprocessor Methods for Computer Graphics Rendering*
ISBN 0-86720-229-7

Wolff, L., *et al.* (eds.), *Physics-Based Vision: Principles and Practice, Radiometry*
ISBN 0-86720-294-7

Wolff, L., *et al.* (eds.), *Physics-Based Vision: Principles and Practice, Shape Recovery*
ISBN 0-86720-296-3